# THE FOURTH ESTATE
# AND THE CONSTITUTION

# THE FOURTH ESTATE
# AND THE CONSTITUTION

*Freedom of the Press in America*

LUCAS A. POWE, JR.

UNIVERSITY OF CALIFORNIA PRESS
BERKELEY    LOS ANGELES    OXFORD

University of California Press
Berkeley and Los Angeles, California

University of California Press, Ltd.
Oxford, England

© 1991 by
The Regents of the University of California
First Paperback Printing 1992

Library of Congress Cataloging-in-Publication Data

Powe, L. A. Scot.
   The fourth estate and the constitution: Freedom of the
   press in America / Lucas A. Powe, Jr.
      p.   cm.
   Includes bibliographical references and index.
   ISBN 0-520-08038-6
   1. Freedom of the press—United States.   I. Title
KF4774.P69   1991
342.73'0853—dc20
[347.302853]                                      90-45465
                                                      CIP

Printed in the United States of America
1   2   3   4   5   6   7   8   9

The paper used in this publication meets the minimum
requirements of American National Standard for Information
Sciences—Permanence of Paper for Printed Library Materials,
ANSI Z39.48-1984. ⊛

*For Monika and Tom*

# Contents

# Preface

Surprising though it may seem, for all practical purposes the modern constitutional law of freedom of the press began with the Supreme Court's constitutionalization of the libel in *New York Times v. Sullivan* (1964). Prior to 1964, press litigation invoking the First Amendment was haphazard and, like most defense litigation, reactive. With *New York Times*, the Pentagon Papers controversy in 1971, and reporters' claim (which the Court rejected in 1972) to a constitutional privilege not to disclose confidential sources of information, the press self-consciously came to see itself as an institutional (and therefore repeat) litigant. As the NAACP Legal Defense Fund brilliantly demonstrated with school desegregation, institutional litigants view courts, especially the Supreme Court, as the forum of choice for creating and then guaranteeing an increasing array of new protections. The press proved no different as it presented a new cast of First Amendment issues for (what it always expected to be) the Supreme Court's judicial imprimatur. While a few older cases—most notably *Near v. Minnesota* (1931), the first case to hold that a statute violated freedom of the press and a central text on the traditional aversion to prior restraints as well as the circumstances where they may be permissible—remain important, it is only a slight exaggeration to view 1964 as year zero for discussions of the constitutional issues that are currently central to the press's performance of its Fourth Estate functions.

Equally surprising, no constitutional scholar has yet written a book dealing exclusively with the post-1964 developments in the constitutional law of the Fourth Estate. It is both trite and accurate

ix

to note that issues relating to a free press play a central role in our democracy; yet because of this gap in the literature, the non-specialist who desires information will find it all but impossible to study the issues in any systematic way. One possibility would be to sort through an excellent though imposing academic literature, issue by issue, and hope to see a comprehensive and coherent whole at the end. If that prospect is too daunting, a second solution would be to rely on discussions of the press by the press, in spite of all the attendant biases and omissions therein. Neither option is satisfactory. Thus my hope is that this book can provide the willing reader, regardless of background, with an understanding of the parameters of the constitutional discussion of the Fourth Estate, if not in the same depth as the academic literature, at least on the same terms.

This book had its genesis in a discussion with my friend and colleague Sandy Levinson immediately after I had finished *American Broadcasting and the First Amendment*—indeed, just as I was leaving Austin for Maui. Sandy suggested that I turn my attention to *Miami Herald v. Tornillo* (1974), the case in which the Supreme Court eliminated the possibilities of even minor broadcast-style regulation for the printed media. Sandy accurately noted that I had, in my writings on broadcasting, assumed *Tornillo* was correctly decided, and he suggested that it was about time I showed rather than assumed that to be so. While enjoying the beaches, I concluded he was right, and on return I researched and wrote a critical review of *Tornillo*, which appeared in the 1987 *Supreme Court Review* (and is the basis for Chapter 9 of this book). It was a short step from writing about freedom of the press in the context of *Tornillo* to deciding that a general volume on the various constitutional issues relating to freedom of the press was both needed and feasible.

In writing this book, I have followed the model of *American Broadcasting and the First Amendment*. Some chapters are historical, others address issues, and the final two attempt to put the earlier discussions into a larger, more theoretical context. This book, as the title makes clear, is about the constitutional law of the press. Thus while shield laws, sunshine laws, and freedom of information acts have a greater impact than the Constitution on press access to places and information (the topic of Chapter 6), my focus is on the Constitution, not statutory developments.

Like *American Broadcasting,* this book, too, is aimed at both those in the field and the general nonlegal audience. *American Broadcasting* explicitly assumed the existence of a rich print tradition into which broadcasting could be assimilated. What follows is a look at the varied contours of that tradition, some of which I find more expansive than the prevailing literature does, some of which I find less expansive than my friends in the Fourth Estate would believe.

An author incurs many pleasant debts. It has been my good fortune to have been teaching for years at a law school where my work overlaps with that of so many of my colleagues. As a result I have had the benefit of insights from a number of people. Douglas Laycock and Sandy Levinson have read and critiqued the entire manuscript; David Anderson, Richard Markovits, and David Rabban have read specific chapters relating to their specific interests. They made my tasks easier and strengthened the book in the process. The same holds for Tom Krattenmaker at Georgetown University Law Center and Dwight Teeter of the Mass Communications Department at the University of Wisconsin at Milwaukee, two scholars whose suggestions both saved me from errors and forced me to express my ideas more clearly. I must single out David Anderson for a generosity above and beyond the academic norms, for he has allowed me access to his ongoing libel research. When, in Chapter 4, I refer to his proposals and analysis, the reference is to an article that David is still in the process of polishing (and that may, when published, be different than described). I think his willingness to share so freely typifies why The University of Texas Law School is such a pleasant place to work.

Beyond so many colleagues with whom ideas can be exchanged, I have benefited immeasurably from Roy Mersky's superb staff at the Tarlton Law Library of The University of Texas, especially Marlyn Robinson and Barbara Bridges. So, too, Dean Mark Yudof has facilitated this book by continuing summer research grants as well as a long research leave at just the right time.

I have had excellent research assistance by four hardworking students who have willingly memorized the lengthy walk from the law school to the libraries on the rest of the campus: Carol and Erica Krennerich, DeeDee Drays, and Kirk Peterson. Their cheerful assistance was much appreciated.

Finally, I would like to acknowledge the permission of the University of Chicago Press, which holds the copyright to L. A. Powe, Jr., _Tornillo_, 1987 _Supreme Court Review_ 345, for allowing its adaptation in this book.

# Introduction

John Peter Zenger's name is synonymous with freedom of the press; Tom Patterson's is not. Zenger, a New York printer, achieved fame when his lawyers left him in jail while they won his seditious libel case in 1735. Patterson, the owner-editor of the *Denver Times* and the *Rocky Mountain Daily News,* was a United States senator who dared to protest a judicial coup d'état at the turn of the twentieth century. Unlike Zenger, he is obscure. At best he is forgotten; at worst his fame never extended through a collection of colonies or an entire nation. History, as losers are wont to learn, is not always fair, and Patterson lost.

The facts of the Zenger and Patterson cases provide an excellent point of departure for discussing freedom of the press as well as an appropriate context for exploring the content of the First Amendment's guarantee. Each raises issues—the limits of dissent and the locus of decision making about those limits—that go to the heart of a democratic society. Although *Zenger* was by far the earlier of the two—Patterson's case was decided over a century after ratification of the First Amendment—an achronological discussion allows us to inquire what, at a minimum, freedom of the press must protect. Once that is established, we can proceed to question how much more than that minimum the First Amendment encompasses and to what extent, if any, society can compel the press to perform its appropriate roles.

## I

Without local control, Denver suffered under de facto colonial rule where formal state control dovetailed with the socioeconomic control emanating from the Denver Club, the bastion of the business elite who dominated the Colorado Republican party, which in turn dominated the state government. The principal local issues concerned the lucrative utility monopolies that fatted the business elite while slighting details such as service.[1]

Home rule was at the vortex of money, power, and legal control. Reformers saw it as a means of bringing better government and breaking the utility monopolies. The Denver Club perceived it as a threat. The reformers, with Patterson's active editorial support, prevailed in 1902 with a home rule amendment to the state constitution. Its immediate impact, however, was to create a pair of symbiotic cottage industries: Denver elections and Colorado Supreme Court decisions on the validity of those elections. The multifaceted elections of November 1904 proved the most interesting and provided the occasion for Patterson to learn that a protester against electoral theft might be at the legal mercy of those benefiting from the challenged transaction.[2]

In that election the voters enlarged the membership of the state supreme court and apparently sent the unpopular incumbent Republican governor, James Peabody, to a 9000-vote defeat at the hands of the two-time former Democratic governor, Alva Adams. With the state about to pass to the Democrats, William G. Evans, president of the Denver City Tramway Company and the principal Republican boss of the state, masterminded a dazzling stratagem, utilizing all three branches of government, to preserve Republican political and economic power. Just days before Adams's inauguration, Peabody nominated Republicans for the newly created supreme court seats, and the Republican state senate immediately confirmed the appointments even though the seats would not come into existence for two months.[3]

Chapter 2 will look at events of the late 1790s in detail. To anticipate for a moment, this is even more outrageous than John Adams's lame-duck appointments in 1801 that led to the famous United States Supreme Court case of *Marbury v. Madison,* for at least Adams was filling positions currently in existence. Evans's plan, however, was to do the century-old Federalist effort one better.[4]

Almost simultaneously, through injunctions involving the vote count, the Colorado Supreme Court cast a cloud over a number of

Denver precincts, with the immediate result that six Denver Democratic legislators were disabled from taking their seats when the legislature convened. Alva Adams took office, but the Republicans carried their claim that Peabody had won to the legislature—which they still controlled, thanks to the supreme court action preventing the six Denver Democrats from taking their seats. The legislature, after investigation of the vote count, determined that Peabody had won. But no one besides Peabody himself wanted him to be governor; part of the deal required that he tender a postdated resignation prior to his inauguration. The resignation was effective the next day, at which time his lieutenant governor took office. Colorado thus had three governors in the twenty-four hours of March 16–17, 1905. It is as if the Congress in 1801 had declared John Adams, not Thomas Jefferson, elected, and Charles C. Pinckney had become the third president.[5]

Validating Evans's plan was only part of the Colorado Supreme Court's involvement in guaranteeing that it was good business to control as many branches of government as possible. The state government, including the newly enlarged supreme court, now resembled an operating subsidiary of the mining and smelting interests, railroads, and Denver utility companies. The first dividend came due in June 1905, when the court voted to set aside a home rule election of county judges on the grounds that the state constitutional requirement of a republican form of government was violated when Denver set the number and terms of such judges (as the home rule amendment permitted). The decision, whereby parts of a voter-approved constitutional amendment were held unconstitutional as a violation of the very document that was being amended, seemed so obviously wrong that it had to portend a worse future. It looked like the first step in wholly eliminating home rule and Denver's ability to control its own destiny—and its private utility monopolies.[6]

Patterson, a leading supporter of home rule, was outraged by the supreme court's theft of the Denver elections. He immediately editorialized in his *Denver Times:* "The people of St. Louis and San Francisco, who have been enjoying the full benefits of just such a system of government as the [home rule] amendment provides, will be astonished to learn that they no longer live in a republic—for the Colorado supreme court holds that such a government is so unrepublican that it cannot be tolerated in Colorado." Patterson's irony was well directed; the supreme court's decision was absurd. He asked, "What next?" and suggested how to find out: "If someone will let us know what next the utility corporations of Denver and the political machine they control will demand, the question will be answered."[7]

The following day the *Rocky Mountain News* carried a cartoon of the five members of the court majority beheading the losing litigants in the home rule election case. The caption read: "If the Republican Party has overlooked anything from the Supreme Court, it will now proceed to ask for it."[8]

Next came a letter to the editor of the *Times*. "Publicus" had the answer. The Republican sponsors of the supreme court were acting to protect "millions upon millions" from their municipal investments. The home rule requirement of voter approval for refranchising municipal utilities created a major obstacle to securing the booty. The Republican bosses therefore planned the "total destruction" of home rule so that a compliant city council that could "always be depended upon to give them what they demand and will pay for" would renew the money-making franchises.[9]

Given the enormity of the Colorado Supreme Court's actions, and the typical excesses of turn-of-the-century journalism, Patterson's response was amazingly restrained, especially for a prominent populist who loathed the utility monopolies. Restrained or not, those supporting the status quo could hardly be pleased with a figure as prominent as Patterson publicly stating that the supreme court was subservient to the utility companies, which, rather than the people, ran the Colorado government.

Denver's two Republican newspapers called for the supreme court to hold Patterson in contempt of court for his statements that impermissible political considerations were motivating the court. In response, Patterson published a reaffirming editorial that took personal responsibility. He had either written or approved each of the pieces: "I believe they were fair and just criticism, and fully warranted by what has transpired." That same day the Colorado attorney general, acting on instructions from the chief justice, issued an order for Patterson to show cause why he should not be held in contempt of court. Patterson's forum shifted from the city of Denver to the Colorado Supreme Court.[10]

If either William G. Evans or the term-and-a-day James Peabody had sought redress against Patterson, their only recourse would have been a libel suit. In such an action the Colorado Constitution guaranteed the right to defend a libel suit on the grounds that the alleged libel was true. Although Patterson might have had a difficult time proving truth, the public would have been treated to a spectacular trial; and if Patterson had prevailed, the legitimacy of the Denver Club's control over the state might have been weakened or destroyed. But neither Evans nor Peabody sued Patterson. Instead, the attorney general acting for the Colorado Supreme Court mounted the assault. And the legal issue was not libel but contempt of court. Yet on the facts "contempt" was nothing but a label for criticism that stung; indeed, to use the old common-law term, what Patterson had done was akin to seditious libel, where truth was no defense either. Patterson had effectively criticized government, thereby diminishing its authority—a point underscored by his response to the contempt charge; he stated that, because he believed in the truth of all he wrote, he was never more convinced of the justice and necessity of publication. Taking advantage of his situation, as only a person headed for defeat can, Patterson argued that the judiciary, as the "sacred" guardian of liberty in the country, retains the confidence of the people only by staying within the limits prescribed by law. If there is integrity and reciprocity between the people and the courts, "there will be little provocation for criticism either of the courts, or by the courts, of the public press."[11]

Everything turns on the if. Patterson held that the court had broken the sacred trust and therefore provocation was proper, and he grasped the opportunity to repeat his charges and reassert their truth. It was on the issue of truth he wished to fight; the contempt charge gave him the legal necessity to do so, and on its face the Colorado Constitution gave him the legal right: "Every person shall be free to speak, write or publish *whatever he will on any subject,* being responsible for all abuse of that liberty; and in all suits and prosecutions for libel the truth thereof may be given in evidence."[12]

In holding that part of the home rule amendment was unconstitutional, the Colorado Supreme Court had begun to behave as if its motto were "What's the constitution among friends?" And now events had gone too far for constitutional niceties to intrude. Patterson may have had all the persuasive points, but he had put the supreme court's very legitimacy at issue, and the court had all the power. Although the court's long opinion is short on the reasoning that might support its various conclusions, it explicitly held that the truth was not a defense to a charge of contempt. The conclusion that an action for contempt was not covered by the quoted constitutional provision seems to flow from the nature of the action. The court reasoned that because the power to punish contempt of court is an inherent power, not granted or even mentioned by the constitution, it is therefore not limited by the constitution. Thus, had he criticized anyone but judges, Patterson would have been allowed his defense of truth; but when the facts required Patterson to point his finger at the judiciary, the state constitution became a piece of irrelevant parchment.

If the Colorado Supreme Court justices appeared overly assertive of their prerogatives, their sentencing of Patterson showed remarkably good judgment. The court was hardly in need of a powerful and articulate martyr; escalating this fight would have jeopardized whatever popular respect the justices retained. Patterson's punishment was a $1000 fine—a slap on the wrist for a man of his wealth.[13]

Seeking the more neutral forum of the United States Supreme Court, Patterson appealed, but to no avail. Justice Oliver Wendell Holmes concluded for the Court that the First Amendment has nothing to do with protecting truth. The First Amendment protects only against prior restraints (that is, having to seek approval before publishing); it does not prohibit subsequent punishments. Thus Patterson did not need to seek approval from governmental censors before he wrote his editorials; but the First Amendment, as Holmes viewed it, incorporated the Blackstonian English view that there was no bar on legislation punishing the printed word. Holmes offered a typically pithy epigram summarizing the law on truth and falsity: "The preliminary freedom extends as well to the false as to the true; the subsequent punishment may extend as well to the true as to the false." In 1769 William Blackstone in his classic *Commentaries on the Laws of England* had similarly written: "The liberty of the press is indeed essential to the nature of a free state: but this consists in laying no previous restraints upon publications, and not

in freedom from censure for criminal matter when published."
Even false information can be purveyed without prior governmental approval, but should a government believe that certain
information is contrary to the public welfare it may punish its
spread—even if the information is 100 percent true. That was the
English common law; that, Holmes said, was American constitutional law.[14]

Therefore, Colorado had legitimately punished Patterson even if
his message was wholly true. It did not matter if the Colorado
Supreme Court had participated in a coup d'état; if the justices
wished to silence their critics, the United States Constitution was no
bar. And if it was no bar in Patterson's case, when would it be?

## II

Patterson had his day in court and lost. No matter what Justice
Holmes said or did not say, Patterson was railroaded. That at first
looked to be Zenger's fate as well; but although his day in court was
longer in coming, it was ultimately more successful.

Patterson was an activist. What was published in his newspapers, even if not written by him, reflected his politics. Zenger, by
contrast, was a conduit. A Palatine German whose father died
during their immigration, he had been apprenticed to New York's
public printer. Now, as an independent printer, he published what
others wrote. His *New York Weekly Journal* was the product of a
local spoils fight between the newly appointed colonial governor
William Cosby and the family of Lewis Morris, lord of the manor
of Morrisania in Westchester County.[15]

Cosby arrived in New York in August 1732 intent on restoring
his ebbing fortunes. This meant selling the provincial offices at his
disposal and, necessarily, creating enemies. One was Rip Van Dam,
who had been acting executive awaiting Cosby. The new governor
demanded that Van Dam conform to an intermittent tradition and
grant Cosby half of Van Dam's salary for the period prior to
Cosby's arrival. When Van Dam refused, Cosby got the provincial
council to authorize the New York Supreme Court to hear the
dispute as a court of exchequer.[16]

That court voted two-to-one to accept jurisdiction. Chief Justice
Lewis Morris publicly dissented against both the legality and the

propriety of the action. Cosby, not content with a simple win, dismissed Morris from the court, creating a full-scale political battle. Morris vowed to drive Cosby from New York. He successfully organized a local opposition in New York City and publicized the governor's every problem. But since Morris's faction could not win elections outside of New York City and Westchester, Morris was unable to break Cosby's control of the council.[17]

Zenger's *New York Weekly Journal* was created in November 1733 to intensify the attacks on Cosby. Because it was funded by the Morrisites, Zenger published what they wrote. As Stanley Katz's excellent exposition of the background notes, "on the whole the *Journal* was looking for trouble." The trouble would be laid at Zenger's door. Lewis Morris and James Alexander (who was the guiding hand of the *Journal*) were immune because, since the letters attacking the governor were pseudonymous, the identity of the attackers was unknown—unless Zenger talked. And a printer was paid in part for his silence.[18]

Zenger's *Journal* was making history in several ways. It was the first partisan opposition newspaper in the colonies. The *Journal*'s partisanship and its systematic attacks on the Cosby administration required justification. At first the *Gazette*, Cosby's captive newspaper (captive because of government contracts), ignored the *Journal;* but that soon proved impossible, and issue was joined. The *Journal* republished extracts from the Radical English Whig essays published as *Cato's Letters,* which emphasized the need of a free press to keep the public vigilant and the people in power honest. The *Gazette* countered with the virtues of the law of libel: " 'Tis the abuse not the use of the press that is criminal and ought to be punished." The law of seditious libel fitted Zenger's press nicely; it was publishing both stories and satire designed to bring the government into disrepute. Indeed, the *Journal* had been founded to do just that.[19]

The *Journal*'s assaults on Cosby avoided seditious libel charges for a year, because the January 1734 grand jury refused to return an indictment. When the next grand jury met the following October, the jurors agreed that two songs published as a broadside attack were indeed libelous, but professed inability to discover the author or printer; so Zenger avoided indictment again.[20]

Thwarted by the local grand jurors, the governor tried the more favorable forums of the council and the provincial assembly. Only the council would go along; it ordered four issues of the *Journal* to be burned by the common hangman, and a reward for the identity of the pseudonymous writer was authorized. A warrant for Zenger's arrest was issued by Chief Justice De Lancey (who had gained his post at Morris's expense), and Zenger was soon in jail. Zenger's lawyers, especially James Alexander, for whom Zenger was covering, immediately tried to obtain bail. But De Lancey set the bail at an extraordinarily high £400 (Zenger stated that his net worth was under £40, "the tools of my trade and wearing apparel excepted"). The Morrisites could have raised the bail, but they chose not to. In the political coin, Zenger was now worth more in captivity than free.[21]

For Zenger, however, release was anticipated as soon as the January 1735 grand jury term expired without an indictment. Although no indictment was returned, everything quickly changed. Instead of abiding by the grand jury decision, the attorney general moved by information; this procedure, equivalent to a grand jury indictment without the grand jury, looked high-handed under the circumstances. Zenger was now in jail for the duration.[22]

The governor's decision to play hardball and disregard the grand jury altered the posture of the case. Zenger's predicament now looked sympathetic. But however sympathetic the jurors might be, their role was all but irrelevant in a seditious libel case where the printer's identity was known. That is because a case of seditious libel addressed only two questions: Was the material printed libelous; that is, did it tend to bring the government into disrepute? And did the defendant print (or write) the material in question? Only the second issue was for jury determination. The first issue was exclusively "a matter of law" and therefore was to be decided by the judge. Furthermore, at common law truth was no defense, although it was not entirely irrelevant. As the attorney general accurately informed Chief Justice De Lancey, "supposing [the *Journal*'s criticisms] were true, the law says that they are not the less libelous for that; nay indeed the law says their being true is an aggravation of the crime."[23]

Zenger's predicament could not have been worse; he was in jail awaiting a trial in which his chances were nil. Because the charge was printing certain issues of the *Journal* and everyone knew Zenger was its printer, he was a sure loser. A grand jury might have saved him by refusing to indict, but when the attorney general moved by information the last safeguard was erased.

Zenger thus appeared to be a defendant without a substantive defense. Then, just as now, that necessitated trial tactics based on procedural defenses. Alexander questioned the validity of the judges' commissions. If the ploy were successful, it would prevent a trial. Instead of obtaining a ruling, De Lancey disbarred Zenger's attorneys. Hard as it was to imagine, Zenger's chances of getting out of jail sank even lower, although a request for court-appointed counsel was granted.[24]

Zenger may have hit his nadir when even the court clerk got involved on the prosecution side. Zenger's court-appointed counsel had successfully moved for a "struck" jury (created by striking off those potential jurors whom counsel does not accept) of free-holders; but the clerk provided a jury list not so limited, which contained the names of men in the governor's employ. The court-appointed lawyer challenged the list, and Zenger received a prop-erly limited jury (which as constituted had at least six members clearly identified with the Morris faction). Alexander, meanwhile, had been searching for a new lawyer and had obtained the services of Andrew Hamilton of Philadelphia (hence the future phrase "Philadelphia lawyer").[25]

When no substantive defense exists and procedural defenses fail, the only choice left is to put the victim on trial. Here Hamilton succeeded brilliantly—the "victim," Governor Cosby, was gen-uinely unpopular in the city. Hamilton began his defense to the jury with an obvious (but, to a jury, quite plausible) misstatement. He claimed that when he first read the information, he had no idea that the governor was the party under discussion. He thought that the case was about "an overzealous printer who had misconstrued the actions of some in authority and that the Attorney General had overreached." But, Hamilton told the jurors, he had now learned from the attorney general's remarks that the case originated by an order of the governor and council. He noted that the courtroom was full, so the case must be important. But, he reminded the jury, the governor was not the king: "Is it not surprising to see a subject upon his receiving a commission from the King to be a governor of a colony in America, immediately imagining himself to be vested with all the prerogatives belonging to the sacred person of his Prince?" Cosby, not the attorney general, was overreaching.[26]

Hamilton had previously conceded that Zenger was the publisher of the *Journal* issues in question; in so doing, he had set the tone of the defense: "I cannot think it proper for me (without doing violence to my own principles) to deny the publication of a complaint which I think is the right of every free-born subject to make." The attorney general, well knowing the law, believed the concession to be tantamount to a guilty plea because, as the chief justice quickly ruled, the truth of the published attacks was irrelevant. But Hamilton rightly noted that although the attorney general had told the jury that the information characterized these attacks as being "scandalous, and tend[ing] to sedition," the attorney general left out an important particular: "He omitted the word *false*. . . . This word *false* must have some meaning, or else how came it there?" Here Hamilton returned to his previously losing argument that truth was a defense: "I will agree that if he can prove the facts charged upon us to be false, I'll own them to be scandalous, seditious, and a libel."[27]

The attorney general made a two-part response. First, he need not prove anything, since Zenger "confessed the printing and the publishing." He should have quit there, but he went on to ask: "How can we prove a negative?" Seizing the moment, Hamilton responded, "We will save Mr. Attorney the trouble of proving a negative and take the *onus probandi* upon ourselves, and prove those very papers that are called libels to be *true*."[28]

Now Hamilton was back arguing with De Lancey, who ruled that the truth of the alleged libels was not to be put in evidence. After an exchange that left the positions unchanged, Hamilton responded that the cases the prosecution relied upon were "Star Chamber cases, and I was in hopes that practice had been dead with the Court." They were not. But given the reputation the Star Chamber acquired under the early Stuarts as a court using streamlined procedures and designed to suppress political opposition, its law may have been dead with the jurors.[29]

Having lost every way he turned, Hamilton now appealed to the jurors, stating that they were chosen because they were "supposed to have the best knowledge of the fact that is to be tried": "According to my belief, the facts which we offer to prove were not com-

mitted in a corner; they are notoriously known to be true; and
therefore in your justice lies our safety." One way or another
Hamilton would drive home the truth of the criticisms Zenger
published.[30]

Hamilton interwove the jurors' knowledge, their need to do
justice, and Zenger's safety through a long closing argument in
which he emphasized that truthfully criticizing colonial malad-
ministration was a natural right. "It is a right which all freemen
claim, and are entitled to complain when they are hurt; they have a
right publicly to remonstrate the abuses of power, in the strongest
terms, to put their neighbors upon their guard against the craft or
open violence of men in authority." Contrasting the colonies with
England, Hamilton tried to suggest that Cosby was more sensitive
to criticism than the English Crown. Indeed, relying on the changes
in religious tolerance over the preceding two centuries, Hamilton
noted sarcastically, "I think it pretty clear that in New York a man
may make very free with his God, but he must take special care
what he says of his governor."[31]

Hamilton told the jurors that they had a duty not to delegate
their decision to another. If Zenger printed the truth, he told them,
"you ought to say so." By the time he reached his closing, it was
apparent that the earlier reference to "our safety" was not to
Zenger's but to that of all colonists, including the jurors: "When
our neighbor's house is on fire, we ought to take care of our own."
Conveniently forgetting that he had earlier protested ignorance of
the magnitude of the case, Hamilton maintained that, despite his
age and infirmities, it was his duty to go anywhere in the land to
protect the subject from governments trying "to deprive a people of
the right of remonstrating (and complaining too) of the arbitrary
attempts of men in power."[32]

De Lancey gave the expected jury instructions at the end, but to
no avail. The jury "in a small time" returned with its verdict of not
guilty, "upon which there were three huzzas in the hall which was
crowded with people." Zenger had won—although while his lawyer and others celebrated that evening, Zenger spent one more
night in jail; he was not released until the day after the verdict. The
verdict, however, was a potent symbol in North America throughout the eighteenth century. No one lost sight of the need for a press

that is free to criticize oppressive governments and the ability of juries to guarantee that freedom.[33]

The Morrisites had defeated the governor, but it was a victory only in their stronghold. They could not prevail elsewhere, and the English government staunchly refused to restore Lewis Morris to his judgeship. When Cosby died a half-year after the trial, his principal advisor was selected as the new governor. The Morrisites now showed what the fight had been about. The principle was not freedom of the press or the right of political opposition; the principle was money. They "grasped greedily" for the spoils of the new administration, and Morris wound up as governor of New Jersey. The factional fight vanished without a trace, although the Morrises (as distinguished from the Morrisites), with their wealth, remained prominent through the time of the drafting of the Constitution.[34]

## III

Both *Zenger* and *Patterson* raise the most basic issue of a free press: the right to publish the truth about the government, however critical, and spread the message to one's fellow citizens. Freedom of the press in the eighteenth century was largely a story of seditious libel—the proposition that government may punish its critics for words that it perceives as threats to its survival (and legitimacy), whether the criticism be directed at the government itself or, more likely, at its officials. Caustic criticism of a government, especially one whose legitimacy is insecure, may well have the effect the law ascribes to seditious libel: weakening and damaging the government. Furthermore, history shows that the more thin-skinned the governors, the more they perceive criticism as a threat to the government's existence. Beyond doubt that is the effect that the Morrisites intended to have on Cosby. Patterson's situation was more complex—he wanted to force the Colorado Supreme Court to withdraw from its attack on Denver home rule (which it did). Patterson assumed that if the court withdrew, the Denver voters would check the city's public utilities on their own. In both cases, publicizing the truth about pernicious government policies was necessary to achieve the goals of the government's critics.

There may be more varied and interesting free press issues than truthful criticism, but they cannot come to the foreground until a legal system settles this basic one. A genuine democracy, where elections count and the losers accept the results, is impossible if the citizens must wonder whether truthful criticism of the government will result in a brush with the law inflicted by those being criticized.

Zenger was freed because the jury accepted Hamilton's urging and delivered the verdict of not guilty. Had the jury followed Chief Justice De Lancey's instructions and simply found that, by Hamilton's admission, Zenger did publish the writings in question, Zenger would have been in virtually the same position that Patterson occupied 171 years later. De Lancey was intimately tied to Governor Cosby, serving at Cosby's pleasure (this was the basis for Alexander's motion that De Lancey's commission was invalid); the Colorado Supreme Court was in the enviable position of judging its own case.

From Patterson's perspective, no forum could have been worse than the one he got. Whether a Denver jury would have acquitted him may be an open question; that he would have had a chance of acquittal is not. And conversely, had Zenger been tried in a venue where Governor Cosby enjoyed substantial support, his criticisms of the governor would probably have been less appealing; indeed, the jurors' conception of truth might well have differed from Zenger's. The chances that the jury would have followed the judge's instructions would therefore have been much greater.

The two cases highlight a fact every lawyer knows: law is not self-enforcing. No matter how much society attempts to sanitize the judicial process, human beings are the instruments of law enforcement. People like Justice De Lancey and the judges on the 1905 Colorado Supreme Court will always be part of the system and anything but neutral. Such judges will see their function as being a part of the enforcing and legitimizing arm of the state.[35]

The realization that judges may be part of the problem rather than the solution to the dispensing of impartial justice qualifies the initial issue of democratic discussion: whether journalists may write critically and truthfully for their fellow citizens. The right in question is in fact a right to have the issues relating to truth tried fairly, that is, by the writer's peers. Presumably this means that if the writing is critical and the government unpopular, a jury acquittal is likely to follow, vindicating the right to criticize. As a corollary, if the government is popular, a jury may find the criticisms false (or unjustified) and therefore convict the critic, who will be unpopular. A jury may thus operate as a majoritarian check on an unpopular government, but not on a popular one. If this seems like a rather limited right of a free press—well, it is. But even this limited right does not exist in many countries; it is the starting point for the creation of a right to freedom of the press.

The First Amendment should have something to do with all this. Yet we must note that Zenger, who could not invoke the First Amendment, won—and Patterson, who did invoke it, lost. The anomaly is explained in Justice Holmes's opinion for the Court in *Patterson*. The First Amendment does not grant the right to print truth or the right to criticize government; it simply guarantees, as did the English common law, the right to publish free of the need to request government permission (no prior restraints). What happens after publication (subsequent punishment) is something else again. Should publishers violate the law, they are responsible.

Thus Patterson did not need to ask permission of the Colorado Supreme Court—or any other governmental body—before publishing his critical articles. But if the articles were found to be in contempt of the court they criticized—and they were—then he was responsible to the law. Under Holmes's theory, Zenger was lucky—as indeed he was in real life—for the First Amendment would not have protected him even if it had been in existence. Only a jury could have granted him the defense that his alleged libel was true; and this is precisely what happened.

*Patterson* holds that the state may punish writings as it pleases. The First Amendment is no bar because it protects only the right to publish, not the publication itself. The publisher always runs the risk that criticism of government may go too far. If Holmes's position in *Patterson* is correct, the historical First Amendment was concerned exclusively with incorporating the great transformation of the seventeenth century that did away with government licensing of the press. A prohibition on licensing guarantees that if printers are committed enough to run risks, they may publish and circulate anything. The dissemination of information is therefore possible. But the elimination of licensing emphatically does not end other legal means of controlling the written word.

Too often the history of civil liberties, freedom of the press included, is written from the Whiggish perspective of progress un-folding; but the realities are different. As *Patterson* demonstrates, at the end of the nineteenth century the Supreme Court did not view the First Amendment as a guarantee of political dissent. Yet Dwight Teeter's study of revolutionary-era printers, described in Chapter 1, demonstrates that the press of the revolutionary era not only took on Great Britain, but attacked patriot policies as well. William Cushing, chief justice of Massachusetts, rhetorically noted to John Adams in 1789, "Without this liberty of the press could we have supported our liberties against british administration? or could our revolution have taken place?"[36]

Times change; perceptions of freedom of the press change. Had Patterson attacked a revolutionary-era judiciary, he might have succeeded. Had he lived to write in the second half of this century, he would have succeeded. Civil liberties enjoy times of great cele-bration and times of strain. Freedom of the press is no exception, although we may hope that the strengths it has shown over the past quarter-century will serve us well into the next one. What follows is a discussion of the celebrations, strains, issues, and theories that constitute the modern understanding of freedom of the press.

*Part One*

■  ■  ■

# Traditions

# Overview

A book about freedom of the press written by an American law professor necessarily deals with freedom of the press under the First Amendment of the United States Constitution. Furthermore, even when I disagree with the Supreme Court, I must acknowledge that its pronouncements are an essential ingredient in any discussion. These two obvious points necessitate some common background for discussion, a commonality that I realize various readers will not have at the outset. In Part One, I attempt to provide that background without writing a full history of freedom of the press in the United States. In choosing "Traditions" for the title, I have used the plural intentionally. As a society—and more significantly, as a legal system—the United States has at varying times been more or less hospitable to claims of freedom of the press, depending in no small part on how caustic and legitimate they were perceived to be and how secure the body politic was. I have written one chapter each on two different traditions and treatments of freedom of the press. In both legal argument and common discussion, the views of the Founding Fathers are invoked, with what often seems an incredible regularity, to justify various meanings of freedom of the press. That, too, is a tradition, and no book about freedom of the press could ignore the framing of the First.

The first chapter is the obligatory bow to the events and ideas, especially from the Declaration of Independence to the First Congress, surrounding the drafting of the First Amendment in the year after ratification of the Constitution. I have attempted a synthesis of the excellent academic literature of the 1980s, especially that of my two colleagues David Anderson and David Rabban, who, I believe, have best explained the events and ideas behind the First Amendment. Additionally, I have prominently integrated some of Dwight Teeter's less available work on the revolutionary-era printers. Anderson's research emphasizes the importance of the continuous drafting of press clauses in the fundamental documents of the era and of the concomitant reiteration that guarantees of freedom of the press were essential to the well-being of the citizenry of a republic. Rabban underscores Anderson's conclusions by his own adaptation of republican historiography and its emphasis on American adoption of the Radical English Whig opposition ideology. When the writings of Anderson and Rabban are combined, they supplant the prevailing academic view that freedom of the press had a decidedly more limited meaning in the 1780s.

Chapter 2 deals with the Sedition Act controversy and with some aspects of the suppression of dissent during World War I. These are well-known episodes, of course—indeed in many respects better known than the decade following World War II. That decade did not produce press litigation, whereas these earlier periods did. It is important to understand how periods of repression were justified constitutionally; not to illustrate a (false) Whig view of progress unfolding, but rather to demonstrate how easy it has been for public figures to justify significant limitations on democratic debate. Because it has been so easy in the past, I am reluctant to believe it will not be almost as easy in the future. I hope that my analysis of the constitutional arguments made during the Sedition Act controversy, as well as those that appear in some less familiar World War I cases (*Frohwerk* and the *Milwaukee Leader* case), will provide some new information even for the specialist. However, the basic analysis of these two historical episodes is familiar ground for those in the field, and my conclusions about both the Sedition Act and the attack on dissent during World War I follow the existing scholarship.

Chapter 3 covers the seven years from 1964 to 1971, beginning with the constitutionalization of libel law and ending with the frantic effort to lift the injunctions preventing publication of the Pentagon Papers. The chapter concentrates on these two landmark cases less for legal doctrine (which will be treated in the opening two chapters of Part Two) than as political and social statements about the Supreme Court, society, and dissent. In between I offer a highly truncated look at the Court's transformation of other areas of First Amendment jurisprudence. In my judgment, in no other period could one look at the Supreme Court's First Amendment work and more readily conclude, as Harry Kalven did in his posthumous masterwork, *A Worthy Tradition,* that the First Amendment was "working itself pure." No other period manifested a tradition of protecting dissent better than this short, but remarkable, era.

## Chapter One

# The Framers and the First

One would think that the document announcing ratification of the Bill of Rights would have a special prominence in bicentennial celebrations and would, perhaps, be a fit subject for public readings like Washington's Farewell Address. But then one reads the letter of the secretary of state to the state governors announcing the ratification of the Bill of Rights and such thoughts evaporate. "I have the honor to send you herein enclosed," the usually eloquent Thomas Jefferson wrote,

two copies duly authenticated, of an Act concerning certain fisheries of the United States, and for the regulation and government of the fisherman employed therein; also of an Act to establish the post office and post roads within the United States; also the ratification by three fourths of the Legislatures of the Several States, of certain articles in addition and amendment of the Constitution of the United States, proposed by Congress to the said Legislatures, and being with sentiments of the most perfect respect, your Excellency's &c.[1]

The ordering in Jefferson's transmittal is quite consistent with the view that the Bill of Rights originated in a desire to kill the Constitution. The goal of the Antifederalists was to defeat, in any way possible, ratification. Pointing to the failure to include a declaration of rights was the most effective way of creating opposition to the Constitution. That it was a ploy is demonstrated by the fact that the Antifederalists were far less interested in the "necessity" of a Bill of Rights after the Constitution was ratified than they were when it might have been defeated. Thus Jefferson got it right: fish were more important, and the Bill of Rights ran a poor third.[2]

Yet if the Antifederalists thought of the Bill of Rights as a potential deal breaker, and thereby lost interest when the Federalists adopted the cause as their own, the power of the felt need for such guarantees testifies to an underlying importance. Something about a newer and more efficient government necessitated the types of protections already incorporated against state governments. This era of constitution drafting had grown well accustomed to enshrining fundamental rights that government could not reach. Thus, while the Antifederalists would have liked the whole Constitution sent back to the drawing board, most Federalists came to agree that a bill of rights was not incompatible with their handiwork and would enhance the document.

James Madison then made good on the Federalist pledge by steering the Bill of Rights through the First Congress as a priority item. Whether Madison's conversion to the need for a Bill of Rights, which he initially doubted, was intellectual progress or the need to avert political defeat at the hands of a prominent Anti-Federalist candidate, James Monroe, may be open to question; but once he publicly committed himself, he made good on his promise. Like everyone else, he never doubted that a guarantee of press freedom would be included in any Bill of Rights; it "had been too integral a part of revolutionary ideology for anyone to dare disavow it" and there was "not one recorded objection" in the Congress to protecting freedom of speech and the press.[3]

If there were no recorded objections, neither were there recorded positive discussions in the Congress on the meaning of freedom of the press. The lack of discussion has seemed in retrospect persuasive evidence that the framers were incorporating, rather than fundamentally altering, what they perceived to be the legal status quo. But what was it? Nonlawyers often think such questions have ready answers, and often they do. But not always. Especially in periods of legal fluidity, one should be wary of believing that a momentary snapshot offers a full portrayal of the law. The second half of the eighteenth century was certainly one of those fluid periods, and it is simply impossible to turn to discussions by the framers, let alone a mythical collection of "Revised Laws of the Several States" for definitive answers on the scope of freedom of the press.

Justice Holmes taught us over a century ago that the life of the law is experience. Thus I propose to look at the events leading to and surrounding the adoption of the First Amendment to gain insight into how the revolutionary generation understood the press. First, we will look at the laws and constitutions of the newly independent states. Then we will look at the behavior of printers during the revolutionary era, because no group can be assumed to be more aware of the law in force than those who would expect to bear its brunt. The examination of press behavior leads into a look at the behavior of government officials and then to a study of the transformed meaning of sovereignty, the very touchstone of the American Revolution. Finally, with that as background, we will look at the actual choices made with respect to freedom of the press in the Constitutional Convention and the First Congress (which proposed the Bill of Rights).[4]

## I

The disintegration of the royal governments in 1775, the call from the Continental Congress in May 1776 to the states to exert "all the powers of government . . . under authority of the people of the colonies," and, of course, the Declaration of Independence created obvious practical problems. Those relating to the military headed the list. But the events also created theoretical problems which could not be ignored because they carried real practical consequences. When the colonies severed their relationship with Great Britain, where had sovereignty—that is, ultimate theoretical entitlement to rule—gone? Sovereignty may seem abstract, but real issues, such as who makes the laws—and therefore what laws—turn on where sovereignty is located. Thus it was necessary to answer the question, Where is sovereignty located?[5]

Were the former colonies in Locke's state of nature? Had they briefly passed through it? Just what were the applicable laws? Were they those of both man and nature, and if the former, where had they come from? Forrest McDonald aptly observes that "independence—the very existence of the United States—was unequivocably justified in the Declaration itself by an appeal to 'the Laws of Nature and Nature's God.' . . . That opened a can of worms."[6]

Although the patriots approaching the theoretical question came to slightly different conclusions, the practical question was an-

swered with considerable similarity. As the Berkshire Constitutionalists of Western Massachusetts argued, the Revolution had thrown
the people "into a state of Nature" and they would remain there
until "the formation of a fundamental Constitution as the Basis and
ground work of Legislation." During the Revolution eleven of the
thirteen states, soon to be joined by the unrecognized state of
Vermont, drafted constitutions. Sovereignty in England rested in
Parliament; but Americans, who had come to find the Radical
English Whig ideology appropriate to their situation, held that
sovereignty was in the people, who through constituent conventions would create new governments as necessary.[7]

Constitutions provide outlines of governance. Ordinary laws,
and by default the common law, fill in huge blanks to govern day-
to-day affairs. All states save Connecticut filled the void of applicable laws to govern individual behavior by determining, through
statute or constitution, that the common law should continue in
force until changed. Given that there was no explicit rejection of
Blackstone's view of the English common law of press freedom—a
printer had the right to publish but was fully accountable subsequently for what was published—Leonard Levy, an influential
scholar of the framing of the First Amendment, has concluded that
seditious libel remained part of the American legal tradition after
independence. The First Amendment quite possibly was intended
to do little more than protect the press against prior restraints,
according to Levy.[8]

Levy's misgivings about the continuing possibility of seditious
libel prosecutions would clearly be alleviated by a statement that
the law of seditious libel, being incompatible with American institutions, does not constitute part of the imported common law.
No such statement has ever been found. The question remains,
however, whether a lesser statement, with a similar import, might
exist.

The methods of continuing the English common law could have
rejected some of it; there was a possibility that while much of the
common law came in, seditious libel was out. Georgia by statute
and the newly independent Vermont by its constitution received the
common law, but only so much as was not repugnant to the state
constitution. What Georgia and Vermont made explicit would necessarily be implicit in other states with new constitutions. Good

though the common law might be, it would not control any question that the state constitution settled otherwise. In other states, such as Virginia, the reception statute expressly received "the common law of England . . . until the same shall be altered by the legislative power." States with such statutes would not be appropriate candidates to have rejected seditious libel. These various methods of receiving the common law encourage a more thorough look at the remainder of the laws of the states, especially the new constitutions.[9]

With two exceptions, the new state constitutions (including that of Vermont) were not silent on freedom of the press. Every state that embedded a declaration of rights into its new constitution included freedom of the press as one of the protected liberties. Virginia led the way, in language that repeated, with slight modification, that of the Radical English Whigs John Trenchard and Thomas Gordon: "That freedom of the Press is one of the greatest bulwarks of liberty, and can never be restrained but by despotick Governments." Massachusetts also included a variant of Trenchard and Gordon in its press clause: "The liberty of the press is essential to the security of freedom in a state: it ought not, therefore, to be restrained in this Commonwealth."[10]

Pennsylvania's constitution was unique because of its radically democratic features; its press clause was also unique because Pennsylvania was the only state that explicitly mentioned freedom of speech as well as freedom of the press: "That the people have a right to freedom of speech, and of writing, and publishing their sentiments; therefore the freedom of the press ought not to be restrained." Additionally, in the body of its constitution, Pennsylvania had a second press clause, one that recognized the importance of the press for enlightening the citizens about the working of government: "The printing presses shall be free to every person who undertakes to examine the proceedings of the legislature, or any part of government."[11]

The nine states (plus Vermont) that adopted press clauses spoke more directly about freedom of the press than they did about their adoption of the common law. Even assuming, as a minority might have, that a constitution and the common law were on equal footing as law, a common-law rule of construction—that the particular controls the general—would give the press clauses primacy over the common law when the question turned to seditious libel. The only way the press clauses would not have primacy would be if there were no conflict between them and the common law of seditious libel. This is virtually inconceivable, for the Radical Whigs, from "Cato" in the 1720s to Joseph Priestley and Richard Price in the generation that lived through the American Revolution, stressed that freedom of political expression provided the most effective way for the people to safeguard their sovereignty and their liberties. Yet the inconceivable is what Levy asserts: freedom of the press, even if copied from the Radical English Whigs (with their complete rejection of Blackstone) nevertheless meant the "narrow conservatism" of Blackstone.[12]

Those who adopted the state constitutions did not speak to this point during the Revolution. They were too busy with other, more pressing tasks. But their new constitutions were based on a radically different theory of government than that manifested in Great Britain and justified by Blackstone's *Commentaries*. Blackstone, recording the aftermath of Britain's Glorious Revolution, recognized the transference of English sovereignty from the Crown to Parliament. Americans, following the Radical English Whigs, cut the middlemen out and placed sovereignty in the people. Rejecting Blackstone, Americans maintained instead that sovereignty derived from the people's continuous assent.[13]

Continuous assent meant continuous scrutiny. The sovereign people needed information and the ability to discuss freely how their government was performing. It is no surprise that they, with "Cato," saw a free press as a "bulwark of liberty" essential to their newly created constitutions. Levy asks us to believe that revolutionary Americans were operating with one view of sovereignty at a constitutional level and with a different one at a practical level. A far more economical position is that revolutionary Americans were consistent, that changes in sovereignty resulted in changes in the scope of a free press.[14]

The very fact that the vast majority of states drafting constitutions found that express recognition of a free press was important speaks more clearly to the issue of press freedoms than generalized statements about receiving the common law—especially when major portions of the common law, at least as theretofore practiced in the colonies, were retained only until new legislation was adopted.

Nevertheless, arguing from inferences can take only so far. Although not without its own ambiguities, press behavior does offer bits of hard evidence about the meaning of freedom of the press.

## II

To a nonlawyer it might seem strange to turn to the practices of journalists to discover the law. But to lawyers that makes good sense. No one is more likely to know what the expected legal norms are than those who risk feeling the brunt of the law. Another Holmes dictum is his definition of law as predictions of what the courts and other public officials will do in fact. This is the *experienced* law. If there are differences between law on the books and law in action (the latter representing the norms of the society, waiting for the law on the books formally to catch up), the behavior of those being regulated provides a workable barometer.

The eighteenth-century press—and the petty merchant-printers that ran it—did not bother with late-nineteenth- or twentieth-century notions such as independence from government. Although it may be too strident to call the eighteenth-century press a kept press, those printers did want to get close to sources of revenue. Income came, not from subscriptions, but from printing contracts, and the most lucrative ones were those from governments (although religious contracts were also available and often lucrative as well). As would be expected, a "subsidized press was in large part a controlled press"; a printer's defiance of those who paid for the printing could result in the bankruptcy of the operation.[15]

After the French and Indian War both external and internal pressures eroded the older deferential system. Some printers were not hopelessly dependent on government largess, and Zenger's earlier example found more emulators. With tensions between the mother country and the colonies increasing, so, too, did criticisms of officialdom.[16]

Printers "seemed to glory in the fact that the Revolution was at hand." And well they should, for their profession was changing with the times. The older "often servile dependence" on government largess, which had been eroding, was broken. Whether the government liked it or not, during the War for Independence, it had a relationship of interdependence with printers; the government itself needed presses to print laws, journals, and proclamations. There was, in fact, "more official printing business than has been commonly recognized."[17]

The result was, as the colonial historian Merrill Jensen observed thirty years ago, a "debate among Americans about constitutions, governmental policies, and politicians [that] continued with unabated fervor." Even Levy describes a "nearly epidemic degree of seditious libel . . . infecting American newspapers after Independence." But the central point is that the law of seditious libel, which in any event had not been used successfully in decades, did not become a weapon during the war. For those supporting liberty, there was liberty of expression. To be sure, Loyalists often found themselves without the same degree of liberty. Extralegal means shut their presses; legal means drove many from their homes. Jensen, after conceding that "the newspapers . . . who supported Great Britain were suppressed," excuses this by plausibly noting that "any nation new or old, would do the same thing whatever its laws might be" during a struggle for its independence. But there was active political debate about the issues facing the newly independent states, and it is worth looking at the conduct of that debate within the free, critical, and often partisan press.[18]

Philadelphia was the largest city in the colonies, and it had the most printing presses. Furthermore, it was the site of the Continental Congress as well as the Pennsylvania Assembly, the latter operating under a much criticized—because it was highly democratic—constitution. Dwight Teeter's pathbreaking studies of the Philadelphia printers illustrate the uses of the newfound freedom to criticize, including those that brought two printers, Benjamin Towne and Eleazer Oswald, to test the existing limits of the law.[19]

The war effort, quite naturally, provided the areas of contention. Timely information often could not be had. Printers working long hours did not search for news; they let the news come to them. In part for that reason, but more likely because George Washington was in command, overall military strategy was not a contentious press topic. Even before his successes, Washington was a demigod, above reproach. If printers were inclined to cross that line, second thoughts cautioned against it. Only the irascible Oswald, an artillery officer whom General Washington had passed over for promotion, dared to criticize the great man's military abilities. For his pains, he was confronted by a mob. To his credit, he seized pistols and challenged the mob's ringleader to a duel. Soon after this, however, he moved on to Philadelphia, where he established his *Independent Gazetteer* and received the assistance of Robert Morris, the superintendent of finances.[20]

Although Oswald could not always be controlled, he immediately came to Morris's defense when controversy arose over Morris's making information public about the nation's problematical finances. Oswald's defense of openness and his attack on secrecy would find an echo over two hundred years later in the opinions of Justices Black and Stewart in the *Pentagon Papers Cases*. Defending Morris, Oswald attacked the idea that discussing finances in public would aid the enemy: "Do you suppose the enemy are deaf to the clamours of our creditors and our army, or blind to the state of our affairs? . . . The enemy has known every Thing, and nobody has been duped but our citizens."[21]

Tom Paine had earlier, and with less justification, discussed in the press what many felt ought to be kept private. During the early part of the Revolution he was a "frequent and intemperate" contributor to the Philadelphia press. But writing in the *Pennsylvania Packet* behind the transparent pseudonym of "Common Sense"—Paine's pamphlet *Common Sense* had made his reputation and he was fond of it—Paine revealed a secret better kept: France had been providing clandestine aid to the Americans before the Franco-American alliance became official. Paine knew this because he held the rewarding job of secretary to the Committee on Foreign Affairs in Congress. The French minister quite naturally complained about the unfortunate disclosures. Delegates to Congress, who surely knew the identity of "Common Sense," ordered that "Mr. John Dunlap [printer of the *Packet*] and Mr. Thomas Paine attend immediately at the bar of this House." Dunlap named Paine, and Paine confessed. Although forced to resign, Paine quickly was hired as the secretary of the Pennsylvania Assembly.[22]

Only a few were in the position to publicize that which other public men wished secret and, given the ability of members of the Constitutional Convention to keep their proceedings secret, it is not surprising that there are few examples of publicizing secret information. But other aspects of wartime behavior did face public scrutiny. One example was the behavior of Congress during the troop mutiny of 1783. Another was the handling of financing the war. In both of these cases writers attacked public men and their actions in ways that might well have drawn prosecutions for seditious libel were officials inclined to assert such powers. That they did not tells us at least as much about the actual understandings of the time as a perusal of old statute books or legal commentaries.

Unpaid troops became increasingly restless after the fighting ceased. Philadelphia had its mutiny in late June, 1783. Delegates to Congress looked out the windows of the State House (which they shared with the assembly) and saw the building surrounded by soldiers. Congress wished protection by the state militia, but Pennsylvania President John Dickinson believed the militia would prove unreliable. Madison wrote that the delegates felt no danger from premeditated violence; at the end of an unproductive daily session Congress safely adjourned in midafternoon, passing by the soldiers who "in some instances offer[ed] mock obstruction." Congress met again and formally requested protection from the state. When it was not forthcoming, Congress clandestinely abandoned Philadelphia, leaving behind with its printer a proclamation setting forth its reason, namely, the lack of protection.[23]

The mutiny itself quickly collapsed. "Congress' disappearance from the city, coupled with the circulation of handbills complaining of the failure of Pennsylvania to protect Congress, took the starch out of the mutineers." Then the printed recriminations began. The mutiny became the ostensible reason for articles that criticized everybody and everything: Congress, the Articles of Confederation, the mutinous soldiers, the militia, and the president, council, and assembly of Pennsylvania. If the state took its share for failure to act, Congress was hardly immune from charges of cowardice. Oswald's *Independent Gazetteer* sided with the army as it discussed the "commotion" which had "excited the most dreadful apprehensions in the minds of Congress, who the soldiers have long considered, like their paper currency, in a state of depreciation, having no solidity or real worth."[24]

Oswald's reference to paper currency brings out a major target of the revolutionary printers' wrath. Nowhere did the press better represent the hostility many Americans felt toward a select few believed to be lining their pockets at the expense of the many. News of the rapidly depreciating currency, along with charges and countercharges of monopolization and profiteering, appeared in the papers. A blunt statement came in the second issue of the *Independent Gazetteer,* where the vice-president of Pennsylvania was accused of embezzling state funds; he was "like Dolon of Troy, whose very features bespeak treason against the majesty of honesty." Francis Bailey's *Freeman's Journal* took the charges to a different level. The *Journal* was not concerned about the honesty of the New York delegate, James Duane. That would be too mild. Instead, the *Journal* asserted that Duane, a proponent of the national bank, chose as his associates Tories and traitors like Joseph Galloway, Silas Deane, and Benedict Arnold. If America prevailed, he would be wealthy and respected. And if the Revolution failed, "the British funds must be exhausted to tender him an adequate reward."[25]

Dr. Benjamin Rush, writing in the *Pennsylvania Packet* as "Leonidas," accused many government officials of embezzlement and fraud, noting that "the man of ancient patrimonial estate is outbid for everything by a deputy quartermaster's clerk. See him lay down *his*—I retract the word—your ten thousand dollars for a farm. There is no end to his purchase." Listing the reasons why paper money kept depreciating, he included the charge that Congress "acted as if . . . [it] thought there was no connection between private and public virtue. How many of your officers have lately been called from billiard tables and taverns to execute the most important commissions under you?"[26]

"Leonidas" brought forth an immediate, angry reaction in Congress, with Elbridge Gerry of Massachusetts demanding that the *Packet*'s printer, John Dunlap, be brought to the bar of Congress. Gerry's opinion was countered by others, including Virginia's Merriwether Smith, who read excerpts aloud and agreed with "Leonidas." Defending Dunlap, Smith argued that "when liberty of the Press shall be restrained, take my word for it, the liberties of the people shall be at an end."[27]

Benjamin Towne, however, presented a more complex situation. Although many opponents of Pennsylvania's constitution were accused of being Tories, Towne and his *Pennsylvania Evening Post,* despite an anticonstitution tone, avoided the charges and thus avoided suppression. But the *Evening Post* "was curiously devoid of controversial comments" while the British were near Philadelphia in 1777; and once they occupied the city, the *Evening Post* switched its ostensible allegiance to the British (and because of the better currency was able to lower its price from four to three pence). The *Evening Post* became a strident Loyalist paper claiming that the leaders of the rebellion had created a tyranny unparalleled in history. Ironically, despite Towne's "flawlessly" Tory line during occupation, a rival printer received most of the British patronage.[28]

When the British abandoned Philadelphia in mid-1778, Towne switched his paper's stance again. That allowed him to continue publishing, but one of the first items he printed must have caused him to wonder for how long. After the patriots reoccupied the city, Towne had the eerie chore of publishing the supreme executive council's proclamation of June 15, 1778, which listed as a traitor: "Benjamin Towne, printer."[29]

Towne lived to print another day. Eventually he surrendered himself to be tried for high treason, but the proceedings were called off (probably because he was regarded as a paunchy, weak-willed fool). This allowed him to be reminded of alternative constraints on the press. The *Evening Post* soon published a piece by Whitehead Humphreys, who adopted the famous Radical English Whig pen name of "Cato," making nasty references to Tom Paine's dismissal from his post as secretary of the Foreign Affairs Committee. "Cato" in a series of questions, two having the answer "Nobody knows" and the rest "Tom P——," charged that Paine was a Tory who had betrayed state affairs, possibly for pay, but definitely to aid the British. Paine responded without a pen name, threatening Towne should he not reveal "Cato's" identity. After another barb from "Cato," Paine's Pennsylvania allies seized Towne and successfully reasoned with him to identify "Cato" by placing a noose around Towne's neck. (When the mob then visited Humphreys, he successfully reasoned with them by waving a musket from an upstairs window.)[30]

The dispute between Humphreys and Paine was part of a larger dispute between Pennsylvania's Constitutionalists and Republicans. As a result, the unprincipled Towne had allies and became a "small scale celebrity" whose name was used to embarrass Paine and the Constitutionalists as violators of freedom of the press. So, too, "Leonidas" had instant defenders when he attacked government corruption. As Teeter has noted, the pluralistic nature of politics in Philadelphia—where both Congress and the assembly were beset by internal factions—meant that a printer would always have ready-made defenders of his actions. Most press controversies thus took on a political, rather than legal, form.[31]

The exception, of course, was for Loyalists: the line was drawn at support for Great Britain. For those who spoke the speech of liberty, there was liberty of speech. For the Loyalists there was suppression. As a result, highly seditious statements such as those of Benjamin Rush's "Leonidas" or Bailey's charges of treason passed without legal notice. But there was a line; treason—in the nontechnical sense of advocating the British cause—was not tolerated. That was the difference between Benjamin Towne's potential (but avoided) fate and that of the patriot Benjamin Rush. The Loyalists were suppressed, but not so the patriots. Whether it would have been different had more printers tried to attack Washington for ineptitude, there is no way of knowing. What is known is that there was only one recorded prosecution for seditious libel during the revolutionary era.[32]

It was against Eleazer Oswald, the one non-Tory printer who had attacked George Washington. But the charge of seditious libel came from Pennsylvania's Chief Justice Thomas McKean—for attacks on Pennsylvania's Chief Justice Thomas McKean. McKean was no stranger to controversy. Despite Pennsylvania's prohibition on dual office holding, he served as the state's chief justice as well as the delegate from Delaware to the Continental Congress. Neither press criticisms nor a vote of the assembly could cause him to drop one of his offices. A letter-of-the-law man, he argued, accurately if not endearingly, that he held but one office in Pennsylvania.[33]

Oswald and McKean each represented one of the two Pennsylvania political parties. When McKean levied heavy fines against two army officers and lectured them about military arrogance, he hit a sore spot of Oswald's, who lashed out at what he perceived to be the unequalled excessiveness of the fines. Oswald did not stop there; he added that McKean had "acquired an intuitive knowledge, an infallible rule by which you can perfectly comprehend the merits of every case by hearing one side only." Less than two weeks after the *Independent Gazetteer* censured McKean, he ordered Oswald arrested for seditious libel.[34]

Oswald was undeterred. He not only printed a vituperative account of being haled before McKean, he published a letter by "A

Friend to the Army" that accused McKean of being a war profiteer, "a noted speculator in distressed Soldier's certificates." Oswald was again arrested, on a second charge of seditious libel. Still undeterred, he referred to the Constitutionalist party [McKean's] as the "Skunk Party," repeatedly taunted McKean by equating him with the infamous Judge Jeffreys, and in correspondence attacked the law of seditious libel: "I am to have a public Trial . . . as a *Libeller*. The infamous English law doctrine of Libels being introduced by the more infamous Judges and Lawyers, in an American Court."[35]

In fact he was to have no trial at all. On the day the grand jury took up his case, the *Independent Gazetteer* published some helpful hints about what a grand jury might do, concluding "in short there is no telling where the evil would end, if we once admit this dangerous and ridiculous doctrine. A good Grand Jury will always be cautious in proceeding." Oswald had a very good grand jury. It voted sixteen to three not to indict. Incensed, McKean instructed it to reconsider in conjunction with the second bill, based on the "Friend to the Army" letter; he stated that it was the job of a petit jury and the court, not the job of the grand jury, to determine the actual libel. The grand jury again supported Oswald, who then published the grand jury proceedings complete with criticisms of McKean's attempt to override the grand jury's refusal to indict and his failure to extend to the grand jury the customary expressions of thanks.[36]

We can now understand better John Adams's observation that "there is nothing that the people dislike that they do not attack. . . . They attack officers of every rank in the militia and in the army, members of congress, and congress itself, whenever they dislike its conduct." They attacked because they felt free to do so. Only Loyalists had no freedom of expression (and many of them, by the time Adams wrote in 1780, had emigrated to Canada or returned to Britain). To Levy it is a great mystery "why many courageous and irresponsible editors daily risked imprisonment." Maybe, as Oswald's case suggests, they didn't.[37]

## III

That the grand jury refused to indict Oswald was hardly a historical anomaly. The simple fact is that by the Revolution, seditious

libel was basically only a theoretical restraint on the press. Harold
Nelson's important study found but nine attempts to use seditious
libel in the entire colonial period. Of those only a single one was
successful, and that occurred before Zenger's highly publicized
success. Nelson left open the possibility that more attempts to use
seditious libel might be unearthed; but despite significant incentives
to do so, no scholar has found additional attempted prosecutions.
The lesson learned from Zenger—and repeated by Oswald—was
that a jury could protect popular speech. Thus, had McKean attempted to initiate prosecution without a grand jury indictment,
Oswald would have been acquitted anyway.[38]

Nelson's conclusion that Zenger's case ended seditious libel as an
actual threat holds true. On the eve of the Revolution there were
attempts to revive the law of seditious libel to silence patriot support, but not surprisingly, no grand jury would indict.[39]

The situation was different when the charging official was not a
Crown attorney but the legislative body of a colony. The legislatures viewed themselves as appropriate representatives of the people, and they claimed and exercised the right to punish for contempt without the need for either grand or petit juries. Nelson
found that punishment for breach of legislative privilege (that is,
for contempt) was "the most efficacious of all colonial controls."
There were over twice as many examples of the use of legislative
privilege to punish printers as there were attempts to use seditious
libel; and the former, unlike the latter, not needing juries as inter-
mediaries, were successful in punishing printers. But with the Revolution the practice apparently died; between 1776 and 1791 there
are no recorded attempts to punish by a prosecution for contempt.[40]

As we have seen, during the Revolution John Dunlap, printer of
the *Pennsylvania Packet,* was twice involved in controversies with
Congress and once called to the bar. At that time, however, he was
on the congressional payroll as its printer and was being asked
to confirm what everyone knew, that Tom Paine was "Common
Sense." When the issue was the identity of "Leonidas," however,
Dunlap no longer was a kept printer; and when Gerry argued for
calling him to the bar, the response instead was speeches "declaim-
ing on the virtues of a free press."[41]

Levy is correct that at least until 1782 neither printers nor other propagandists argued that the existence of the law of seditious libel or of contempt for breach of legislative privilege was incompatible with a free press. But it would be a mistake to believe that printers and propagandists embraced restraints on their presses. To be sure, at a theoretical level, the propriety of *some* line between the acceptable and the forbidden was recognized. But that line was typically somewhere else.

The point is easily shown from *Cato's Letters,* the most widely read, reprinted, and important transmission to America of the Radical English Whig ideas on government and the press. Cato clearly and repeatedly emphasizes that there is always reason to fear government ("the People, for One Injury that they do their Governors, receive Ten Thousand from them"); that only corrupt or wicked magistrates have anything to fear from press scrutiny; and, of course, that freedom of speech and the press are essential to liberty. Nevertheless, Cato takes an obligatory bow toward the law of seditious libel. England's laws are "very good" and if they are "prudently and honestly executed" then those who libel "ought not to escape Punishment."[42]

But anyone reading *Cato's Letters* could tell that Trenchard and Gordon were only going through the motions in such passages. Cato asserts that "no Man in England thinks worse of Libels than I do," but does not really want to punish them: "I would rather many Libels should escape, than the Liberty of the Press should be infringed." The assertion is demonstrably false, a patina of deniability should the authors subsequently have a serious discussion with a government official. A fair reading of *Cato's Letters* is that much of seditious libel ought to go. Yet Cato pulls up short from his own logical conclusion, and instead offers more limited suggestions to improve the "very good laws" of England. A century ahead of his time (on the east side of the Atlantic), Cato argues that given the public interest in true information about the workings of government, truth should be admitted as a defense to seditious, but not personal, libel actions.[43]

Trenchard and Gordon and the other Radical Whigs had little impact in England, but they were enormously influential in America. Through the Radical Whigs the English struggle against tyranny became linked with the American movement for independence, a linkage facilitated by the personal friendship of figures such as Joseph Priestley and Richard Price with prominent American patriots. The essays in *Cato's Letters* were immensely popular because their views of magistrates resonated with the colonists' experiences. They were praised and copied with regularity in the colonies. (The *Boston Gazette* reprinted Cato's essay on free speech seven times between 1755 and 1780.) Their popularity and their transmission of Radical English Whig views on the relationship of governed and governor presented a view of sovereignty that was incompatible with the Blackstonian view of the underpinnings of seditious libel. Although the colonists' views on sovereignty diverged from the established Blackstonian views, there was little—until independence—that the colonists could do. They could not, for example, change the common law. They could have decided to cut back on the prerogatives of the local legislatures, but that was hardly realistic. Of all the defects that might have been articulated, cutting back on the one locally representative branch of government could not have been high on anyone's list.[44]

Thus printers were brought to the legislative bar. There, they did not waste time on the self-defeating argument of lack of legislative power (although, of course, they could have taken the revolutionary step of denying legislative legitimacy as a way-station on the road to jail); instead, printers offered apologies, relied on due process arguments, or accepted the punishment—with legalistic skill, they employed the argument most likely to succeed in the immediate case.[45]

With independence, at least initially, came change. Although neither seditious libel nor legislative contempt prosecutions were used during the bulk of the Revolution, in Levy's view they remained a threat—thus he was left wondering why there were so many courageous printers. Because he consistently ignored the reality of civic republicanism in America, he failed to see that new institutions, conforming to the new views of sovereignty, were leaving older solutions in their wake. Thus, while the Radical English Whigs were primarily concerned with executive abuses, Americans increasingly transferred the Radical Whig fear of government authority to their own legislatures. And, of course, many of the legislative actions in the 1780s that facilitated the Constitution reinforced this new American fear.[46]

Levy recounts the decision in Congress not to summon James

Dunlap to the bar for the "Leonidas" essay and quotes statements supportive of a free press, such as Merriwether Smith's closing observation: "When the liberty of the press shall be restrained, take my word for it, the liberties of the people will be at an end." But in so doing he asserts, without more, that Smith meant "restrained" in the Blackstonian sense. This, indeed, is Levy's essential point, that Americans only had a Blackstonian conception to work with and until an alternative was put forth, they had to see press issues in Blackstonian terms. This seems implausible—both because of the adoption of Radical Whig ideology and because it was possible to see press issues in vastly more libertarian terms than Blackstone while still retaining some concept of seditious libel.[47]

Oswald's obvious concern was avoiding jail time and, as recounted earlier, the day the grand jury met he offered it Zengerian instructions via his *Independent Gazetteer*. More significantly, in November 1782 his paper also printed an essay that for the first time challenged the very existence of seditious libel. "Junius Wilkes" explicitly recognized that the distinction between prior restraint and subsequent punishment would not matter once it was realized that the operation of the law in either case penalized the printer in such a way that he would be hesitant to publish: "The danger is precisely the same to liberty, in punishing a person *after* the performance appears to the world, as in preventing its publication in the *first* instance." This is an exaggeration, because subsequent punishment occurs after the information has become available to the public at large, as it never does with a prior restraint; nevertheless, "Junius Wilkes" made a breakthrough by realizing that the printer, facing punishment either way, may not care whether the punishment is administered previously or subsequently.[48]

When "Junius Wilkes" wrote that the press should be "perfectly free and unrestrained" he was not using empty rhetoric. He justified his conclusion in several ways, reflecting the Radical English Whig heritage. First, the press "exposes and defeats the *end* and *objects* of tyranny and misrule." There is reason to fear government and assume, because of the function of the press, that those holding public office are not likely to be its friends. Second, the people, not the rulers, are sovereign. Public officials are "merely public servants and stewards, and, as such, accountable at all times to the people."

Finally, the risk of injury to the innocent is an "unavoidable inconvenience" of a free press. Men know they will receive criticism when they seek public office; their remedy is additional publicity: "Like the spear of *Telephus,* the same weapon that wounds can heal."[49]

What "Junius Wilkes" did was put all the republican pieces together: fear of government abuses; sovereignty in the people and not the rulers; and the consequent need of a free press to preserve the liberties, and therefore the sovereignty, of the people. Had he stopped here, he would have done enough. But "Junius Wilkes" took one additional step. He tied his republican theory into the new republican creation—constitutions. The Pennsylvania Constitution of 1776 justified "publications which respect the conduct of public servants; and, when they even appear false and groundless, it is rather an inconvenience . . . a kind of *damnum absque injuria* [harm without legally cognizable injury]." This use of the Pennsylvania Constitution was seconded by another of the writers protesting McKean's actions against Oswald. Yet these concepts of what the state constitution meant could not be authoritative without the assent of judges, including McKean.[50]

It should not be assumed that everyone was moving linearly in their conclusions that the new republican institutions necessitated a fresh look at issues left in abeyance for years. Sometimes other concerns were more pressing. For instance, McKean still wanted Oswald's scalp; and at the end of the decade he got it. In the process he tried to update the law regarding the press while maintaining harmony with republican government.

The second tangle began with a private libel suit against Oswald that Oswald believed was inspired by his enemies as a means of hampering his opposition to the proposed federal constitution. When an offer of a retraction in exchange for dropping the suit was rebuffed, the *Independent Gazetteer* charged a conspiracy against Oswald. McKean then brought him before the supreme court, arguing that his efforts to prejudice the libel case against him constituted contempt of court. Oswald's lawyer argued freedom of the press and called for a jury trial, but to no avail. In an action for contempt of court, as Tom Patterson was to learn a century later, the defendant has no right to a jury trial. Thus there were no buffers between McKean and Oswald.[51]

McKean lectured Oswald that the state constitution gave no rights to defame or to disrupt the workings of government. Although McKean quoted liberally from Blackstone, he agreed that the state constitution went beyond the simple prohibition of prior restraints. In an intriguing fusion of Cato and Blackstone, McKean shifted from the republican concern of false attacks on good government to the position that courts should distinguish between attacks on government made in good faith and those "which are intended merely to delude and defame." It took little time for McKean to conclude that his old adversary published with "bad motives," since the articles had the tendency "of prejudicing the public [about the case] and of corrupting the administration of justice." Oswald was fined and sentenced to jail for a month.[52]

Oswald's battles with the Pennsylvania chief justice thus produced agreement that the state constitution went beyond Blackstone, even if there was a large split between the press propagandists and McKean on its distance from Blackstone. McKean stopped at what Norman Rosenberg has aptly labeled a "neo-Blackstonian" view, that republican institutions should only be criticized with good motives. The printers were less tame. Both of these positions were vetted at the end of the decade in Massachusetts, this time in private correspondence by two of the leading figures of the era, John Adams, drafter of the Massachusetts Constitution's press clause, and William Cushing, the chief justice of the commonwealth.[53]

Cushing initiated the correspondence with a thoughtful letter asking Adams's opinion as to how far the Massachusetts press clause authorized publications to cast aspersions on the conduct of public officials "when such charges are supportable by the truth of the fact." Cushing's letter noted that the Massachusetts Constitution's language applied to subsequent punishment as well as to prior restraints. And like "Junius Wilkes," Cushing recognized that "fear of jails . . . from the examining of the conduct of persons in administrations . . . will be as effectual a restraint as any *previous* restraint."[54]

Cushing tied the existence of a free press to the success of the Revolution. "Without this liberty of the press could we have supported our liberties against british administration? or could our revolution have taken place? Pretty certainly it could not, at the time it did. Under a sense and impression of this sort, I conceive, this article [the press clause] was adopted." Liberty of the press could not harm honest officials or a good government. But beyond truthful comment, Cushing drew the line. "When the press is made the vehicle of falsehood and scandal, let the authors be punished with becoming rigour."[55]

Adams responded to precisely the question addressed: the issue was settled adversely to truth-as-a-defense in England, "but it is a serious Question whether our Constitution is not at present so different as to render the innovation [truth] necessary?" Adams then noted the importance of discussion because of annual elections in the state. This led him to agree with Cushing that a jury should decide the issue of truth, and if the jury found that the publications were true and were published for the public good, they would readily acquit.[56]

Adams's response combined the positions of Cushing and Mc-Kean, stopping far short of that of "Junius Wilkes." Yet they have several points in common. First, all agreed that the state constitutions were relevant to the issue of the scope of the received common law. Second, the pervasiveness of the Radical Whig influence created the belief wherein all (possibly excepting McKean) held a free press essential to the system of government that the independent states had created. Third, all were willing to apply the previous two conclusions to a recasting of the law of libel to fit the needs of a republican state. Where they split was on how far that recasting should go. Here Adams seems quite close to McKean in believing that one should only criticize with good motives; "Junius Wilkes" would have found that limitation inconsistent with republican government; Cushing was in between, believing with Cato "that truth sacredly adhered to" was "favorable" to republican governments. Had there been more experience with political libel, there would have been a better opportunity for a position to jell prior to the ratification of the First Amendment. But events of the late 1780s had forced different issues to the fore.[57]

## IV

By 1787 Americans had not only debated thoroughly the issue of republican government and the need to create constitutions; all but those in Connecticut and Rhode Island had also experienced the process of constitutional creation. This common local experience now moved to the national level. There are both differences and similarities in the drafting of state constitutions and of a national constitution, but one difference dwarfs them all. With the Revolution, there had to be state constitutions, but a national constitution was not inevitable.

Whatever one might think about the importance of declarations of rights, the issues facing the delegates in Philadelphia in the summer of 1787 were, in context, even more important. Even with all the hindsight we can muster, we still must marvel at the delegates' ability to create compromises to deal with state versus national powers, small versus large states, and slavery, which pitted the interests of the South against those of the North. Any one of these issues could have derailed the enterprise.

There might have been time to add a declaration of rights to the Constitution, depending on how fast agreements could have been reached at the end of the summer after the essential compromises were in place. But delegates naturally were willing to spend only so much time away from their homes, and an operative premise of all of them was that they were creating a limited government (how limited would be a contentious issue; that it was limited was not). A declaration of rights was seen as unnecessary, indeed wrong-headed, since the constitution did not grant the federal government power to infringe on important rights.

Thus when George Mason and Elbridge Gerry tried to create a committee to draft a bill of rights, it was rejected by unanimous vote. A like effort by Charles Pinckney was referred to a committee and never heard of again. Pinckney and Gerry then proposed only a press clause. Roger Sherman answered with the familiar, dominant, and winning argument: "It is unnecessary—The power of Congress does not extend to the Press." The proposal died.[58]

When the Constitution moved from the Convention to the several states, the issue of a bill of rights, necessarily with a guarantee of press freedoms, became more urgent. The Constitution contained a number of sharp-edged words and phrases which reeked of centralized, nationalized power—taxes, army, general welfare, coupled with the "elastic clause" allowing Congress to do whatever it deemed "necessary and proper" to the achievement of these great ends—terms that frightened Antifederalists. Anything that could defeat the Constitution became important to both sides, and once the ratification debate moved from the sure states, the absence of a bill of rights gained increasing importance.

At first the Federalists viewed the bill of rights issue as, in Alexander Hamilton's words, an effort "to frighten the people with ideal bugbears, in order to mould them to their own purposes." Because the Federalists believed that the new government had no powers over the press, a press clause made no sense. James Wilson, who ranks second only to Madison in importance as the architect of the Constitution, explained: "The proposed system possesses no influence whatever upon the press; and it would have been merely nugatory, to have introduced a formal declaration upon the subject; nay, that very declaration might have been construed to imply that some degree of power was given, since we undertook to define its extent."[59]

The Federalists believed their argument was logically unassailable. When Hamilton asked "why declare that things shall not be done which there is no power to do?" Federalists agreed. But the Antifederalists were afraid of the new and more efficient government being proposed. The "necessary and proper" clause signified the possibility of implied powers, and the Antifederalists needed no prodding to conclude that implied powers would be used to increase national dominance at the expense of both the citizenry and the states. Thus the Antifederalists wished to defeat the Constitution. But if they could not, then they had to live under it. A bill of rights would make it safer.[60]

After the five easy state ratifications, demands for a bill of rights were made in every other state. New York and Virginia were the key states; at least one had to ratify for the new union to be viable. Both did; and each called for a bill of rights. New York, one of the few states without its own declaration of rights, suggested a press clause that was the first to group freedom of the press with rights to assemble, petition, and instruct representatives. Virginia's, instead of following the language of its own declaration of rights, suggested a press clause that used the Pennsylvania model: "That the people have a right to freedom of speech, and of writing and publishing their sentiments; that the freedom of the press is one of the greatest bulwarks of liberty and ought not to be violated." When, a year later, James Madison introduced his proposed bill of rights in the First Congress, he used almost identical language. By then Madison had come to understand the merits of the Antifederalist argument. The Federalist error had been to focus on the lack of any express power to restrict the press (or establish religion or violate other liberties), and to overlook the risk that delegated powers might be exercised in ways that would accomplish the same undesired ends. On June 8, 1789, Madison delivered a seminal speech in the House of Representatives, presenting his proposals for a bill of rights and justifying the need for amendments by adopting the Antifederalist argument on implied powers: "The powers of the General Government are circumscribed, they are directed to particular objects; but even if the Government keeps within those limits, it has certain discretionary powers with respect to the means, which may admit of abuse to a certain extent." He went on to give the example of a general search warrant as a means of enforcing revenue legislation (a Fourth Amendment issue), but he could just as easily have given the example of press regulation during wartime as a means of maintaining domestic morale. In the course of the speech he made clear that the judiciary would be expected to enforce the guarantees: they would "consider themselves in a peculiar [i.e., special] manner guardians of these rights." Madison's conversion to the Antifederalist understanding of implied powers guaranteed that a bill of rights would address the most pressing issues of the federal government's potential abuse of implied powers to invade essential liberties.[61]

Madison, in fact, proposed two press clauses in the First Congress. The first tracked the Virginia convention's: "The people shall not be deprived or abridged of their right to speak, to write, or to publish their sentiments; and the freedom of the press, as one of the great bulwarks of liberty, shall be inviolable." Although that clause, given the universality of its language, could have applied to the states as well as to the national government, Madison apparently did not think it did, because his second press amendment was entirely so directed: "No State shall violate the equal rights of conscience, or the freedom of the press, or the trial by jury in criminal cases." This was the only amendment Madison proposed that was directed at the states. Madison indicated that if there was reason to limit the federal government, "it was equally necessary that they should be secured against the State Governments." The House agreed (without a recorded vote) and this measure went to the Senate, where it was rejected—and because of Senate secrecy at the time, that it was rejected is all we know.[62]

Madison's first proposed press clause was ultimately successful, although only after a number of changes. In committee, Madison's speech and press protections were combined with his separate clause protecting rights of assembly and petition, to read: "The freedom of speech and of the press, and the right of the people peaceably to assemble and consult for their common good, and to apply to the Government for the redress of grievances, shall not be infringed." In this form the proposed amendment passed the House but, as with the Senate, the vote is unrecorded.[63]

Because there is no record of the Senate debates, all that is known is that several important decisions were made. One was a proposed change in the House version that jumps out: to modify the press clause by language that the press should be protected "in as ample a manner as hath at any time been secured by the common law." It is not known who proposed this, or why, or what was said. Had this language been adopted, there would be little doubt of Blackstone's relevance to the framers' intent; and it is conceivable that constitutional argument, if not outcomes, would have been different. The language also demonstrates that the framers were capable of finding language that would have codified the common law—and that they rejected doing so.[64]

Next came a new version of the amendment, this time beginning with the more familiar language, "That Congress shall make no law, abridging the freedom of speech, or of the press, or the right of the people peacefully to assemble and consult for their common good, and to petition the government for a redress of grievances." With this change, the press clause now read parallel to the religion clause as adopted by the House, which began "Congress shall make no law. . . ." A few days later the Senate combined the two clauses, dropped the phrase "and consult for their common good," and sent the Bill of Rights back to the House. The House then called for a conference committee, which wound up accepting the bulk of the Senate changes, including the press clause. The conference committee also acceded to the Senate in dropping Madison's press clause that applied to the states.[65]

We know what happened; we know too little about what was said. Apparently there was no debate about incorporating protections for a free press in the Bill of Rights; every single version that was considered contained these. We know that various linguistic formulations were discussed, which implies that the choices ultimately made were made consciously. The rejection of Blackstone is unlikely to have been inadvertent.

The move from Congress to the states adds little to our knowledge. There must have been debate in the state legislatures over the Bill of Rights, because the first two proposed amendments were rejected. But newspapers of the period said little about the debates; correspondence talked about procedure rather than substance. A press clause was hardly likely to be controversial, given its inclusion in every suggestion of a declaration of rights.[66]

## V

So, what did the First Amendment mean to the framers? Surprisingly, unlike so many other constitutional questions, this one can be answered with remarkable certainty. The First Amendment meant exactly what its plain language would suggest to an ordinary reader: Congress was completely without power to pass laws that would abridge either freedom of speech or freedom of the press. Despite the paucity of recorded discussion, I write with such assurance for a simple reason. Everyone said so and no one offered a suggestion to the contrary.

Let us go back for a moment to review the debate on freedom of the press from the Constitutional Convention through ratification of the Bill of Rights. James Wilson and Alexander Hamilton said forcefully and consistently that the theory of the constitution being drafted was that there was no power granted to the federal government to pass a law dealing with the press. The Antifederalists did not disagree; they did not believe the Constitution carried such a power. Rather, they, more than their Federalist opponents, were fearful of usurpation. They believed that once in operation, the federal government would find it irresistible to go beyond its limited boundaries. When that unfortunate day occurred, the rights of

the people would be in jeopardy. For the Antifederalists, the demand for a bill of rights, including a press clause, was for additional
protection against the constant danger of usurpation.

Madison, as we saw, became a convert. Whether other Federalists did is not clear, but at a minimum they changed their mind on
the issue of whether enacting a bill of rights would be dangerous—
as James Wilson had previously articulated. Madison's June 8
speech addressed these fears and offered the Ninth Amendment's
protection of unenumerated rights as the solution. Once the Federalists concluded that it would not be dangerous, they implemented
the promise that had been made to carry the Constitution through
the more divided ratifying states. The press clause would be yet
another barrier against a potentially overreaching legislature.

This places Madison's proposed second press clause in perspective. Because there was no federal power to pass laws abridging the
freedom of the press (even prior to the First Amendment) only the
states were in a position to do so. Thus Madison's second proposal
dealt with the likely "abridgers" and would have limited them as
well. The Senate, and ultimately the House, determined that the Bill
of Rights should restrict the national government only, and Madison's second clause was rejected. Thus the federal Constitution, as
amended in 1791, said nothing about how the states might deal
with their own printers.

If the question is whether the First Amendment was intended to
preclude Congress from adopting the English law of seditious libel,
then the answer is yes. If the question is whether the First Amendment was intended to preclude Congress from adopting any version
of the law of seditious libel, the answer remains yes. The First
Amendment was intended to be an additional structural provision
to keep the federal government within its prescribed boundaries.

Within a decade the federal government would jump those
boundaries with the Sedition Act of 1798, discussed in the next
chapter. A consequence, whether intended or not, of the Sedition
Act controversy is that subsequently the Supreme Court, historians, and lawyers would ask of the First Amendment a question it
was not intended to answer: what did the First Amendment say
about the *scope* of freedom of the press?[67]

The First Amendment was not intended to answer that question,
because that question was left entirely to the states. Nevertheless,

because this wrong question has dominated the legal history of the First Amendment, it is worth attempting to answer it; but we must recognize that there will necessarily be ambiguities in answering a question that the framers never asked.

The most restrictive available meaning of freedom of the press was Blackstone's. Yet the issue of prior restraints had been an English, not an American, concern; given the revolutionary-era constitutions and press, it is simply inconceivable that the framers were worried about finalizing an English battle that had been decided in the mother country a century earlier when, in the aftermath of the Glorious Revolution, licensing was dropped. Even Adams's and McKean's restrictive interpretations went beyond Blackstone. Levy, who once asserted that the framers' notion of freedom of the press was limited simply to no prior restraints, has now abandoned this view.[68]

During the revolutionary era, Americans had an experience with a licentious, lively, and, by eighteenth-century standards, free press. "The revolutionary state constitutions, the ratifying conventions, and the First Congress produced numerous expressions [that] leave little doubt that press freedom was viewed as being closely related to the experiment of representative self-government." But the framers had not worked out all the details. One reason was ideological. Another had to do with the framers' own experiences.[69]

In America, the Blackstonian view of sovereignty lay in shambles. Americans, both individually and collectively—after their initial agreement with the views of the Radical English Whigs, who deeply distrusted government powers—held to differing ideologies. Some were classical republicans; others looked to Locke. Although we can see "a sharp dichotomy between two identifiable traditions [republicanism and liberalism]," they did not. "None of the Founding Fathers ever had any sense that he had to choose between Machiavelli and Locke." Because the Founding Fathers held diverse views and did not feel compelled to choose, there are strands pointing in different directions. Because they did not feel a need to choose, we cannot be sure that our choices for them would be theirs. Freedom of speech and the press fit differently into republican and liberal theory; but the framers had not worked this out, and other events would preempt their doing so.[70]

The framers had not sorted out their own beliefs on freedom of the press because no issue forced them to do so. "By 1791, Americans had simply not seen enough political libel suits to debate legal boundaries at any great length." Reputations were important and men did not lose their right to reputations by holding public office. Thus personal, rather than political, libel suits were clearly permissible. From our perspective two hundred years later, it is easy to see that a line between the personal and the political is difficult, and maybe impossible, to draw. But that is our experience, not theirs.[71]

Much of the debate on the meaning of the First Amendment has followed Zechariah Chafee to focus on whether the framers intended to abolish the law of seditious libel. For the reasons already mentioned, this is necessarily a dead end. The federal government would not have the power to pass a seditious libel statute; that power, if it could exist in a republic at all, could only be in the states.[72]

If the seditious libel question is not legally or analytically helpful, it nevertheless has been fruitful in forcing scholars to learn more about the eighteenth-century press and the various responses thereto. This has helped us understand that at varying times there have been stricter and looser definitions of seditious libel, and it is impossible to pin a single definition on the framers. If Chafee's question is rephrased to ask whether the framers wanted a press to be free to criticize the government, then the answer is surely yes. But if the question is whether the framers believed there was a point at which malicious criticism of government went so far beyond the pale as to be criminally punishable, the answer is still surely yes.[73]

In between there is a lot of room for press criticism of government, and it was here that the framers' free press had been operating. Everyone, from Federalist to Antifederalist, had come to see that a free press was of great value to representative self-government. Remember Cushing's conclusion that without a free press the patriots could not have sustained their liberties against the British. Where this draws a legal line is unclear, but it does suggest that criticism had to go a long way before it would cease to be appropriate. The framers "could only have meant to protect the press with which they were familiar and as it operated at the time. They constitutionally guaranteed the *practice* of freedom of the press."[74]

*Chapter Two*

# Freedom of the Press
# in Times of Crisis

Even if the exact dimensions of the area of unprotected expression were left for the tests of experience, the framers had created an edifice with impressive foundations. From civic republicanism they took a fear of government, coupled with the necessity of participation; from the emerging liberalism they took the view that the individual is the best judge of how to write and speak. The integration of these traditions should have given the First Amendment a strong impetus—much like the one that vested property rights enjoyed—in the young republic.

The tests of experience, however, arrived too soon. Property may be a threat to some governments, but freedom of expression can be perceived as a threat by all governments; and less than a decade after ratification of the Bill of Rights, internal and external events combined to make political dissent appear to the Federalists as something akin to treason. The events surrounding the Sedition Act of 1798 initiated a darker First Amendment tradition, one that would recur periodically when governments perceived a need for all citizens to be, in the words of a federal district judge, "friendly to the Government, friendly to the policies of the Government." Repetitions occurred in the South as the Civil War approached, in World War I and its aftermath, during the early Cold War, and, on a lesser scale, in the South during the late 1950s and early 1960s. Chapter 2 splits its focus between the Sedition Act and World War I, because much of the effort to limit dissent during these periods was directed at the print media rather than speech, and at the national rather than the local level.[1]

## I

When the citizens of a republic exhibit civic virtue, neither faction nor political parties will exist, or so civic republicans believed. Yet splits, first over Hamilton's ambitious domestic programs and then over the threatened export of the French Revolution, were driving the American elite into faction and, ultimately, parties. The members of the ruling elite had much in common, especially in their determination to preserve republicanism; yet, united on so much, they saw difference, and with difference came distance and concern.[2]

Each party found in the other's actions the potential subversion of republicanism. The party of Washington and Hamilton—the Federalists—thought the opposing party leaned too far toward "democracy," a term the Federalists associated with legislative excesses and social instability. Unleashed, democracy would lead to despotism. The concern of Jefferson, Madison and their followers was the opposite. Too much distance from the rulers to the ruled, too much pomp and ceremony, was the road to monarchy and aristocracy and the subversion of the republic.[3]

Virtually everyone had hailed the beginnings of the French Revolution, at least in public. But when the revolution spilled over its borders and plunged Europe into war, it placed pressures on the United States that the young American republic was ill-prepared to bear. France was America's ally and its guarantor against recolonization by Great Britain. Yet the latter was America's largest commercial trading partner. Trying to maintain neutrality between the two warring great powers was difficult, not only in action but also psychologically, because of the universal "assumption that the ultimate fate of America lay in Europe" rather than at home. The strains caused by the shifting European tide created unfortunate tensions at home as the distrust of faction built with "each camp associating the other with the most ominous illegitimacy of all, an attachment to a foreign power."[4]

A dramatic manifestation of the European influence on America was the rapid creation of the Democratic-Republican Societies along the East Coast in 1793. Modeled loosely after the Jacobin

Clubs of France but with a solid ancestry going back to prerevolutionary American associations, these societies "filled the air with celebrations and pronouncements that intermingled enthusiasms for France and advocacy of liberty at home." The Democratic-Republican Society of Philadelphia, the country's most important, pledged in its statement of basic principles "to cultivate the just knowledge of a rational Liberty, to facilitate the enjoyment and exercise of our civil Rights, and to transmit, unimpaired, to posterity, the glorious inheritance of *free Republican Government*."[5]

The societies believed in an active citizenry "discussing without fear, the conduct of the public Servants, in every department of Government." Eugene Link, the leading historian of the societies, emphasized the prevalence of their "strikingly forthright" defense of freedom of expression. Implementing the Radical Whig ideology, which emphasized the inherent tendency of government to abuse power, they offered its republican antidote—popular citizen vigilance and debate. No individual citizen could perform the watchdog function alone. Therefore the societies "took it on themselves to monitor the government, pledging to warn the general public in times of actual danger to their liberties."[6]

Reaction to the societies was sharply divided. Jeffersonians easily identified with the societies' American roots and their manifestation of appropriate civic behavior. George Washington—the object of much of the vigilance and, for the first time in his storied career, scorn—had a different view of the Democratic-Republican Societies. He hated them, believing they were "self created," by which he meant self-elected and therefore in clear violation of republican principles. Washington's Federalists saw the societies as importing Jacobinism to North America and accused them of attempting to gain power for a minority in the guise of acting for the people.[7]

The Democratic-Republican Societies and the response to them mirrored a concurrent development of the press. From around 100 newspapers at the beginning of the decade, the number jumped to about 250 by its end. Printers, if only to fool themselves, formally subscribed to the concept of press neutrality; but in operation the press was anything but objective. Probably no period in our history witnessed such an irresponsibly partisan press. To the Republicans this was a necessary check on the aristocratic tendencies of the government. "Good rulers will not shrink from public enquiry," as one Democratic-Republican Society noted. Federalists, however, were coming to view partisan attacks on their policies in a more sinister light, as efforts to split the citizens from their government, to undermine republican constitutions, and ultimately to subvert the republic.[8]

Some Federalists, coalescing around Hamilton, saw ties between the newspaper falsehoods about the administration, the growth of "seditious" organizations (the Democratic-Republican Societies), and domestic anarchy such as the Whiskey Rebellion. These Federalists urged action against a licentious press that they believed no stable government could tolerate. As Joyce Appleby writes, once the societies came under attack, issues of freedom of expression came to the fore and stayed there for the rest of the decade. The issues "represented a complex of new and old concerns: the relationship between dignity and authority, the blurred line between public and private realms, and the competence of ordinary people to deliberate on weighty matters of state."[9]

Despite hostility to the Democratic-Republican Societies, the Washington administration consciously decided to take no action. Hamilton's views, however, gained wider currency in the aftermath of the XYZ Affair as the Federalists came to believe that it was necessary, maybe opportune, to move against the Republicans— the "French party" as Monsieur Y had referred to them; the "internal foe" as the Federalists soon came to call them.[10]

## II

Diplomatic relations with France deteriorated with Jay's Treaty. When Washington replaced James Monroe with Charles Cotesworth Pinckney as ambassador in Paris, the French refused to recognize Pinckney, thereby breaking diplomatic relations between the countries. By the time Pinckney informed the State Department, John Adams was president. Adams then sent John Marshall and Elbridge Gerry to join Pinckney to negotiate for a restoration of ties. Negotiations with Talleyrand, the French foreign minister, went nowhere. But three unofficial agents of the French government—X, Y, and Z—made it clear that unless the Americans paid a bribe and guaranteed a loan (in advance) to the Directory, negotiations could not proceed. The envoys naturally refused.[11]

Adams received coded dispatches declaring the mission a failure in early March 1798, and a day later he informed Congress. Two weeks later, after fully decoding all the messages, Adams advised Congress that no settlement was likely, and he called for new military expenditures. Jefferson thought Adams's message was "insane" and Republicans demanded that Adams lay before Congress the dispatches from France. It is always a mistake to ask a hostile witness a question when you do not already know the answer. The Republicans were about to learn this basic lesson.[12]

The dispatches were political dynamite. The growing concern about party attachment to a foreign power seemed confirmed by one of the dispatches, which detailed Y's boast that France had its own party in America and if the envoys attempted to unite the American people in resistance to France's demands for money, they would fail: "The diplomatic skill of France and the means she possesses in your country, are sufficient to enable her, with the French party in America, to throw the blame which will attend the rupture of the negotiations on the Federalists."[13]

Although the envoys had informed Y that he was mistaken, the Federalists at home now had evidence that, as they suspected, the Republicans—dragging their feet with respect to the affront to national dignity—were "traitors." This view was given additional impetus in June when Benjamin Franklin Bache's opposition newspaper *Aurora* printed a conciliatory letter from Talleyrand before the secretary of state had sent the letter to the president (and two days before the president informed Congress of its receipt by the government). Federalists, now pushing the Sedition Act through Congress, immediately claimed that Bache's "French paper" had printed the letter on orders from the Directory.[14]

Because both the United States and Great Britain "were threatened by the same danger—the 'Terrible Republic' and a disloyal domestic faction—the Federalists argued that methods which worked in Great Britain would be equally effective in this country." Starting in the Senate as a bill providing for the death penalty to anyone giving aid and comfort to France, the Sedition Act (formally entitled "An Act in addition to the 'Act for Punishment of Certain Crimes against the United States'") wound up as a liberal, state-of-the-art sedition act. Unlike the law newly passed in Britain, which finally accepted the Zengerian outcome of genuine jury participation, the American law went even further and provided that truth would be a defense to the crime. Nevertheless, the Sedition Act barely passed a bitterly divided Congress. The Republicans voted nay, but they were outnumbered by the Federalists.[15]

It is important to note, however, that just as 1798 was not 1789, and just as James Lloyd, who introduced the initial bill in the Senate, was not James Madison, the Federalists of 1798 were not the framers—of either the Constitution or the First Amendment. By 1798 the legislative turnover since the two events was largely complete. Of the ninety-five members of the First Congress, only eighteen remained in 1798; and of those, only ten voted for the Sedition Act. Neither Lloyd nor the House drafter Robert G. Harper nor the other Federalists who dominated the proceedings creating the Sedition Act had been present at the founding.[16]

The Republicans had no difficulty understanding that they were to be the targets of the new Federalist policy. They fought as best they could in Congress; but since they were outnumbered and a wartime hysteria was in the air, defeat was unavoidable. The enactment of the Sedition Act confirmed the fears of the Antifederalists of 1787 that the federal government would try to usurp a power it did not have. Yet the Federalists of 1798 believed they were acting constitutionally and had little difficulty articulating their constitutional theories.

The Federalist constitutional theory had to clear two hurdles. First, in response to the obvious question, "Where does the power come from?" they had to tie the Sedition Act into the body of the Constitution. Second, they had to meet the further objection that, even if they were correct on the power point, the First Amendment precluded such a federal law.[17]

Number 84 of the *Federalist Papers* had noted that only "men disposed to usurp" would contend that there was a power granted to restrict the press. But the Federalists of 1798 were going to claim such a power, and that meant they were going to give a constitutional argument supporting it. Although the debate was brief, and the reporting in the *Annals of Congress* sketchy, three different explanations for congressional power were given by Harper and his principal lieutenants, James Allen and Harrison Gray Otis: (1) the power was inherent; (2) it was necessary and proper to the preservation of the Constitution; and (3) it was an amplification of the already existing power in the federal courts to punish common law crimes. All three explanations underscored the Federalist grab for power.[18]

Proponents of the Constitution had never wavered from the position that it was a constitution of delegated and enumerated powers. Congress had what was given, no more (and no less except if otherwise restricted). Inherent power, a power existing because the government exists, is antithetical to the theory of delegated and enumerated powers. Yet Otis argued that "every government has the right to preserve and defend itself against injuries and outrages which endanger its existence." Given the hysteria that the Federalists found and fanned, their belief that the existence of the republic was at stake is credible. There may be circumstances—as even Abraham Lincoln noted—where forgetting the Constitution is necessary in order to preserve it. But the inherent-powers theory is one that, by finding power outside the Constitution, may subvert the limitations of the Constitution. Only as a last resort—and the nation was not yet reduced to last resorts, as it would be when the Civil War exploded on Lincoln—could such an argument be anything except *Federalist* 84's "usurpation."[19]

Unlike inherent powers, the phrase *necessary and proper* is an express grant "to make all Laws which shall be necessary and proper for the carrying into Execution the foregoing powers, and all other Powers vested by this Constitution in the Government of the United States, or any Department or Officer thereof." Textually it invites reference to the delegated powers of the Constitution. Harper, however, used the clause as an alternative means of bolstering the inherent-power argument. Instead of making a textual argument that the Sedition Act was necessary and proper to supplement the war power in the time of crisis with France, he argued that the Sedition Act was necessary and proper because government could not function "if sedition for opposing its laws, and libels against its officers, its proceedings, are to pass unpunished." Harper's argument was just the type that the Antifederalists had feared and used to justify their opposition to the Constitution.[20]

The argument that Congress could codify common-law crimes, while attractive, was not without its own troubles. First, Supreme Court Justice Samuel Chase on circuit had just hinted that there was no federal jurisdiction over common-law crimes, a view that the full Court would embrace in 1812. There were, however, contrary opinions among Federalist judges in 1798. Second, if the federal courts did have such jurisdiction, then why was it necessary for Congress to pass a law confirming that jurisdiction? Alternatively, if the federal courts did not have such jurisdiction, where did the congressional power to grant it come from?[21]

The Federalist constitutional arguments were those of frightened men who knew where they were going. They had the votes (44 to 41 in the House), and they had an explanation for their actions that was satisfactory to that majority. In retrospect, the explanation appears to be just what the Republicans said it was, a pretext for usurpation.

## III

Once the Federalists disposed of the issue of power, they had no troubles with the First Amendment, because, they asserted, the First Amendment was not a limitation on congressional power; instead it confirmed the existence of the very power the Congress had exercised. Freedom of the press meant no prior restraints, but allowed subsequent punishment. That was exactly what the new state-of-the-art Sedition Act did. Furthermore, as noted earlier, the Federalists' ideology had been evolving during the decade, and by 1798 they were able to offer a full neo-Blackstonian explanation for their law against lies.

The Federalists may have moved from the idea of the Constitution as exclusively containing delegated powers, but they did not move from the bedrock idea that sovereignty flowed from the people. In the decade since ratification, the Federalists had come to believe that popular sovereignty could be undermined by lies about the government. "To mislead the judgment of the people where they have no power [in a monarchy] may produce no mischief. To mislead the judgment of the people where they have *all* power, must produce the greatest possible mischief." Furthermore, because everyone agreed that the states were appropriately republican, and the states retained the common law of seditious libel, it was not possible to argue with consistency that seditious libel law could not coexist with republican principles. Indeed, the Federalists were going farther; the law of seditious libel was a necessary part of republicanism.[22]

The Federalists held that an attack on government was an attack on the people themselves. Elections were the exercise of popular sovereignty; but after an election, the people delegated power to those elected. Those public officials then needed protection from unjust criticism in order to govern effectively. An attack on a public official was therefore an attack on the people. Supreme Court Justice Samuel Chase perfectly summarized this neo-Blackstonian Federalist position:

Since ours is a government founded on the opinions and confidence of the people, if a man attempts to destroy the confidence of the people in their officers, their supreme magistrate, and their legislature, he effectively saps the foundation of their government. A republican government can only be destroyed in two ways; the introduction of luxury, or the licentiousness of the press.

Unstated, but implicit in the argument, was the assumption that the government meant the governing majority. A decade earlier Hamilton had written in *Federalist* number 71 that "the representatives of the people, in a popular assembly, seem sometimes to fancy that they are the people themselves; and betray strong symptoms of impatience and disgust at the least sign of opposition from any other quarter." The Federalists of 1798 had done exactly this. Opposition to Federalist policies was opposition to the government and therefore opposition to the people, a position that Hamilton now enthusiastically embraced.[23]

The Federalists identified opposition to their policies with support of France, and their name for the Republicans—the "internal foe"—expressed their view that the Republican party was a threat to the republic. Jefferson had forecast that the Federalists would turn on the opposition. Federalist leaders like Harper, who believed philosophers were the "pioneers of revolution," and John Allen made clear in their speeches that they believed the political statements of the Jeffersonians properly constituted a crime under their proposal. Even a congressman, Matthew Lyon of Vermont, was convicted under the act. To the Republican targets it did not matter that the Sedition Act was more liberal than Great Britain's recently liberalized law of seditious libel. A seditious libel law, whether liberal or strict, was a tool of the governing majority to beat down opposition.[24]

Two facial aspects of the law made its partisan nature unmistakable. First, its expiration was tied neither to the duration of the potential hostilities with France nor to the end of the enacting Fifth Congress. Instead it expired on March 3, 1801, the last day of the Adams administration. Second, the act made it a crime to "write, print, utter or publish . . . any false, scandalous and malicious [statement] against the government of the United States or either house of the Congress of the United States or the President of the United States with intent to defame." Conspicuously omitted was any like protection for the vice-president, Thomas Jefferson. From the law's perspective, he was fair game; had it been otherwise, Alexander Hamilton, as well as the leading Federalist editors, would have transgressed the act as freely and frequently as the leading opposition editors.[25]

The unsuccessful opposition to the bill was led by the able Jeffersonian House leader, Swiss born—and therefore potential Federalist target if the Naturalization Act were amended—Albert Gallatin. Noting the "temporary majority in Congress," Gallatin offered an analysis that would be vindicated by history. "This bill must be considered only as a weapon used by a party now in power in order to perpetuate their authority and preserve their present places." Prosecutions under the Sedition Act, initiated largely by Secretary of State Timothy Pickering, fully confirmed Gallatin's views. Benjamin Bache of the *Aurora* escaped conviction only by his premature demise in the yellow fever epidemic of 1798. His successor William Duane was convicted, as were two other prominent opposition editors, Thomas Cooper and James Callender. Four of the leading opposition newspapers were prosecuted; three of them were forced to cease publication, two permanently. The papers selected for prosecution—the *Aurora,* the *Boston Independent Chronicle,* the *New York Argus,* the *Richmond Examiner,* and the *Baltimore Examiner*—were precisely those from which most of the lesser opposition papers copied their political material. Whether in good faith or not, the Federalists attempted to decapitate the opposition press, while, as Gallatin observed in the Sixth Congress, scandalous misrepresentations by Federalist papers were untouched: "How has it been executed? Only by punishing persons of politics different from those of the administration."[26]

The Sedition Act trials showed, as their counterparts in Great Britain also did, that the Zengerian inclusion of full jury participation was no guarantee of a free press. Juries might be stacked or, as was the case on both sides of the Atlantic in the 1790s, anti-French hysteria might be such an overriding concern that the jury would easily convict for the exercise of legitimate dissent. Nor was the defense of truth, available only on our side of the Atlantic, a factor. In no case brought under the Sedition Act did a defense of truth prevail. Prescient as always, Gallatin had accurately forecast that truth would be too elusive to be useful: "And how could truth of *opinions* be proven by evidence?" If an individual wrote that the Sedition Act was intended not for the public good, but rather "solely for party purposes," would a jury "composed of the friends of that Administration hesitate much in declaring the opinion ungrounded or, in other words, false and scandalous and its publication malicious?" Opinions cannot be proven true, even in the best of times; and the 1790s were not the best of times.[27]

## IV

Defeated in Congress, defeated in the 1799 congressional elections, defeated by a Federalist judiciary actively participating in the Sedition Act prosecutions, the Jeffersonians retreated to the few places they had strength, Southern legislatures. There, especially in Virginia and Kentucky, through Madison and Jefferson (who were echoing Gallatin's and John Nicholas's losing arguments in the House), the Republicans used their control of the legislatures to create a forum to counter with their own constitutional theories. They also offered a novel remedy—nullification—for the "deliberate, palpable and dangerous" usurpations of authority (the Virginia Resolution's apt label for the Sedition Act).[28]

It was not difficult to demonstrate that Congress had grasped a power not delegated. But the Republicans were answering all constitutional arguments, and this meant that the Federalist view of the role of criticism in a republic would not go unchallenged. The Jeffersonians, too, had been thinking about freedom of expression during the decade, especially in conjunction with the earlier debate over the Democratic-Republican Societies. Not surprisingly, the Jeffersonians saw the consequences of popular sovereignty in a markedly different manner than the Federalists.

The Federalist argument that criticism of the government was criticism of the people was countered by arguments from Nicholas and Madison on a far different theory of popular sovereignty. As Madison explained in his famous *Report on the Virginia Resolutions,* the "essential difference between the British Government and the American constitutions" provides the "clearest light" on why neither the British view of no prior restraints nor the Federalist view that publications could be punished for their criticisms of government was compatible with limited government in the United States. In Britain, rights against encroachment are "understood" as confined to the executive. Parliament is the "omnipotent" guardian of the people "against executive usurpation."[29]

"In the United States the case is altogether different because the people, not the government, possess the absolute sovereignty. The legislature, no less than the executive, is under limitations of power." Because of this difference from Britain, American theory on the press necessarily had to be different. The abolition of prior restraints might be a sufficient check on the royal prerogative there, but under American constitutions the press must be free "not only from the previous inspection of licensers, but from the subsequent penalty of laws."[30]

With his explicit equating of prior restraint and subsequent punishment—it would be a "mockery to say that no laws should be passed preventing publications from being made, but that laws might be passed for punishing them in case they should be made"— Madison agreed with Gallatin's view of freedom of the press. Their views, along with that of Nicholas, were built on the Radical English Whig view of sovereignty that rejected Blackstone and his theories. Leonard Levy concluded that the debates on the Sedition Act and Madison's *Report* represent a sudden breakthrough of libertarian thought; but this is to overstate their novelty and ignore the implicit rejection of Blackstone already existing in American theory.[31]

Just because Blackstone's theoretical position on sovereignty had been rejected, this did not mean that all the interstices were worked out immediately, or even that people recognized all the logical implications of their new beliefs. It took the drastic step of Federalists attempting to secure the national government as their own preserve to bring the full implications of the meaning of citizen sovereignty to the fore. It is not that the generation living through the 1790s lacked other demands for their time. The conclusion that Gallatin and Madison voiced in the Sedition Act controversy had been latent in the theories going back to Oswald's battles with McKean in Pennsylvania and the more recent debates over the Democratic-Republican Societies.

This is not to say that they were the only conclusions that could be drawn from the experiences of the prior quarter-century. The splits of the 1790s, including splits over the degree of reverence (and possibly longevity) that should attach to the Constitution, brought forth differing views on the amount of criticism of government that a new republic could withstand and still survive; meanwhile, the opposition press was busy creating an empirical record. The Sedition Act, even if adopted in hysteria and with motives that cannot withstand examination, was an outgrowth of the maturing of alternative views on the relationship of citizen to government. Both the Federalist and the Jeffersonian views could point backward to antecedents; both sides could claim support among the framers (although neither would cite the framing because that generation believed that the views of those drafting and ratifying a document were not relevant in ascertaining the meaning of the words they chose); neither side could claim a lay-down victory because the newly independent nation had not had the time to think the issues through and come to a definitive solution, even if one was possible.[32]

As a historical matter the Antifederalists had feared the national government might exercise a power to pass a press law, and the Antifederalist position was that if such an exercise occurred it was wrongful. They were right. But 1798 was not the last time that the Constitution in crisis times would prove to be, contrary to Madison's hopes, only a "paper barrier."[33]

## V

While Jefferson and Madison were correct on the issue of congressional powers, their Virginia and Kentucky resolutions and the Virginia report, as helpful guides to the meaning of the First Amendment, suffered a double historical blow. One was their move, especially Jefferson's, from congressional usurpation to its remedy. The other was that they did not, because they could not, foresee that future First Amendment debates would not implicate the issue of the constitutional source of legislative power. Twentieth-century laws impacting the press are justified as either "necessary and proper" to the furtherance of a delegated federal power or else passed by states which, by reason of their police power, have the necessary powers—subject only to constitutional provisions limiting power.

The Virginia and Kentucky resolutions and Madison's Virginia report not only asserted that the national government had usurped powers, but going beyond the claim of right, they offered a remedy. The milder statements Madison drafted for Virginia looked to the state legislatures to declare the meaning of the Constitution. That novel constitutional theory was at least as great a move from the Constitution as was the Sedition Act. But Jefferson, for Kentucky, went even farther with his claim that a state had the right of nullification.[34]

When Madison and Jefferson moved from right to remedy they undermined their own claims for adherence to the Constitution. It is not surprising—although an older, wiser Madison protested—to find that the "Spirit of '98" was claimed by other Southerners in the four decades of national crisis culminating in the imposition of the Fourteenth Amendment as the price of military victory in the Civil War. The theoretical justifications for freedom of the press simply became lost and forgotten amidst the more radical—and for a time, useful—theoretical justification for nullification and state power to withdraw from the union.[35]

The next difficulty with the Republican position was more constitutionally rooted, and therefore more lasting, than the nineteenth-century detour to nullification. It is not enough that everyone agree there is no power to pass a press law and that the "necessary and proper" clause does not provide any independent justification to do so. Congress might pass a law clearly implementing a delegated power and nevertheless restrict the press. Madison flirted with this problem in the Virginia report, when he argued that Congress, having claimed an implied power to suppress insurrections, could not go on to claim an implied power to prevent them "by punishing whatever may lead or tend to them." To do this, Madison argued, would be to claim far too much.[36]

What Madison did not do—and he did not have to, because by

the time he wrote the Virginia report the potential for war with France had evaporated with the French navy at the Nile—was consider whether Congress could pass wartime measures that would necessarily restrict what the press printed. If Congress did so, then Congress would be exercising its delegated powers and therefore not simply passing a press law. What then?

One thing is plain. The way the debates over the new Constitution and its lack of press guarantees were structured would be of little help, because Congress would be exercising a specifically delegated power. Instead, the First Amendment claim would come to the fore; and here, at least, the governing elites had not thought of the solution because they had not thought of the problem.

Nor, of course, was there reason for them to think about what would happen if a state passed a press law. That changed with the Fourteenth Amendment. With its passage, the United States Supreme Court would face cases where the issue of power was not relevant because the issue of affirmative power had already been settled in the state courts. Only the First Amendment, applicable to the states because of the Fourteenth, mattered. *Patterson*, discussed in the introduction, while a transition case, is nevertheless illustrative. Although Holmes first wrongly concluded that the Fourteenth Amendment did not protect rights of press freedom—a point corrected two decades later—he nevertheless decided the case as if the Fourteenth Amendment did protect the press. Recall that Holmes concluded that the guarantees of freedom of the press were simply the transmission of Blackstone's common law of no prior restraints into the United States Constitution. In the century since the Sedition Act, the framers' move from Blackstone had been largely forgotten. What that era's legal research could find easily was Blackstone's *Commentaries* and McKean's contempt judgment against Oswald. Holmes was notoriously quick in his judicial writing, and here his haste produced the erroneous conclusion that freedom of the press in the United States, as in England, simply meant no prior restraints. As he aptly summed up in a 1922 letter: "I simply was ignorant."[37]

Holmes's analysis never questioned Colorado's substantive power to do as it pleased. Under American law, state governments have whatever powers their state constitutions grant. The right of a state to act as a matter of state law cannot be questioned by a federal court. The latter can only apply federal constitutional limitations, typically the Fourteenth Amendment, to state actions. To put this in the context of the founding, any state—if its constitution permitted—could have passed a press law in 1792. Because Madison's state press clause was rejected, the Bill of Rights was no bar. As *Patterson* showed, all that changed once the Fourteenth Amendment came into being, because it extended to state governments the restrictions that the Bill of Rights imposed on the federal government. Nevertheless, there was a theoretical difference between state and federal cases. In state cases, only the restrictions of the federal Constitution applied, whereas federal cases could also, as the Sedition Act controversy showed, raise the question of whether Congress acted in pursuance to a constitutional grant of authority.

Even on the federal level, however, the Sedition Act controversy over affirmative power was to be a historical anomaly. In twentieth-century cases—beginning with those coming out of federal wartime censorship—if the federal government wished to pass a law, it was considered to have the power to do so unless the First Amendment trumped. Thus federal cases and state cases became identical, with each focusing exclusively on how far the constitutional guarantee of freedom of the press restricted legislative action. The Sedition Act controversy remained relevant on the First Amendment issue. No one wished to replicate 1798 and the Federalists' attempt to perpetuate themselves in power. But few in the government wanted the populace up in arms against the war either.

# VI

Even before the United States entered World War I in April 1917, preparations for entry had been under way. Ultimately, government policy was to conscript both men and minds for the fight, virtually matching Elihu Root's view at the outbreak of the war that "we must have no criticism now."[38]

In the Justice Department, lawyers were thinking to the future while remembering the past. During the Civil War there had been considerable opposition to the draft and it was correctly assumed that that would be the case again. Attorney General Thomas W. Gregory noted a year later that "when war broke out we had no real, substantial set of laws with which to confront the emergency."

The Justice Department wanted laws that would repress "political agitation . . . of a character directly affecting the safety of the state."[39]

The administration had three legislative goals: one would authorize the president to censor information that "might be useful to the enemy"; the second would prohibit "willfully" making false statements to interfere with military success or "willfully" causing insubordination in the military or obstructing the draft; the third would render "nonmailable" any publications that transgressed the provisions of the second. The first was hotly debated, narrowed, and then ultimately defeated; the second was passed virtually without debate; the third was enacted after considerable debate.[40]

What the administration wanted most—the "teeth" of its proposals—was presidential control over defense information. President Wilson saw this as "necessary for the protection of the Nation." He believed that while the "great majority" of newspapers would exercise "patriotic reticence" there were some that would not, and it was "imperative" that the president have powers to do something about them. The "great majority" of newspapers were not as enthusiastic as Wilson about his desire to censor them, and they mobilized to defeat the proposal.[41]

The censorship provision was attacked on two fronts: because it was a prior restraint, and because it could be a means to suppress criticism of government policy. Critics were uneasy about granting even a wartime president such powers; and although the administration acceded to a specific limitation precluding restrictions on "any discussion, comment, or criticism of the acts or policies of the Government and its representatives, or the publication of the same," fears were not allayed. Harold Edgar and Benno Schmidt, in their careful study of the legislative history of the Espionage Act of 1917, were ultimately unable to determine whether First Amendment concerns or political anxiety about the grant of powers predominated in the House; but the combination resulted in a House vote instructing its conferees to delete the censorship provision.[42]

Most of the litigation under the Espionage Act involved the provisions that prohibited willfully making false reports with intent to interfere with the armed forces or willfully causing insubordination or obstructing recruiting of the armed forces. Yet in the extensive debate, little attention was directed to this section. The

House deleted a Senate provision that prohibited willfully causing "disaffection" because, in the words of Judiciary Chairman E. Y. Webb, "disaffection" was overly "broad," "elastic," and "indefinite." In discussing the prohibitions in general, Webb assured his colleagues that the provisions "guarded" all true speech, a point that the conviction of Eugene Debs, to name only one, later proved wholly wrong.[43]

Debs, the leading labor figure in the nation, and the Socialist party's presidential candidate from 1904 to 1912, was convicted for giving an outdoor speech in Canton, Ohio, about "socialism, its growth, and a prophecy of its ultimate success." Although a leading opponent of the war, his discussion of the issue was mild. He said that his listeners were "fit for something better than slavery and cannon fodder" and that he was proud of three jailed socialists who had been convicted for failing to register for the draft. Beyond belying Webb's assurances, Debs's conviction—and its unanimous affirmance in an opinion by Justice Holmes—indicated that no one who criticized the war could be assumed immune from conviction. From jail, Debs received almost a million votes in the 1920 presidential election. Prosecuting Debs was as if the Nixon administration had prosecuted George McGovern for his speeches against the Vietnam War.[44]

The provisions of the Espionage Act making certain items nonmailable combined aspects from each of the two prior provisions. First, nonmailability tracked the "obstructing the armed forces" section (although it also went beyond it); and second, for all practical purposes nonmailability is censorship. But in contrast to the fate of presidential control over defense information, on this provision the administration prevailed. There was already a precedent with the Comstock Laws—named for Anthony Comstock's post–Civil War efforts to cleanse the American mind of any impure thought—for giving power to the Post Office to exclude certain harmful materials from the mails. And, although those affected might not notice any difference, excluding printed matter from the mails is not a prior restraint in the same way that presidential censorship would have been; censorship would prevent any circulation of the information, whereas exclusion from the mails affected only what needed the mails for transmittal. Yet these reasons are too tenuous to account for allowing nonmailability while forbidding presidential censorship. David Rabban persuasively argues that the legislative history "suggests that the majority wanted to restrict antiwar speech it considered dangerous, while protecting major newspapers and other nonthreatening expression." Thus it was not that Congress trusted postmasters more than the president; that is preposterous on its face. Rather it was that the nonmailability provision better expressed a "judgment about the appropriate wartime boundary" of acceptable reporting. As Postmaster General Albert Sidney Burleson later stated, "there is a limit."[45]

The debates on the Espionage Act did reflect the traditional hostility to censorship. But as Rabban notes, another underlying feature was an effort to draw boundaries, to separate good speech from bad. Efforts to preclude mail censorship were unsuccessful, and even congressmen who opposed giving postmasters power to block publications agreed that advocating opposition to the war effort ought to be punished; but their problem with the proposed legislation was that postmasters would mistakenly exclude "legitimate" publications. Thus even congressmen taking the anticensorship position indicated objections to publications that might harm the war effort. It is hardly surprising that the majority who prevailed were even less protective of First Amendment interests. As Representative James Robert Mann of Illinois noted: "A whole lot of people here and elsewhere seem to think that if a man does not agree with you he is a traitor and is guilty of treasonable utterances."[46]

Historians have noted that in the Progressive Era, "freedom of expression did not rank high in the hierarchy of values." Freedom of speech and freedom of the press were perceived as linked to other liberty issues, such as freedom of contract, and were seen as a hindrance to the need "to discipline American society" and create "a tight national cohesion." The traditional view is that there was an "absence of a libertarian concern with protecting basic freedoms" and that the "war hysteria" was "unchecked by a tradition of civil liberties." Mark Graber demonstrates, however, that what he identifies as a tradition of "libertarian concern with protecting basic freedoms" was part of *conservative* libertarian tradition that most Progressives were repudiating (and that future historians would forget). The needs of wartime mobilization simply reinforced the emphasis of many Progressive nationalists on national unity and subordination of the selfish individual to the social order. Thus, although the Espionage Act did not incorporate the boldest efforts at censorship, its underlying premise was that criticism of wartime policies could and should be limited.[47]

## VII

The Espionage Act produced *Schenck* and *Debs,* the Supreme Court cases traditionally seen as the beginning point in modern discussions of freedom of expression. Schenck, an important official of the Socialist party, was convicted for mailing to men accepted for military service a document charging that the draft violated the Thirteenth Amendment (prohibiting slavery) and that entry in the war was simply an effort to assist "Wall Street's chosen few." Debs's speech extolling socialism, opposing militarism, and praising several "comrades" who were in jail for draft resistance has already been mentioned. For all that the record of the case shows, possibly the most damaging piece of evidence was his address to the jury stating: "I have been accused of obstructing the war. I admit it. Gentlemen, I abhor war. I would oppose the war if I stood alone." Sandwiched between these two cases was a third, involving a German-language newspaper in Missouri and a defendant so obscure that even his position with the newspaper is unknown.[48]

Jacob Frohwerk combined with Carl Gleeser to prepare and publish the *Missouri Staats Zeitung* in Kansas City. The two German immigrants were charged with conspiring to violate the Espionage Act in a series of articles printed during the second half of 1917. Justice Holmes, again for a unanimous Court, found these articles "not much" different from that sent by Schenck. The first of the articles carried the essential thrust of them all: "We can not possibly believe it to be the intention of our administration to continue the sending of American boys to the blood-soaked trenches of France." What followed was nothing original, just the standard antiwar litany: it was a rich man's war but a poor man's fight, designed to fatten the great trusts and protect the loans of Wall Street; the Germans have an unquenchable spirit and were fighting a defensive war, thus presenting no danger to the United States;

Americans were being sacrificed only in the interests of England. "We say therefore, cease firing."[49]

*Frohwerk*'s facts raise directly the issue of whether or not public opposition to the war was criminalized in the Espionage Act, and if so, whether the First Amendment precluded that legislative choice. *Schenck,* decided a week earlier, provides the beginning point. Recall that the Espionage Act required specific intent; that is, before a person could be convicted a jury must find that he or she intended "willfully" to encourage obstruction of the draft. *Schenck* simply found intent from publication, concluding that "the document would not have been sent unless it had been intended to have some effect, and we do not see what effect it could be expected to have upon persons subject to the draft except to influence them to obstruct the carrying of it out." Holmes was equally direct on the First Amendment point, holding that freedom of speech was not absolute and war was a limiting factor on an individual's rights. *Schenck* coined the "clear and present danger" test, according to which "the question in every case is whether the words used are used in such circumstances and are of such a nature as to create a clear and present danger that they will bring about the substantive evils that Congress has a right to prevent."[50]

In *Frohwerk* it turned out that Schenck's targeting those about to enter the military may not have been relevant. On its facts, there was no showing that the *Missouri Staats Zeitung* aimed specifically at potential draftees. Yet that did not matter, because "on this record it is impossible to say that it might not have been found that the circulation of the paper was in quarters where a little breath would be enough to kindle a flame." The case against Frohwerk was thus weaker than that against Schenck on both contested points; the recipients of the writings and the intensity of the writing. Nevertheless, the First Amendment protected neither the writing nor the defendant from a jury's finding that Frohwerk violated the Espionage Act.[51]

Holmes wrote in *Frohwerk* that "we do not lose our right to condemn either measures or men because the Country is at war." Yet *Frohwerk,* more than either *Schenck* or *Debs,* contradicts that very statement. The cases hold that the circumstances of war do matter and do affect the scope given to antiwar dissent. Apparently war itself is likely to create a clear and present danger that antiwar

writings will hinder the war effort, thereby producing a "substantive evil that Congress has the right to prevent." Holmes never
asked when it was legitimate to discuss the causes of war. Before a
war begins? That would be interesting. After the war ends? That,
alas, will be done with frequency. But when it really matters is when
discussion of war policy matters—that is, when such discussions
can influence government policy.[52]

Holmes's statements about the right to condemn a war are thus
hollow rhetoric. Frohwerk was sentenced to ten years in jail, and
the *Frohwerk* opinion all but limits discussions of war policy to
those who support the war; those who do not may be convicted if a
jury wishes to attribute forbidden motives to their discussion, a
circumstance all too frequently found. Just as with the Sedition Act
of 1798, when a time of national crisis existed, juries functioned as
instruments of the government, and the pressures to conform to the
official governmental line became too much. Once again it bears
noting that Zenger was tried by a jury in a community agreeing
with his side. In a democracy that possibility becomes, as Frohwerk
(and Tocqueville) could have noted, increasingly unlikely.

Even the government attorney who prevailed in *Frohwerk* knew
an injustice had been perpetrated. In private correspondence he
wrote that Frohwerk's articles advocated change in existing governmental policy "as distinguished from advocacy of obstruction of
existing policy, and seemed to me therefore to fall within the protection of the constitutional guarantee of free speech and press."
Frohwerk was, he concluded, "one of the clearest examples of the
political prisoner."[53]

## VIII

If the "obstructing the armed services" provisions of the Espionage
Act could be used to jail antiwar dissenters such as Frohwerk, it
should hardly come as a surprise that the nonmailability provisions
had a similar use. Postmaster General Burleson, a confidant of
Wilson, was known for his "ability and efficiency," and he was in
charge of dealing with antiwar publications that used the mails.
According to Josephus Daniels's diary, Burleson said at a cabinet
meeting that he "wanted something done" about Tom Watson, the
Georgia Populist, who was writing articles against the draft; and

two weeks later he urged "drastic action" against a newly formed peace group that was trying to obtain a statement of peace terms. These are not the statements of a man who takes dissent lightly—even though Daniels's diary noted in the first case that it was impossible to "go after all the DFs [damned fools]" and in the second that the better policy was to do nothing and "let them show their impotence." That was not Burleson's style, however; and when the problems fell under his jurisdiction, he acted.[54]

By mid-July, issues of at least a dozen socialist publications, including *The Masses,* the *New York Call,* and the *Milwaukee Leader,* had been excluded from the mails under the nonmailability provision. Complaints began coming into the White House. Max Eastman, Amos Pinchot, and John Reed of *The Masses;* former congressman and conservative socialist Victor Berger of the *Milwaukee Leader;* Hearst columnist Arthur Brisbane; Wilson's friend Grenville Macfarland of the *New York American;* and Herbert Croly and Walter Lippmann of *The New Republic*—all wrote, expressing a similar concern; that the Post Office was exceeding its statutory powers in moving against all antiwar criticism. The poignant letter from the journalists of *The Masses* noted that they could not obtain from the Post Office any specific complaint against an article; rather postal officials asserted it was the "general tenor" of the magazine that rendered it unmailable. The authors stated that *The Masses* had been studious not to violate the law, because the editors were "anxious in [the] crisis to put their opinions before the public." But without knowing how they had run afoul of the Post Office, they did not know how to attempt to conform their dissent to acceptable standards.[55]

Wilson forwarded the letters to Burleson, often asking for a response, and urging caution or suggesting that Burleson act with more leniency: "very careful weighing," "expressed doubt," "must act with utmost caution." But ultimately Burleson prevailed; Wilson wrote, "Well, go ahead and do your duty." In one case Burleson wrote on the bottom of Wilson's note that he had turned down the request. "Pres[iden]t expressed doubt but yielded." Twice, however, Burleson responded to Wilson more fully; and these responses give a fair picture of what he thought his powers were.[56]

The letter from *The Masses* stated that the magazine had been suppressed even though it had tried to stay within the law, and that the Post Office would not tell them what they had done wrong, mentioning only the "general tenor" of the magazine. Burleson responded to all the points. First, he was precisely legal. No social-ist publication had been suppressed or suspended; rather, particu-lar issues which were unlawful had been refused transmission in the mail. Second, Burleson stated that the reason they were found unmailable was that "they contained matter which would interfere with the operation or success of the military or naval forces of the United States, or would promote the success of its enemies, or would cause insubordination, dissent, disloyalty, mutiny, or refusal of duty in the military or naval forces, or would obstruct the recruiting and enlistment service of the United States, or that such matter advocated or urged treason, insurrection or forcible re-sistance to some law of the United States." Burleson was simply quoting to Wilson the relevant provision of the Espionage Act; this was hardly responsive to the authors' point that no one would tell them how they had run afoul of the law. It is clear, however, that Burleson thought that point spurious. "The terms of the law are perfectly plain, and publishers should have no difficulty in avoiding a violation." But some publications, such as *The Masses,* went beyond mere criticism to obstruction. Four months later in his other major response to Wilson, Burleson sounded an identical note. After directly quoting the Espionage Act, he stated: "These are the things prohibited by the law I am directed to enforce." Criticism of government policy was protected as long as the person was "loyal to the United States."[57]

If Wilson's letters are to be credited, Burleson persuaded him. Wilson wrote to one correspondent that Burleson "wanted to do the right thing," to another that Burleson was "inclined to be most conservative" in the exercise of his powers. But Burleson's state-ments during the cabinet meetings were a better gauge than his responses to Wilson. Burleson believed there was no power to suppress proper criticism; but he found the criticism in the socialist press to be improper. Furthermore, given the way he stretched the laws in the *Milwaukee Leader* case, he provides apt illustration of why we should fear censors who assert that they are merely doing their duty.[58]

In his response to Wilson about the *Masses* letter, Burleson took the dryly legal position that there had been no suppression of the magazine, just an exclusion from the mails of those issues found to violate the law. However excessive his actions may have been, they plausibly accorded with the nonmailability provisions of the Espionage Act. But in the *Milwaukee Leader* case Burleson went much further and used instead the Mail Classification Act of 1879. Briefly, that act created four classifications for mailable material; one of these, second class, applies to newspapers and magazines which are "regularly issued at stated intervals." Second-class mailing privileges are really a huge subsidy to those who qualify, a subsidy justified because of "the historic policy of encouraging by low postal rates the dissemination of current intelligence." Without such a subsidy, periodicals would be significantly more expensive to subscribers.[59]

What Burleson did to the *Leader* was yank its second-class mailing privileges, affecting some 9000 of its subscribers. Burleson's theory was as ingenious as it was threatening to a free press. He argued that because he had found the *Leader* frequently violated the Espionage Act in the recent past, it could be expected to do so in the future. And because issues violating the act could not be mailed, the *Leader* would no longer be "regularly issued at stated intervals" for mailing. Therefore, it no longer qualified for second-class mailing privileges. In his responses to Wilson, Burleson had emphasized that he was just following the directions of clear law. With the *Leader*, Burleson was not following the law, he was making it.[60]

When Berger was informed that the *Leader* was to be denied second-class privileges, he wrote Burleson that such actions would obviously weaken those socialists who advocated evolutionary tactics and would thereby strengthen the revolutionaries. Burleson was unmoved: "The instant you print anything calculated to dishearten the boys in the army or to make them think this is not a just or righteous war—that instant you will be suppressed." When Berger pressed for guidance, he was advised to ignore the war entirely.[61]

With such advice being offered, it is not surprising that the *Leader* lost at the hearing to which it was statutorily entitled. As a result, its out-of-town subscription rate dropped by 85 percent. Nevertheless, it survived; indeed its circulation in Milwaukee grew after the Post Office action. Sure that it was a target, and maybe anticipating his own future indictment as well as trying to soften the government, Berger ordered the *Leader* to shift its editorial policies. Fewer editorials would be published; they would be double-checked, and the readers would be left to draw their own conclusions. "We will say nothing we don't think, although we think a great deal that we can't say." As his indictment with four other national officers of the Socialist party only ten days before the Wisconsin senatorial primary—which he mistakenly thought he might win—showed, the government was unrelenting.[62]

Nor was the Supreme Court a better forum than the administrative hearing. Three years after the war ended—a fact underscoring Justice Brandeis's warning that this case did not at all turn on the war powers of government—the Supreme Court sustained Burleson's actions. Its reasoning was direct. Second-class mailing was a privilege that the government could withhold. "The Constitution was adopted to preserve our Government, not to serve as a protecting screen for those who while claiming its privileges seek to destroy it." In one paragraph "without going much into detail" the Court explained how the *Leader* had so abused its privileges that they could be taken away. Without the slightest trace of irony, the Court gave as an example the *Leader*'s denunciation that the Food Control Law was "Kaiserizing America." Apparently the justices had forgotten that only one week earlier they had held that the very same Food Control Law violated the United States Constitution.[63]

## IX

Crisis times make protecting any freedoms, especially public dissent, difficult. Nor is this a lesson from a quaint and forgotten past. It is true that I have focused on events occurring in the distant past. I chose to do so because the World War I cases involved the press, they have intrinsic interest, and the hysteria of seventy years ago can be viewed with detachment. But I could have used the 1950s instead and replicated the discussion with majoritarian arguments about the need to protect the United States from a Communist fifth column. Crisis times happen, and the pathology they give rise to is unchanging.[64]

The events I have related show that during a period of crisis it becomes all too easy to see vigorous opposition to majoritarian policies as something akin to treason. Thus the Federalists saw the Republicans as the French party, the internal foe. The socialist press during World War I was perceived as pro-German, not loyal to the United States. Once opposition to government policy can be identified with opposition to the United States, the First Amendment is not seen as any great bar to action—although it may, as in the Espionage Act debates, block the most excessive proposals for censorship.

Furthermore, everyone is involved, not just the policy-making branches of government. Joseph Gilbert, an important figure in Minnesota's Non-Partisan League, had given an antiwar speech with a number of angry questions about how democratic the United States was, grouped under his topic sentence: "We are going over to Europe to make the world safe for democracy, but I tell you we had better make America safe for democracy first." The Supreme Court believed democracy in the United States was working just fine, thank you. "The war . . . had been declared by the power constituted by the Constitution to declare it, and in the manner provided for by the Constitution. It was not declared in aggression, but in defense, in defense of our national honor, in vindication of the [now quoting Wilson's war message to Congress] 'most sacred rights of our Nation and our people.'" Gilbert's denunciation of the war was thus "false, a deliberate misrepresentation." How dare he.[65]

The Supreme Court, agreeing with Wilson, was echoing a federal district judge in Iowa who sentenced a defendant to twenty years for circulating a pamphlet urging voters not to reelect the congressmen who had voted for conscription. The Espionage Act was passed to "protect the feeling and spirit of the American people against the work of those who defy authority; it was not intended for ninety-five per cent of the American people, but necessary for the few who will not heed the judgment of the ninety-five per cent; who assume to know more than all the others put together." If young men can be conscripted to die for a cause, do those at home have any lesser duty? Jury behavior held no; the right to a jury trial for antiwar dissent became simply a right to be convicted. Thus a Vermont minister was convicted for distributing a pamphlet teaching that Christians should not kill in wars, while a group of South Dakota farmers met a similar fate because they petitioned the governor to change his decisions on draft exemptions. In a time of national unity all, from high to low, participate.[66]

The crisis mentality, finding the First Amendment no bar, also fails to see that freedoms are affected. *Frohwerk* asserted that criticism of war policy was legitimate; Burleson stated that public officials were not immune from appropriate criticism. But "appropriate" becomes synonymous with tame. Policies can be criticized, but only on terms acceptable to those who approve of the policies. Thus the line drawn in the Espionage Act debates left the major newspapers, with their likelihood of nonthreatening expression, in the clear, while restricting the antiwar speech of those who were intensely opposed to intervention. Not surprisingly, the more that individuals believe a policy is fundamentally wrong, the more likely they are to be considered beyond the pale. Their writings are perceived as "creating hostility to, and encouraging violation of," the majority's policies. Furthermore, Gallatin's apt point from the Sedition Act debates is proven correct again and again: safeguards of truth are of no help when a person enters the realm of opinion. As Gilbert learned, to question President Wilson's version of events was to willfully misrepresent. The majority not only criminalizes dissent; it brands dissenters as liars, further separating them from the body politic.[67]

The message is that dissenters should play by the rules, directing their efforts to amending or repealing offending policies. But, like Holmes in *Frohwerk,* the messenger never asks how. When a solid majority favors a policy and has the votes to maintain it until a future election, there is no way to change that policy except by attempting to create significant vocal opposition to it. Yet this is precisely what the restraints preclude. Maybe the Catch-22 is not unintended.

What are we to make of a tradition with so little tolerance of dissent? One response is that it is precedent, and as such it could justify similar actions in the future. An alternative response is that it is well in our past and the lessons learned offer confidence for the future. It depends. Political agitation may well lead to lawbreaking; it may also lead to a change of government. The Federalists of '98 serve as an apt reminder that a majority may well fear a change of government far more than an outbreak of lawlessness.

## Chapter Three

# Freedom of the Press
# from *Times* to *Times*

Harry Kalven wrote that "the greatest fascination of law study is to watch some great event from the real world intersect with existing legal doctrine." Appropriately, Kalven was discussing the civil rights movement, the impetus that forced the Supreme Court to undo much of the First Amendment law it had created for the anticommunist litigation in the 1950s.[1]

## I

On February 1, 1960, four black college freshmen in Greensboro, North Carolina, went to the downtown Woolworth's, sat down at the whites-only lunch counter, and, after being refused service, stayed all day. Sit-ins had begun. Seven weeks later, the *New York Times* editorialized: "The growing movement of peaceful mass demonstrations by Negroes is something new in the South, something understandable." The *Times* urged Congress to "heed their rising voices." Two weeks later Bayard Rustin and Harry Belafonte decided to use the latter phrase as a lead to a fund-raising appeal to assist with Martin Luther King, Jr.'s rising legal fees.[2]

King's was a life filled with firsts; he was, among other things, the first citizen in the history of Alabama to be charged with felony tax evasion for perjuring himself when he signed his tax returns. This first was all the more notable because when he moved from Montgomery to Atlanta he had been assessed for back taxes, and rather

than fight, he paid. That should have ended everything right then
and there. Even if it had not, the worst a taxpayer could expect under the circumstances would be misdemeanor tax evasion charges.
Alabama, which was in the process of attempting to ban the
NAACP, upped the ante and now appeared intent on sending the
civil rights movement's most eloquent leader to jail as a greedy
preacher who had lied to cheat the government.[3]

King's problem was that his bank records were a complete mess.
Attempts to straighten them out were transferring money from
King to those helping him. His accountant, a trustee at his father's
Ebenezer Baptist Church in Atlanta, was running a tab that equaled
a year of King's salary to go over the two tax years in question.
Five lawyers weren't coming free either. The Northerners believed
King's Southern lawyers were charging beyond their competence;
the latter were complaining about the Northerners' unwillingness
to disclose their rates. Against this background, Rustin and Belafonte set out to raise money for King's defense by taking out a full-
page ad, in the name of sixty-four prominent citizens, in the *New
York Times* to solicit funds. The ad ended by calling on "men and
women of good will" to do more than "applaud." They should give
material support as well. They did. The ad, which cost $4800, paid
for itself many times over.[4]

Soon the ad would be creating legal fees even more times over,
but in the meantime King's perjury trial was fast approaching. His
lawyers, who may have believed him guilty and laughed behind his
back at his claim of innocence, delivered their unhappy prognosis
that a jury would convict and there would be little chance of getting
an appellate court to upset a jury verdict. Fortunately, William
Ming of Chicago brought a young member of his firm who had a
tax and accounting background, Chauncey Eskridge, to assist with
the defense. When Eskridge gingerly talked with King, he learned
that although the bank records were in shambles, King had kept
meticulous notes in a diary. A night with the diary and an adding
machine convinced Eskridge that King was more honest than any
man he had ever hoped to meet.[5]

Now there was a clear trial strategy and, although it would not
have been wise to place even a hedged bet, the Alabama jury, after
three hours and forty-five minutes of deliberation, acquitted King.
Even he could not explain it: "Something happened to the jury." It

would be a different story when the *New York Times* ad received its day in the Alabama courts.[6]

The ad began with an appeal: "three needs—the defense of Martin Luther King—the support of the embattled students—and the struggle for the right to vote"; it then moved on to describe the situation in the South. The first paragraph alluded generally to the "non-violent demonstrations" as a "positive affirmation of the right to live in human dignity as guaranteed by the U.S. Constitution and the Bill of Rights." It charged that in efforts to uphold these guarantees the demonstrators had been "met by an unprecedented wave of terror by those who would deny and negate that document which the whole world looks upon as setting the pattern of modern freedom."[7]

After mentioning the teargassing of demonstrators in Orangeburg, South Carolina, the ad turned, in paragraph three, to Montgomery. It began by complaining of mistreatment of demonstrators who sang in the state capital. It charged that leaders of the demonstration were expelled from Alabama State College, that truckloads of police "armed with shotguns and tear-gas" had ringed the Alabama State campus, and that when "the entire student body" protested by refusing to register, the college dining hall was padlocked in an effort to starve the protesters into submission. Paragraph four made reference to other Southern cities where "young American teenagers" were facing the "entire weight" of the state and police.

The fifth paragraph speculated that "Southern violators of the Constitution fear this new, non-violent brand of freedom fighter . . . even as they fear the upswelling right-to-vote movement" and that they were determined "to destroy the one man who more than any other, symbolizes the new spirit now sweeping the South—the Rev. Dr. Martin Luther King, Jr." The next paragraph asserted that the "Southern violators" had repeatedly "answered Dr. King's protests with intimidation and violence"; it referred to the bombing of his home, assault on his person, his seven arrests, and the pending perjury charge. It asserted that "their real purpose is to remove him physically as the leader to whom the students— and millions of others—look for guidance and support, and thereby to intimidate *all* leaders who may rise in the South." It concluded that King's defense was "an integral part of the total struggle for freedom in the South."[8]

The first indication that the ad might generate more legal fees than it brought in came a week after it ran, when the Alabama attorney general announced that Governor James Patterson had instructed him to consider suing the *Times* and the signatories of the ad for libeling Alabama officials (even though none were specifically named). Then on April 8, Montgomery Police Commissioner L. B. Sullivan wrote four Alabama ministers who were listed in the ad's endorsement section, demanding a "full and fair retraction of the entire false and defamatory matter." As Taylor Branch recounts, these letters came as a "chilling surprise to the four ministers, none of whom had known of the ad's existence, much less that their names had been used."[9]

An identical letter from Sullivan, misdated March 8, was also sent to the *New York Times*. After checking with its Montgomery stringer, the *Times* wrote back that it was "puzzled as to how you think the statements [in the ad] in any way reflect on you." The point was a good one; Sullivan, like everyone else, had not been mentioned by name, nor was there any mention of his job.[10]

Alabama law required Sullivan to request a retraction before suing. It did not require that he continue the correspondence to explain how he felt he had been harmed. On April 19 he let his lawyers do the talking by filing suit against the *Times* and the four Alabama ministers, demanding $500,000 in damages. That was ten times higher than the highest libel award that the Alabama Supreme Court had ever sustained.[11]

A day later the Alabama attorney general recommended that "proper public officials" follow Sullivan: "File a multi-million dollar law suit." His price advice was unheeded, although Sullivan's fellow commissioner Frank Parks, Montgomery Mayor Earl James, and former commissioner Clyde Sellers followed Sullivan's lead precisely. Then on May 6 the mayor of Birmingham and the city's two commissioners each filed $500,000 suits against the *Times* based on stories Harrison Salisbury had written in early April. Similar suits, again based on Salisbury's stories, were filed by three Bessemer officials.[12]

The toppers were yet to come. On May 9 Governor Patterson wrote the *Times* demanding a retraction. Unlike Sullivan, Patterson indicated why he thought the ad implicated him. Not only was he governor, he was also ex officio chairman of the state board of education. This time the *Times* printed a retraction: "To the extent that anyone can fairly conclude from the statements in the advertisement that any such charge [of wrongdoing by Patterson] was made, the New York Times hereby apologizes." It wasn't enough. Patterson filed suit for one million dollars, naming King as a defendant as well. Finally, the distinguished *Times* correspondent Harrison Salisbury, who had written two stories on conditions in Birmingham and Bessemer, was hit with a forty-two-count indictment for criminal libel. The *Montgomery Advertiser* accurately informed its readers: "State and city authorities have found a formidable legal bludgeon to swing at out-of-state newspapers whose reporters cover racial incidents in Alabama."[13]

Although CBS was also hit with libel suits out of Birmingham, it was the *Times* that was seeing the "legal bludgeon" up close and personal, in a state where it could legitimately claim to be a stranger. Only 394 (out of 650,000) copies of the *Times* came in daily, some 35 to Montgomery. Moreover, only two of its regular reporters, Salisbury and Atlanta-based Claude Sitton, had even been in the state in 1960 (and as a result of the lawsuits, on the advice of counsel, Salisbury, Sitton, and other *Times* reporters were instructed to stay away from Alabama). If Alabama courts had jurisdiction over the *Times*—and the courts would hold that they did—then trouble lay ahead.[14]

Jurisdiction aside, both Sullivan and the *Times* had problems. Sullivan's was basic; he had to convince a jury that an ad mentioning neither him nor his position libeled him. The *Times*'s problem was that there were indeed several technical, and one more substantial, factual errors in the ad. Under Alabama defamation law—which was the same as that in the majority of American jurisdictions—these errors would strip the *Times* of the common-law defense of truth, because that defense existed solely for perfectly true statements. The errors in the underlying statement of facts also negated the common-law defense of fair comment. The *Times*'s fate would presumably be in the hands of an Alabama jury no more admiring of it than was the 1918 Ohio jury that had blandly convicted Eugene Debs, the leading Socialist of his time.[15]

The ad's technical errors were just that. Paragraph three said the students sang "My Country 'Tis of Thee," when in fact they sang the national anthem. Paragraph six said King had been arrested seven times—three too many. Police never "ringed" the Alabama State campus, although they were deployed nearby in large numbers. A large portion, but not "all," of the student body participated in the demonstrations. A more serious error was the charge that the dining room had been padlocked to starve the protesting students into submission. That simply was not so, and the only students who were barred from eating were a relatively small number who lacked the necessary documentation.

Still, Sullivan had to prove identity, defamation, and damages, the issue of identity being his greatest hurdle. It would be a jury question, and Sullivan's goal was to demonstrate that references to police in the ad would be interpreted as referring to him in his official capacity as the police commissioner. Thus in paragraph three, the ad stated that in Montgomery "truckloads of police armed with shotguns and tear-gas ringed the Alabama State College Campus. When the entire student body protested . . . their dining hall was padlocked in an attempt to starve them into submission." Then in paragraph six the ad referred first to "Southern violators" and then to the seven arrests of King. Sullivan contended that since arrests are normally made by the police, the references to "they" and "Southern violators" would be read as describing the Montgomery police, and hence him, as lawbreakers and people who would padlock a dining hall to starve students. If Sullivan could convince the jury that the words "they" and "police" referred to him, then, surprising as it might seem, he could be home free; the ad's references to brutality, harassment, and illegality by the police were clearly defamatory, and, as we have just seen, the *Times* would be defenseless because the ad's statements were not 100 percent true.

Nor would it be relevant that the *Times* did not write the ad and that the ad's real authorship was undisputed. At trial the *Times* would attempt to disclaim responsibility for Rustin's errors, while Sullivan would have the more enviable position of being portrayed as the "innocent victim of powerful corporate interests in the North." Sullivan's point was the better one, rhetorically and legally: the *Times* had circulated the libel and therefore had legal responsibility for it.[16]

The trial's beginning on November 1, 1960, was most inauspicious for the *Times*. An all-white jury was empaneled, and Sullivan's counsel established the right to use the word "nigger" in the courtroom, on the ground that it was the customary usage of a lifetime. Then followed the establishing of Sullivan's case. Grover Hall, editor of the *Montgomery Advertiser,* testified that most Montgomery citizens would take the ad to be defamatory of Sullivan if they believed the charges. Sullivan's other witnesses testified that they understood the ad to refer to the police department and Sullivan—although none of the witnesses testified that he believed the truth of any of the statements deemed to apply to Sullivan. Naturally Sullivan took the stand, and on cross-examination he helped his own case when in separate answers he stated, "Certainly I feel it reflects on me," and "I have endeavored to try to earn a good reputation and that's why I resent very much the statements contained in this ad which are completely false and untrue."[17]

None of Sullivan's witnesses thought less of him because of the ad. That was not relevant, however, because of a unique facet of libel law, again common to most American jurisdictions: damage, falsity, and malice could be presumed without being proved. Such "galloping presumptions" can produce amazing results. Thus, whereas the jury was to decide the issue of identity—and they found that the ad did refer to Sullivan—the judge properly ruled that no damage need be shown. Sullivan was entitled to a presumption of general damages, based on presumed harm to his reputation—never mind the compelling irony that the ad, if believed, would probably have enhanced Sullivan's reputation in the Montgomery of 1960! Similarly, as the *Times* was unable to establish truth, the trial judge ruled, again properly, that the charges in the ad were libelous as a matter of law. Defamation is a tort of strict liability, so it did not matter that the *Times* did not know whether the facts were untrue. By publishing the ad, the *Times* took its chances. When the jury came back, giving Sullivan every cent he had asked for, the *Times* learned the costs of taking its chances.[18]

Again it bears repeating, as Harry Kalven has so carefully noted, that "Alabama did not create any special rules of law for these defendants. It simply applied the existing principles of the law of libel," namely, (1) whether the statements would be understood as referring to the plaintiff was a question of fact for the jury to decide; (2) the plaintiff could recover damages for statements tending to injure him in his office, without proving actual injury; and (3) the privilege of fair comment did not protect false statements of fact. All this didn't make the *Times* feel any better, and it didn't make Alabama's legal bludgeon look any tamer—a point reinforced on February 1, 1961, when a jury awarded an identical $500,000 judgment to Mayor Earl James in his libel action against the *Times* and the Alabama ministers. Only by successfully, although possibly temporarily, removing the remaining cases from state to federal court did the *Times* prevent additional judgments from rolling in.[19]

If the battles in the Southern streets and in the arena of public opinion were largely draws, the legal arsenal contained in the law of libel enabled the South to make a powerful counterattack. A former vice-president and general counsel of the *Times* reflected: "Without a reversal of these verdicts, there was a reasonable question of whether the *Times*, then wracked by strikes and small profits, would survive."[20]

## II

Preparing for the appeal, the *Times* added the Columbia Law School professor Herbert Wechsler, one of the giants of American legal education, to its Lord, Day, and Lord legal team. That did not, however, forestall a complete defeat in the Alabama Supreme Court in the summer of 1962. In an opinion that referred to "so-called 'demonstrations,'" the *Times* lost point by point. The court even used the *Times*'s unsuccessful retraction to Governor Patterson against it, by noting its failure to retract for Sullivan when "the matter contained in the advertisement was equally false as to both parties." Nor did the court allude once to the fact that the judgment was ten times higher than any libel award it had ever affirmed. It was, the court twitted, "common knowledge that as of today the dollar is worth only 50 cents or less of its former value." Thus there was no reason for the court to mitigate damages.[21]

With the *Times*'s only hope now being the United States Supreme Court, the *Times*'s legal position was, to put it mildly, intriguing. For the Supreme Court to deny review (or to grant review and affirm the Alabama court's judgment) would be to authorize the South to secede intellectually from the Union. With the Supreme Court already the lead player against Southern segregation, it was not conceivable that the Court could sit back and allow the South to silence the Northern press, any more than it would have been conceivable to allow the South to rid itself of the NAACP. Yet there is rarely a 100 percent certainty in constitutional law; and with potential bankruptcy as the downside risk, the *Times* was not in any position to assume that it would prevail, especially when the operative rule of constitutional law in 1962 was that state libel laws raised no United States constitutional issues. Indeed, the legal literature was all but silent on that very point. Sullivan's counsel, M. Roland Natchman, Jr., based his confidence of victory on just this point: "The only way the Court could decide against me was to change one hundred years or more of libel law."[22]

The *Times* decided to put its fate in Wechsler's hands, rather than Lord, Day, and Lord's. Wechsler had a case with wonderful facts but no law. His job was to show the Court how to make the law conform to the facts; he did it by merging the two in an ingenious argument that the Alabama court had functionally, if not formally, applied the law of seditious libel, but without the safeguards included even by the Sedition Act, which required proof beyond a reasonable doubt that defendant had intended to bring an official "into contempt or disrepute." Furthermore, there was no protection against double jeopardy; the *Times* was being punished several times for a single offensive statement, and in amounts vastly exceeding permissible fines under the Sedition Act. The jury's actions had turned impersonal denunciation of an agency into actionable defamation. The libel law thus applied had "transformed the law of defamation from a method of protecting private reputation to a device for insulating government against attack." All nine justices agreed.[23]

Justice Brennan's opinion for the Court tracked Wechsler's seminal argument, formally resurrected the Sedition Act—one hundred sixty-three years after it expired—and slew it properly: "Although the Sedition Act was never tested in this Court, the attack upon its validity has carried the day in the court of history. . . . Because of the restraint it imposed upon criticism of government and public officials, [the Sedition Act] was inconsistent with the First Amendment."[24]

Beyond reflecting Wechsler the advocate, the opinion combined the insights of the philosopher Alexander Meiklejohn on the necessities of political speech with those of William Brennan, lawyer and jurist, on the practical effects of litigation. It was a stunning combination. By holding the Sedition Act retrospectively unconstitutional, the Court embraced the centrality of speech about public affairs. Citizens, as Meiklejohn had so long argued, must be free to criticize their government; political speech is necessary to a properly functioning democracy, and the government may not win a debate by using its powers, courts, and legitimacy to silence its critics. No topic should be out of bounds, no matter how much the government wishes to create boundary limits.[25]

To Meiklejohn's concept, Brennan added his own flourish: that the risk of being sued for libel by public officials chilled freedom of discussion. Brennan's "chilling effect" was made more chilling by the fact that the verdict against the *New York Times* was a thousand times higher than any permissible fine under the Sedition Act; risking such liability might give any publisher pause. And he recognized that there was a chilling effect even though truth was a defense in libel suits. Persons wishing to make factual assertions in a controversial area might be deterred, not because they do not believe their statements true, but because they doubt whether the statement can be proven true to the satisfaction of a jury. Beginning with his 1958 opinion in *Speiser v. Randall,* Brennan had been instructing the judiciary on the consequences of the risk of error in litigation, creating an awareness in the law of the law's own limitations in accurately making determinations. No matter how perfectly a lawsuit is conceived, no matter how talented the lawyers, no matter how certain the existence of a fact, there is always the risk that the fact finder may err in its determinations. And the more controversial the area, the more unpopular the party, the greater the likelihood of factual error slipping into litigation. Brennan's concern with errors in fact finding dovetailed with his efforts to create awareness that some legal rules by their very existence might cause would-be participants in debate to engage in self-censorship.[26]

In *New York Times v. Sullivan* Brennan brought these strands together to demonstrate that the traditional libel laws, operating to protect public officials, necessarily had a chilling effect on public debate. Although chilling-effect analysis often requires the Court to speculate about whether and to what extent a chilling effect may exist in a particular context, the political context of Alabama in the early 1960s demonstrated convincingly that, absent federal intervention, opposition speech would be silenced.

When the Court moved from its rationale of the importance of criticizing the government and the concerns over chilling effect, to the translation of that rationale into operative legal doctrine, it announced four new rules: (1) Public officials may not recover damages for defamatory falsehoods relating to their official conduct unless they can prove that the statements were made with "actual malice"—that is, either with actual knowledge of falsity or with "reckless disregard" of whether the statements were false. (2) Actual malice must be proved with "convincing clarity." (3) A jury may not infer that criticism of the conduct of underlings is criticism of the supervising official. (4) Judges—both the trial judge and those exercising appellate review—must engage in independent review to satisfy themselves that the evidence in the case is constitutionally sufficient. By themselves (1) and (3) would have required reversal of the Sullivan case; but to make sure that the message was loud and clear, the Court exercised its judgment under (2) and (4) to further hold that the evidence was constitutionally insufficient. Had the Court not done so, there was the real risk that an Alabama jury would find whatever facts were necessary to justify the imposition of liability. Bull Connor, in fact, won his libel judgment after the decision in *New York Times v. Sullivan,* when a federal jury found actual malice in the careful reporting of Harrison Salisbury. It took a trip to the United States Court of Appeals for the Fifth Circuit to set aside that judgment.[27]

The Court had thus entered a brand-new area of law and dramatically constitutionalized it. Furthermore, it had reached back to settle a long-dead controversy over the Sedition Act. But the opinion also contained an intangible, as Kalven perceptively observed. It had given momentum to First Amendment adjudication.[28]

It might be assumed that First Amendment adjudication did not need momentum, because it already had plenty. This view stems from the traditional writings that treat First Amendment adjudication as if it were a wonderful example of the Whig concept of progress unfolding. According to this tradition, the World War I cases such as *Schenck, Frohwerk, Milwaukee Socialist Democratic Publishing,* and *Debs* were wrongly decided, as were the subsequent *Gitlow* and *Whitney* decisions; but thereafter the cases are seen as being decided according to the brilliant dissents authored by Holmes and Brandeis. Beginning in the early 1930s, the Court began to protect First Amendment rights, and with the legacy of Holmes and Brandeis providing the necessary guidance, the Court made the United States the most speech-protective nation in history. First with radicals, then with Jehovah's Witnesses, and finally with labor, the Court expanded the areas of First Amendment protection.[29]

The principal problem with this Whig history of the First Amendment is that it must ignore the 1950s and early 1960s, when the protections accorded to organized labor all but vanished, and the Court sanctioned the McCarthy hysteria in cases involving reds and pinks. For over a decade, with a modest blip around 1957, the Court found the First Amendment not offended by the national demands for conformity. In the process, the Court gutted and then basically ignored Holmes's "clear and present danger" test, the supposed doctrinal cornerstone of the Holmes-Brandeis legacy; and ultimately it replaced that test with a balancing test, which in operation always found that the First Amendment interests were outweighed by the need to root out domestic communism wherever it might be found. Just two years before *New York Times v. Sullivan,* the Court had initially voted five to four to require the NAACP to answer Florida's questions about supposed Communist infiltration, questions that could have ended the NAACP's ability to function in the South. Only a stroke felling Justice Frankfurter caused the decision to be delayed and then changed (upon his replacement by Justice Goldberg).[30]

For almost fifteen years the Supreme Court had genuflected to the need for self-preservation as "the ultimate value of any society." *New York Times v. Sullivan* killed that. The Sedition Act was unconstitutional; the clear and present danger test, either strict or gutted, was unmentioned; balancing was ignored. Instead, the Court wrote that the case, indeed all First Amendment cases, must be considered "against the background of a profound national commitment to the principle that debate on public issues should be uninhibited, robust, and wide-open."[31]

## III

The Supreme Court demonstrated its commitment to *New York Times v. Sullivan* by plunging into its newly constitutionalized area with rare energy. First and most important, it expanded the class of plaintiffs who had to meet the new standards before they could recover damages. Second, it policed actions by lower courts, which often seemed to wonder if *New York Times v. Sullivan* were not simply a civil rights case in disguise, and it strengthened the core of the rules.

When the former supervisor of a municipal ski area sued over statements (not naming him) suggesting mismanagement when he had been in charge, his own claim that the public would know to whom the account referred was used by the Court to justify categorizing him as a public official. Then, in a pair of cases wherein one political candidate was called a "former small-time bootlegger" and another was mistaken for his brother and therefore reported as having been indicted for perjury, the Court held that the First Amendment also protected statements that did not refer to job-related actions, because for public officials everything was relevant to electoral politics.[32]

From public officials, the Court moved to public figures. General Edwin A. Walker had commanded the federal troops desegregating Little Rock but was forced to retire from the military over public disputes with President Kennedy, whom he accused of "collaboration and collusion with the international Communist conspiracy." His background brought him to Oxford, Mississippi, and the riots at Ole Miss in the fall of 1962, when James Meredith was admitted by court order and federal intervention. As if atoning for being right in Little Rock, Walker rallied the students: "[Mississippi Governor Ross] Barnett yes, Castro no. Bring your flags, your tents and your skillets! It is time! Now or never." The Associated Press had assigned a young reporter to cover the events; he had successfully posed as a student during the riot and almost immediately sent a dispatch stating that Walker had personally led the charge against federal marshals and encouraged the rioters to use violence. Walker, while admitting his presence and speaking to the students, stated that he had counseled restraint, that he exercised no control over the crowd, and that he emphatically did not take part in the charge against the federal marshals.[33]

A Texas jury believed Walker and found that the Associated Press dispatch had libeled him—to the tune of $500,000 in compensatory damages and another $300,000 in punitive damages.

The trial judge, however, refused to award punitive damages, because there was no evidence of malice on the part of the defendant. The judgment was affirmed on appeal, with the court finding *New York Times v. Sullivan* inapplicable. "Truth alone," the trial judge had noted, "should be an adequate defense."[34]

The Supreme Court unanimously disagreed; the First Amendment imposed limitations on libel suits by public figures as well as public officials. Chief Justice Warren's opinion explained the rationale most fully when he noted that increasingly "distinctions between governmental and private sectors are blurred." Governmental power has become centralized, but so too has private power. "In many situations, policy determinations which traditionally were channeled through formal political institutions are now originated and implemented [in the private sector and] only loosely connected with government. This blending of positions and power has also occurred in the case of individuals so that many who do not hold public office at the moment are nevertheless intimately involved in the resolution of important public questions or, by reason of their fame, shape events in areas of concern to society at large." As with *New York Times v. Sullivan,* the Court directed a verdict in favor of the defendant—the press.[35]

Kalven's seminal article on *New York Times v. Sullivan* had ended by predicting that "the invitation to follow a dialectic progression from public official to government policy to public policy to matters in the public domain, like art, seems to me to be overwhelming." The Court caught the mood, too. George Rosenbloom was arrested, tried, and acquitted on obscenity charges. He then successfully sued WIP-AM for libel, winning a judgment of $25,000 compensatory and $750,000 punitive, the latter being judicially reduced by two-thirds. WIP, relying on a phone call from the captain of the Philadelphia Police Special Investigations Squad announcing Rosenbloom's arrest, had characterized him as a "smut distributor" and "girlie book peddler." The Supreme Court, in contrast, characterized Rosenbloom as "a distributor of nudist magazines in the Philadelphia metropolitan area," thereby adding no additional insult to its conclusion that the distinction between public and private was too artificial: "If a matter is a subject of public or general interest, it cannot suddenly become less so merely because a private individual is involved, or because in some sense the individual did not 'voluntarily' choose to become involved. The public's primary interest is in the event; the public focus is on the conduct of the participant and the content, effect, and significance of the conduct, not the participant's prior anonymity or notoriety."[36]

In just seven years the Court had entered and constitutionalized a new area and concluded that robust debate on public issues was of such transcendent importance that libel judgments could not be allowed unless the plaintiff could show that the defendant made the decision to publish in reckless disregard of falsity. Furthermore, in other cases the Court held that neither "ill will" nor publishing without investigation, despite an obvious risk of serious harm to reputation, could constitute actual malice or reckless disregard; the plaintiff had to show that the defendant either knew that what it was printing was false or "in fact entertained serious doubts as to the truth." The Court also continued its jury supervision; it held in one case that in context the word "blackmail" was not defamatory because the plaintiff—and the jury—should have understood it was "no more than rhetorical hyperbole, a vigorous epithet." Finally, in one of the more striking extensions of the new doctrine, one that arguably presaged *Rosenbloom,* the Court held that a "false light" privacy claim (one that alleges publicity that places the plaintiff in a false, although not necessarily defamatory, light) also had to be tested by the standards set forth in *New York Times v. Sullivan.* By 1971, the Court's rules could be seen as culminating in the conclusion that if a newspaper published the information, it was necessarily a matter of public importance and therefore constitutionally protected.[37]

## IV

The attitudinal change occurring in the shift from "self-preservation" to creating a climate for robust debate was instantly obvious in the litigation, still occurring a decade after McCarthy's fall, to sanitize public life from supposed Communist influences. In the three years after *New York Times,* the Court demolished the basic strands of the needless loyalty-security program. Some cases were easy. Thus a requirement that those wishing to receive literature from countries such as China or North Korea had to sign in at the

Post Office went down quickly with the recognition that being forced to ask to receive materials designated as "Communist political propaganda" was bound to deter. *New York Times* had invalidated a long-dead federal statute. *Lamont* killed a live one; this was the first time an existing federal statute had ever been declared unconstitutional for violating the First Amendment's expression clauses.[38]

New Hampshire had its attorney general operating as a one-man un-American activities committee. A prosecution for refusal to answer the bingo question—"Are you now or have you ever been a member. . . ?"—resulted in a Supreme Court opinion suggesting the question could be split into two, with a negative to the first part possibly precluding the need to answer the second. The Court also noted the staleness of the desired information, something that would also have been true in the 1950s about activities during the 1930s. Each of these points cut inroads in the ways witch-hunters had behaved during the 1950s. In other cases, the Court also applied its criminal-law requirement of intent—that membership in the Communist party could only be punished if there was specific intent to further the party's illegal purposes—to loyalty oaths, thereby invalidating all but the most innocuous. Finally, by a similar technique the Court invalidated a federal law prohibiting Communist party members from working in a defense facility.[39]

There was an air of tidying up about such finishing off of the ought-to-be-dead relics of McCarthyism. Tidying up was not, however, limited to McCarthyism. The Court was making similar moves with obscenity, World War I–like wartime opposition, and the legacy of Holmes and Brandeis.

It is much easier to describe what the Court was doing with obscenity than to state either the law or what the Court thought obscenity was. Indeed, it may only have been Justice Stewart's excess candor in stating that he could not define obscenity "but I know it when I see it" that set him apart from his brethren. He had not seen it for years (despite an influx of exhibits to the Court), and neither, it appeared, had the other justices. Although 1966 produced two affirmed convictions, genuine rarities, the trend of obscenity law was unmistakably toward restricting prosecutions. The justices learned that they could not define obscenity in any intelligible terms. Indeed, the *Redrup* case—where the opinion simply stated the individual view of each of the seven justices in the majority and then announced that, whichever view was applied, the materials were not obscene—made a virtue out of incapacity. The Court created a new verb, to Redrup: defined as reversing an obscenity conviction without providing any reasons.[40]

Redrupping was later supplemented by the holding of *Stanley v. Georgia*—that the Constitution forbids criminalizing the possession of obscene material (however defined) in the home—to create a rule regarding obscenity: consenting adults could have whatever they wanted; nonconsenting adults and children could be protected; and knowing what obscenity is could be avoided. This combination was put on hold and questioned in 1971, when the Court refused to declare the federal obscenity laws unconstitutional and authorized a ban on commercial importation of admitted hard-core pornography, but it would be two more years before it became clear that the *Redrup-Stanley* pincers was not the Court's chosen solution for what Justice Harlan called the "intractable" problem of obscenity.[41]

It was with regard to the legacy of World War I and Holmes and Brandeis that the Court's new moves most clearly underscored that something dramatically different was occurring. In 1965 Julian Bond, the young black communications director of the Student Nonviolent Coordinating Committee, was elected to the Georgia legislature, which then refused to seat him because he had made remarks opposing the Vietnam War and supporting draft resisters. Like *New York Times v. Sullivan* in the Alabama courts, it was a decision that *had* to be reversed, even though what Bond had said was at least as culpable as anything Eugene Debs said in his Canton speech during World War I. The Court unanimously held that *New York Times* gave legislators, no less than citizens, the right to speak out on controversial issues, including the gut issues of war and peace. In so holding, the Court was not only recognizing the necessary sweep of its recent decisions but also interring the repressive sweep of its World War I decisions.[42]

*Bond*, of course, could be explained as another civil rights case. But *Brandenburg v. Ohio* could not, since Clarence Brandenburg was a Ku Klux Klan leader convicted under a "criminal syndicalism" statute for a rally at a farm in Hamilton County, Ohio. The significance of the case lies not so much in the reversal of Branden-

burg's conviction as in what the Court did. First, it squarely over-
ruled *Whitney v. California,* which had occasioned the famous
Brandeis dissent on the purposes of free speech. Second, purporting
to operate within the idea of "clear and present danger" as handed
down by Holmes and Brandeis and applied previously by the
Court, the opinion announced the most speech-protective test that
the Court had ever agreed to: a state may not "forbid or proscribe
advocacy of the use of force or of law violation except where such
advocacy [1] is directed to inciting or producing [2] imminent
lawless action and [3] is likely to incite or produce such action."
Had the *Brandenburg* test been applied to the Communist cases of
the 1950s—which the Court blithely cited—not a single conviction
could have occurred. Because the area of law involved in *Brandenburg*—advocacy of illegal action—was one that every constitutional law professor taught, everyone could immediately see the
fundamental changes the Court announced. *Bond* was neither a
fluke, nor a civil rights case, nor even a stopping point.[43]

Finally there was Paul Cohen, who walked into a Los Angeles
courthouse wearing a jacket with "Fuck the Draft" inscribed on the
back. The prevailing wisdom was that the F-word was absolutely
beyond the pale, a view powerfully supported by Justice Black—
who, trapped by his well-known position that all speech and writing was absolutely protected, was forced to declare that the writing
on Cohen's jacket as not speech at all, but conduct instead. Cohen
did not just use the F-word; he used it to show both the intensity of
his feelings and his contempt for the values of the generation that
had brought the Vietnam War to America, all with a wonderful
economy—try to find a better antiwar slogan that fits on the back
of a jacket. To the Court's credit, five justices understood. Justice
Harlan wrote one of his great opinions protecting Cohen and his
right to phrase his message in his own terms:

To many, the immediate consequence of this freedom may often appear to
be only verbal tumult, discord, and even offensive utterance. These are,
however, within established limits, in truth necessary side effects of the
broader enduring values which the process of open debate permits us to
achieve. That the air may at times seem filled with verbal cacophony is, in
this sense, not a sign of weakness but of strength. We cannot lose sight of
the fact that, in what otherwise might seem a trifling and annoying
instance of individual distasteful abuse of a privilege, these fundamental
societal values are truly implicated.[44]

A year before *New York Times,* Bob Dylan wrote "The Times They Are a-Changin'"; it was impossible not to see the change following *New York Times.* There was some backing away in obscenity law in 1971—a year after *I Am Curious (Yellow)* became the first mass-audience X-style movie—and the Court balked at sanctioning draft-card burning as an acceptable antiwar protest; but the Court's decisions generally pushed for a newer, farther boundary. It is no wonder that Kalven, whom the Court was citing for the meaning of what it was doing, emerged at the forefront of First Amendment scholarship; it was his dialectic dominating First Amendment law.[45]

V

Then came the most massive security leak in American history, precipitating what former Secretary of Defense Clark Clifford called "an event of outstanding significance." Since coming to Washington in 1945, he "had never seen anything like it." James Reston, chief of the *Times*'s Washington bureau, informed his New York editors that it was "the biggest story of the century." Although that appellation was much like each decade's "wine of the century," as an accidental prediction of the two weeks of litigation it is hard to beat.[46]

In the spring of 1967 a disillusioned Robert McNamara, without White House approval, commissioned a study of how the United States had come to where it was in Vietnam. A Vietnam History Task Force produced seven thousand pages, forty-seven volumes of documents detailing the origins and development of America's involvement in the Vietnam War. Fifteen sets of the documents, which came to be known as the Pentagon Papers, were produced. One set was kept in a locked safe in the secretary of defense's office; another was at the Rand Corporation in Santa Monica. There Daniel Ellsberg, a former hawk who had become a guilt-ridden dove, copied the documents and then spent a frustrating year trying unsuccessfully to persuade some leading politician to go public with them. He believed that the information they contained was so explosive that it would bring a dramatic shift in public opinion on the war. So did Richard Nixon's national security advisor, Henry Kissinger.[47]

Failing with politicians, Ellsberg finally turned to a *New York*

*Times* reporter, Neil Sheehan, and ultimately gave him all but the four very sensitive diplomatic volumes. Once Sheehan and the *Times* editors were satisfied with the content and authenticity of the documents, the operative assumption was, in Harrison Salisbury's words, that *"The Times* had to publish the story." The *Times*'s Lord, Day, and Lord lawyers were not so sure. Louis Loeb, who, Salisbury notes, "had taken to wearing a small, enameled American flag in his lapel" to signify his patriotism and support for Nixon's war policy, was adamant that the *Times*'s duty was to go to the government. Loeb's counsel underscored the complexity of the decision to publish. But the decision was made; and late Saturday afternoon, June 12, 1971, the presses started to run with the historic Sunday edition.[48]

The front page began with a large picture of Tricia Nixon being escorted by her father to her wedding in the Rose Garden. Next a large headline, "Vietnam Archive: Pentagon Study Traces 3 Decades of Growing U.S. Involvement," introduced Sheehan's story. Below it was another story, by Hedrick Smith, "Vast Review of War Took a Year." The only use of the word *secret* on the front page was in Smith's story, where he reported that while the *Times* had most of the Pentagon Papers, it lacked "the section on the secret diplomacy of the Johnson period."[49]

Thrilled by their scoop, the *Times* editors and reporters waited for the reaction. Initially there wasn't one. By chance, the future principals Robert Mardian, head of the Justice Department's internal security division, and Kissinger were both in California until Monday. Furthermore, as a history of U.S. involvement in Vietnam, the Pentagon Papers undermined the public positions of the Kennedy and Johnson administrations; the initial response at the White House was that the story was a Democratic party problem. More surprising, there was no response from the press or those opposed to the war either. Sheehan did not get a single call on Sunday. Neither did managing editor Abe Rosenthal or Washington bureau chief Max Frankel. Salisbury reports having lunch with a group of avid *Times* readers, cocktails with a second group, and dinner with another; and yet "not one mention of the Pentagon Papers. My God, I said to myself, the story is a bust!"[50]

The second installment appeared on Monday morning; and that day the decision was made to go "full court" against the *Times* in order to demonstrate the government's resolve to protect its secrets. The reasons for this decision are still not wholly clear, but they presumably include Kissinger's desire to be tough on Ellsberg (with whom he had had prior dealings) and the upcoming, highly secret, trip to China. Monday evening, Nixon called Attorney General Mitchell at the latter's Watergate apartment, where Mitchell and Mardian had been preparing a telegram to the *Times* requesting no further publication and a return of the documents. Nixon gave his okay, and the telegram was sent to the FBI for transmittal to the *Times*. The FBI sent it to a fish company in Brooklyn instead. Improving with experience, they got it to the *Times* on the next try.[51]

At the *Times,* Loeb again urged against further publication; most others, especially in-house counsel James Goodale, urged the opposite: if the *Times* gave in, it would never be the same. Hearing the arguments over the phone in London, the publisher, Punch Sulzberger, gave the go-ahead. Goodale knew that meant heading to court, and he asked Loeb to get ready to defend. Loeb turned him over to Eisenhower's former attorney general, Herbert Brownell, who expressed shock that the *Times* was defying Mitchell and stated that the firm would not undertake the defense. Meanwhile the text of the *Times*'s response was being hammered out and was phoned to James Reston for his input. Reston was at the time dining with McNamara. On hearing the phrase that the *Times* would abide by "decisions of the courts," McNamara interjected, "not the courts—the *highest* court." That was too strong for the *Times,* which split the difference: "We will abide by the decision of the court." These decisions made, Goodale set out to round up Professor Alexander Bickel of the Yale Law School for the defense (Wechsler being unavailable), and the lead story for Tuesday's paper was hastily changed from Sheehan's continuation to an announcement of the confrontation between the *Times* and the Nixon administration: "Mitchell Seeks to Halt Series on Vietnam but *Times* Refuses."[52]

Major litigation typically takes years. The *Pentagon Papers Case* took fifteen days, beginning with a hearing Tuesday before Judge Murray Gurfein, sitting for his first working day since Richard Nixon appointed him to the federal bench. The government argued that further publication must be prevented because of serious injury to foreign relations and the national defense. But no American court had ever enjoined publication of a newspaper, and Bickel asked if Judge Gurfein wished to be the first judge to do so— especially when the government's affidavits were merely conclusory and had not carried the high burden of proof that was necessary to justify a prior restraint. Gurfein, who kept saying "we are all patriotic Americans," requested that the *Times* voluntarily cease publication while the case proceeded. When the *Times* refused to cooperate, a visibly angry Gurfein issued a temporary restraining order and set Friday as the day for hearing the case.[53]

The *Washington Post*—"still feeling," in Sanford Ungar's apt words, "egg on its well-respected, well-connected face"—used Gurfein's temporary injunction to play catch-up. Ellsberg, dismayed that the *Times* was obeying Gurfein's injunction, provided the *Post* with over four thousand pages of the documents. After its own internal debate, made more serious by a pending public stock offering and the ownership of radio and television stations (complications not facing the *Times*), the *Post* nevertheless went forward over its lawyers' objections.[54]

The *Post*'s Friday publication came as a complete surprise to the government lawyers and made the case against the *Times* harder. How could Gurfein enjoin the *Times* for national security reasons if the *Post* were free to publish the same materials? Furthermore, as Bickel noted, the government had claimed that any additional publication would pose a grave danger to national security, and yet "the republic stands. And it stood for the first three days." The government promised to take action against the *Post* "if it appears necessary" (and it immediately would). But the government's problem, both before Gurfein and before Judge Gerhard Gesell in the about-to-be-created *Washington Post* case, was pointing to information in the Pentagon Papers that could lead a judge to believe that publication would create a grave danger to national security. Because no one in any important government position had read the documents, hard information was lacking. To an executive branch used to bowing to absolute White House authority, saying so was enough; to an independent judiciary it might not be.[55]

But maybe no one would know that the government had such a problem. The hearings were conducted in camera (that is, in secret); all anyone on the outside could know was that the government appeared very serious about matters that, it asserted, significantly affected foreign affairs and the national defense. Yet the best the government did behind the closed judicial doors came in a supplement to an affidavit of Admiral Noel Gayler, director of the National Security Agency (NSA). He testified that a certain document revealed that the NSA had the ability to intercept North Vietnamese communications and break their code. This was serious stuff. But George Wilson, the *Post*'s defense correspondent and the principal technical advisor to the lawyers, recognized the cable and knew that he had seen it before. "Suddenly it became clear to me. I had seen it on page thirty-four of the 1968 Senate Foreign Relations Committee hearings on the Tonkin Gulf. It was on the left side of the page." Furthermore, Wilson had a copy of those hearings in his pocket, which the *Post* attorneys read to the stunned judges and government attorneys. The government's *Washington Post* case had collapsed.[56]

Ultimately, both Gurfein and Gesell ruled for the newspapers. The government appealed each ruling. On Wednesday, June 23, the respective courts of appeal ruled against the *Times* and for the *Post* (with the injunction against publication continued until Friday evening to allow the government a chance to appeal). If there had been doubt before, the conflicting rulings meant that the Supreme Court would necessarily cast the deciding vote.[57]

The stakes were high. Never before had publication of a newspaper been enjoined. Yet the political incentives all pointed to Nixon at least acquiescing in publication of the Democrats' embarrassing folly. The government's adamant opposition to publication suggested that publication of the Pentagon Papers could indeed hurt the nation, not just the government—a point echoed by Malcolm Wilkey's dissent in the *Post* case: publication "could result in great harm to the nation . . . the death of soldiers, the destruction of alliances, the greatly increased difficulty of negotiation with our enemies, the inability of our diplomats to negotiate." Instead of shortening the war, as Ellsberg hoped, publication could prolong it.[58]

The Supreme Court's year (October Term 1970) was essentially over. Justice William O. Douglas had been at his summer home in the Cascades for over a week. All that remained for the other eight justices was a final conference on Friday, June 25, to mop up the term and a perfunctory sitting on Monday to announce its end. But everyone at the Court knew that the *Pentagon Papers Cases* were on history's fastest judicial track and that the split in the courts below made some Supreme Court action inevitable. The system could not leave the *Times* enjoined and the *Post* free to publish.[59]

Continuing the breakneck pace of the cases, both sides rushed to get to the Court before it adjourned for the summer, and the necessary papers arrived late Thursday. At the Friday morning conference the justices voted five to four to hear the cases. An unprecedented Saturday morning sitting was scheduled with double the usual time for oral argument; briefs would be exchanged before argument. Douglas flew East to attend, having phoned in his vote to deny review in the *Post* case and lift the stay in the *Times* case—thereby joining Black, Brennan, and Marshall.

Both sides wrote two briefs, one open and one secret. Solicitor General Erwin Griswold had stayed up all night, first forcing Admiral Gayler to pare down what he considered the most sensitive materials to as few as possible and then writing the secret brief, which discussed the eleven remaining items. Unbeknownst to the newspapers or their counsel, Griswold also filed a secret motion to hold the oral argument in camera. The Clerk of the Supreme Court informed Bickel of the motion just before oral argument so that Bickel could be prepared if and when it came up. That proved unnecessary; Chief Justice Burger announced to a packed courtroom (1500 hopefuls had begun to queue up shortly after daybreak for the 174 seats) that the government's motion for argument in camera had been denied by a six-to-three vote, with Burger, Harlan, and Blackmun dissenting. That would prove to be the identical division on the merits when the vote was taken in Conference later in the afternoon.[60]

Because the vote on the merits held the injunction to be a violation of the First Amendment, logic dictated lifting the injunction as quickly as possible; time and effort were not spent on producing a majority opinion. Instead, each justice repaired to his chambers to produce an opinion. As always, it was no contest as to who finished first. Douglas was done by Sunday night and flew West on Monday, while the other eight continued writing.[61]

At 2:30 P.M. on Wednesday, June 30, the Court convened and announced the result in a laconic per curiam opinion drafted by

Brennan: any prior restraint comes to court with a heavy burden of proof, and the government did not carry that burden. Then followed an opinion by each of the nine justices. Most interesting were those of the dissenters, who showed their anger at the haste with which the case was decided, their willingness to accept (at least temporarily) the government's claims at face value, and their fear of the consequences of publication. Burger noted that the *Times* spent several months delaying the public's "right to know" while it studied the "purloined" documents, yet it now demanded an instantaneous decision. The Court's precipitous actions agreeing with the *Times* had created a "parody of the judicial function." Harlan, easily the most careful of the justices, quoted Holmes for his dubious proposition that great cases make bad law and complained that the Court "has been almost irresponsibly feverish in dealing with these cases." Blackmun's dissent concluded that publication would probably prolong the war and cause "further delay in the freeing of United States prisoners." Should these likely consequences occur, "then the Nation's people will know where the responsibility for these sad consequences rests."[62]

Both the *Post* and the *Times* were elated at the victory. The *Post*'s managing editor, Eugene Patterson, jumped on a desk and stated: "We win, and so does the *New York Times*." The *Times*'s managing editor, Abe Rosenthal, listening in the crowded third-floor newsroom to an open phone from Washington, shouted: "It's a glorious day. We won it. We've all won it. We've won the right to print." But Sheehan's stories ended as they began, almost unnoticed. China, "lost" for twenty-two years, had been "found" in a condition apparently safe for an American president. When the administration announced on July 15 that Kissinger had returned from a secret trip to China and that Nixon would go there for a summit, everything else was history.[63]

China did not, however, end Nixon's interest in the Pentagon Papers. He perceived that he had lost a battle—the press had "won the constitutional right to profit [by] the publication of stolen documents under the First Amendment. This right is superior to the right of our soldiers to live"—but he could win the war. Ellsberg would pay. And with that conclusion Nixon initiated the chain of events we know as Watergate, the real "story of the century" and one that belonged to the *Post*, not the *Times*.[64]

## VI

The seven years encompassing the two *New York Times* decisions were remarkable. Neither before nor since has there been such an outpouring of law on freedom of speech and the press. And never has it been so protective of the interests of dissent and so skeptical of government claims of the social harm that supposedly would be forthcoming if the expression were allowed.

The lead cases came in an ironical order. *New York Times v. Sullivan* protected falsity to protect truth. The *Pentagon Papers Cases* then protected truth to expose official lies.

In *New York Times v. Sullivan* Brennan reasoned that unless some falsity were allowed, those wishing to discuss an issue would be impelled to guard their statements too carefully for fear of the consequences of accidental error. Brennan's emphasis on reality and his understanding that would-be speakers do not find the legal consequences of speaking irrelevant forced the Court to pay more attention to the actual way the legal system collides with freedom of expression. Truth could have been guaranteed at the cost of a drastically limited range of discussion, a range assisting the status quo, whatever it is—from segregation to continued war. As Justice Stewart recognized, "an informed and critical public opinion alone can . . . protect the values of democratic government. . . . For without an informed and free press there cannot be an enlightened people."[65]

Another lesson from *New York Times v. Sullivan* was that the exercise of First Amendment rights necessarily carries with it some harm to society—generally to specific people. Although often overlooked, the point is a fortiori; if there were no perceived harm, there would be no need to attempt to limit both the topics and the form of discussion. Nevertheless, once it is understood that exercising rights of expression hurts, the claim that any specific type of expression causes harm should be seen as a given, rather than as a reason to curtail the exercise of First Amendment rights. In no other period has the Court been so willing to allow harms to occur because it felt that protecting society from those harms would unduly curtail important discussion.

Fifty years earlier, Joseph Gilbert was jailed for questioning the causes of World War I; in the *Pentagon Papers Cases,* the two newspapers not only questioned the origins of the Vietnam War, they did so using the government's own secret documents. The juxtaposition of the cases is more stark when it is realized that unlike *Gilbert,* where no genuine harm could have come from the statements about the origins of the war, in the *Pentagon Papers Cases* the justices recognized that publication of the papers might prolong the war and therefore additional American youths might be killed; yet with the new understanding of the meaning of a free press, that was a risk to be run.

Citizens cannot control or change government policies without information about the policies. In World War I, Gilbert was branded a liar; in Vietnam, it was Presidents Kennedy and Johnson (and later Nixon) who were branded liars. The Court's changed perception was that the official version of events could not be imposed. It is not officials, be they elected or appointed (even for life), but citizens who make the choices. The press necessarily plays an essential role in a democracy: "The press was to serve the governed, not the governors. [It] was protected so that it could bare the secrets of government and inform the people. Only a free and unrestrained press can effectively expose deception in government."[66]

Those words, from the last opinion of Justice Black's distinguished career, did more than summarize his views. They spoke for what the Court had been doing: protecting those who challenged entrenched authority, removing the government as an intermediary in establishing the acceptable level and style of criticism, and allowing citizen-critics the opportunity to challenge at will the established truth. Freedom of expression from *Times* to *Times* recognized fully the conclusions of Chief Justice Charles Evans Hughes on security in a democracy: it is necessary "to maintain the opportunity for free political discussion, to the end that government may be responsive to the will of the people and that changes, if desired, may be obtained by peaceful means. Therein lies the security of the Republic, the very foundation of constitutional government."[67]

*Part Two*

■   ■   ■

# Issues

# Overview

At times everything seems to grate on the press: injunctions against publication, severe questioning about how a defamatory story was put together, big libel verdicts, questioning about confidential sources, and involuntary court appearances generally. Yet those watching the watchdog have not been applauding the legal system either; they have noted its inability to allow defamed plaintiffs to recover and the lack of effort to bring competition to monopoly newspapers and media conglomerates. The four chapters in Part Two discuss the most contentious contemporary legal issues involving the press: libel, injunctions, access, and antitrust. I should note that there are some omissions. The issues of Chapter 6, "Access to Information and Places," have proven easier to solve by statute—shield laws, sunshine laws, freedom of information acts—than by constitutional adjudication. But my focus here, as elsewhere, is on the Constitution. Additionally, it may come as a surprise that privacy is omitted; but the legal (as opposed to ethical) issues involved in discussing the private lives of elected officials are nonexistent. Just as I am omitting pornography, so too I leave the private lives of entertainers to the grocery store lines and to others.

*Chapter Four*

# Libel

As measured by ink spent, no legal issue so infuriates the press as does libel. Whether it is whopping jury verdicts (routinely set aside by the trial judge or appellate court) or the litigation's focus on the decisions of reporter and editor, the promise of *New York Times v. Sullivan*—wide-open discussion of public affairs without the fear of huge liability for error—has faded through the years. Yet those injured by press errors fare no better, as virtually all libel plaintiffs take home nothing except their loss in court.[1]

Much of the current state of libel law is associated with the untimely and unfortunate transformation of the Warren Court into the Burger Court. The new chief justice, whose hostility to the press was acidly expressed in his *Pentagon Papers* dissent and reaffirmed periodically on public occasions, presided over a decade and a half of libel litigation that, unlike in the Warren Court, the press often lost. Nevertheless, it is wrong to blame either Burger or his court for the current state of libel law. As both logic and experience showed, the system had gone awry, so that the framework of *New York Times v. Sullivan,* rather than offering a solution, became the problem. The *New York Times* decision correctly defined the problem as setting reputational interests against the chilling effect; and it balanced the two, with enough weight accorded to reputation to preclude the elimination of all remedies for damage—if the press "in fact entertained serious doubts as to the truth of its publication," *New York Times* holds that the First Amendment is no bar to an award of money damages. Nevertheless, in its early days the "actual malice" standard seemed high enough to preclude all but a minuscule number of judgments.

Such was the state of the law in 1974, when the academic community suffered a great loss with Harry Kalven's untimely death. That same year his dialectic progression was cut down by the pen of Justice Powell in *Gertz v. Robert Welch, Inc.* But because the dialectic introduced the possibility of an unchecked press debasing the political dialogue by falsehoods and chilling the entry of superior talent into politics, as well as creating a more robust public debate, whether its death was untimely was debatable and debated.[2]

*Gertz* seemed to set libel law on a new path. Abandoning *Rosenbloom,* the Court concluded that private figures entwined in public events should not be required to prove actual malice, as are public figures (such as General Walker). Private individuals, the Court believed, are more entitled to protection than those in the public spotlight because the latter—the Court wrongly concluded—have more access to the media for the necessary corrections. The Court nevertheless moved beyond the existing common law in two ways. First, it rejected liability without fault. If the defendant had made an innocent error, it should not be forced to pay; some level of fault—negligence—was made a precondition to recovery. Second, damages could not be presumed. The state had no interest in imposing damages for injuries not suffered, at least when the defendant acted without actual malice; therefore, the plaintiff in such cases could receive compensation only for actual damages. Justice Powell defined actual damages to encompass not only harm to reputation, but also personal humiliation and mental suffering. However, the Court held that if a private plaintiff could prove actual malice, in the *New York Times* sense, then the jury could award punitive damages.

*Gertz* distinguished between public and private figures, with the latter having an easier path to vindication than public figures. The distinction was unsettling for the press. The path for private figures was not only easier in theory; it proved easier in fact, as the press suffered a string of defeats at the Supreme Court. The defeats then seemed to be magnified by the filing of three highly publicized multimillion-dollar cases by public figures: Israel's defense minister, Ariel Sharon; the former commander of American forces in Vietnam, William Westmoreland; and the chief executive officer of Mobil Oil, William Tavoulareas. There need not have been a connection between the loss of the private-figure cases and the potential liability in the public-figure cases, but the press saw one, and this created a feeling of despair in the media.[3]

But the assumptions of judicial hostility were wrong. In *Bose Corporation v. Consumers Union* the Court reaffirmed the duty of appellate courts to scrutinize carefully all jury determinations, even in a case wholly divorced from the world of robust political exchange that is at the heart of the Kalven-Meiklejohn tradition. In *Philadelphia Newspapers v. Hepps* the Court concluded that the plaintiff in public-figure cases had the burden of proving falsity: if there is doubt about the truth of a statement, that doubt cuts in favor of the press. And finally, the Court unanimously ruled against the Reverend Jerry Falwell in his suit against *Hustler* magazine claiming that a tasteless parody of himself (and a Campari "First Time" ad) had caused him emotional distress. The dramatic unanimity in *Falwell* and the fact that Chief Justice Rehnquist chose to write a strong opinion on behalf of *Hustler*'s rights, guaranteeing that satire would receive full constitutional protection, signaled the close of the period of concern about whether the Court might seriously turn the clock back on libel laws.[4]

In the meantime, lower courts took on their constitutional responsibilities to merge First Amendment considerations into this body of press law that had, prior to *New York Times,* been so long immune from constitutional scrutiny. At common law the press had always been privileged for accurate reporting of what occurred in judicial proceedings, even if the repetition of a defamatory (and false) statement caused harm to the plaintiff. The United States Court of Appeals for the Second Circuit extended this privilege to "neutral reporting" of other charges without regard to whether they were made in official proceedings. As the court explained, "when a responsible, prominent organization makes serious charges against a public figure, the First Amendment protects the accurate and disinterested reporting of the charges, regardless of the reporter's private views regarding their validity. What is newsworthy about such accusations is that they were made." Finally, taking up from the Court's statement in *Gertz* that "there is no such thing as a false idea," courts more rigidly distinguished statements of opinion from erroneous statements of fact. To be sure, there is a fuzzy line between fact and opinion, as Gallatin realized so clearly in the Sedition Act debates. This, however, merely underscores the necessity of giving a broad constitutional scope to statements that are, in the words of Robert Bork in one of his finest opinions for the DC Circuit Court of Appeals, "rhetorical hyperbole." Libel law should deal with mistaken facts, not mistaken views. Subsequently the Supreme Court concluded that it would not constitutionalize an exception for expressions of opinion, but that statements that "cannot reasonably be interpreted as stating actual facts" are fully protected. The Court specifically noted that "imaginative expression" and "rhetorical hyperbole" had added much to the discourse of the nation and would be wholly protected.[5]

This brief summary could not fully cover all the interstices of the current law, which has been aptly described as "a mysterious labyrinth for those seeking to clear their names and a costly and unpredictable burden for the speakers the First Amendment is designed to protect." Rather than flesh out the full law of libel, it is more useful to turn, first, to how a libel suit looks from beginning to end; second, to what problems are illustrated thereby; and third, to the solutions that may be available. During the mid-1980s, when everything seemed up for grabs, the spectrum of suggestions ranged from gutting *New York Times* to the exact opposite, following the suggestion of Justices Black and Douglas that all public-figure libel suits violate the First Amendment, with numerous more nuanced suggestions in between. My goal is to demonstrate, first, that the balances created by *New York Times* have taken unintended turns; and second, by reviewing the best proposals for change, to explore ways, consistent with the *New York Times* balance, to better protect innocent citizens, the press, and the integrity of "uninhibited, robust, and wide-open" public debate.[6]

## I

The CBS documentary on General Westmoreland's undercounting of enemy troops and the *Washington Post*'s stories about Mobil's Tavoulareas setting his son up in business were so well publicized that they immediately spring to mind; but tough investigative stories are not typically the ones that produce libel litigation. They are done with too much care. Instead, "it's the routine stories that rise up and bite you in the ass." Libel litigation is marginally more likely to result from inside-page stories than from those on the front page.[7]

As citizens, we read more about libel than almost any other type of noncriminal litigation, and the easy conclusion is that because we read about it there must be a lot of it happening. There is also a staggering number of articles in legal journals dealing with libel; some three articles are written for every five published judicial opinions, an astonishing ratio. Yet for all the written words, libel is all but an insignificant blip in the statistics of American courts. We just read more about it because it affects the press, and the press assumes, with becoming myopia, that anything that affects it is important to us, too. Given this assumption, it is useful to know how libel litigation really looks.[8]

We know much more about libel litigation than we did, because of an exceptionally impressive study by the Iowa Libel Research Project, headed by two journalism professors (Gilbert Cranberg, formerly the highly respected editorial page editor for the *Des Moines Register,* and John Soloski) and a law professor (Randall Bezanson, now dean at Washington and Lee University) who studied all defamation cases filed in the decade after *Gertz* and went beyond the judicial opinions by interviewing parties and attorneys in over 150 cases. The study confirms while enriching Stanford law professor Marc Franklin's pioneering data from the 1970s; it represents a wealth of data, some quite surprising, and is essential to any discussion of the area.[9]

Libel is a high-status tort. Those who sue tend to be male, well educated, professional, financially well-off, middle-aged, married, and long-term residents in the community. The majority of those characteristics could be deduced from asking who is likely to be named in newspaper articles. The Iowa study found that 40 percent of the plaintiffs had been candidates for office or had held office by the time they filed their suit. More than three-quarters reported that they had at least above-average visibility in their communities. These statistics make sense. The press is more likely to report the doings of newsworthy individuals; and libel litigation, to the extent it is unaffected by legal rules such as those of *Gertz,* should reflect the type of reporting that occurs. Indeed, the statistics confirm what the big publicized cases were saying. Despite *Gertz*'s allowance of easier recovery for private figures, public-figure libel is where the action is.[10]

There is "a strong correlation between a plaintiff's community visibility and the content of the alleged libelous story. The higher an individual's visibility, the greater the likelihood that the alleged libel will deal with his or her public or political activities. The lower an individual's visibility, the greater the likelihood that the alleged story will deal with his or her business or professional activities." Some 90 percent of all public-figure libel litigation concerns allegations dealing with the professional side of the plaintiffs' lives, whereas half the private-figure libel cases deal with allegations about immoral or criminal conduct in the plaintiffs' nonprofessional lives.[11]

Finally, although a few litigious rogues are sensitive to supposed libels because they are overly sensitive to everything, the average libel plaintiff is not. Two-thirds of libel plaintiffs had never filed any kind of suit before; and nearly three-fourths, at least at the time the Iowa researchers contacted them, had subsequently filed no other suit. But the litigious plaintiff does exist. Some 11 percent of libel plaintiffs were multiple libel plaintiffs.[12]

In what may be the most surprising of the findings, the Iowa researchers assert that most libel suits are preventable even after publication of the offending story. The victim of an alleged libel will typically make contact with the newspaper to explain the falsity of the story before contacting a lawyer. It turns out that whereas the future plaintiffs were merely agitated when they called the press, they were outright angry after they called—and at that point they sought a lawyer to initiate litigation. All the arrogance that critics ascribe to the media seems to come out when the future plaintiff calls to discuss the story. Tavoulareas, for example, was outraged that the *Post* refused to give an inch even after its inaccuracies were pointed out.[13]

Some of the problem is institutional. Newspapers are geared to put out today's news, not to deal with problems created by their discussion of yesterday's news. Furthermore, too many papers have no systematic way of dealing with complaints. Sometimes the relevant editor only finds out after suit is filed because the future plaintiff contacted the reporter, who did not pass it on. Sometimes calls are bounced from person to person; but future plaintiffs get more than an institutional runaround. Newspapers are "organizations conditioned to resist pressure." When the future plaintiff calls, the siege mentality is already in place. The ombudsman of the *Kansas City Star and Times* notes that when a public figure complains, the typical response is to treat the complaint as self-serving and without justification. No one likes to admit error; newspersons, rather than being the exceptions that prove the rule, simply take the rule to a higher order of magnitude. An editor of the *Chicago Tribune* notes that the "rudeness in this business is legendary." The complainant who was told "Fuck you, you're full of shit" can certainly agree.[14]

Rudeness and arrogance send into court cases that could be settled out of court; the individual's contact with the media too often triggers a decision to sue. The lawyer is contacted for representation, not advice—which is perhaps fortunate, because the lawyer will typically lack experience in the libel area and is likely to overstate the chances of success for the plaintiff. As the advertisements on television inform those who may have suffered a personal injury, anyone wishing to be a personal injury plaintiff will usually not be charged a cent unless the attorney wins an award of damages for the plaintiff. For tort litigation, including libel suits, such contingent fee arrangements are typical. No hourly fee is charged, but the attorney takes from 33 to 50 percent of any damages awarded. Despite the notoriously low success rate of plaintiffs in libel actions, most fee agreements are contingent rather than hourly. There is one further anomaly in the Iowa findings. Plaintiffs who were public figures were *more* likely than private figures to have a contingent fee arrangement, even though the rules make it harder for public-figure plaintiffs to succeed. Even if misjudgments about the chances of success are factored in, attorneys ought to realize that the legal rules make it more difficult for public figures to prevail, and therefore the economically sound position for the attorney is an hourly fee arrangement. That attorneys would be willing to subsidize this type of litigation seems explicable only if they anticipate nonfinancial and status rewards from representing public figures.[15]

Private plaintiffs, especially those suing for money damages, are more prone to listen to a lawyer's advice on bringing suit, whereas public plaintiffs often have already made up their minds to sue. In what appears peculiar to libel, plaintiffs frequently change lawyers, most likely for two reasons: First, in libel suits the plaintiff may intend to take both the lawyer and the defendant for a ride; when the lawyer seems a reluctant passenger, she is asked to disembark. Second, lawyers push lawsuits at different speeds; money judgments, especially with contingent fee arrangements, get priority. For the plaintiff who wants an untarnished reputation as much as or more than monetary recovery, the lawyer may not be pushing hard enough.[16]

The media defendant, however, will pay an hourly rate, because defense attorneys do not work on contingent fees. The longer the litigation drags on, the more the newspaper will pay its lawyers. Nevertheless, for many of the same reasons that newspapers find it difficult to admit error, they also find it difficult to settle libel cases out of court; and, without such settlement, attorneys' fees keep mounting. (Additionally, the paper may fear that by settling it will be seen as an easy target for future libel actions and that a reputation for fighting to the very end will deter future suits.)[17]

Another discovery of the Iowa researchers is that plaintiffs "win" by filing suit, not by prevailing. Tavoulareas noted that after the *Washington Post* ran the story about his setting his son up in business, he got a lot of sympathy but little respect: "People you've known for years feel sort of sorry for you. And some are saying, 'Hey, maybe he did something wrong.' But the moment I sued, the attitude of everybody changed—suddenly people started to believe you. My days changed the day I started the suit." The Iowa researchers found similar responses. The vast majority of plaintiffs who lost—including virtually every public official—indicated that they would sue again, *knowing what happened*. To the plaintiffs, the very act of filing suit legitimizes their claim that the story was false. Furthermore, the decision to sue is often accompanied by a desire to punish the defendant—by imposing litigation costs and publicity, not necessarily by obtaining damages.[18]

It would be nice to say that anything else is gravy, but in fact what occurs after filing is likely to be pleasant for neither plaintiff nor defendant (although the plaintiff may take some satisfaction in imposing legal costs on the defendant that the plaintiff, with a contingent fee arrangement, need not bear). Libel suits are seldom settled out of court, and yet three-fourths of them never go to trial.

Within the legal system this means either a dismissal of the case because plaintiff's complaint does not adequately make out that defendant's publication constitutes a libel, or, more likely, a summary judgment. The latter is a legal tool aimed at a quicker resolution of a dispute than a full trial. In libel litigation, the Court will grant a summary judgment when it is clear that even if a plaintiff's factual allegations are true, the defendant will prevail. Summary judgment is especially important from the defendant's point of view, because a full trial generally costs three times more than a case disposed of by summary judgment. A defendant's motion to dismiss or motion for summary judgment is decided on the basis of a legal privilege that protects the defendant; therefore the plaintiff's contention that the offending statement was false is irrelevant at this stage and will not be considered. Even if the defendant will prevail on a pretrial motion, however, the case may not be over; some 60 percent of dismissals and summary judgments are appealed.[19]

Plaintiffs, naturally, wish to fight it out at the trial rather than appellate level. There is no way for plaintiffs to prevail without a trial; moreover, at trial they can enjoy the possible fruits of discovery, a device whereby the legal system orders a party to answer the other party's requests for information about the events in the lawsuit. Without the evidence gained through discovery, it is all but impossible for a plaintiff to prevail. In searching for evidence of actual malice, the plaintiff will ask the reporters and editors what sources they used, what suspicions they may have had about the facts, and why they made the choices they did. The plaintiff will also want all the written evidence relating to the story. Discovery can be both time-consuming and traumatic. Reporters and editors will be compelled to answer hostile questions about their behavior for hours on end. It is a two-way street; the plaintiff will undergo similar searching and unpleasant questioning by defense attorneys. The *Post* attempted to dissuade Tavoulareas from suing because, as he put it, "they'd drag me through the mud in discovery." He was not alone in being willing to risk that in order to sue and obtain vindication. If discovery is unpleasant for plaintiffs, it typically is worse for the press. Document production is time-consuming for both staff and attorneys, and it keeps the defendant's costs mounting. Although the press has argued that the risk of high discovery costs may have a chilling effect on what it publishes, the Court responded that all litigation costs money: "Mushrooming litigation costs, much of it due to pretrial discovery, are not peculiar to the libel and slander area." All defendants hate discovery; the press is no different, nor is it treated differently.[20]

If the plaintiff is fortunate enough to dodge through the pretrial maze, which requires a fair amount of luck as well as a strong case, then things are temporarily going to get a lot better—especially if the plaintiff's attorney has a modicum of intelligence and chooses to try the case to a jury rather than to a judge. When the case goes to trial, everything changes. Issues of truth still do not matter much, but press behavior does; and the predominant focus of a libel trial is on the arrogant press defendant. There seems little doubt that juries, as temporary reflectors of the community's conscience, respond unfavorably to press arrogance. A full 89 percent of cases going to a jury will produce verdicts, some staggering, for the libeled plaintiff. The success rate in front of a judge sitting without a jury is a shade under 50 percent; given that the plaintiff is entitled to a jury if he or she wants one, both the statistics and the undercurrent of community hostility to the press make it clear that no attorney should forego the opportunity. Why some have done so is a mystery.[21]

As the great American philosopher Yogi Berra noted, "It ain't over 'til it's over," and in libel, like other litigation, the end is roughly four years from the beginning. Where libel differs from other litigation is that, jury verdict notwithstanding, the plaintiff and plaintiff's attorney are unlikely to pocket any cash. Indeed, once the verdict breaks six figures the odds on reversal of the judgment, which are already very good, become overwhelming. To be sure, a reversal will take time, and time is money (at least for the newspaper that has to pay its attorneys); but it will happen. Discarding only two awards, one for a quarter of a million and the other for half a million (remember that the data ended in 1984), the Iowa researchers found that the average successfully sustained libel judgment was a mere $20,000. This can usefully be compared to the costs of defending the cases. Counting staff time as zero, newspapers with circulations between 50,000 and 100,000 pay $54,000 to defend the average case; newspapers with circulations over 400,000 pay ten times that amount. And the really big cases can easily see legal fees in the millions. Nevertheless, attorneys' fees are much more a cost of doing business for the big boys than for a small paper sitting close to the economic margin.[22]

Robert Sack noted that the "few plaintiffs who succeed resemble the remnants of an army platoon caught in an enemy crossfire. Their awards stand witness to their good luck, not to their virtue, their skill or the justice of their cause." While all that is true, he could have gone a bit further and said: "Yes, Virginia, if you are a media defense attorney, there is a Santa Claus; it's your client, which unintentionally, but surely, harms some of the people it writes about." Because media attorneys (like Sack) work at an hourly rate for clients who can pay, libel litigation gives them every person's dream: a chance to do well by doing good.[23]

## II

Although *New York Times v. Sullivan* emphasized the need for speech to be "uninhibited, robust, and wide-open," no modern discussion could fail to note that the falsity flowing from that robust debate may lead to an impoverished discourse where truth never quite has a chance to catch up and some speakers are reluctant to engage. "Uninhibited" catches the underlying premise of *New York Times,* that debate is necessarily improved by the removal of inhibitions. In the ensuing years it has become apparent that not all inhibitions are bad and that the need for information about the workings of government is frustrated rather than assisted when falsehood enters the debate. Furthermore, would-be public officials understand that a press armed with a constitutional hunting license will view them as fair game and that they will be required to put up with any distortions about their records and their lives that might occur. To the extent that some good citizens are deterred from entering public service, the functioning of our democracy is harmed. Additionally, for those who do enter public service and suffer wrongful damage to their reputations, the rules impose real costs.

The tensions between press freedom, public debate, and reputation are reflected in the legal rules intended to protect those interests. That much was foreseeable. What the Court could not have foreseen was that it might have created the worst of all possible worlds, where the rules designed to free the press from a chilling effect nevertheless do not keep it warm enough, while reputational interests, recognized by other rules, remain consistently frustrated. A quarter-century of litigation since *New York Times* has led to the ironic situation where the law of libel protects neither the press nor the individual. Libel has become a lose-lose proposition.

No one disputes that reputational interests suffer under *New York Times*. As we have seen, most plaintiffs sue because that is the only way they can make their claim that they were wronged by a story. What many plaintiffs want first and foremost is for a falsehood to be corrected. But at least two major factors prevent the truth from coming out. First, the press just doesn't admit error—and the operation of the rules reinforces the "we stand by our story" posture of the press. Second, it is easier for the press to win on issues of legal privilege than of truth (even when the story is 100 percent true), and that is necessarily the favored line of defense. Thus three-quarters of the cases filed never make it to trial, but are disposed of by the conclusion that the plaintiff cannot produce the requisite evidence to overcome some press privilege (typically the *New York Times v. Sullivan* privilege of publishing defamatory falsehoods as long as this is done without actual malice). In all these cases the plaintiff will lose regardless of how false the statements were, and there is nothing the plaintiff can do about it. Once the cases do go to trial, most plaintiffs will win a money judgment, and with it a ruling that the statements were false; but for the few who cannot overcome the privileges of the press (for example, by proving actual malice), the trial result will be a well-publicized loss, with no finding that the statements were nevertheless false. The message is clear. Whatever the popular view may be, truth and falsity have precious little to do with libel litigation.[24]

The few cases that reach a jury also bear witness to the proposition that reputation, at least in any sense that is commonly understood, has virtually nothing to do with libel litigation either. Elmer Gertz, a liberal Chicago lawyer, had his reputation go to juries twice. The organ of the John Birch Society had labeled him a Leninist and had charged him with an attempt to frame a police officer for a murder; the harm to his reputation among associates and in the community was valued first at $50,000 and then, on retrial, at $100,000. Maybe the doubling was caused by subsequent inflation, but why the conduct of *American Opinion* had become so outrageous between juries that it needed to be punished to the tune of $300,000 in punitive damages the second time around was never explained.[25]

Only five companies received a Dun and Bradstreet financial report erroneously stating that Greenmoss Builders had filed for bankruptcy. Each received a correction from Dun and Bradstreet eight days later, and none took any action on Greenmoss during that period; a classic example of no injury. But libel law presumes injury, and the jury presumed it at $50,000 and then tagged an extra $300,000 in punitives to make sure Dun and Bradstreet got the message.[26]

*Penthouse*'s story about a baton-twirling Miss Wyoming who levitated men by oral sex initially got Kimerli Jayne Pring, a real baton-twirling Miss Wyoming, a fancy $26.5 million ($25 million of it in punitives). But the trial judge, recognizing that the jury had gotten a bit carried away, showed the wisdom of Solomon by cutting the judgment in half. The Tenth Circuit Court of Appeals, with an identical recognition about the jury, plus the realization that no one could seriously take the story as applying to Pring (who denied all its particulars), showed the wisdom of the Constitution by taking the other half away.[27]

The *Washington Post* published a story on how William Tavoulareas, in fatherly fashion, had engaged in favoritism toward his son by setting him up and then sending Mobil business his way; the story was worse in its headline than its substance. The jury thought that reputational sting worth $250,000 and they added $1.8 million in punitives—just the amount, it so happens, that Tavoulareas testified he had spent in legal fees.[28]

Then there was Mary Alice Firestone, whose well-publicized society divorce trial was full of stories of adultery. Apparently upset that her son would know, she sued *Time,* which had erroneously stated that the ground, rather than the groundwork, for the divorce was adultery. She got $100,000 (in 1973 dollars) for the distress that caused her—although, in one of the greatest-ever moves in a libel trial, her attorneys specifically withdrew any claim of injury to her reputation.[29]

It does not warm newspapers up to learn that of these examples, only Gertz and Greenmoss got to keep their awards. Nor does it help that the Iowa researchers found the average successful case for the plaintiff to be worth a piddling $20,000. Recently there seems to be a damages explosion in tort verdicts, with sympathetic plaintiffs being allowed to reach deeply into the pockets of corporate defendants. Newspapers know catastrophe can arrive with just one big hit. The entire industry is aware that a $9 million judgment against the *Alton (Illinois) Evening Telegraph* sent the paper to bankruptcy court (although a subsequent settlement allowed the 38,000-circulation paper to stay in business). Libel is special only in arousing more than a sneaking suspicion that the plaintiffs really weren't hurt that badly.[30]

The press may be partially to blame for the damages spiral. When Westmoreland sued CBS for $120 million, everyone in the legal community (and presumably the press) knew the number was picked out of a hat. But all news reports of the case bandied about the amount "$120 million" as if it had meaning. (In much the same way, the press idiotically notes that if a criminal defendant is "convicted on all counts" and given the maximum sentences, the defendant could be sentenced to [say] 98 years in jail, when anyone familiar with the system—as the press certainly is—knows that the sentences will be concurrent, and therefore with time off for good behavior the defendant will in fact serve a sentence of 14 months.) By always reporting the ridiculous amount *asked,* the press may well be influencing both future plaintiffs and current juries about what they ought to believe is reasonable. This type of self-fulfilling prophecy is one the press could easily do without.

There is, of course, William Shakespeare's fine insight that reputation is an individual's prized possession, worth more than mere money. Robert Post has brilliantly illuminated the dignity aspect of reputation, its nonfinancial basis, and how jurors are providing damages for the affront to the plaintiff's dignity interest—an interest that is not objectively quantifiable. Yet "incalculable" and "unmeasurable" need not be defined as astronomical. What is occurring is not the monetary repair of reputational harm, but rather punishment of a press by a community that finds it in great need of improved manners.[31]

Punitive damages—which by law are designed to punish defendants—exacerbate the problem. How a jury chooses the amount of punitives varies, but as *Tavoulareas* illustrates, at a minimum jurors seem to use them to cover all plaintiff's expenses. Furthermore, once a jury finds actual malice, and therefore can award some damages, "an award of punitive damages is almost a foregone conclusion." Yet because punitive damages are to punish, they are largely unsupervised in normal tort litigation, although supposedly either the trial or appellate court should set them aside when they are so disproportionate as to raise the presumption that they were awarded out of passion or prejudice. In libel cases, there is the chance they may be awarded because the press is unpopular generally or because the story in question touched an unpopular subject. Although the First Amendment ought to foreclose either possibility, it does so only if judges will set aside the awards, as they typically do; but that area of guess is hardly the "breathing space" *New York Times* attempted to secure.[32]

In the vast majority of situations, it is impossible to punish the press—or aid reputation—because these cases will never get to a jury. But in the rare case that does, the plaintiff sometimes hits the jackpot (until an appellate court intervenes). The tort rules systematically undercompensate, or fail to compensate, virtually all defamation injuries and then wildly overcompensate a handful.

To what end? After all, the rationale for constitutionalizing libel and actively supervising juries is the need to protect the press from the chilling effect of substantial liability. Yet just as the libel rules do not provide for a means of truth to come out at trial and are out of whack in restoring reputational harm, so, too, they fail to reduce the chilling effect. One terse answer is that the only way to really reduce the chilling effect is to abolish the tort of defamation (that is, libel and slander). Then, being truly free, the press can be genuinely warm. Justices Black and Douglas took that position, but that seems eras ago, and too much has happened in the ensuing years. There is no way that the Court is going to declare the press immune from libel liability. But the fact that the Court will not go all the way does not mean that it cannot deal with the problems its own decisions, as implemented by the remainder of the legal system, have created.

While the problems that the libel rules pose for the press are complex, they ultimately can be subsumed under a single heading: money. Libel litigation, as we have already seen, allows attorneys for the media to make out like bandits. Newspapers can insure against some of the costs of libel, but even though that is a necessary cost of doing business, it is expensive, and the coverage is not complete. As long as the press has to guard against the possibility of multimillion dollar verdicts, there will be a pretty cool breeze blowing. These verdicts may be rare, but they happen; and two reasons for their occurrence stand out: the uncoupling of damage awards from injuries (and the availability of punitive damages) and the nature of the trial.

My colleague David Anderson has persuasively demonstrated that the nature of the modern libel trial feeds the damage awards. It took time, however, for this insight to come forward; for a while, after it became clear that the Court was serious about *New York Times,* it was thought that plaintiffs would find the "actual malice" requirement to be an impassable hurdle. Although the hurdle has turned out not to be impassable, the actual-malice rule of *New York Times* does prevent many cases from coming to trial and offers a theoretically potent defense weapon for those that do. Furthermore, libel plaintiffs were traditionally informed that they faced a searching scrutiny of their reputation and a real likelihood of being bloodied even in a victory. But a wholly unanticipated aspect of the actual-malice rule was that it turned the libel trial away from what the defendant said about the plaintiff to a scrutiny of how the press put the story together, what reservations the reporters and editors may have had about parts of the story, and why they chose to say one thing rather than another. Furthermore, if confidential sources (a topic in Chapter 6) were used in preparation of the story, the rules may lead to a judicial order to disclose the source—or face a judicial statement to the jurors that they may conclude the source did not exist. Most tort litigation tries the defendant; libel used to be different, but the actual-malice rule brought libel into the mainstream of tort litigation in this respect. It is now the defendant's conduct, rather than the plaintiff's reputation, that is on trial.[33]

Proving actual malice requires evidence about the reporters' and editors' states of mind. Obviously self-serving statements by the reporters need not be the end of the inquiry. Thus, as previously mentioned, discovery in a libel case will be an extensive rummaging through the defendant's procedures and thoughts in putting together the allegedly libelous story. It usually will turn on inferences drawn from circumstantial evidence, although inquiring into how the reporter thought may provide the needed links. The press attempted to block such an inquiry in a "60 Minutes" case. *Herbert v. Lando* involved extensive discovery, and eventually CBS had had enough. Producer Barry Lando answered most questions directed toward him during discovery, but drew the line at why he had pursued certain leads and not others and why he believed some interviewees were more honest than others. Nor would he discuss his conversations with Mike Wallace about the preparation of the program. All of this was rolled into a claim of editorial privilege: that a plaintiff could not inquire into the state of mind of the reporter. The Second Circuit Court of Appeals actually agreed with this argument.[34]

The Supreme Court, however, was less than impressed. If the plaintiff could not inquire into the defendant's state of mind, then the plaintiff could not acquire the requisite evidence to meet the *New York Times* standard. Yet when *Herbert v. Lando* came down, the press went nuts. It was "Orwellian." It would "almost literally put lawyers into editors' chairs." It imposed "an intolerable chilling effect." It made it "more hazardous to exercise [press] freedoms." *Herbert v. Lando* could have tempered discovery to better recognize First Amendment values, but its logic was that of *New York Times*. The tone of press complaints does look childish. Marc Franklin in the *Stanford Law Review* and Justice Brennan in a speech both noted the incredible overreaction of the press; indeed Brennan chided it for its "bitterness" and "acrimonious criticism," even though he had dissented in *Herbert v. Lando*. But the press may well have intuited what would subsequently be clearer. Too much damage is done to the First Amendment by trying press behavior to a jury.[35]

The dynamics of a trial focusing on the practices, care, motives, and views of the press—especially when, as is likely, the story is false—invites punishment of the press. Indeed, the jury especially will have every motivation to lash at the arrogant institution when the jury disapproves as well of the story covered. A good plaintiff's lawyer will be able to paint the dispute as a contest between good and evil, and the necessary evidence to prove actual malice leaves no doubt which side is evil. Inflaming jury passions against an arrogant and maybe unpopular press is not consistent with the First

Amendment. There has been a shift from juries being protective of the press two hundred years ago, when the colonial governments were unpopular, to juries not offering protection when it turns out that the press is unpopular.

The *New York Times* rule, when it results in a summary judgment, works in the press's favor and leaves the plaintiff's reputation where it found it. In an actual trial, the *New York Times* rule turns the tables by its focus on press behavior; this focus is likely to inflame juries and invite punishing the press. A noted attorney who represents plaintiffs in libel actions has observed that "the public believes that the media generally look at themselves as answerable to nobody, and the public wants the media to be answerable like any other institution." A newspaper ombudsman notes that the public can understand mistakes: "What they can't understand is the extremes to which many reporters and editors go to keep from saying 'We were wrong.'" When the jury is given the evidence to infer actual malice it acts on it, and thus Anderson observes that "it is not surprising that the *average* jury award in cases where actual malice is found exceeds $2,000,000."[36]

For Fred Schauer, the money is a cost of doing business. Schauer notes that some negligent reputational harm will inevitably be inflicted by the press as it serves its function of assisting in public debate. He then notes that if a pharmaceutical manufacturer accidentally puts a drug on the market that causes harm, the tort liability system will make it pay. Indeed the possibility of erroneous liability will likely cause some pharmaceutical companies to cut back on product development or to delay marketing a beneficial product. Why, Schauer asks, should the pharmaceutical company pay while the press escapes paying for the harms it inflicts?[37]

Schauer, who has written some of the best analysis of the chilling effect, wishes to pose the serious problem of how the laws reduce chill and at what costs. Besides noting that freedom of the press, but not of pharmaceutical companies, is enshrined in the First Amendment, one answer to his question is that the capitalist system gives the pharmaceutical company powerful incentives to engage in research and development and to market new products. Financial incentives for newspapers, especially monopoly ones, to take risks are hardly as compelling. Schauer counters that the press will take all the necessary risks because of its "good faith sense of mission"—

but for those, including many in the press, who are appropriately skeptical, a little empirical data on how good faith substitutes adequately for financial incentives would be appreciated.[38]

Beyond the matter of incentives or the lack of them, there are two further answers. One is that a negligently manufactured drug will typically harm a number of individuals, whereas a libel harms only one. The second, about which a considerable amount has already been said, is that the jury's determination of damages is likely to be higher for the reputational harm suffered by the libel plaintiff than the physical harm (including possibly death) suffered by the pharmaceutical plaintiff. There are few paralyzed libel plaintiffs.

To recapitulate, the operation of the *New York Times* rule has produced a strange landscape. Issues of truth and falsity rarely surface, and the vast majority of plaintiffs do not have their reputations cleared. For those few that get to a jury, however, trying the press can lead to a nice, albeit usually momentary, windfall. And finally, the possibility of having to pay out that windfall, coupled with the necessary legal fees to avoid doing so, keeps the chill right on the press even though appellate supervision generally cuts the verdicts to size. Libel law, having been wholly remade in the wake of *New York Times,* needs to be rethought again. It is not that the Court misunderstood what to balance; rather, it is that the balance it achieved systematically weakens all the values it attempts to protect.

## III

The initial rethinking, if not elaborate, was candid. The principal cost of a libel suit is the defendant's attorney's fee, even though plaintiffs nearly always lose. Why should an almost certainly losing litigant be able to impose these costs on an unwilling party? The answer, "he shouldn't," seems straightforward enough and so, too, the obvious solution therefrom. The loser in libel litigation should pay the winner's legal fees—just as in the British system.

Leaving aside the delightful irony of seeking First Amendment guidance from a legal system that accords no special protections to freedom of expression, the idea of shifting attorneys' fees will be remarkably successful—if the goal is to discourage libel litigation. Because contingent fee arrangements at present relieve plaintiffs of the responsibility to pay even their own legal fees, the specter of the potentially steep and virtually certain defense bill will be sufficient to stop most plaintiffs right in their angry tracks. To be sure, these proposals would have the defendant pay the plaintiff's fees should the defendant lose, but that is merely the symmetry noted a century ago by Anatole France: the law in its majestic equality "forbids rich and poor alike to sleep under the bridges, to beg in the streets, and to steal bread."[39]

Fee shifting is simply a way to prevent a type of litigation. The British require the loser in libel litigation to pay, because the British require the loser in all litigation to pay. The American system has been built on the different foundation that all parties should bear their own costs. The most notable exception in the American system is civil rights and civil liberties litigation, where, by federal statute, a governmental body that loses the litigation is required to pay the plaintiff's fees, but not vice versa. The assumptions of the federal statute are, first, that we should encourage governments to behave, and second, that plaintiffs are performing an important public service in forcing government to conform to constitutional norms. However much we love the First Amendment, libel litigation is not so one-sided. Litigation may harm the press, but false reporting harms both reputations and public debate. Fee shifting blocks some potential plaintiffs' already limited access to redress; it would overprotect the press by functionally eliminating even meritorious litigation. It is a backdoor method of ending libel litigation, and it is hardly surprising that no one takes it seriously except the true believers in a 100 percent perfect press.[40]

Fee shifting to discourage plaintiffs turns out to be almost perfectly mirrored by a proposal that would actually increase suits against the press. Seeing the current chill as leaving the press too warm, its antagonists would gut *New York Times* by replacing the actual-malice rule with a negligence rule. Because in practice a jury will always find negligence if it finds factual error, the negligence standard would create an open season on newspaper treasuries as well as severely dampen press willingness to report on questionable activities of the government. If a stronger government, more able to lash at its critics, is the goal, this proposal makes sense. But the First Amendment grants the press a larger role than cowering before its official "betters"; and returning a modern press (with modern jury verdicts) to a pre–*New York Times* legal standard would take from the American people a major institutional check against government wrongdoing. Like fee shifting, giving government officials additional weapons against the press plays well only before an audience of true believers. The proposal is doomed by its failure to see that there must be a balance between reputation and a free press.[41]

If libel litigation cannot be eliminated, as many in the media would love, maybe it can be rationalized. If giving the press some breathing space is a legitimate goal—and that ought to be granted—then the single biggest problem is damages. This should have been clear in *New York Times*. If Sullivan had been awarded $500 and the other pending cases looked as if they would reach a similar end, the outcomes would have been offensive, but they would not have had the appearance of an effort by the South to silence national criticism of its retrograde policies. The Court wrote *New York Times* as if damages were not a real problem. In retrospect, this was clearly an error (as Justices Harlan and Marshall, but alas, not their brethren, saw in 1971). The awards discussed in the prior section demonstrate that the Court's failure to deal with damages, the engine driving the chilling effect, led it seriously astray. Any sensible discussion of modern libel law has to look at the bottom line.[42]

With the possibility of punitive damages being used as toppers for an already inflated view of reputational harm, it is no wonder that the press perceives a chilling effect. The Iowa researchers' finding of an average take-home verdict of $20,000 (and significantly less after attorneys' fees and expenses) bears some relation to the realities of reputation, however the injury is measured. The six- and seven- and eight-figure verdicts do not.

Reputational loss that leads to income loss ought to be fully compensable. When humorist John Henry Faulk was colored red during the McCarthy era and therefore blacklisted by the entertainment industry, he suffered a huge, identifiable financial loss. Under the existing rules, damages were presumed; under the present suggestion he would have to prove loss, but to the extent there was a financial loss, he should be able to recover. But the traditional common-law approach of presuming damages from the fact of defamation is, in today's world, just a way to authorize an uncompensated taking of the defendant's property to give a windfall to the plaintiff and her attorney. We all suffer losses in our lives, and there seems no logical reason why a loss of reputation should (in money terms) be greater than the breaking of an irreplaceable family heirloom or the destruction of a home and its furnishings in a flood or tornado. A libel plaintiff should be required to prove with some specificity the actual harm that she suffered. If she cannot, then she should not be able to recover damages. By requiring a plaintiff to prove harm, trial judges and appellate judges would be in a better position to supervise the jury's initial conclusions about both the existence and the value of the harm the plaintiff suffered.[43]

What was just suggested would exclude damages for a dignity injury. If such awards are retained, then at least they should be limited—for example, to $100,000 (which offers enough to feed the plaintiff's attorney too). Such caps are not unheard of in tort law, especially in areas where jurors are prone to play Santa Claus; some new medical malpractice statutes impose a cap on damages for pain and suffering, and older worker's compensation statutes have always included such caps. The advantage of caps is that when they exist, both sides can rationally calculate how much time and effort a case is worth. As Anderson notes, when the potential recovery is unlimited, both sides are likely to spend more on the litigation than the case is actually worth. Realistic damages (although Faulk's case demonstrates that proven damages can be high in the very unusual situation where the defendant makes it impossible for the plaintiff to continue his or her employment) would limit defense spending, the single largest factor in libel costs, and thereby serve well as a means of reducing the chill of litigation.[44]

It should go without saying that holding damages to a realistic figure requires doing something about punitive damages. No serious proposals to reform libel law fail to include the elimination of punitive damages. Punitives not only chill; they offer the opportunity, quite literally, to punish. Any mistakes in overwielding that weapon necessarily impinge on the First Amendment. Although the Court has held that punitives in general tort litigation do not violate the "excessive fines" clause of the Eighth Amendment, it ought to rule that in libel cases they violate the press clause of the First Amendment. The potential of unlimited punishment for publication cannot be squared with the premises of the Constitution.[45]

Once the easy parameters of holding damages in check and recognizing that plaintiffs have rights, too, are understood, the serious rethinking begins. Limiting recoveries, like fee shifting, risks becoming little more than a stalking-horse for more media rights to run roughshod over innocent reputations. Rethinking, therefore, necessitates a further calculus.

No proposed libel reform has been accompanied by more publicity than that produced under the direction of Rodney Smolla (head of the Bill of Rights Institute at William and Mary) for the Annenberg Washington Program Libel Reform Project. Although other proposals were offered earlier, Annenberg's backing and publicity guarantee this one the necessary hearing on the merits. The cornerstone of the Annenberg plan, adopted from the earlier proposals of Marc Franklin, is the concept of reducing libel litigation to a declaratory judgment action. Declaratory judgments simply declare what the facts and rights are, without any award of damages. Annenberg's proposal, like Franklin's, looks to an especially speedy disposition of the case, with trial occurring within six months of publication. Furthermore, because declaratory judgments do not involve money, they all but eliminate the chill on the press. If the Iowa researchers are correct in their conclusion that plaintiffs really just want the truth out, then the declaratory judgment should satisfy them.[46]

Like Franklin's, the Annenberg proposal looks to early nonjudicial settlement. The plaintiff would first have to go to the paper and demand either a retraction or a right of reply. Only if the paper failed to print conspicuously an adequate retraction or reply (as defined) could the plaintiff file suit. At this point the plaintiff would have the choice of seeking either a declaratory judgment or damages (for actual injury only). So far, Annenberg largely tracks Franklin. The real difference is that Annenberg's proposal would make it unlikely that any plaintiff could successfully sue for damages, because the plan would authorize the press, *at its option*, to turn a plaintiff's action for damages into a declaratory judgment action. Thus no matter how severely the plaintiff was injured or how egregiously the press had behaved, a paper in its sole discretion could deny the plaintiff damages by demanding use of the declaratory judgment remedy.

The Annenberg proposal places the ascertainment of truth as

virtually the sole objective of libel litigation. It looks first to retraction or reply—the plaintiff must request this remedy and be refused before going to court—and then to a statement of rights in the form of a declaratory judgment. It is one thing to let an injured plaintiff choose a simplified declaratory judgment remedy to establish truth. It is quite another thing for the newspaper to force an injured plaintiff to this remedy. Yet that is what the Annenberg proposal does. Finally, as a pro-press topper, the proposal looks to fee shifting in the declaratory judgment action. Thus a plaintiff who is denied (by the defendant) a right to sue for damages, and who then loses in the declaratory judgment action, would wind up picking up the paper's reasonable legal fees.

Somehow, some media attorneys don't think this is enough, and Gilbert Cranberg quotes some as calling the proposal a "draconian onslaught against the First Amendment." How could educated people be so wide of the mark? The explanation is easy once you know Thomas Reed Powell's famous definition of a lawyerlike mind: the ability to think of one of two inseparably connected things without thinking of the other. The attorneys quoted appear to be showing that the converse of Powell's definition is equally true. The best explanation for their ridiculous conclusion is that they have wholly internalized the fact that the First Amendment is responsible for their fat wallets—so that an attack on the latter is perceived as an onslaught on the former.[47]

An alternative explanation for the overreaction may be the conclusion that (regardless of legal costs and any consequent chill) the press is winning those libel suits now brought because of the *New York Times* privilege, and should a declaratory-judgment alternative be substituted, the press will lose because the stories that provoke libel suits are either false or matters of opinion that a misguided jury could find false. Under this view, the First Amendment interest is measured by press victories in litigation. This is a doubly wrong conclusion. First, it ignores the public interest in true information. Second, it ignores the press's interest in litigation alternatives that cost less and therefore chill less. The press accurately perceived in the mid-1980s that its First Amendment interests were not prevailing, even though it won almost all libel litigation. Thus Eugene Roberts, editor of the *Philadelphia Inquirer,* stated that the Westmoreland and Sharon cases were but the tip of the iceberg and that the "actual malice loophole" provided a tool of harassment for public officials to use with the help of friendly, antimedia juries. That insight, tied into attorneys' fees and the chill from a potential big hit, suggests that either the press must be guaranteed an impossible 100 percent victory rate or the rules must be changed. Given press mistakes—which candid editors admit happen too frequently—a guarantee of victory is impossible. That means that alternatives such as declaratory judgments are the only option. The press might discover it could win even though its attorneys lose both cases and fees.[48]

The Annenberg proposal largely removes the chill on newspapers by assuming that only truth matters, not harm. But not all plaintiffs sue merely to set the record straight, and maybe more than a few who told the Iowa researchers that money did not matter at all were engaging in a cost-free, self-serving deception. These plaintiffs would be left high and dry by the Annenberg proposal, but not by the one pioneered by Franklin during the 1980s. He offered a simplified, truth-seeking option for plaintiffs, the declaratory judgment remedy. Franklin would not allow discovery, because it would be unnecessary. The press already has the information on which it based its story; the plaintiff knows the facts about himself; and the requirement that the plaintiff go first to the paper eliminates the possibility of surprise at trial. For plaintiffs who fit the Iowa researchers' model, it looks like an attractive option. If they are willing to litigate factual truth only (with the opportunity to collect attorneys' fees should they prevail), why shouldn't the newspaper?[49]

The best reasons for opposing a truth-only declaratory judgment are that truth is more slippery than we think; that jury findings on the issue will turn out to be unreviewable by appellate courts more sensitive to First Amendment interests; and that jury second-guessing of the press is unseemly and may weaken the media's credibility, thereby undermining their checking function on governmental officials. Assuming for the sake of argument that all that is true, a plaintiff's-option declaratory judgment would still improve the press's relative position. Media lawyers will disagree; but their position seems less an illustration of sober reflection than of the proposition that the better is the enemy of the good. The press would prefer never to litigate, and if by chance forced to, then always to win. When the press ceases injuring citizens by false-hoods, that happy day will be closer. Until then, the Franklin proposal deserves the attention granted to its Annenberg competitor.

But what if the plaintiff is injured, angry, and wants a real trial? Few ideas have surfaced that do not reflect a tilt toward one of the parties, and it may prove impossible to avoid some tilt. Damages, especially punitives, are what fuel plaintiffs' efforts; yet they must be limited because otherwise the chilling effect on the press cannot be brought under control.

One suggestion, tentatively offered by David Anderson, a leading academic in the area who has also represented both plaintiffs and defendants in libel cases, offers a potential solution. It requires plaintiffs to prove actual damages (allowing dignity awards *only* when economic injury is proven—a possible loophole that could run up damages), but takes away their need to prove actual malice. It thus takes from the press its principal protection of privilege, in exchange for limiting the amount of damages that can be assessed. Everything else, including leaving the entire burden of proof on the plaintiff, remains as is. For injured plaintiffs it offers the chance—subject to proof and the limitations of defenses such as neutral reportage—to receive compensation for injury. For the press it limits the amount a jury can award and shifts the trial focus from the defendant's behavior (the focus that currently allows plaintiffs' attorneys to put the press on trial) to issues of truth. Both sides give up a considerable amount, but the key is fairness to each. This would deescalate libel litigation in much the same way Franklin would with his declaratory judgment approach and to the same end: a trial focusing on truth rather than press misdeeds.[50]

## IV

Thus far, one question has been avoided, and possibly a wrong answer to another has been assumed. Are these proposals constitutional, and will they solve all the problems? The questions have fairly easy answers: yes, the proposals are constitutional; no, they won't make libel problems vanish.

Sometimes the press has reacted to proposals to change some of the rules aiding them as if those were the ones graven in constitutional stone. This response is wrong on two counts. First, it wrongly assumes an era of Black and Douglas and their willingness to go to any lengths to protect the press. Lest it be forgotten, they could not prevail even during the heyday of the most liberal court in American history. Second, the actual malice rule is not in the constitution. It is a rule implementing what is in the constitution: a guarantee of freedom of the press. The guarantee was implemented in *New York Times* by balancing reputational interests and public debate, incorporating a recognition of the press's need for breathing space. If a different set of rules can implement that balance as well as those of *New York Times,* then that different set of rules is no less constitutional. More significantly, if a different set of rules could better implement the balance, then the Court would be wrong not to adopt or approve them. The constitutional balance, not any specific set of rules, is the bedrock of the system. To find what is in that balance we must look not to the implementing rules, but to the language, purposes, and traditions of the Constitution itself.[51]

No reform is a complete panacea. Balancing reputation against the needs of vigorous debate and thereby determining the appropriate breathing space are difficult tasks. It may be that imposing the burden of proof on plaintiffs is too arduous. It may be that anything short of the Black-Douglas view that libel suits are unconstitutional will leave too much of a chill, because to the extent that any proposal has balance, it is impossible to guarantee that the chilling effect will be entirely eliminated. One reason is that libel can be the grounds to fight symbolic battles to a figurative death (perhaps with a wish that it could move closer to literal). A libel suit can be an instant replay of history, much larger than life, in which the goal is not restoring reputation (although that may occur) so much as transforming the present by recasting the past. The high-stakes litigation between General William Westmoreland and CBS, a case that despite CBS's victory may have precipitated its decline as a network, is a prototype of the symbolic use of libel.

The CBS documentary "The Uncounted Enemy: A Vietnam Deception" comes perilously close to charging Westmoreland with treason, and whatever else he may be, no one could seriously think he was a traitor. It is one thing to allege, as CBS did, that the Vietcong and North Vietnamese were undercounted (thereby aggravating the surprise of the Tet Offensive) to deceive the American people. Inappropriate as this behavior is, it is nevertheless a far cry from CBS's thrust that Westmoreland also deceived the Joint Chiefs of Staff and the president of the United States. Like "The Uncounted Enemy," Westmoreland's libel suit was in many ways a replay of a lost war, this time between its major living combatant, Westmoreland, and some of his major foes, the American media as personified by CBS.

What makes the Westmoreland suit unusual and interesting is its replay of Vietnam. Westmoreland, and to a larger extent his attorney, Dan Burt of the Capital Legal Foundation, a conservative public interest law firm, intended to use the case as a vehicle for discrediting CBS News in the present and, by implication, in the past. By winning the case, Burt would substantiate the conservative claim that but for the biased liberal American media, our troops in Vietnam would have prevailed. Although Westmoreland sued for $120 million (and Burt talked of toppling CBS), the suit was less financial than ideological. In no other libel case did the goal of discrediting the defendant seem so completely to dominate. Westmoreland's anger is understandable; he should never have been required to assert, as he has, "I'm no Benedict Arnold."[52]

No reform can eliminate the ideologically driven lawsuit. Even if damages were unavailable, a declaratory judgment could still be used to discredit a media defendant—at a price. In the Westmoreland case—the essential rerun of why we lost the Vietnam War—the truth will never be fully known; the effort to establish the truth is potentially endless. If the plaintiff is willing to run the costs, then discovery is going to result in the defendant running right with him (and the estimate is that CBS may have gone $10 million in defense fees). However, in most cases the vast majority of discovery relates to actual malice, which cannot be put at issue in the proposed declaratory judgment suits. The Westmoreland case may be unique in its ability to run discovery costs up when the issue is truth. It is hard to conceive of many libel cases where the truth of the matter would be beyond the reach of plaintiff's own information and ultimately unknowable.[53]

As discussed above, the availability of unlimited damages is likely to mean that few reasonable calculations about time and the worth of the suit are made. An ideological suit, though to a lesser extent, offers a similar high-stakes game that leaves reason in its wake.

There are two consolations here. First, there is no good reason to believe that many ideological suits are lurking. Westmoreland's was one. It is possible that Tavoulareas's could have been another, although his own statements indicate that he would gladly have taken an early retraction from an arrogant *Post*. Ariel Sharon's suit against *Time* is probably a third. These three cases all came in the mid-1980s, but I think that is just coincidence and not an indication that a new type of lawsuit is in the offing.

The second consolation is that even ideological suits cannot completely ignore the costs of litigation. It is hard to know what to make of the precedent Mobil made when it agreed to buy its managers libel "insurance" to cover possible attorneys' fees; no other group of executives so spent their company's money. More significantly, Westmoreland's case was settled out of court—on terms unfavorable to Westmoreland and under circumstances where those who followed the case knew he had lost—because Dan Burt was running out of conservative money to support his crusade. In retrospect, if Westmoreland could have prevailed before the jury, he would have won big, given the statements that were made about a man who, if rigid and misguided, was nevertheless honorable in his service to his country. If a case like his, carrying great (if speculative) gain as a hope, nevertheless flounders on financing, then few cases driven solely by ideology and the desire for vengeance are likely to succeed. Protracted, hard-hitting litigation takes money, and there is reason not to throw the good after the bad. Just as there are many lessons from Vietnam, some better than others, so there are lessons from Westmoreland's lawsuit. One of the better ones is that even deep pockets may learn that the costs may exceed any hoped-for gain; in Kenny Rogers's words, "You've got to know when to fold 'em."[54]

If ideological libel suits were a problem, one radical solution might be a mechanism whereby the trial judge could declare them to be beyond judicial resolution (as a nonjusticiable political question). One reason to fear Franklin's declaratory-judgment model is that we may not want courts too actively arbitrating the truth of newspaper stories. While I have such sympathies, I believe the benefits of improving the current system significantly outweigh the risks. But it may well be that ascertaining the truth about Vietnam is much better left first to politics and then to history. Allowing judges a discretionary refusal to hear libel suits attempting to re-fight and rewrite political history ought to be considered as a supplement to any libel law reform. Within prevailing doctrine, some further expansion of the concept of unproveable fact could do the job.

When he wrote about libel law in the 1950s, Kalven tried to get his audience to see a constitutional problem lurking therein. He failed. Writing in the 1960s, he dominated the discussion as few academics ever have (or probably will again). The 1970s saw some retrenchment and the 1980s more confusion, as both Kalven's analysis and *New York Times v. Sullivan* broke down in unanticipated ways. The changes in tort law generally and in American juries in particular make it impossible to go back, and yet there are times it seems equally difficult to go forward. Part of the problem flows from precisely what delighted Kalven (as noted in the beginning of Chapter 3): the intersection of the real world, the common law, and the Constitution. The exact solution to the problem may still be hazy and years away, but its contours appear visible. For better or worse, some legislature should adopt a declaratory-judgment remedy and some trial judge should risk reversal by modifying the libel trial along the lines suggested by Anderson. These necessary first steps could help move the Supreme Court out of the dilemma created by its mistaken refusal to understand that the problem in *New York Times* was not a lack of actual malice by the defendant, but rather an excess of money damages to a wholly uninjured plaintiff.

Chapter Five

# Prior Restraints

While the newsrooms of the *New York Times* and the *Washington Post* were celebrating their great victory in the *Pentagon Papers Cases,* they were blissfully unaware that five justices had indicated that a criminal indictment of those responsible for publishing national secrets in the newspapers might be favorably received. That quick cold shower is precisely similar to the effect of the Blackstonian prior restraint doctrine: writing that cannot be stopped by government order—for example, by an injunction—may nevertheless be stopped by the threat of criminal conviction of those responsible for its publication. To be sure, a criminal trial may take a little longer, but then the penalties are greater too. And that is why Madison in his *Report on the Virginia Resolutions* concluded that it would be a "mockery to say that no laws should be passed preventing publications from being made, but that laws might be passed for punishing them in case they should be made."[1]

Prior restraints grew out of the Tudor-Stuart response to the printing press, and the eighteenth-century battles on both sides of the Atlantic over the law of seditious libel were set against the backdrop of the abandonment of this licensing system in the aftermath of the Glorious Revolution of 1688. Blackstone's *Commentaries* summarized the law on the eastern shore of the Atlantic, and, as Chapters 1 and 2 demonstrated, there was full agreement on the western shore that federal licensing of the press was unconstitutional. That agreement did not extend to the second half of Blackstone's doctrine of liberty of the press: the question of subsequent punishment and the permissibility of making seditious libel a crime.

Thus even after his first blast at the Colorado Supreme Court, Tom Patterson was not, and could not have been, ordered to cease publishing such attacks. Indeed he was never told he had to stop. In perfect conformity to the Blackstonian position, he could publish freely—being legally responsible, of course, for any breach of the law. The *Times* and the *Post* were given an identical message.

The prohibition on prior restraints allows the material to reach the public, but also puts citizen critics in the position where they may be severely punished should the material exceed the constitutional privilege. Therein lies the key aspect of the rule against prior restraints: it assumes the speech in question can be properly punished in conformity with constitutional standards. If the writing is already within the ambit of constitutional protection (and if judges do not err), then the rule against prior restraints is unnecessary: the writing being constitutionally protected, it can be neither enjoined nor punished. The prohibition against prior restraints matters only to writings that are not immunized from punishment by the First Amendment.

When Blackstone wrote, the ban on prior restraints was all the protection afforded the press. Two and a quarter centuries later, huge areas of expression are immunized from government interference, and the citizen's ability to criticize caustically is constitutionally enshrined. Thus, despite its wondrous past and its worship by newspapers nationwide, the changes in the law may well have moved the "no prior restraints" doctrine into functional obsolescence.[2]

The possibility must be considered that one of the most hallowed aspects of freedom of the press may have lasted well past its prime. At a minimum the "no prior restraints" doctrine is layered with ironies. Prior restraint may be no more restrictive of civil liberties than subsequent punishment is; and the primary rationale of the doctrine—that to allow prior restraint would chill expression even more than a criminal statute would—no longer remains valid. A further irony is that when prior restraints are legally permitted, they are not always effective, either because the government lacks advance notice of publication, or because unenjoined sources remain free to disseminate the information. The final irony is that ever since the Supreme Court in 1931 created the modern doctrine in *Near v. Minnesota*, national security has been at the forefront of

exceptions to the ban on prior restraints, and yet the national
security cases are typically the ones where the rationale of no prior
restraints has its central core—perceived seditious attacks on government policy. When analyzed, the ironies suggest, first, that much
of the aversion to prior restraints is ill-founded, especially when the
press strays from discussions of government policy; and second,
that the potential for prior restraints to protect national security,
and the consequences flowing from such restraints, justifies the
historical stigma attached to the banning of publication.[3]

## I

The Supreme Court merged injunctions against publication and
other prior restraints in *Near v. Minnesota,* which, astonishingly
enough, was the first case to hold that a law violated the guarantees
of freedom of the press. Before *Near* the historic bad name of prior
restraints came from the excesses of Tudor-Stuart licensing and
from John Milton's impassioned plea in *Areopagitica* against having to receive governmental permission before an author could
publish—"Give me the liberty to know, to utter, and to argue freely
according to conscience, above all liberties." *Near* succeeded (at
least until recently) in equating injunctions with licensing, thereby
attaching the historic disdain for licensing to injunctions. This
merger was made possible because of the unique features of the
Minnesota Gag Law, drafted to deal expeditiously with the problems posed by "an obscene scandal sheet published by some religious nut from Duluth."[4]

The "religious nut" was John Morrison, whose *Rip-saw* was one
of Minnesota's prohibition-era "ragtag scandal sheets" that, once
they selected their prey, were unceasing in their attacks. When
Morrison targeted two state senators, however, he finally hit people
who could implement their belief that "there ought to be a law."
With the drafting assistance of the Minnesota Editorial Association
(the umbrella group for the respectable press) they wrote the Gag
Law, officially titled the Public Nuisance Bill of 1925, which authorized a permanent injunction against any person engaged in the
business of regularly publishing a "malicious, scandalous and defamatory newspaper." A publisher could prevail at trial only by
proving both that the material was true and that it had been

published with "good motives and for justifiable ends." Once enjoined, the publisher would stay enjoined, with a perpetual possibility that freshly published material would result in a quick trip before the judge and then to jail for contempt. The bill unanimously sailed through the senate, was overwhelmingly adopted in the house (87 to 22), and was signed without fanfare by the governor.[5]

Instead of Morrison's *Rip-saw*, it was Jay Near and his *Saturday Press* that furnished the test of Minnesota's Gag Law. In a commendable understatement, the Supreme Court described Near's articles as charging that "a Jewish gangster was in control of gambling, bootlegging and racketeering in Minneapolis" and that law enforcement officers and agencies, including the golden boy of Minnesota politics, County Attorney Floyd Olson, were not doing much about it. Olson, on his way to becoming the three-time Farm-Labor governor, was not a bit amused. Having grown up poor in the predominantly Jewish north side of Minneapolis, he retained his sympathy for those trying to eke out a living, including honest (albeit illegal) small-time gamblers. Olson resolved to "put out of business forever the *Saturday Press* and other sensational weeklies."[6]

The *Saturday Press* was much like the *Rip-saw*; scurrilous attacks were its stock-in-trade. Still, the *Rip-saw* would have been first but for Morrison's untimely death from a blood clot in the brain. Near, although almost destitute, stated: "I have no intention of being so accommodating." Four court dates later—the issuing of a preliminary injunction, an appeal to the state supreme court, a trial that consisted entirely of proof by the state of publication, and a second trip to the state supreme court—Near was zero for four and out of the newspaper business. The trial judge, regarding the *Saturday Press* as a garbage dump in a residential neighborhood, enjoined Near from publishing a "malicious, scandalous, or defamatory newspaper under the name and title of said The Saturday Press or any other name or title." The victorious Olson then orchestrated gratuitous applause from the Hennepin County grand jury, which announced that the *Saturday Press*'s going out of business was not a loss to Minneapolis; indeed, it stated, "the community will be improved." The Minnesota Supreme Court, affirming the permanent injunction, struck a similar note, stating that Near was not restrained "from operating a newspaper in harmony with the public welfare, to which all must yield," and that "defendants have in no way indicated any desire to conduct their business in the usual and legitimate manner."[7]

The quoted language from the Minnesota Supreme Court demonstrates that Near was not under a true prior restraint. First, there was no licensor whose approval need be sought prior to publication; indeed the official was a judge, not a professional censor. Second, there was an adversarial, not an ex parte, proceeding prior to any determinations. Third, the Gag Law was aimed at closing an intriguing loophole in the laws of libel. As long as the libeler was impecunious (like Near), those injured by malicious lies had no real civil remedy. This blends into the fourth point. If Near wished to go legitimate, there was no bar. All that Minnesota wished to do was stop scandal sheets from constantly attacking victims without being accountable. These differences from the English prior restraints were sufficient to cause four justices of the U.S. Supreme Court, in Near's fifth trip to the courthouse, to vote against his claim. A majority, however, through Chief Justice Hughes, applied a functional, rather than formal, approach to prior restraints, and finding that the Minnesota system embodied the evils of prior licensing, it struck down the Minnesota law.

The novelty of Minnesota's law, which impressed the dissenters, troubled the majority. Instead of noting that an impecunious defendant was judgment proof, Hughes noted that the civil laws of libel were available and unaffected. Nor did the statute look like punishment for criminal libel. Instead it operated prospectively to prevent future libels of public officials. Despite Near's concession that libel was unprotected speech, the majority viewed the statute as unnecessarily restricting criticism of official behavior: "The administration of government has become more complex, the opportunities for malfeasance and corruption have multiplied, crime has grown to most serious proportions, and the danger of its protection by unfaithful officials . . . emphasizes the primary need of a vigilant and courageous press, especially in great cities."[8]

This merged easily into the majority's other principal thrust, that the prospective features of the Gag Law operated as censorship through prior restraints. "Where a newspaper or periodical has been suppressed because of the circulation of charges against public

officers of official misconduct, it would seem to be clear that re-
newal of publication of such charges would constitute a contempt
and that the judgment would lay a permanent restraint upon the
publisher." Here Hughes made clear that it was not the form of the
statute but its substance that would control. Thus, in form, Near
would only be guilty of violating the injunction *after* he published
material that was "scandalous and malicious." Technically, this is
subsequent punishment by the procedure of contempt of court.
Hughes, however, wrote that the Court must "cut through mere
details of procedure." Therein lay *Near*'s significance: the majority
concluded that in fact the Minnesota procedure was bound to
operate as a system of prior restraint.[9]

Hughes believed that a publisher in Near's position would necessarily be concerned that any future publication would come before
the same judge who had issued the injunction and might be adjudi-
cated, without a jury or the safeguards of a criminal trial, as a
violation of the injunction. The publisher would have to "satisfy
the court as to the character of a new publication." Although the
chilling effect had not been given its name in 1931, what Hughes
described was classically a chilling effect. To avoid being held in
contempt, publishers would steer wide of the contested area and
refrain from publishing even what they had every right to print.
Alternatively, a publisher might try to clear in advance with the
judge any dubious materials before printing them. In either case
this was, as Hughes noted, "the essence of censorship."[10]

*Near* did not go all the way to embrace the full Blackstonian ban
on prior restraints. Thus in the opinion's most famous passage the
Court implied that national security might well be a ground for a
prior restraint: "No one would question but that a government
[during actual war] might prevent actual obstruction to its recruiting service or the publication of the sailing dates of troops and
transports or the number and location of troops." *Near*'s discussion
of its era's idea of national security meant that when the *New York
Times* was haled into court on Tuesday, June 15, 1971, everyone
knew that *Near* would be the dominant precedent. Bickel made the
point strongly when he asked whether Judge Gurfein wished to be
the first judge in American history to order a newspaper not to print
a story. Although Gurfein did not so wish, and showed himself
aware of the presumptive ban on prior restraints, he felt he had no

choice but to issue at least a temporary order to find out what the case and materials really were about. Solicitor General Griswold made the same point: "The real objective of starting the suit was simply to say 'For God's sake, give us time to find out what this is all about.'" Gurfein's temporary injunction and the one issued Friday in Washington were in fact more like the historical prior restraints than like the injunction in *Near.* What was at issue, and ruled unconstitutional in the *Pentagon Papers Cases,* was the government demand that the newspapers preclear their stories, through either appropriate declassification procedures, justice department approval, or judicial orders of inclusion and exclusion.[11]

Both *Near* and the *Pentagon Papers Cases* "cut through mere details of procedure" to find that the injunctions at issue operated like classic prior restraints by imposing a broad and uncertain area of prohibited publications. The next major prior restraint case, however, inverted the process and allowed form to control the prior restraint issue even when in substance the evils of overbreadth and uncertainty were not present. *Nebraska Press Association v. Stuart* involved a pending murder trial in a rural community, where the trial judge prohibited publication of any of the accused's confession or admissions of other facts strongly implicative of the accused's guilt. Although the range of material covered was both limited and certain, the restraint temporary, and the state interest—protecting the accused's right to a fair trial—high, the Court found that the ban on prior restraints applied to the judge's gag order, making it unconstitutional. *Nebraska Press Association* thus concluded that the form of restraint (an injunction) was sufficient in and of itself to justify a presumptive ban. The justices explicitly noticed that "given the generative propensities of rumors" in a town of 850 people, there was going to be lots of talk about the murder regardless of what the newspapers said or were precluded from saying. Why that did not lead the Court to the obvious point that such talk is constitutional is a great mystery. As noted at the outset, speech that is fully protected under the Constitution, as this clearly was, needs no protection by the doctrine of prior restraints.[12]

*Nebraska Press Association* thus doubly inverted the American doctrine of no prior restraints: it elevated form over substance, and it ignored the essential point that protected speech has no need of the doctrine disfavoring prior restraints. When a doctrine appears to go so haywire in a single case, it provides an occasion for a more careful look at the doctrine and its possible obsolescence in First Amendment adjudication. This is not to say that if a true prior restraint occurs it should not be invalidated; rather it is to state that the blithe merging of injunctions into prior restraints merits reconsideration.[13]

## II

In the sixty years since *Near,* the prior-restraint doctrine has acquired less procedural and more substantive baggage. Furthermore, although injunctions have been merged into licensing, there are differences. For a real licensing system, complete with a requirement of preclearance for all publications, one need go no farther than the Central Intelligence Agency (CIA). All employees are required before beginning work to sign a secrecy agreement promising not to publish "any information or material relating to the Agency, its activities or intelligence activities generally" without prior approval from the CIA. Prior approval means just that: giving the materials to a CIA officer who is authorized to make whatever deletions he wishes.[14]

*Snepp v. United States* held that even though the CIA review is a classic prior restraint—an administrative official reading what an individual wishes to publish and deciding what must go—it is constitutional and may be enforced with an injunction (as well as other remedies). Although the ex-agent is free to publish without submission any general criticisms of the intelligence community, as well as materials already in the public domain, any specifics run afoul of the preclearance requirement.[15]

How the CIA review operates also demonstrates that true prior restraints have the same characteristics over time. The agency has admitted in congressional testimony that it exercises its powers of censorship more heavily when the material to be censored is critical rather than supportive of the agency. Victor Marchetti, an ex-agent, knows this too well. When he submitted for review (under court order) his manuscript, *The CIA and the Cult of Intelligence,* the agency demanded that 339 deletions (some 15 to 20 percent of the entire manuscript) be made prior to publication. The history of prior restraints is a history of administrative overreaction, and the CIA lived up to its role. With commendable zeal the agency attempted to block a statement showing that then Chilean President Salvador Allende had been a major candidate in the election he won: "The Chilean election was scheduled for the following September, and Allende, a declared Marxist, was one of the principal candidates."[16]

After a meeting with Marchetti and his lawyer, the agency dropped 114 objections. Later another 29 went, and still later another 57. After that, with 168 remaining, the agency would not budge. Marchetti then challenged these in court (his appeal from the licensor's decision), and the trial judge held that all but 26 items could be published. The judge stated that there were no explanations of why the 142 other items had been previously classified; and he disbelieved the testimony of four deputy directors of intelligence that the classification had been done prior to reading Marchetti's manuscript. The Fourth Circuit Court of Appeals, which naturally had seen none of the testimony at trial, then told the trial judge that there was "a presumption of regularity" so high it left no room for speculation or conclusions contrary to what the agency said. The 168 items never saw the light of day; the published version of the book contains blank spaces corresponding to the deleted items, with boldface capitals announcing "DELETED."[17]

The authorization of full-scale administrative prior restraints in some circumstances is persuasive evidence that judicial prior restraints, if sufficiently precise, will be held valid in others. The national security cases, whether involving ex-CIA agents or the Pentagon Papers themselves, present the easiest, most obvious application for prior restraints. But Hughes's famous passage suggested that the limits on the Blackstonian doctrine went beyond national security. In full it reads: "No one would question but that a government [during actual war] might prevent actual obstruction to its recruiting service or the publication of the sailing dates of troops and transports or the number and location of troops. On similar grounds, the primary requirements of decency may be enforced against obscene publications."[18]

An unfortunate incoherence to Hughes's statements is not limited to equating the probable immediate death of troops in war to, "on similar grounds," the effects of the distribution of obscenity.

The passage, complete with an earlier citation to *Schenck*, seems to be equating the ability of government to punish subsequently—for obstruction (*Schenck*), for publishing the sailing dates of troop ships (which is quite probably treason), for publishing obscenity— with the ability to issue a prior restraint. While this may make terrific sense, it is the antithesis of the Blackstonian prior-restraint doctrine, which prohibits injunctions to suppress speech that will later be subjected to punishment. *Near's* exceptions allow prior restraints even though, and maybe because, the availability of subsequent punishment is clear. Yet Hughes understood the Blackstonian point, because the premise of his opinion was that Near's *Saturday Press* was legally responsible for its unprotected libelous speech, but nevertheless the *Saturday Press* could not be enjoined.

That some unprotected speech enjoys Blackstonian freedom from prior restraints while other unprotected speech does not demands some criterion for deciding where to draw the line. Hughes provided none; subsequent cases have followed suit. Apart from obstruction of the armed forces, which has been happily ignored (probably because it is impossible to conceive how mere writing could cause such obstruction), *Near's* categories have been treated as givens, but not as defining the only possible exceptions to the Blackstonian rule.

Laurence Tribe has suggested that the cases conform to the rule that the presumption against prior restraints can be overcome "where the expected loss from impeding speech in advance is minimized by the unusual clarity of the prepublication showing of harm." It might be nice to have such a sensible rule, but in at least one case a newspaper was enjoined without *any* clear prepublication showing of harm: the *Pittsburgh Press* simply ran afoul of a determination by the Pittsburgh Commission on Human Relations that gender-specific "Help Wanted" advertisements violated city law. That determination was then enforced by issuance of a cease-and-desist order, which was affirmed by the Pennsylvania courts. The *Pittsburgh Press* was thus enjoined from printing the offending advertisements. At the time the case was decided, the Supreme Court's operative rule was that all "commercial speech"—such as advertisements—was deemed beneath constitutional protection. Since the speech was not constitutionally protected, the case presented a prior-restraint problem. When the newspaper argued that prior restraints chill, the Court responded that the expression was unprotected anyway, so the chill did not matter. Tribe's synthesis can explain some cases, but not this one; which suggests that his synthesis does not describe what the Court is doing.[19]

Although the Court continues with its rubric that prior restraints bear a heavy burden of persuasion, some prior restraints make it. National security can sometimes persuade, because when the information is confidential and important, lives may be lost by publication. In other cases the heavy burden appears to be carried by the conclusion that the writing is beneath concern. Later in the chapter, I will turn to whether injunctions can protect national security and confidentiality; but for now what matters is that the Court has walked a considerable distance from strict adherence to a Blackstonian view. Kalven observed, with reason, that "it is not altogether clear just what a prior restraint is or just what is the matter with it." Excepting the special problems of CIA contracts, where the Court is willing to see would-be authors subjected to full administrative review, the Court may have been turning the Blackstonian rule, which forbids restraints prior to publication, into a modern rule that forbids restraints prior to adjudication. By so doing, much of the procedural detriment of prior restraints vanishes.[20]

As the Court has modernized the rule, it has also severed many of the procedural aspects of prior restraints from *Near*'s era that assisted in reinforcing the stigma of prior restraints. Recall that the assumption from *Near* was that any future publications by Near would be fully scrutinized for transgressions of the injunction, and that if there was any transgression, Near would then be hauled before the issuing judge, who, without jury, would proceed to find the defendant in contempt of court. Although there is ample reason to question whether a jury can be placed in the mood to protect unpopular speech, modern rules require that if a judge wishes to impose a sentence of six months or more for violation of a court order, a jury must be made available at the defendant's option, and the prosecution is required to prove violation beyond a reasonable doubt. At a minimum, enpaneling a jury and trying the case to it makes the prosecution more expensive.[21]

The real difference between enforcing an injunction and enforcing a criminal statute is the "collateral bar" rule, which forbids challenging the legality of an injunction by disobeying its terms. Resting on the need to "respect the civilizing hand of the law," the rule forbids such a challenge even on the ground that the injunction violates the First Amendment. An injunction can be challenged only by appealing to a higher court. Thus the only time that Martin Luther King, Jr., was found by the Supreme Court to have violated the law was when he participated in the Good Friday march in Birmingham in violation of a state court's injunction forbidding the march. On the basis of a vague—and clearly unconstitutional— city ordinance on parade permits, Birmingham officials obtained an ex parte temporary injunction that forbade King to march without first complying with the city ordinance. All the judge required King to do was obtain the permission of the notorious Bull Connor! Instead of either making the obviously futile gesture of going to Connor or taking the time to appeal the injunction, which would have required postponing the march and thus eliminating the symbolism of Good Friday and the Christian Passion, King marched, and was later held to be in contempt of court. Because of the collateral bar rule, King was not allowed to put in issue the injunction's unconstitutionality, and the Supreme Court upheld his conviction for contempt, even though it would hold the city ordinance patently unconstitutional just two years later.[22]

The collateral bar rule is an important procedural aspect of injunctions. But ex parte injunctions in the First Amendment area have subsequently been banned; and the Court has suggested that a "really" unconstitutional injunction does not merit the respect of the collateral bar rule (although it is hard to think of a more unconstitutional one than the Birmingham one). These rulings may provide wedges for doing away with the collateral bar rule. If it is abandoned, the procedural aspects of the law of prior injunctive restraint will have been tamed to conform to the law of subsequent punishments.[23]

## III

When prior restraints have undergone such radical procedural and substantive modifications, what about them continues to merit such a bad name? One answer is that the historic stigma deservedly applies to licensing schemes but not to injunctions, and that we mistakenly think "licensing" when we hear "injunction." For many in the press that is too true. But for others, including the Supreme Court, the reason for disdain of prior restraints is their ability to induce a special chill on expression.[24]

In his posthumously published book, Alexander Bickel expressed the chilling-effect rationale as well as anyone had: "Prior restraints fall on speech with a brutality and a finality all their own. Even if they are ultimately lifted they cause irremediable loss—a loss of immediacy, the impact, of speech. . . . A prior restraint stops more speech more effectively. A criminal statute chills, prior restraint freezes. Indeed it is the hypothesis of the First Amendment that injury is inflicted on our society when we stifle the immediacy of speech."[25]

Yet subsequent punishment chills, too. As we saw in Chapter 3, one of the most important aspects of *New York Times* was to reduce the chilling effect of the common law of libel to a constitutionally acceptable level. If the current disdain for injunctive prior restraints rests on a chilling effect, to make sense it must be on a chilling effect that is greater (or different) than that of a statute that would criminalize publication of the same information. The *Pentagon Papers Cases* provide a useful illustration. The telegram sent to the *Times* demanded that the paper stop publication because of the sensitive nature of the material and the fact that disclosure violated the Espionage Act. Assuming that the materials did violate the law, then those responsible—for instance, managing editor Abe Rosenthal—would be subject to a criminal indictment and the possibility of some years in jail. The *Times* published anyway. Then, when a federal judge on his first working day on the bench enjoined the *Times,* publication ceased—proof of Bickel's dictum that subsequent punishment only chills, whereas prior restraint freezes.

Why would the *Times* obey Gurfein but not Mitchell? One reason is that Bickel told them they had to comply with a court order; the *Post,* of course, complied with the Washington order. Much more interestingly, the leftish *Progressive* magazine also complied with an injunction and did not publish its article on how the H-bomb works while the injunction stood. These actions suggest that there is something genuinely special about a judicial order. It could be the certainty of punishment. If an injunctive prior restraint is violated, it is a very safe bet that someone will be held in contempt of court. But even beyond certainty of punishment, my guess is that respect for the judiciary and commitment to the rule of law cause most press litigants facing an injunction, from the top of the establishment down to the countercultural magazines, to comply. We are a society based on law, and even radicals have been indoctrinated with the view that judges are bastions of liberty, there to do justice by protecting everyone's rights.[26]

That possible criminal penalties did not deter the *Times* or the *Progressive,* but an injunction stopped them in their tracks until lifted, goes a fair length toward making the case for a special chill; but it does not go all the way. Despite these examples, there is much to be said for the chilling effect of criminal sanctions. After all, retribution may be the necessary response to failed deterrence, but the goal of the criminal law is nevertheless deterrence. When the criminal law works—as it does most of the time—it does so by deterring people from actions that they might otherwise attempt. Why else do we stop at traffic lights on uncrowded streets at night?

Erwin Knoll, editor of the *Progressive,* begins his discussion of being enjoined with Samuel Johnson's gallows humor: "Depend upon it, Sir, when any man knows he is to be hanged in a fortnight, it concentrates his mind wonderfully." For Knoll, being subject to an injunctive prior restraint "has much the same effect"; he paid close attention to the meanings of the First Amendment during the six months and nineteen days when he was "deprived of its full protection by court order." Knoll writes as if he is bearing witness to Judge Learned Hand's knowing statement: "I must say that, as a litigant, I should dread a lawsuit beyond almost anything else short of sickness and of death." For nonlawyers who have not experienced a lawsuit, it is probably impossible to grasp how correct Hand is. Litigation impresses itself on the lives of the parties, who find they think constantly about what is happening and rue their lack of control over the event that is shaping their immediate existence. Nor do the effects of litigation end with the lawsuit. Some parties are changed forever by the all-consuming focus of the lawsuit. Humorist John Henry Faulk was not the same even after winning his pre–*New York Times* libel action against those who caused his blacklisting during the McCarthy era. And more recently General William Westmoreland, as a result of his failed libel action against CBS, has seen his military career almost forgotten in his new incarnation as a lay expert on libel law, a mandatory presence on prestigious national panels.[27]

Knoll was enjoined, frustrated, but free (in all respects save one). "Journalists in particular," he wrote, "are swift to sing the First Amendment's praises and invoke its protections. I suspect, however, that few of us can appreciate the constitutional guarantee of freedom of speech and the press as fully as one who has been directed by a court [not to publish]." Heady stuff, but suppose instead that the government had not learned of the *Progressive*'s knowledge of how an H-bomb works until after publication. Unable to enjoin Knoll, the government would have indicted him under the Atomic Energy Act. Knoll bemoaned what he rightly found were high attorney's fees in fighting the injunction. His criminal defense would not have cost a penny less; in fact it would likely have run lots higher, because the ante had been upped and the full panoply of a jury trial would be irresistible. If Knoll had been convicted, he would have faced the prospect of several years in the federal penitentiary. What would he do then, pending appeal? What would he think? I strongly doubt he would find this period anywhere near comparable to the time the prior restraint controlled the *Progressive* and he enjoyed his days (rather than Andy Warhol's fifteen minutes) as a celebrity.[28]

Then, suppose that six months and nineteen days later, the trial judge granted a post-trial motion to vacate the conviction, thereby freeing Knoll. I can only guess, but I would expect that his psychological trauma during that period would have been geometrically higher than while he was enjoined. Losing the right to publish without prior appeal is one thing; but the prospect of losing all rights, especially that of freedom from confinement, is something else again, as Judge Warren also observed when enjoining the *Progressive*. That prospect truly focuses the mind.

Just because Abe Rosenthal and Erwin Knoll escaped prosecution does not mean that I have created a fanciful hypothetical. A few years after Knoll was freed from injunctive restraint, a civilian defense analyst for the navy, Samuel Loring Morison, grandson of the famous Harvard historian Samuel Eliot Morison, provided *Jane's Defence Weekly* with a satellite photograph of a new Soviet aircraft carrier under construction at a Black Sea base. The Soviets already knew about their aircraft carrier; so the harm to the United States could only lie in the demonstration of the capability of the KH-11 reconnaissance satellite that took the photos. Yet, as the United States knew, the technical manual for the KH-11 had already been sold to the Soviets by a real spy, former CIA agent William Kampiles. Nevertheless, Morison was tried, convicted, and sentenced to two years in jail for espionage; his conviction was affirmed, and the Supreme Court refused review. Shortly after Morison's conviction, CIA Director William Casey threatened the *Washington Post* with a criminal indictment after it published an article about "Ivy Bells," a program for monitoring Soviet communications that was allegedly compromised by former National Security Agency analyst Richard Pelton (whose espionage trial was then pending). The *Post* initially postponed the story, then ran an edited version after "Ivy Bells" was mentioned on NBC's "Today" program. Explaining the editing, managing editor Ben Bradlee said that "the highest authority in the land was telling us that we were about to commit a treasonous act. Even if you disagree with that, and I did, that's a red light you go through very slowly." As Bradlee noted, it gets pretty cold when the word *treason* is tossed around.[29]

Bickel's "freeze versus chill" point is pithy, technically correct, but ultimately misleading. At its core it rests on the empirically sound observation that, the *Times* in its *Pentagon Papers Case* notwithstanding, when the enforcing authorities focus on a specific party, that party is likely to become more inhibited than before. Bickel implicitly incorporates the realization that because injunctions appear less expensive than full-scale criminal prosecutions, government attorneys are more willing to use them. This may be true; but the criminal law can both chill, as it did for Bradlee, and freeze. Ask Morison. Bravado such as Knoll's is appropriate for the victor, but he would have been a different man with jail time; at a minimum, while incarcerated, it becomes impossible to roam the nation on the celebrity circuit. The effects of a judicial injunction are immediately appreciated, but when the chilling effect of real criminal sanctions is downplayed, it is possible to miss the important point. Stephen Barnett, the first to seriously challenge the equating of injunctions with prior restraints, placed the chilling-effect argument in perspective. "The pinpointed freeze of a narrowly drawn gag order might produce less refrigeration overall than the broader chill of threatened subsequent punishment, especially if the latter carried penalties or liabilities that were more severe." Both regimes will stop some speech, and there are no good empirical ways of knowing how much. Whatever other reasons there may be for disfavoring injunctive prior restraints, their supposed extra chilling effect ought not to be one of them.[30]

As presented so far in the discussion, prior restraints appear to have one important advantage over subsequent punishments. Assuming the material is harmful, the freeze of the prior restraints should keep the material cabined. Furthermore, unlike the criminal process, prior restraints find themselves (at least before appeal) on a procedural fast track where they not only may obtain efficient judicial review, but may do it before the injury that follows publication, and without the distraction of collateral issues that an experienced defense lawyer might offer to fog a jury's deliberations. Yet ultimately, except in the most unimportant situations, a prior restraint is futile. People can be enjoined. Information, photocopiers, computer disks cannot.

When Gurfein brought the *Times* to a halt, Ellsberg provided 4000 pages to the *Post*. When it, in turn, was restrained, Ellsberg made friendly with the *Boston Globe*. By the time the Supreme Court lifted the injunctions, original Pentagon Papers stories had appeared in the *Chicago Sun-Times,* the *Los Angeles Times,* the *St. Louis Post-Dispatch,* the *Christian Science Monitor,* and the Knight newspapers. Wondering about the efficacy of an injunction, one of the D.C. Circuit judges likened the judicial posture to "riding herd on a swarm of bees."[31]

The same held true with the H-bomb injunction. Howard Morland's article was in numerous hands by the time the government decided to enjoin it. Although Morland was ordered to retrieve all copies, such orders are much like the Utah law forbidding the Great Salt Lake to exceed set boundaries. They work only in times of tranquillity, preferably with an agreed-upon snowfall. Morland reports that friends and associates were contacted by the FBI, but he doubts that anyone turned over their copy of the article without first photocopying it. One copy was in the hands of someone calling himself "Spring Berg," who informed the *Progressive* that he had the article, and if the Supreme Court affirmed the injunction, the article would "be on the streets the next day."[32]

Furthermore, Chuck Hansen, a computer programmer whose hobby was collecting information on H-bomb design, was worried about how the case might affect his hobby. While everyone was preparing the argument in the Seventh Circuit Court of Appeals, Hansen wrote a long letter to Senator Charles Percy, whose Subcommittee on Investigations was already looking into one leak; the letter described how Hansen believed an H-bomb worked. Although Morland asserts there were errors in Hansen's analysis, the government nevertheless classified his letter. Morland made two further observations: "Chuck Hansen had made it," and "Copies of the letter were multiplying like rabbits." Hansen's letter was arriving at newspapers, from the *Daily Californian* and the *Village Voice* to the *Chicago Tribune* and the *Oakland Tribune*. The *Daily Californian* got enjoined; the *Chicago Tribune* said that unless it, too, got enjoined it would print the letter. Finally, the *Madison Press-Connection* made the whole question of injunctions moot by hitting the street with a twelve-thousand-copy special extra edition containing the letter. The government then requested that the *Progressive* case be dismissed; and Morland's article became available for comparison with the quite similar discussion in the *Encyclopedia Americana* by Edward Teller, the father of the H-bomb.[33]

It is theoretically possible that the entire American press might be enjoined. But as live broadcasts from Moscow, Beijing, and Pretoria make clear, we live today in a global communications network. Consider the fiasco in Great Britain when the Thatcher government attempted to block *Spy Catcher,* Peter Wright's book about MI-5, its probable mole (whom he believes to have been Roger Hollis, the head of MI-5 from 1956 to 1965), and the plot of a group of MI-5 officers to destabilize the Labour government of Harold Wilson. *Spy Catcher* was, of course, published in the freer air on the western side of the Atlantic; and prior to Thatcher's throwing in the censorial towel, Her Majesty's subjects could and did acquire it abroad and bring it home. Similarly, at least one copy of Morland's article was taken to Australia prior to the case, and although it was not published, it was well enough known that, after the injunction, the *Honolulu Advertiser* ran a story headlined: "H-bomb Secret Comes Up Down Under." There are obvious lessons there. Does anyone doubt that Ellsberg would have been willing to go to Canada, France, or Sweden to obtain publication of the Pentagon Papers?[34]

Suppose, however, that there was some reason to believe that national security information could be caged by enjoining a manageable number of people. If the injunction is justified, that means the information is dynamite—substantial harm is certain to follow its release. If that is the case, how can we be sure those enjoined will not slip—accidentally, or worse, intentionally? The possibility of substantial certain harm demands more than an injunction. Would surveillance, both electronic and personal, be sufficient? If the information is that awesome, what does that say about risks and risk aversion? If we really think someone has decided to tell all the world's terrorists how to bring the United States to its knees, are we likely to believe that a federal court order saying "behave" will lead to a change of heart? If the person with the information would publish it absent the prior restraint, are we really willing to let her roam, pretending to be secure in the knowledge that her faith in the rule of law will prevent the information from circulating?[35]

This is not to argue that all injunctive prior restraints are futile. The more closely controlled the information, the more establishment-oriented the newspaper, the more likely an injunction will be obeyed. But with national security, where information, politics, and tempers get hot, getting an injunction is probably the easy part; preventing alternative publication is the impossible challenge, a point now underscored by Knoll's conclusion that it was a mistake, not to be repeated, to obey the injunction.[36]

The ironic counterpoint to the futility of the government's seeking an injunction in the mistaken belief it will work is the fact that injunctive litigation may best serve the interests of the press, not the government. Over sixty years ago, Professor Edwin Borchard, who tirelessly championed adoption of the Federal Declaratory Judgment Act, argued to a Senate committee that a civil rather than a criminal action should be available to test citizens' belief that they have a perfect constitutional right to do what a statute appears to prohibit. "Into this dilemma no civilized system operating under a constitution should force any person." A civil action could provide the twin benefits of determining where the constitutional boundary on disclosure of classified information lies, and of eliminating the uncertainty surrounding criminal sanctions. After consideration, the *Times* went forward with the Pentagon Papers story; the *Post* watered down "Ivy Bells" to avoid prosecution; maybe the latter course would not have been necessary.[37]

The civil-liberties basis of the proposed civil action is apparent in the Supreme Court's revolutionary 1965 decision in *Dombrowski v. Pfister,* authorizing injunctive relief against prosecutions where those in Borchard's dilemma claim that the statute under which prosecution is threatened chills their First Amendment rights. Six years later, a counterrevolution prevailed in *Younger v. Harris,* and a constitutional claimant's ability to enjoin enforcement of an unconstitutional criminal statute all but vanished (although the Court subsequently agreed that a declaratory judgment action would be available). For a decade thereafter, the nation's law reviews mourned *Dombrowski,* in an unmatched display of sympathy for an abandoned case, as an essential aspect of civil liberties.[38]

Although there are intriguing parallels between injunctive prior restraints and *Dombrowski,* it would be craziness to assert a successful fit. First, risk aversion among constitutional claimants varies not only between different people, but for the same person over time. The Reagan administration, with its demonstrated willingness to initiate Espionage Act prosecutions, looked more scary to Bradlee and the *Post* than the preplumbers Nixon administration did. (And, of course, "Ivy Bells" was not quite history.) The constitutional right at stake does, after all, belong to the citizen; and if the citizen wishes to exercise it and risk later criminal litigation, we should be wary of the argument that we, or a government attorney, better comprehend the individual's own best interests. As Paul Cohen's jacket illustrates, when First Amendment claims are at issue, speakers and writers have intense desires to communicate what they believe. At times, and the Pentagon Papers situation appears to be one—although street demonstrations are by far and away the best example—the important thing is to seize the political initiative and attempt to change the status quo. Legalities or not, King was right to march on Good Friday, and failure to march, even with a successful appellate vindication, is not the same thing.[39]

All of this said, if the rule against prior restraints cannot be supported by more than what has been discussed, then maintaining it because of a historic stigma is an expensive proposition for society. Injunctive prior restraints may be futile, but as the discussion stands, the reasons for special disdain have seemingly eroded. Yet if the stigma on prior restraints becomes eroded, might not judges begin to overuse them?

## IV

Overuse necessarily means misuse, which can create effects, if not results, much like the chilling effect. In the most persuasive modern defense of the traditional disdain for prior restraints, Vincent Blasi writes that because injunctive prior restraints are predictive—"adjudication in the abstract"—the risk aversion of judges becomes an important determinant of whether the reliance on injunctions will be excessive.[40]

Will judges behave differently in prior-restraint cases—because they are predicting rather than reviewing—as Blasi believes? Other perceptive commentators suggest no. John Jeffries observes that Blasi relied on literature from an earlier era, less protective of the First Amendment, and that the same judges who would decide whether to order a prior restraint would also decide the subsequent punishment. Martin Redish asserts that abstractness would only matter "if the court were to assume the possibility of more harm than would actually have occurred." But Redish assumes an unrealistic perfectionism in judges; his judiciary consists of nothing but honorable lawyers who never err. Would that his assumptions were valid. But even if they are not, we ought to realize that predictions are not exclusively a problem of prior restraints. Thus in *Dennis v. United States,* the major Smith Act trial involving the Communist party leadership, Chief Justice Vinson announced that self-preservation was an ultimate value and there was ample reason to strike at the party now; Justice Douglas properly responded that the Court was quivering from the threat of the Red Army, not of the Communist party in the United States; and Justice Jackson equally properly noted that there is no way to predict accurately the effects of a seditious conspiracy. Mistakes may occur in any context. What matters is whether they are likely to occur more in issuing injunctions before the harm occurs than in litigation afterward; and Jeffries and Redish doubt it.[41]

Blasi, Jeffries, and Redish each discuss the full array of prior restraints; my focus is exclusively on press defendants. This narrower focus helps, although, as with the chilling-effect analysis, any conclusion is necessarily speculative. Knowing how actual situations have been resolved also helps. Thus to flesh out the issues I will discuss three additional cases beyond *Near*, the *Pentagon Papers Cases*, and *Nebraska Press Association*.

First, let us return to the gender discrimination of *Pittsburgh Press Co. v. Pittsburgh Commission on Human Relations*. Enforcement by cease-and-desist orders is part of the standard drafting of local civil rights laws, and Pittsburgh's was no exception. If the *Pittsburgh Press* had refused to hire women or minorities, no one would think the First Amendment violated by an order to cease and desist from such unlawful discrimination. By chance, the *Pittsburgh Press*'s violation took the form of gender-based formatting of its want ads. Once it is judicially established that demanding legally conforming headings is not a substantive violation of the First Amendment, does it matter that enforcement is by a cease-and-desist order rather than a fine? I have seen no one come forward, copy of the *Pittsburgh Press* decision in hand, to announce "this is the dreaded prior restraint." The cease-and-desist order, issued as a result of prior adjudication, is the functional equivalent of subsequent punishment in an area, illegal commercial speech, where the tie between expression and criticism of government policies is close to, or is, nil.

Next consider *Seattle Times v. Rhinehart*, a libel action by the head of the Aquarian Foundation, a "spiritualist Church" believing in the "ability to communicate with deceased persons through a medium," who had been unflatteringly portrayed in newspaper articles and whose donations had begun to decline. During pretrial discovery (forced production of materials requested by the other side) the *Seattle Times* wanted to see financial statements and membership lists, information that it could never otherwise expect to acquire. Rhinehart was in the unenviable position of producing the evidence or losing his opportunity to prevail in his libel action. He chose to produce the material but then got a protective order from the Court prohibiting disclosure by the newspaper defendant. Under these circumstances it is appropriate for a trial judge to prohibit the newspaper from using any discovery-acquired information for any purpose other than litigation. It is not surprising that the Supreme Court was unsympathetic to the complaint by the paper that the prohibition violated its First Amendment rights. The protective order operates as a prior restraint, but if a court could not impose it, discovery could operate as a state-sanctioned illegal search and seizure—which would discourage civil litigation against the press.[42]

With the *Progressive*'s H-bomb article, the stakes really go up. When asked at the *Times*'s oral argument in New York to give an example justifying a prior restraint, Bickel offered as an example the situation where the "hydrogen bomb turns up." He was not alone. Ellsberg, among others, felt Morland's quest to write about the technical aspects of the H-bomb was irresponsible and likely to assist countries not noted for their peaceful inclinations. The government agreed with that wholeheartedly, and from the bench Judge Robert Warren stated that he would have to think "a long hard time" before he gave "the hydrogen bomb to Idi Amin" (today it would be Saddam Hussein). Yet Morland had no access to classified information; he worked only with available library materials and interviews. This was irrelevant under the government's theory, which is that all information about the atomic technology is "born classified" and can only be revealed if the government declassifies it. Although the establishment press initially screamed editorially at Knoll and Morland, it reluctantly fell into line to protest the prior restraint. What made the injunction against publishing jarring was, first, the assumption that the human imagination can be cabined— Morland once mumbled, "I think the government wants to classify the inside of my head"—and, second, the reluctant realization that discussions about H-bombs in the nonscientific press, however irresponsible they seem, may be intended as policy discussions. Indeed it is hardly surprising to learn that Morland is a unilateral disarmament activist, one who believes a faulty Pentagon computer is more likely to set off a hydrogen bomb than "Pakistan or Peru."[43]

Leaving aside the tremendous change in the substantive content of the First Amendment since *Near*, *Pittsburgh Press* and *Nebraska Press Association* remain importantly different from *Progressive, Inc.*, or the *Pentagon Papers Cases*. Once the *Pittsburgh Press*'s gender-based want ad headings are ruled (a) illegal under the ordinance and (b) not protected by the Constitution, there is nothing left to argue over. Whether enforcement is by cease-and-desist order, with a fine as the likely penalty for noncompliance, or by criminal prosecution, also with a fine as the likely penalty, there is no issue left for the newspaper to litigate. And the penalties are functionally the same: the prior adjudication has operated fully as a subsequent-punishment trial would; and predictive consequences are irrelevant, because the rule of decision—illegal commercial speech banned—operates without regard to the actual consequences of expression. Maybe the case demonstrates that at the margins, even the supposed bright-line boundary between prior restraint and subsequent punishment becomes blurred.

*Nebraska Press Association* may be something else again. The prior-restraint analysis wholly obscured the outrage of telling a newspaper it cannot write truthful information derived from material lawfully in its possession about a crime of immense public concern. The order forbidding publication could never have withstood a constitutional challenge even if it had been in the form of subsequent punishment. Although *Nebraska Press Association* stands alone at the Supreme Court level, it may be unfortunately typical of a subterranean stratum of cases, where a trial judge issues a quick temporary injunction, only to lift it (or have an appellate judge do so) almost immediately. Even allowing for the large number of misclassified cases under the heading of "Prior Restraint," the magazine of the Reporters Committee for Freedom of the Press reports more than the occasional prior restraint issuing, if only for a few hours. Under these circumstances, a prior restraint would prove easier to obtain than subsequent punishment—for the simple reason that the latter is generally impossible to obtain. This would stand the old prior-restraint doctrine on its head; but to the extent that it may apply to some temporary injunctions, it is genuine support for maintaining the stigma on prior restraints.[44]

Situations like those in *Nebraska Press Association, Rhinehart,* and *Pittsburgh Press* are not likely to involve risk aversion. Once the applicable rule of constitutional decision is settled, there is every reason to assume, with Jeffries and Redish, that the decision, whether by prior restraint or subsequent punishment, will come out the same; there is no attempt to guess about the harm from the publication. It is different, however, in the national security area.

Let us look at procedure, especially speed, once again. The *Progressive* did not have the clout for a judicial-speed-of-light track, as the *Times* and the *Post* did, but the trial phase was fast enough. The government obtained a temporary restraining order precluding publication pending a hearing, which was held a week later, with an injunction then issuing. Criminal cases cannot go anywhere near that fast, and no defense attorney would allow it. Furthermore, the bulk of the expert witnesses—a necessity in national security cases—are, in one way or another, on the government payroll and easily obtainable by the government. Not so the defense witnesses. Even from supposedly sympathetic scientists around the nation, the "answers ranged from polite demurrals to outraged refusals," although eventually the *Progressive* found someone who would cooperate. The *Post* in the Pentagon Papers litigation was incredibly lucky that it had George Wilson in the courtroom, able to respond to Admiral Gayler's supplemental affidavit about the cable that allegedly revealed code-breaking capabilities, by recalling that the cable had already been published. But generally in a contest of affidavits, the prestige of high government officials is hard to beat.[45]

Finally, in some cases the government may feel compelled to "do something now," and a prior restraint, despite its inevitable bad publicity, is probably not going to generate as much bad publicity as prosecuting and jailing editors would; further, it is likely to be the most economical way of meeting the need for immediate action. Recall that neither Morland nor Knoll nor the others who published H-bomb information were ever indicted, despite confident assertions that they had violated the Atomic Energy Act. I am not sure to what degree, but in a fast-tract national-security injunction case, the government has advantages that can be maximized by speed and therefore may be peculiar to prior-restraint litigation. It may be that the heavy presumption against prior restraints then counters the government's initial advantages. If so, the decisive fact will be how the dynamics of the litigation affect the judges.

Let me begin with Gurfein's response to the government request for an injunction. When the *Times* would not voluntarily halt, Gurfein issued his temporary injunction so that he could find out what was at issue. He then held a hearing and decided the government had not made out its case. On appeal, the Second Circuit Court of Appeals determined that the government should get another chance to prove its case. In Washington, although the *Post* prevailed, the outcome before the DC Circuit Court of Appeals might well have been different had it not been for Wilson's memory. Yet amazingly, Wilson was needed because the government was adding materials on appeal. The very idea that one of the parties should be able to bring forth new evidence in an appellate court is foreign to our system of adjudication; had it been a criminal case, the government would not have been able to supplement the evidence in this way. The behavior of the Fourth Circuit Court of Appeals in Marchetti's battle with the CIA was similar. Despite not having heard the evidence, and therefore not being able to test credibility, the Fourth Circuit decided that the trial judge had been wrong in disbelieving the deputy directors of intelligence. Unable to do this directly, the Fourth Circuit erected a presumption that it then found had not been overcome. Whether in *Marchetti* or the New York phase of the *Pentagon Papers Cases,* had the litigation been criminal, a ruling for Marchetti or the *Times* could not have been touched on appeal. Only the fact of its being civil litigation gave the government a second chance. Furthermore, especially in the Second Circuit's ordering Gurfein to hear the government again, there appears to be present a significant factor of risk aversion. Erroneously deciding in favor of the press could harm all of us.[46]

Risk aversion was right up front in the *Progressive* litigation. Judge Warren's opinion stated that a "mistake in ruling against the United States could pave the way for thermonuclear annihilation for us all. In that event, our right to life is extinguished and the right to publish becomes moot." This statement illustrates what the more generalized discussions of prior restraint in the literature overlook, that the dynamics of prior-restraint litigation moves the decision on whether to publish from the newspaper editor to a judge. With the movement of the decision to publish necessarily comes some movement of the responsibility for consequences. Warren's statement could not be more explicit about his own risk aversion, and part of that comes from his view of consequences. The day he granted the temporary injunction he took responsibility for the consequences of publishing. The issue was not whether the *Progressive* or Morland would give irresponsible third-world countries the secret, it was that Warren would have to think a long hard time before—in his words—"*I gave* the hydrogen bomb to Idi Amin." At trial he would learn that Idi Amin's Uganda lacked the necessary industrial capabilities to build the H-bomb; but the same could not be said of Iran, Iraq, Pakistan, and the Koreas. I do not know how others would decide, but—with a caveat about the ineffectiveness of injunctive relief, already mentioned—I do not find Warren's decision surprising.[47]

Judges are not editors; judges are used to deciding post hoc; and the posture of a national-security prior restraint forces guesses about the unknown future. If the consequences are as grave as in *Progressive,* what do we expect? And if Ellsberg would not publish, why should a federal judge? Yet Morland believes that discussions of nuclear disarmament necessarily favor the government by their abstract quality, whereby listeners may find the effects beyond comprehension because the bomb is beyond comprehension. Those who argue that there is no social value in information that the Supreme Court might find unprotected are wrong. Whether or not Morland's information could constitutionally be punished does not necessarily affect its value in debate; and at a minimum, as Morland fully grasped, Morland's being able to explain how an H-bomb works gives him a more authoritative voice in the public debate than he otherwise could have had.[48]

A central tenet of those who query the need for a ban on injunctive prior restraints is that the same judges will behave similarly in prior-restraint and in subsequent-punishment situations, a circumstance belied by actual behavior in the cases. Furthermore, the psychology of the situation may become wholly reversed in the criminal case if the judge believes the issues are close. In a prior-restraint case, the judge will not want the responsibility for the consequences of publication. In a subsequent-punishment case, the judge may not want the responsibility for sending an editor to prison. It is myopic to assume that the dynamics of prior-restraint litigation will have no distorting effects on the process. Such an assumption slights the great insight of *Speiser v. Randall:* that in litigation, error inevitably occurs—and an error in issuing an injunctive prior restraint will prevent the information from entering the public debate. It is equally myopic to assume that no worthy speech can be prosecuted; it is not clear that the details of "Ivy Bells" or of how an H-bomb works are not worthy speech—even if divulging the information would subject the authors to criminal sanctions.[49]

## V

Blackstonian prior restraints, as *Near* demonstrates, were tightly intertwined with the law of seditious libel. Citizens must have the right to question government. In barring prior restraints, the focus properly is on the legitimacy of dissent. *Near,* in fact, contains Hughes's powerful passage about the need for a vigilant and courageous press to expose corruption in the great cities—a too-frequent accompaniment of the "Noble Experiment" of drying out America. The *Saturday Press*'s attacks may have been scurrilous, but underneath they rubbed at reality.[50]

Nevertheless, the Supreme Court's move from policy to law began the blurring of the doctrine of prior restraint. *Near* tied the appropriateness of a prior restraint into the appropriateness of subsequent punishment; and with that tie, the doctrine began to lose its intellectual coherence and started down the path to its current mode, where sophisticated First Amendment scholars hold that deterring unprotected speech is appropriate because the rules of subsequent punishment have defined that speech as lacking in value. The press, on the other hand, remains committed to the view that prior restraints are anathema. When the *Progressive* case exploded, the press was very edgy, both because it feared a huge defeat and because of quite commendable beliefs that internal restraint is appropriate. The dynamics of prior restraint, as that case illustrates, offers evidence that the press's reflex loathing of prior restraints may be more on target than the more sophisticated questioning of the need for a modern bar on the use of prior restraints.

Bickel's hydrogen-bomb hypothetical turns out not to be the example of a needed prior restraint, but rather the key case demonstrating that reasons to be wary of prior restraints still exist, even though the supposed chilling effect has receded into insignificance. While the *Progressive* was a highly charged case—often characterized as "how to build an H-bomb" (rather than how an H-bomb works, a subtle but important distinction)—there is little reason to believe it is atypical on the issue of injunctive prior restraint in the area of national security. The government's first reaction is horror. It then more successfully marshals its experts, while the defense's begin to pull away. Before a judge, the government can magnify the potential harm to the national interest (and it is, after all, our government). We are all patriots, said Gurfein. There is "no plausible reason why the public needs to know the technical details about hydrogen bomb construction to carry on an informed debate," said Warren. Why not write the article as a patriot, removing the offending information?[51]

Morland thought Knoll was a typical lefty mush-head who uttered slogans without substance. Morland wished to be different. His possibly overstated point is that technical information is essential. It demystifies the H-bomb, makes it imaginable, thinkable—like a gun. Furthermore, it allows one to join debate as an equal, where the government's official position—"national security does not permit us to explain the deep ways" to those of you questioning us—is eroded. Technical sophistication adds persuasiveness to political argument—although there may be debate on how much it adds—and Morland will be more effective than Knoll on issues of unilateral disarmament.[52]

In an era where military spending and military preparedness dominate our national agenda, we should recognize the relationship between Morland's article and the ability to challenge government. Edward Teller had published on the H-bomb workings, and the *Progressive* subsequently learned that the best diagram of an H-bomb appeared in a 1976 issue of Lyndon LaRouche's US Labor Party newspaper, *New Solidarity*. It was when similar facts came out in an article questioning national policy that the government acted. Although the government would reply that it is not the questioning, but rather how Morland questioned, the similarity of that response to the Wilson administration's response to its war critics (detailed at the end of Chapter 2), is not only intriguing, it is telling. If Morland violated the law by acquiring information legally and then sharing it, his criminal trial would be interesting indeed.[53]

Contrary to his obligatory public assertions, Knoll actually wanted the *Progressive* to be enjoined, because of the media attention. Nevertheless, by channeling Bickel's hypothetical as an actual prior restraint rather than as a criminal action, the *Progressive* reinforced the reasons for a special hostility to prior restraints. Information, even that which legal rules deem of no value, is essential to public debate and potential change. There is, as Blasi remarked in a somewhat different context, a "common tendency to find virtue in the status quo." The need to challenge the status quo, and to do so on the citizen's rather than the government's terms, provides a continuing reason for a special hostility to prior restraints.[54]

Postscript, November 29, 1990: At least some of the foregoing was placed at issue by the temporary restraining order issued by a federal judge to prevent the Cable News Network from airing tapes it had been given containing telephone conversations between Manuel Noriega and his attorneys. CNN initially refused to comply and aired one of the conversations while the case moved first to the Eleventh Circuit and, following affirmance there, to the Supreme Court, where the Court rejected, as it had before in *Nebraska Press Association,* a request for expedited review.

Supposed harms from airing the tapes fall into two categories: impairing a fair trial or breaching the attorney-client privilege. The former is frivolous; a nation that can find jurors who never heard of Oliver North can do the same for Noriega. The attorney-client harms have more substance but still are speculative because (1) Noriega might be acquitted, (2) prosecutors might successfully isolate themselves from the disclosures, (3) the taped discussions might not have anything to do with what would eventually occur at trial, or (4) the tapes may discuss only things the government already knows, such as the identity of government witnesses. To be sure, the judge needed the temporary restraint to acquire a less speculative estimate of harm, but given the likely ambiguity of the harm, the Supreme Court's prior restraint jurisprudence ought to have precluded even the temporary order that let the trial judge review the tapes and decide for himself.

After the judge reviewed the tapes, he lifted his order and ended the unfortunate episode (subject to a possible contempt hearing for airing the one tape). His initial risk aversion was understandable: Noriega's trial will be the biggest case of his career. Nevertheless, CNN had acquired the tapes legally, did not prejudice the case, and added information to a continuing debate about the consequences of invading Panama. That is why editors rather than judges should decide whether to publish.

*Chapter Six*

# Access to Sources
# and Information

Highest in the pantheon of press heroes is James Madison, father of the Constitution and the press's favorite amendment. Fittingly enough, he also wrote one of the most powerful statements on the importance of a free press, one that has been quoted with fervor and regularity over the past two decades: "A popular Government, without popular information, or the means of acquiring it, is but a Prologue to a Farce or a Tragedy; or, perhaps both. Knowledge will forever govern ignorance: And a people who mean to be their own Governors, must arm themselves with the power which knowledge gives."[1]

The press can bask in the glory Madison reflected, albeit largely by failing to know, and therefore not needing to forget, that Madison was praising public education, specifically a liberal appropriation by the Kentucky legislature. Original context aside, however, Madison's apt merging of an informed citizenry and republican government speaks powerfully to the needs of both public and press. From the Radical English Whigs to modern Supreme Court justices, the essential relationship between the press, an informed citizenry, and the needs of self-government has been clear—for if the citizens are kept in the dark, they cannot make the essential choices postulated by democratic government, and as the Supreme Court recognized in the bicentennial decision of *Buckley v. Valeo*, "the people are sovereign."[2]

Both *Near* and *New York Times* were designed to facilitate the informed citizen's full participation in the country's governance.

Holding that truth as a defense was insufficient because of the potential chill on the "citizen-critic of government," *New York Times* resonated with Alexander Meiklejohn's view that in a democracy the citizens, rather than their elected agents, are the essential public officials. *Near,* of course, looked to ensure that government could not prohibit the publication of statements about its behavior, regardless of their truth.

Discussion of public affairs must be, as *New York Times* held, "uninhibited, robust and wide-open." But that is not enough. It must also be informed. Meiklejohn wrote that "when a free man is voting it is not enough that the truth is known by someone else, by some scholar or administrator or legislator. The voters must have it, all of them. The primary purpose of the First Amendment is, then, that all the citizens shall, so far as possible, understand the issues which bear upon our common life." In our modern society information is power, and the government has, for both proper and improper reasons, attempted to protect information, releasing it only when those in power deem its release to be in the national interest. A spectacular illustration occurred in the summer of 1989, when the B-2 Stealth Bomber went from never-seen and top secret to all over the news and congressional committees as the Bush administration attempted to persuade a skeptical Congress and public that any airplane could be worth over half a billion dollars a copy.[3]

In this context the willingness of others to supplement the official information—"handouts" is the pejorative—is essential. Obviously, Robert Woodward's "Deep Throat" and Watergate come to mind. But every Washington reporter attempts to keep a stable of happy sources, and this results in some blockbuster stories. Thus Seymour Hersh of the *New York Times* described in 1974 a large-scale CIA operation directed against the domestic antiwar movement, a disclosure resulting in major congressional hearings and restructuring of the agency. Two reporters for the *Chicago Sun-Times* broke the story of the Abrams M-1 battle tank fiasco: it could not go into most combat situations without an accompanying bulldozer to dig it in and out of protective ground cover. George Wilson, a decade after his brilliant courtroom display countering Admiral Noel Gayler's affidavit in the DC Circuit Court of Appeals, disclosed a $750-billion mismatch between the cost of the Reagan rearmament program and the amount the administration had yet requested from Congress. Rowland Evans and Robert Novak reported that American intelligence had discovered an immense radar system in Siberia that flagrantly violated treaty obligations to the United States. (Although many liberals thought this story nothing but right-wing propaganda, the Gorbachev administration actually confirmed the point.) And Woodward, in yet another coup, revealed that the Reagan administration's secret disinformation campaign designed to destabilize Muammar el-Qaddafi's regime was in fact deceiving the American public and our nation's allies. Without people on the inside willing to risk loss of their jobs in order to disclose such folly, none of these important disclosures might have occurred.[4]

Meiklejohn, and more recently Thomas Emerson, with their emphasis on the public as sovereign, properly focus on the need for the citizen to have relevant information—such as Hersh, Wilson, Woodward, Evans and Novak, and others are constantly providing through their unauthorized access to information the government would rather keep secret. This, in turn, has powerful echoes at the Supreme Court, where Justices Stevens and Powell have stated that "without some protection for the acquisition of information about the operation of public institutions the process of self-governance contemplated by the Framers would be stripped of its substance." The rhetoric is powerful; for better or worse, however, it far outstrips reality.[5]

The rhetoric speaks to individual decision making. But the reality, both in fact and by the express language of various provisions of the Constitution, is that decision making in our democracy is placed in the hands of our elected representatives and their appointees. There is a powerful claim that the elected representatives need all essential information before they can decide intelligently; but rhetoric aside, that claim attenuates considerably, although it does not vanish, when it is applied to the voters. Furthermore, the problem is compounded when the elected representatives, who have the necessary information, come to the conclusion that the information, if disseminated, would be harmful to the nation. Why should a lone unelected citizen who happens to have access to the information be allowed to impose a contrary decision?

*Near* answered the question about whether a newspaper with

information could publish. It assumed, as do all true prior-restraint cases, that punishment might appropriately follow. In this chapter, that assumption will be further questioned. In addition, since information does not simply grow and wait to be harvested, we will look at two essential means of gathering it: access to places and cultivation of people.

## I

Although presidents have often perceived the fact as an unfortunate failure, the United States, unlike Britain, has no Official Secrets Act. Publication of government information, even if properly classified, is not an offense per se under the criminal laws. As we saw in Chapter 2, President Wilson sought such a provision during World War I, but Congress refused to adopt it. Only with the Atomic Energy Act of 1954 (which Knoll and Morland were threatened with) and the Intelligence Identities Protection Act of 1982 has Congress adopted statutes specifically criminalizing mere publication of specified information. More general laws were proposed late in the Eisenhower administration, again by Senator Stennis in 1962, and most recently in the mid-1970s overhaul of the Criminal Code; but all failed. As former CIA Director William Colby testified, Congress "has drawn a line between espionage for a foreign power and simple disclosure of our foreign policy and defense secrets, and decided that the latter problems are an acceptable cost of the kind of society we prefer."[6]

Colby's observation correctly treads the line of constitutional power. Few would argue, and no court would likely agree, that there is a First Amendment right to disclose secret information. Yet disclosure—leaks—is a way of life in the nation's capital. There seems general agreement that without leaks it would be impossible to understand government, especially diplomacy and national security. Congress has the power to prohibit disclosure, but except in a few specified categories it has refrained from exercising that power.

While the previous two paragraphs are correct as far as they go, they unfortunately do not go far enough in describing the Criminal Code. Begin with the realization that theft of government property—conversion, in legalese—is obviously a crime. Indeed, the specific section of the Code, section 641, makes it a crime to take "anything of value." Might that not include photocopying a document? And of course, however nice leakers are, we take a rather dimmer view of those leaking to a foreign power; we label their actions spying, which is prohibited by section 794 of the Espionage Act. Its companion section, 793, goes considerably further, prohibiting disclosure to any unauthorized person. This might at first glance appear to be an Official Secrets Act, but section 794 is aimed at the leaker, not those who publish. Finally, we should not forget regulations, like those of the CIA, which preclude those with access from disclosing information without permission.[7]

These statutes and regulations, either separately or, more likely, in combination, might prove effective, not in stopping all leaks, but in deterring some. Furthermore, they at least offer the government an additional hunting license, complete with an opportunity to make an example of the unlucky quarry. In upholding the CIA secrecy contract, the Supreme Court stripped Snepp of all his profits from his book. If he and the thousands of others who have signed such contracts wish to leak, it will likely be "for free"— which means to newspapers rather than book publishers.

At the instant the leakers move from books to newspapers, they meet Morison, the defense hawk who was convicted of espionage and theft. Morison, of course, was no spy, and therefore section 794 was not applicable. But he did provide copies of a defense briefing and a satellite photo to *Jane's Defence Weekly*. His conviction was affirmed under both section 793, because whoever received the copies was necessarily unauthorized to do so by the US government, and section 641, because what he did was technically—and more important, legally—conversion.

As it has steadfastly done in this area, the Supreme Court ducked and refused to review Morison's case. Had it decided to review the case, it could have interpreted the statutes as not reaching leakers; or it could have, and my guess is would have, affirmed. In either event, the Court would not have created a First Amendment immunity from appropriately drafted legislation. It would only have dealt with the question of whether Congress had properly authorized punishment of the action at issue. In *Haig v. Agee,* with emphasis on the importance of national security, the Court had sustained stripping an ex-CIA agent of his passport because of his consistent efforts to disclose the identities of agents in the field. The result and reasoning of *Haig* are broad enough to sustain the subsequently adopted Intelligence Identities Protection Act.[8]

Reality prevents the conclusion that the leakers have a First Amendment right to disregard legislative determinations of when confidentiality is necessary—not to mention the betrayal of the trust whereby they obtained access to classified information. Leakers cannot be laws unto themselves. Society has rights, too, and one of those must be the right to demand faithfulness in those it trusts. In so doing it provides important incentives for those in government to respect secrecy, at least when their superiors wish the information kept private.

When secret information reaches the press, the line changes radically. As we have seen, *Near* and other cases virtually guarantee that the press may publish without fear of an injunction. More relevant, however, is what protections the First Amendment provides after the press has published. We know that Daniel Ellsberg was indicted for passing the Pentagon Papers to the press, and we know that the newspapers, despite some contrary bluster, were not indicted for publishing them. We know that Philip Agee lost his passport after he persistently identified CIA agents in the field (and today he would be subject to criminal sanctions); we do not know what will happen if a newspaper crosses that line. Maybe, in Laurence Tribe's apt phrase, there is a "rough 'law of the jungle'" at work, whereby the leaker is, if necessary, fed to the animals so that the newspaper will survive. It is vastly easier to understand that publishing information in your possession is an exercise of freedom of the press than that either pilfering documents or disclosing confidences in breach of trust is an exercise of freedom of speech.[9]

The easy constitutional rule would be that the press may publish all truthful information it noncoercively acquires, subject only to the laws of treason. But the Supreme Court, like Richard Nixon, has concluded that to do the "easy" thing would be "wrong." Despite upholding the press in every single "privacy" case and in other, noncopyright, contexts where it has published truthful information noncoercively obtained from government sources, the Court has avoided sweeping rules and has always assumed that somewhere down the line may lie a situation where the press ought not publish. Indeed, one might have thought the *Progressive* was such a case; but as with the publishers of the Pentagon Papers, nothing happened to either Howard Morland or Erwin Knoll.[10]

Three cases, *Landmark Communications v. Virginia, Florida Star v. B.J.F.,* and *Seattle Times v. Rhinehart,* are illustrative. In *Landmark Communications* and *Florida Star,* the newspaper published confidential information: the name of a judge involved in disciplinary proceedings in the former; the name of a rape victim (accidentally and against the newspaper's own policies) in the latter. Although the issue was the same in each case, the Court's analysis was different. In *Landmark Communications,* a criminal case, the Court held that Virginia failed to prove a clear and present danger from disclosure—and since disclosure would necessarily harm the judge, the implication of the holding is either that the harm was insufficient or that it simply could not be prevented by a sanction on the press. In *Florida Star,* a civil privacy case, the Court relied on its previous holdings regarding disclosure of the names of victims and juvenile offenders to invalidate the $100,000 in damages awarded the victim, because the paper had lawfully obtained the information through government disclosure. The decision recognized, as had *Landmark Communications,* that the state is in the best position to protect against disclosure through "careful internal procedures."[11]

*Florida Star* declined to rule that publication is protected so long as the material is truthful. The Court was uneasy about future cases—alluding, as always, to *Near*'s national security problem as well as to libel of private figures. Neither example seems as supportive of its holding as *Rhinehart,* where, as noted in the previous chapter, the Court held that information acquired through discovery during litigation cannot be published unless the information is also disclosed in open court. *Rhinehart*'s balance demonstrates that there are some circumstances where it is too unfair to allow the press to publish (without sanction) information that it has. And one could extrapolate from *Rhinehart* that if the press broke into a building and pillaged files—or planted bugs—and later published, then the publication could be taken as insult upon injury.

But these examples of coercive acquisition of information are a far cry from the issue, ducked ever since the *Pentagon Papers Cases,* of the press publishing information which was unlawfully taken by a third party (which at the federal level, because of section 641, may be just about everything). Nevertheless, looking at results rather than the reasons offered for them, the rough law of the jungle works fairly well; it precludes sanctions where the press did not coercively acquire the information, while leaving the potential deterrent of criminal penalties hanging as a very last resort. Justice Stewart, if not the Court, has suggested this approach; and past practice indicates that it ought to take a blockbuster disclosure— maybe "Ivy Bells" would have been it had Bradlee not caved— before sanctions against the press rather than against the actual source could be constitutionally permissible. But even then, the better rule would be that the press, but not the leaker, enjoys a First Amendment immunity to tell the public what its government is doing. Surprising as it may seem, my suggested better rule receives legislative support from the Intelligence Identities Protection Act of 1982. This law covers anyone (and therefore the press) who, "with reason to believe that such activities would impair or impede the foreign intelligence activities of the United States, discloses any information that identifies an individual as a covert agent"; but it has an important proviso: that disclosure be part of a "pattern of activities intended to identify or expose covert action." The proviso appears to limit the operation of the law to publications such as the *Covert Action Information Bulletin,* thereby leaving the regular press alone.[12]

## II

Saying the government must prosecute the leaker, not the press, might be a nifty Catch-22. What if the government does not know who the leaker is—and, obviously, someone at the newspaper does. What should the newspaper, or its reporter, do when the government asks "Who did it?"

The immediate response will be: protect the source. Imagine if Woodward had named "Deep Throat," the Watergate source without whom Richard Nixon would have been a two-term president. Had Woodward disclosed at any time, it is inconceivable that Potter Stewart (in Woodward's book, *The Brethren*) or William Casey (in *Veil*) would have opened for him the two most secretive agencies of government. Obviously, most reporters will never have Woodward's luck; yet all in the capital cultivate sources, and most government officials reciprocate, as they come to understand that culti-vating reporters may result in favorable coverage. Leakers typically view the press as a resource, and they leak for all sorts of reasons: glorifying their own importance; discrediting others; obtaining a credit to cash in later; and, most frequently, to influence, either positively or negatively, some policy. As Martin Linsky wonder-fully summed it up: "[Although] leaks have a negative connotation, one person's leak is another's profile in courage."[13]

The reasons are sufficiently diverse so that leaks are an everyday occurrence. Seemingly everyone leaks, although a recent study, whose author thought the figure understated, found that 42 percent of all senior government officials admitted leaking materials to the press. Statistics confirm the intuition that leaking is more prevalent now than it was fifteen years ago, and more prevalent then than fifteen years earlier. For the most part, leaking is without risk, because it is tacitly authorized, widespread, and generally not im-portant enough to result in an investigation. Even if the leak does matter and might get the leaker fired or worse, the confidential relationship between the reporters and their sources allows a leaker to deny being the culprit without fear of contradiction—unless the reporter can be made to talk.[14]

Even a court order could not get Marie Torre of the old *New York Herald-Tribune* to reveal her source. She may have been pro-tecting a confidential relationship and providing the public with much-needed information, but the news that CBS executives would not employ Judy Garland because of her drinking problems was definitely not the type of information Meiklejohn thought a democ-racy needs. The Second Circuit Court of Appeals, in an opinion by visiting Sixth Circuit Judge (and Justice-to-be) Potter Stewart, did not think so either. In Garland's defamation and breach-of-contract suit against CBS, Torre refused to name her source even when the judge ordered her to do so. She was held in contempt of court, served ten days, but remained silent. Torre's article was hardly a matter of national security; and it occurred well before the fruition of the symbiotic relationship between Washington reporter and government official. So, too, did the next few cases, all of which stayed in the state courts. Then in the early 1970s, with the re-porter-Washington-source relationship well in place, the issue of reporter's privilege—the legal right to maintain confidentiality without fear of punishment—came to the Supreme Court.[15]

It did not come from Neil Sheehan refusing to identify the already known Daniel Ellsberg or from Woodward hiding "Deep Throat's" identity. Indeed, it did not involve Washington, DC, national security, or foreign affairs at all. Instead, the cases involved the Black Panthers and the emerging drug culture. Earl Caldwell, a black reporter for the *New York Times,* had been transferred to San Francisco because the Panthers were becoming increasingly distrustful of white reporters, at least in part because FBI agents had posed as reporters. "Because the Panthers feel oppressed by established institutions, they will not speak with newspapermen until a relationship of complete trust and confidence has been developed—often slowly and meticulously." Caldwell managed to do that and as a result was able to write informative stories. Paul Pappas of a New Bedford television station had a one-shot relationship with the Black Panthers in their headquarters one night during what was euphemistically called "civil disorders." Pappas was allowed to come to Panther headquarters for an anticipated police raid, which he could photograph and report on as he wished; but he promised not to reveal anything should the raid never materialize—and it didn't.[16]

In between was the *Louisville Courier Journal*'s Paul Branzburg with his access to the central Kentucky drug scene. Branzburg's beat was the drug culture. Two of his articles, written fourteen months apart, detailed differing aspects. One described the profitable extraction of hashish from marijuana, wherein one of his sources opined he did not know why he was letting Branzburg do the story—"To make the narcs (narcotics detectives) mad, I guess." Correctly, as it turned out. In the other he attempted to provide a "comprehensive survey" of the "drug scene" in Frankfurt. In a two-week period, he interviewed "several dozen drug users" for the article.[17]

Caldwell was one of the few people who could provide hard information on the increasingly violent and beleaguered black militants, especially the Panthers. Over two dozen Panthers had been killed in shootouts with police. Yet, unlike the Student Nonviolent Coordinating Committee (Caldwell drew the parallel in one article), the Panthers had staying power in the ghetto; probably because, as Caldwell noted, they were from the ghetto and were going to jail one way or another in any event. At a time when Panther leader David Hilliard had stated in a public speech, "We will kill [President] Richard Nixon," Caldwell quoted him as saying the only solution to an oppressive government was "armed struggle." Caldwell's article also noted that in police raids caches of weapons, including high-powered rifles, had been found, because the "Panthers [had] picked up guns."[18]

All three reporters were called to testify before grand juries about the criminal activities of their sources. Pappas and Branzburg appeared and refused to testify. Caldwell did not even appear, categorically asserting, "If I am forced to appear in secret grand jury proceedings, my appearance alone would be interpreted by the Black Panthers and other dissident groups as a possible disclosure of confidences and trusts and would . . . destroy my effectiveness as a newspaperman." The establishment press, identifying with Caldwell, took his case as their own. Affidavits filed in his behalf and agreeing with his conclusions read like a who's who: Walter Cronkite, Marvin Kalb, J. Anthony Lukas, Dan Rather, Eric Sevareid, Mike Wallace. Whatever differences there might be in the cases, the Court tossed them together (and to the shock and dismay of the press, which had grown accustomed to "the Caldwell case," put them all under the name of *Branzburg v. Hayes*) and treated them as indistinguishable, even though Branzburg had clearly witnessed the commission of a crime, whereas Caldwell and Pappas had not.[19]

Forcing reporters to appear before a grand jury and disclose sources will necessarily deter some newsgathering. Some otherwise willing sources would not talk to a reporter if their identities could subsequently be learned, and some reporters would be unwilling to pledge confidentiality if it meant that they would be forced to choose between their promise and a personalized trip to jail (and as one of my colleagues teaches his students, if either you or your client is going to jail, make sure it is not you). Even the Department of Justice, seeking the information from Caldwell, agreed there would be a chill. But as the discussion of libel demonstrates, a chill by itself is only a starting place. The dispositive questions are how much of a chill? and how important are other, countervailing values?[20]

Justice White, for the majority, conceded the chill, but found its scope quite speculative; he appeared unwilling to give it much credence, especially after he granted that there was some constitutional protection for newsgathering and that the case was not about indiscriminate demands for disclosure. Because chills are always speculative, White's hostility to the argument seems out of place. Quite possibly it stemmed from the choice of argument made on behalf of the claim of privilege.

No one argued for an absolute privilege—a right not to disclose under any circumstances. The reason no one made this argument is that it was a sure loser. No rights are that absolute—including even the Fifth Amendment privilege against compulsory self-incrimination and the attorney-client privilege—and therefore to make such an argument would be a sign of unreasonableness. Unfortunately, the reasonable choice—contending for a qualified privilege, which could be overcome under certain (hard to achieve) circumstances—presented a different problem. The empirical basis for the privilege was that sources had to have up-front assurances that the reporter would not disclose their identities. This empirical claim logically leads to an absolute privilege. But the legal contention was that a qualified privilege would do; yet necessarily this would mean that a reporter could not give the guarantees that the empirical claim said a source would need. As the Court responded, "if newsmen's confidential sources are as sensitive as they are claimed to be, the prospect of being unmasked whenever a judge determines the situation justifies it is hardly a satisfactory solution to the problem." In fact, "only an absolute privilege would suffice"; and the press was eschewing that argument. With the empirical premise at war with the legal argument, the claim was in lots of trouble.[21]

Beyond finding the chill too speculative, the Court emphasized that what was at stake were grand jury investigations of criminal activity. The Court waxed poetic about the nature of grand juries (playing an "important" role in providing "fair and effective law enforcement aimed at providing security for the person and property"), the duty of all citizens (complete with a pre-Watergate footnote including within the term even the president) to give the grand jury their evidence, and a reminder that it was criminal conduct at issue. "Only where news sources themselves are implicated in crime or possess information relevant to the grand jury's task need they or the reporter be concerned." And if they are involved in criminal conduct, "their desire to escape criminal prosecution, while understandable, is hardly deserving of constitutional protection." Nor was the Court impressed by the idea that the press's duty should be deemed complete by bringing the issue to the attention of the authorities through publication. Embracing the world of action over that of contemplation, it wrote: "We cannot seriously entertain the notion that it is better to write about crime than do something about it."[22]

The Court ended by noting that "the administration of a constitutional newsman's privilege would present practical and conceptual difficulties of a high order." Who, after all, qualifies as a "newsman"? When should the privilege apply? What should be seen as a good enough reason to force the reporter to disclose? These, the Court opined, are questions better left to the legislature. The press, with its resources, ought to be able to take care of itself there.[23]

*Branzburg* is both unusual and transitional. It is unusual because the decision turned not so much on the Court's rejecting the constitutional claim that there was a need for confidentiality as its rejecting the remedy and doubting its own ability to fashion coherent rules in advance. Furthermore, *Branzburg* was a five-to-four decision, with three dissenters fully accepting the press position and Justice Douglas, in a fit of sheer mindlessness, willing to give the press a privilege so absolute the reporter need not even show up to claim it. And, above all, it was the case that began the press's transformation of Justice Powell into the Sainted Lewis (only a slight exaggeration) by the time he was to be replaced by the mephistophelean Robert Bork. Powell did surprisingly little in his first step toward beatification, writing a simple page-and-a-half concurring opinion "to emphasize what seems to me [as the deciding fifth vote] the limited nature of the Court's holding." He agreed the newsmen were "not without constitutional rights with respect to the gathering of news or in safeguarding their sources." What Powell asserted was that a "case-by-case" approach was the appropriate method of balancing the needs for information against the constitutional rights of the press. There was nothing inconsistent between Powell's separate opinion and that of White; hard and fast rules could be avoided, but in individual cases, when a source deserved protection, a judge might grant it.[24]

*Branzburg,* decided in June 1972, was doubly a transitional case. First, it is a precursor of the move from *Rosenbloom* to *Gertz,* toward applying different rules to public figures and to private individuals. Had the grand juries been seeking information from reporters about dealings with public officials, matching the facts of litigation with all-star supporting affidavits asserting that confidentiality helped the press gain information from government officials, the result might have been different. Second, *Branzburg* radiated a new skepticism about the creation of additional rights and the ability of the judiciary to administer them. Furthermore, the Court's administrative worries were not unrealistic.

Who should be granted the privilege? Tom Wicker, writing for the *New York Times?* Surely. Tom Wicker researching and writing a book about the prison riot at Attica? Hmmm. Tom Paine? History demands a yes. Everyone? Has to be no. Why Paul Branzburg and not Ralph Nader (who, after all, has proven an excellent investigator)? What about anyone writing eventually for publication? That is a good line, but what if the publication is entitled the *Cosa Nostra Ledger?* All of these questions are answered in some fashion by some administrative schemes that issue press credentials. But however much the Constitution supposedly follows the flag, does it also follow the credentials criteria for admission to presidential news conferences?

For the most part the press has not been concerned with the "who" questions, because those discussing reporter's privilege have always been secure in the knowledge that they would be covered. Because most reporters can instantly identify with the need for a privilege, the press has never reconciled itself to *Branzburg* and, naturally, has never stepped back to enjoy the irony that it would like to claim for itself a right it fully believed (and believes) should be denied to the president of the United States (because if Richard Nixon had had the complete presidential privilege he asserted, his tapes would never have been turned over to the Grand Jury or Congress). Illustratively, at the end of 1988 a reporter for the *Wall Street Journal* and a media lawyer wrote a law review article,

detailing the need for a privilege to protect confidential relation-
ships developed inside the Beltway. Yet not once, in an otherwise
impressive display of documentation, did they offer an example of
the actual need for a privilege in those circumstances. As Caldwell's
all-star group of supporters and that law review article demonstrate, it is easy to make a solid claim for the privilege. It is a lot
tougher, however, to show that it is needed, even in the key situation; and few reporters have even deigned to discuss how it might
work in the world beyond the Beltway.[25]

Speaking for too many journalists, Theodore H. White wrote
that "had the jurisprudence [requiring reporters to disclose sources
to criminal defendants because of the latter's Sixth Amendment
right of compulsory process] prevailed in 1974, the attorneys of
Messrs. Mitchell, Haldeman, and Ehrlichman could have demanded that Woodward and Bernstein give up their notes and so
reveal the identity/identities of 'Deep Throat' or go to jail." Although inelegantly put, White's point is that if *Branzburg* had
existed in 1974, then Woodward and Bernstein might have been
faced with jail time to protect "Deep Throat." White, whose grasp
of history is usually secure, ignores the elementary fact that 1972
occurred two years before 1974. Like others, he apparently cannot
remember that Watergate came after *Branzburg,* and yet the administration (which had both the incentives and propensities to do
so) never placed Woodward in a situation of having to choose
between some jail time and disclosure. That has always proven to
be the case, from Richard Burt's disclosure for the *Times* that
President Carter was about to cancel the neutron bomb (a leak
that undid the cancellation) to Leslie Gelb's disclosing, also in the
*Times,* that the United States had contingency plans for deploying
nuclear weapons in Canada, Iceland, Bermuda, and Puerto Rico,
though it had not informed the host governments of these plans.
Washington leaks, from Ellsberg's through Morison's, may be spectacular, but they do not result in reporters being told to disclose
their source on pain of punishment.[26]

The government leak situation properly worries the press. It
most directly affects the ability to provide information about what
government is doing in a context where the government has the
necessary resources to find criminal behavior without comman-

deering a reporter. The First Amendment should protect the press in these circumstances, but there are other foreseeable cases where blanket protection of the press would fail to take account of relevant interests mandating disclosure.

One foreseeable example takes us back to the first case of a claim of privilege, Garland's defamation action. Let us update the case to make it a little more contemporary. Suppose that the press prints a libelous story, assertedly relying on confidential information, which the public-figure plaintiff can prove is false. What is at issue is whether the paper printed the story with reckless disregard as to its falsity. If there is no source and the reporter just made it up, then the plaintiff will prevail. If there is a source, then the identity of the source may well open issues of the source's veracity, as well as issues of how much checking the reporter did. None of these issues can be addressed without knowing who the source is, and it is hardly surprising that judges in these circumstances (wherein the plaintiff has already made a substantial showing that the story is both untrue and defamatory) will conclude that the source must be named. For reasons I expressed in Chapter 4, the *New York Times* rules have proven inadequate; but as long as the courts are required to work within them, it is irrational to suppose that when a case arises such as I have outlined, reporters will not be forced to disclose.[27]

Thus far I have not addressed what will happen should the reporter refuse. Typically, as with Marie Torre, it will mean some jail time for contempt. The reporter can choose whether to disclose or go to jail. It is interesting to recall the comment of my colleague that if faced with a choice between you and your client, you'd better make sure it's not you who goes to jail. Reporters, either because of a different professional norm, or because circumstances force them to take their promises more seriously, will often make the non-lawyerly choice and go to jail themselves. As long as they are willing to do so, then sources can have some assurance of protection. The jailed reporter will always be released at the end of a criminal trial. In the case of a refusal to provide grand juries with information, the situation is more complex; but once a reporter demonstrates a determination not to divulge regardless of time spent in jail (which could go six to eighteen months), then imprisonment is typically terminated, because its purpose is to create an incentive, not retribution. Jail time is not fun; but it is not forever either.[28]

The situation is different, however, in libel suits. In such cases, if reporters refuse to name their sources, judges typically respond in the same way they respond to any failure to produce evidence—the jury will be instructed to presume that the evidence would be harmful to the nonproducing party. In these circumstances that means the jury will be told to presume the reporter had no source—and such a presumption is likely to be fatal to the paper's libel defense. This may prove to be another defect in libel litigation, quite similar to *Herbert v. Lando,* but until the current rules are changed it is all but inevitable. And it is fair: confidential information is often subject to forced disclosure in litigation, and many forced disclosures are more sensitive than the naming of a confidential source. One need only recall *Seattle Times v. Rhinehart* to note that the press plays a similar game, too, and that in appropriate circumstances protective orders may limit the ways in which disclosure may be used (thereby attempting to preclude retaliation against the source).

Another foreseeable situation is when a reporter may have evidence that would assist a criminal defendant (who is entitled by the Sixth Amendment to compulsory process for obtaining witnesses in his or her favor). In 1966 a number of mysterious deaths occurred in an Oradell, New Jersey, hospital. A decade later, on the basis of a letter stating that the chief surgeon of a hospital had murdered thirty to forty patients, *New York Times* reporter Myron Farber investigated the deaths and wrote several stories carrying the results of his investigation. An outgrowth of the stories was a murder indictment against Dr. Mario E. Jascalevich, who was charged with poisoning five patients. The defense naturally had a keen interest in Farber's investigation, since without Farber's stories the defendant would not have been facing such unhappy prospects. The trial judge issued a subpoena ordering Farber and the *Times* to produce Farber's notes and documents for the judge's inspection. When Farber and the *Times* refused, they were found in contempt, Farber eventually being jailed and the *Times* required to pay fines totaling $285,000.[29]

Farber's case was complicated by the fact that New Jersey had a so-called shield law, and the trial judge's order did not conform to the law. The New Jersey Supreme Court did not make matters any better. It ruled that before the shield law could be overcome, the trial judge must hold a hearing where the defendant must show that the material would be relevant for the defense and was not available from other sources. It then ruled that the failure to hold such a hearing in Farber's case was irrelevant, because if there had been a hearing Farber would surely have lost. The New Jersey court simply forgot that an elementary point of due process is that we do not conclusively presume that a person would lose at a hearing that has never been held. Furthermore, a reasonable construction of the shield law would be that the legislature had already decided that reporters' sources and notes require protection; if the defense needs them, the rights of the defendant and those of the reporter need not conflict, because both can be upheld by dismissing the prosecution.[30]

Having said all that, let us revisit Farber's case without the Shield Law. The claim then would be that the need for confidentiality is so important that Farber and the *Times*, and society, are willing to see Dr. Jascalevich wrongly convicted of murder (or wrongly freed— you choose) rather than disclose the information. The *Times* editorialized: "To betray one such source would jeopardize them all. How many reporters will be trusted to choose jail?" I have no answer for that question, but I can answer the unasked question about why Dr. Jascalevich should go to jail if Myron Farber is holding information that would set him free. The answer is quite simple: He should not. We live in a civilized society (even if reporters are not always civil), and it is not a high price to pay for that civilized society to require even unwilling people to testify for the accused in criminal cases, because that helps ensure that innocent people are not convicted.[31]

Farber understood press theory well. To protect his sources and information he went to jail for an indefinite period. He showed decidedly less interest in lawyering, expecting Jascalevich's defense counsel to accept his word that nothing he had could help the defense. It may be true, as Farber claims, that "a reporter has only so many tools with which to work." But a lawyer, whose client stands trial for murder because of the reporter's stories, does not have unlimited tools either. Even FBI material about confidential sources and wiretaps cannot be withheld from defense counsel, because, as the Supreme Court knows (and Farber rejects), only the lawyer can tell what is or may be useful and how it will fit into an overall judgment on the case. These determinations can be made only after seeing the data; they cannot, as Farber would have it, be made in advance. Although Farber makes nothing of it, an out-of-court exchange between him and the defense counsel is illustrative of the point. Farber tried to assure the defense counsel he was not in a conspiracy against Jascalevich. The lawyer responded, "Mr. Farber, I believe you. But maybe I have a larger perspective on the case."[32]

Forty days in jail behind him, Farber was released when the case went to the jury. Two hours of deliberation later—in what must approach a record for speed after an eighteen-week trial—the jury returned its verdict of not guilty. Four years later, Farber published a book on the Jascalevich case, and also on his case: "*Someone Is Lying.*" It ends with Jascalevich's statement that justice was done; but it is not clear that Farber thinks so.

An unanticipated aspect of the constitutional claim of privilege came years after *Branzburg,* when papers started "burning" sources—publishing confidential information after agreeing not to. In the case of William Casey and that of Potter Stewart, Woodward explained that "agreements of confidentiality cannot extend to or from the grave." In the case of Oliver North, *Newsweek* was incredulous when it heard North blast leaks during the Iran-Contra hearings and refer to the leak regarding interception of the airplane carrying the *Achille Lauro* hijackers as "very seriously compromising our national security." Maybe it did, but as *Newsweek* revealed, "the Colonel did not mention that details of the interception, first published in a *Newsweek* cover story, were leaked by none other than North himself."[33]

But suppose reporter and editor disagree on whether or not to maintain confidentiality? This occurred with an election-eve story in the Twin Cities, when the Democratic Farm-Labor ticket was running away with the race for governor and lieutenant governor. Republican operatives decided to leak newly discovered documents that the Democratic candidate for lieutenant governor had been convicted of shoplifting twelve years earlier. Editors at the *Minneapolis Star Tribune* and the *St. Paul Pioneer Press Dispatch* correctly decided the leak was a Republican dirty trick, and printed not only the story but the name of the confidential source who leaked to their reporter. As a result, the source was fired from an advertising agency where he was public relations director, and he sued the newspaper for breach of contract, that is, of the promise of confidentiality made by the newspaper's reporter. The press naturally believes that "ethical, not legal, considerations" should determine whether it is appropriate for a newspaper to burn a source. That position is strongly supported by the fact that it is an editorial decision to publish the name that triggers the complaint. Yet ethics and law are not so separate: inducing someone to provide material on a pledge of confidentiality and then violating the pledge, with significant harm to the source, is not behavior to be encouraged.[34]

Initially, two lower Minnesota courts ruled that each of the papers violated a valid contract and should pay for the harm it caused. The trial court went even farther and authorized an award of punitive damages on the basis that the promise was fraudulent. Because the action was for breach of contract, the courts held, the First Amendment was irrelevant. That conclusion is simply wrong, as a quick look back to Chapters 3 and 4 makes clear. A mere common-law label—"contract" rather than "libel"—does not make the Constitution disappear. Rather, just as in the judicial decision to force disclosure of sources, consideration must be given to the totality of factors. In the Minnesota case, the factors included that the source, a very experienced political operative, was inducing the promise of confidentiality without divulging the nature or datedness of the information; that he did not disclose to the reporters that he was spreading his story like shotgun pellets (because he feared some papers might not find it newsworthy and others might balk at the dirty-tricks quality); and that the Republican campaign was lying in denying its role in the disclosure. The Minnesota Supreme Court corrected the errors, holding there was no contract at all, and if there were it would violate the First Amendment.[35]

Burning sources, hiding behind fictitious sources in libel cases, withholding information to make it more likely a criminal defendant will be convicted—all in the name of freedom of the press. What the cases add up to—especially when there is no need to subtract an indictment for leaking classified information inside the

Beltway—is the wisdom of the Supreme Court's *Branzburg* decision. A general privilege to withhold would do neither the press nor
the public a service. Specially tailored decisions, reflecting both the
needs of a free press and the legitimate need to have access to a
reporter's information, will serve both press and public by allowing
a reporter to respect confidences in the vast majority of circumstances. *Branzburg* never held that the First Amendment did not
protect the relationship between reporter and source; it did hold
that not all confidences are of the same magnitude. Anthony Lewis
of the *Times* correctly wrote that "nothing in *Branzburg* or *Farber*
allows exposure for exposure's sake," and if there were any indication that a request for confidential information was based on the
desire to break the relationship rather than the desire to have the
information, then to enforce the request would be unconstitutional.[36]

## III

When Justice Stevens wrote that "without some protection for the
acquisition of information about the operation of public institutions the process of self-governance contemplated by the Framers
would be stripped of its substance," he was dissenting from the
Court's refusal to grant the press special access to prison facilities.
At a time when reports on prison conditions would create page-one
news against the desires of the captors, the Court was adamant that
the First Amendment could not open closed doors.[37]

The amazing outgrowth then became, not just closed prisons,
but closed judicial proceedings as well; in *Gannett v. DePasquale,*
the Court awarded its justice seal of approval to the practice. It held
that the Sixth Amendment's guarantee of a public trial belonged
not to the public, but to the defendants; they could, accordingly,
waive that guarantee if they thought it in their interests to do so.
*Gannett* held that such a waiver did not violate the First Amendment rights of either the public or the press, because the trial judge
properly assessed the competing interests when he concluded that
the defendants' right to a fair trial must prevail. As the defendants
argued, the "unabated buildup of adverse publicity" was simply
too much.[38]

Sounds like yet another sensational murder trial. And indeed it did have all the necessary ingredients: a bullet-ridden boat; a disappearance, but no body; and one of the two defendants being only sixteen and a juvenile under the laws of the state of capture. But the case was not big news everywhere. The *New York Times,* for one, ignored it.

Three friends had gone fishing on Seneca Lake near Rochester, New York. One never came home; five days later his two friends were found with his pickup truck in Michigan. On July 22, 1976, the Gannett morning and afternoon newspapers in Rochester, with a circulation of somewhat over 1000 in Seneca County (population 36,000), reported the arrest. There was a story each of the next three days: the arrestees' waiver of their right to challenge extradition to New York; their leading police to a buried gun; and their arraignment in Seneca County. A week later the papers carried two stories, one on the indictment and the other on the pleas of not guilty. That was it. Despite the great plot, there was no sensationalism; and only a single 1959 picture of the missing man, who had formerly been a policeman in a Rochester suburb, had been printed.[39]

The facts are such that the likelihood of a plea bargain seemed overwhelming—especially since 90 percent of all criminal cases are disposed of without trial. All that was needed was a preliminary hearing to determine whether the state would be allowed to use the defendants' confessions as well as the gun. The outcome of the hearing would determine the level of offense likely to be agreed upon in the plea.

That hearing came three months after the initial pleas of not guilty were entered. In that ninety-one-day period, not a word about the case appeared in the Gannett papers. Yet at the beginning of the preliminary hearing, the trial judge granted the defendants' motion to close it to the public. The hearing was held, and subsequently Seneca County maintained its perfect 1976 record of no criminal trials—the defendants pleaded guilty to lesser included offenses.[40]

Gannett's reporting did not represent anything out of the ordinary. These were not defendants who were being tried and convicted in the press. If Gannett could be excluded from this hearing, then probably the press could be excluded any time the parties wished and the trial judge agreed, even from the actual trial.

That, indeed, was Justice Rehnquist's point in a separate opinion. He felt the Supreme Court had quite properly given trial judges carte blanche to close their doors. Since the Sixth Amendment right to a public trial was personal to the defendant, no reasons whatsoever had to be shown for the defendant to obtain closure. Nor should First Amendment claims fare better. "It is clear that this Court repeatedly has held that there is no First Amendment right of access in the public or the press to judicial or other governmental proceedings." If the press was interested in a "sunshine law" it should look to the legislature, not the First Amendment.[41]

In what seemed an overnight transformation of practice, judges nationwide accepted the Court's offer and went behind closed doors to hear cases. In the year following *Gannett* there were 272 motions to close criminal proceedings, and well over half were successful. In the majority of cases, whether successful or not, trial judges treated the motion to close as nothing out of the ordinary and thus offered no reason for their grant or denial of the motion. Most motions, like that in *Gannett,* sought to close pretrial hearings (typically the dispositive stage of the case), but according to the Reporters Committee for Freedom of the Press, there were also 33 closed criminal trials in that year.[42]

One of the tersest acceptances of the power *Gannett* placed in judicial hands came in Virginia, whose supreme court affirmed the closure of a murder trial in a single sentence, citing *Gannett.* John Paul Stevenson had been indicted for the knife murder of Lillian Keller. He had been staying temporarily with his brother-in-law (also indicted) in a room next to Keller, a live-in manager of a motel. The murder weapon was found in their room, but without fingerprints. Stevenson's Maryland driver's license had been found in the victim's room, and the police, using it, obtained a blood-stained shirt from Stevenson's wife that was matched to the victim. At trial Stevenson and his brother-in-law were found guilty and sentenced to prison.

Stevenson appealed, and the Virginia Supreme Court ruled that testimony about the bloodstained shirt was hearsay and should not have been allowed at trial. Eight months later Stevenson's retrial commenced; but a juror asked to be excused, and there being no available alternate, Judge Richard Taylor declared a mistrial. A week later Taylor declared another mistrial, apparently when one prospective juror told others about the earlier reversal of Stevenson's conviction, which had been reported by the *Richmond News Leader* in its story about the previous mistrial.[43]

The prosecutor was not about to quit. The third attempt to retry Stevenson occurred three months later. Before the trial, Stevenson's lawyer moved that the courtroom be closed to the public, stating that he did not want information being shuttled between spectators and witnesses during any recesses, and that he did not want jurors to get any information from newspapers. Taylor agreed, and the court was closed.[44]

With the courtroom clear, the commonwealth presented its case. Then the defense moved for yet another mistrial. The judge excused the jury, and in the presence only of the court reporter, the prosecutor, and the defense counsel, he threw out the commonwealth's case. A barely audible dictabelt indicates that Taylor said something like "the prosecution's case is filled with holes." There was no mistrial this time. The judge entered a verdict of not guilty and Stevenson went free.[45]

*Gannett* had set off a storm of protest when it came down. If it allowed secret trials and acquittals without reasons given, such as that granted by Taylor, then it was seriously flawed. Furthermore, in an unprecedented display of public backpedaling, four justices made extracurricular comments on the case during the summer, the most intriguing being Chief Justice Burger's assertion that lower court judges were misreading an opinion that "referred to pre-trial proceedings only." The Court's flight from *Gannett* and from Rehnquist's apparent carte blanche was made official the next term, when every justice save Rehnquist voted to reverse the Virginia Supreme Court's conclusion, in *Richmond Newspapers v. Virginia,* that *Gannett* authorized closing Stevenson's trial.[46]

Simply to note that there was no opinion for the majority is too misleading; rather, there were six opinions for the seven judges voting with the majority, and no opinion commanded more than three justices. The opinions of Chief Justice Burger (joined by White and Stevens) and Justice Brennan (joined by Marshall) made the fullest attempts to explain the result, and they have proven to have the most staying value.

Ironically, Burger's opinion was a replay of the losing side in *Gannett.* The opinion, like Blackmun's dissent a year earlier, referred respectfully to the long, "unbroken, uncontradicted history" of open criminal trials. Citizen access to trials "historically has been thought to enhance the integrity and quality of what takes place." Well and good, but all of that could have been said a year earlier to open the hearing in *Gannett;* what was new was that the Chief Justice added a brut ipse dixit, that the First Amendment was the guarantor of continued openness "in the context of trials," together with a disclaimer, that it mattered not whether one spoke of a "right of access" or a "right to gather information." Beyond the long history of openness and its recognized importance, however, there was nothing to indicate why the First, rather than the Sixth Amendment, should have served as the vehicle of decision.[47]

Because Brennan's opinion explained that puzzle, it is by far the more satisfying. Relying on a recent speech he had made at the Rutgers Law School, Brennan wrote that the First Amendment plays an essential *"structural* role in securing and fostering our republican system of self-government." By focusing on structure, Brennan looked to the "indispensable conditions for meaningful communication" and echoed Meiklejohn and Emerson, quoted in the introduction to this chapter. Fortunately, Brennan recognized that the rhetoric has "theoretically endless" reach. To create the necessary boundaries, he suggested that "practical necessities" must be considered. Fleshing this out, he, too, was impressed by the long tradition of openness of criminal proceedings, and he added that "the value of access must be measured in specifics." Because rhetoric can always make the case for openness, Brennan asked instead how important openness is to the proceeding in question. Again, given Anglo-American history, that question answered itself.[48]

In a brief concurring opinion, Justice Stevens called *Richmond Newspapers* "a watershed case": never before had the Court held that the public had an entitlement to the acquisition of newsworthy information. Although Stevens's message was probably more intended for lower courts, the press has taken it to heart.[49]

Press joy over *Richmond Newspapers* nicely counterpoints the earlier despair over *Branzburg* and *Farber.* Each reaction was excessive. *Branzburg* and *Farber* did not annex the press as an investigating arm of the state, and *Richmond Newspapers* did not turn the First Amendment into a sunshine law. Although the Supreme Court can create a new constitutional right any time the mood strikes, it is worth remembering that no one thought the First Amendment granted a right to confidentiality of reporters' sources until the *Herald-Tribune*'s entertainment writer brought the claim forward, 169 years after the First Congress framed the language of the amendment. When *Branzburg* rejected the claim, the Court was taking nothing away from the press but a dream; however evil and awful—and "terrifying" to Theodore H. White—the decision may have been, it simply restated what had always been the case. *Richmond Newspapers*, on the other hand, presented the example where Virginia was taking from the public and the press a right long held, exercised, and believed essential in our society. Instead of validating Virginia's stark reversal of the presumption of open trials, the Supreme Court validated, as with *Branzburg*, the status quo ante. The distinction between misfeasance and nonfeasance may be slippery, but sometimes it is clear; and when it is, misfeasance is quite properly perceived as the more wrongful.[50]

If the context of *Richmond Newspapers* suggests that its rule may be narrower than it appears, so does reality. Despite all the good things that flow from public access to government proceedings, there are times and places for secrecy. Even when we celebrated the revolutionary bicentennial in 1976, speeches hailed less the revolution than the stable legal order established after 1787. No speaker could offer enough praise of the Constitution and of the framers who conceived it—in secret. All historians agree that without secrecy there would have been no constitution, because the opponents of the key compromises would each have had the opportunity to mobilize separate opposition and scuttle the document—which had enough trouble being ratified anyway. Are we now to hail a document conceived in secrecy as dedicated to the proposition that government business must always be conducted in the open? Maybe, but I doubt it; and at a minimum the drafting of the Constitution in secrecy should offer a caution light, one that the Supreme Court may indeed have an incentive to turn red.

The sacred cow of all secret decision making is the Supreme

Court's own Conference, wherein the justices discuss argued cases and tentatively cast their votes. Every justice for the past two hundred years would have agreed that the Conference must remain private. Yet for years, as Justice Scalia most recently complained, Conference has consisted not of discussion or efforts at persuasion, but of short speeches announcing how each justice will vote. *The Brethren* may have demystified the Court for a wider public, but the various criticisms of the book's washing the Court's linen in public never suggested that the authors got it wrong. When Potter Stewart can lead four other justices in leaking about the sacred institution and what occurs, maybe the time has come to say the obvious: the Court's decision making probably would not be either different or worse if done in public view. Just how would someone justify members of a deliberative body agreeing to join the majority opinion before they have even seen the dissent (as happens almost always)? But ending the secrecy is not going to happen or even be considered, because secrecy will always have nine friends at the Supreme Court.[51]

While I am thus skeptical about *Richmond Newspapers* as a full-fledged sunshine law, it is nevertheless important in preventing the judicial behavior exhibited by Judge Taylor and by the trial judge in *Gannett*. The Supreme Court's Conference may not be an open institution, but trials are; and *Richmond Newspapers*, while possibly doing no more than open closed trial doors, at least has done that. In subsequent cases the Supreme Court has ruled that the public cannot automatically be excluded from the courtroom when an underage victim of sexual offenses takes the stand; from jury selection; and, even in the face of a claim about denial of a fair trial, from preliminary hearings when they function as a trial. In extending *Richmond Newspapers*, the Court has eschewed absolutes and indicated that it would approve closure when higher values were at stake and when the closure is narrowly limited to preserving those values. Thus it is doubtful that civil cases could be constitutionally closed. The end of the line, however, is at grand juries, where the Court has been careful to emphasize continuously that "the proper functioning of our grand jury system depends upon secrecy." While that may be a questionable conclusion, it fits with the historical explanation and serves to reinforce a melding on the approaches of Burger and Brennan in *Richmond Newspapers:* from Burger a respect for the tradition, from Brennan a consideration of the "practical necessities" of the situation.[52]

## IV

The Scotsboro Boys, blacks in 1931 Alabama charged with capital rape (of a white woman), were tried without according them counsel—a legal lynching. The Supreme Court intervened by holding, in *Powell v. Alabama*, that under the circumstances counsel was necessary. Three decades later, in *Gideon v. Wainwright*, the Court held that counsel was necessary in all felony cases. In between, however, the Court struggled with a rule that held that counsel was necessary only when there were special circumstances that made the case too complex for the defendant (with some assistance from the judge) to handle his or her own case. After a decade and a half it became clear that capital cases always have special circumstances. But it still took another fifteen years for the powerful rhetoric about the function of counsel to come to fruition in *Gideon*. Yale Kamisar, in an early comment on *Richmond Newspapers*, referred to the commentaries that treated the case broadly as a sunshine law decision: "*Someday* the views they advance may be the law of the land. In the meantime, however, many more battles will have to be fought. *Someday* we may look back on *Richmond Newspapers* as the '*Powell v. Alabama*' of the right of access to government controlled information—but it was a long, hard road from *Powell* to *Gideon*."[53]

My guess is that it will be an even longer, harder road. There is language in *Richmond Newspapers* to ease the journey. Burger would have liked to limit his opinion to trials and nothing else, but as Brennan noted, logic pushes farther. "The explicit, guaranteed rights to speak and to publish concerning what takes place at a trial would lose much meaning if access to observe the trial could be foreclosed arbitrarily." There is nothing inherent in trials that prevents Burger's observation from being transferred to any government institution.[54]

What will operate as a check is Brennan's emphasis on practicalities. The Supreme Court, in fact almost everyone, recognizes a place for secrecy in our society. This means there is an immediate countervailing principle to openness already in place. The fundamental need for counsel in criminal cases was far clearer, and only the cost of providing it was offered as a countervailing principle. Furthermore, every criminal case presented the possibilities of "special circumstances" requiring counsel, so that the operative rule between *Powell* and *Gideon* produced litigation. Treating *Richmond Newspapers* too broadly, and forgetting that secrecy, too, has its place—which the press, apparently unaware of the irony, knows from its own claim in *Branzburg*—would turn every closed meeting into a violation of the First Amendment. There is today a lot of freedom of information act and sunshine act litigation. That is fully appropriate; laws on the books should be enforced, even if government officials would have it otherwise. But to treat *Richmond Newspapers* broadly would add to all of this extensive litigation a constitutional claim that could be pushed beyond the statutory one. Practical necessities suggest that courts will not be overly receptive to that solution.[55]

The press's right of access to people and places has proven more difficult to establish than the right to publish, but this should not be surprising. Our Constitution, noble document that it is, was nevertheless written in the late eighteenth century. It has kept up well through much of our history, but the establishment of the welfare state has created strains. Through most of our history, liberty has been conceived negatively as preventing the state from doing harm to the citizen. It is only in the past few decades that liberty has also been seen positively, with the state having a facilitative role. Yet despite the new realizations, and despite justices with the best of intentions, it has proven all but impossible to create a constitutional jurisprudence of entitlements. Press claims for access have fared somewhat better than others, in large part because the court closings (as opposed to the closed prisons) could be litigated as a state intrusion on a long-held privilege.

Although interconnected in the structure of communication, the claim of confidentiality is a negative claim and could have been accommodated. The claim as presented failed largely because it was too difficult to administer. In narrower contexts, where the issue can be reduced to aspects of governmental intrusiveness, it fares better.

The ties between access and confidentiality, beyond their necessary relationship to acquiring information, are that both can be defended with powerful First Amendment rhetoric and each lacks helpful stopping points. Justice White noted that newsgathering qualifies for First Amendment protection, while he simultaneously rejected the privilege asserted. The failed-access cases carry a similar message of recognition of the First Amendment claim coupled with an inability to implement it. There is more of a constitutional dimension to the general claim than judges can competently enforce. This being the case, other governmental officials have an important duty to facilitate the acquisition of information by the press—as shield laws, sunshine laws, and freedom of information acts recognize—and an equal duty on judges to broadly construe legislative efforts to implement these inchoate rights. In this respect it is especially troublesome that the New Jersey courts in *Farber* failed to realize that the legislative mandate allowed accommodation of both First and Sixth Amendment rights, by dismissal of the prosecution if the withheld evidence was essential. The legislatures do not often lead; when they do, judges need not be grudging in their interpretations. Finally, government efforts, from whatever source, to block willing dissemination of information should be interpreted as barriers to the necessary functioning of the press in our democratic society.

## Chapter Seven

# Antitrust

The Hazelwood East High School's newspaper, the *Spectrum*, usually has six pages. But the May 13, 1983, issue consisted of only four. Right before publication the principal (who routinely read and approved articles prior to publication) ordered the deletion of two major articles, one on three pregnant students, the other on a student's reaction to her parents' divorce. Five years of litigation later, the Supreme Court held the First Amendment was no bar to the principal's decision.[1]

However strange it initially seems, the Court got it right. James Reston may have given Neil Sheehan the necessary go-ahead on the Pentagon Papers story, but the final decision was made by publisher Punch Sulzberger. Had he decided, for whatever reason, to kill the story, Sheehan would have had no legal recourse, because what appears in the *Times* can be dictated neither by the government nor by the *Times*'s reporters. The ultimate locus of authority is with the publisher. The claim by the suburban St. Louis teenagers that they should have legal rights to decide what is published is one that no working adult reporters could hope to enjoy.

The students were taught three civics lessons. School officials are often sensitive. Some constitutional rights cannot be shared. And control, in a capitalist society, accompanies ownership. In A. J. Liebling's apt phrase: "Freedom of the press is guaranteed only to those who own one." This conclusion is often repeated by those who are less than enamored with the press, because Liebling captures, in ways fundamentally different from James Madison, other essential truths—about exclusivity, class bias, and, implicitly, the fear of manipulation.[2]

## I

Liebling's "The Wayward Press" columns in the *New Yorker,* between 1945 and 1963, often poignantly described the development of a single-newspaper city. At the turn of the century there were over 2000 daily newspapers, and the numbers kept growing for the next two decades; some five hundred communities had competing daily newspapers; and almost all were owned by individuals with no other media holdings. The aftermath of World War II saw a decline to 1750 papers. In the ensuing three decades the decline halted because new starts (in places such as Cocoa Beach, Florida, and Maui) offset failures in some of the largest cities in the United States: New York, Philadelphia, Cleveland, Baltimore, St. Louis, Washington. In the past decade there has been a new consolidation, dropping the number to about 1650.[3]

Sometimes papers died because of competition or lack of readership. Sometimes they were killed. The afternoon *Detroit News* in 1960 "bought and instantly put down the *Detroit Times.* This was a clean suppression, without pretense. The *News* did not even bother to call itself the *News-Times,* but added, like a scalplock, to its masthead "including the best features from the *Detroit Times*— '18 extra comic strips.'" The price tag for the *Times* was $10 million, not bad for a paper "forced by rising costs to shut down." In reality, however, the *News* was not buying a newspaper, it was buying an afternoon monopoly. Hearst abandoned Detroit with the sale of the *Times,* then gained a monopoly in Albany in a swap with Gannett, in which Hearst killed its two Rochester dailies, leaving that city to Gannett. Similarly, in 1962 Hearst killed its morning Los Angeles paper while Chandler did the same for its afternoon paper, leaving Hearst's *Herald-Examiner* an afternoon monopoly and Chandler's *Los Angeles Times* a morning monopoly. Instead of competing afternoon papers and competing morning papers, fewer and fewer American cities had *any* competing papers. The number of cities with competing papers fell to 51 in 1963, to 37 in 1973, and to 30 in 1983; and it is now below that.

When profitable newspapers die, as Liebling demonstrated, rising costs are a smokescreen to cover the value of monopoly profits for the survivor.[4]

While Liebling often chronicled the slow decline of the American daily, his New York City home, with its diverse array of papers, was of special interest to him. Writing in 1949, he noted that over the previous eighteen years, five newspapers had gone out of business. "If the trend continues, New York will be a one or two paper town by 1975." He was wrong; it kept several.[5]

Even before Liebling died in 1963, another trend, long in existence, was superimposing itself on top of the single-paper monopolies. Simultaneous with the arrival of local monopoly was the emergence of national chains. (Frank Gannett hated "chain" for its obvious bondage connotations and strove, with success among newspapers, to have "group" substituted.) Virtually nonexistent at the turn of the century (8 groups controlling 27 papers), by 1935 there were 63 chains owning 328 papers, which included 40 percent of total US circulation. Just twenty-five years later, about a third of all newspapers were chain owned. The trend has continued, and by 1986 the five largest groups controlled 27 percent of daily newspaper circulation, with all chains controlling about 77 percent (although Gannett, the largest at 8.8 percent, is well below the 13.6 percent Hearst held in 1935).[6]

Chain ownership raises the possibility of regional monopolies and national oligopolies. Additionally, as ownership became more concentrated, a related phenomenon further constricted the flow of information in the American press. Chains, their protestations to the contrary notwithstanding, were often the death knell of serious local reporting and individualized (as opposed to canned) editorials, thereby diminishing the "robust" debate that *New York Times* had found at the heart of the First Amendment. Jerome Barron's writings, beginning with his seminal 1967 article, "Access to the Press—A New First Amendment Right," focused on the homogenization of the press and proposed various novel remedies.[7]

Yet the forces pushing toward concentration were neither abating nor limited to newspapers. Ben Bagdikian became an important spokesman in the 1980s against the newer forms of integrated press oligopolies that dwarfed those existing during Liebling's lifetime. Writing in 1983, even before some of the spectacular media mergers (such as Capital Cities/ABC; GE/RCA, where NBC is a subsidiary; and Fox/Murdoch), he portrayed a world in which just fifty corporations own more than half of the newspapers, magazines, radio and television stations, book publishers, and movie studios. When he updated the book four years later, the fifty corporations had been reduced to twenty-nine. At the beginning of the 1960s, the five hundred largest companies listed in the *Fortune* 500 included nine media companies; when Bagdikian wrote, the number had jumped to twenty-one. Bagdikian's description of the media as a "Private Ministry of Information and Culture" explicitly captures the feeling of helplessness in the face of media power, with its potential manipulation of the marketplace of ideas. Given the historic association of freedom of the press with American democracy, the not unnatural concern is that the threats that concentration poses to a fully vibrant press are also threats to democracy.[8]

Liebling's dismay over the death of competing newspapers and Bagdikian's fear that huge media conglomerates will set the terms of debate raise a crystal-clear question. Given the constraints of the First Amendment, is there anything the legal system can do to counter this growing concentration of private power?

## II

The only helpful experience of dealing with media monopolies is that of the Federal Communications Commission (FCC). In 1938 Genessee Radio, operator of the sole radio station in Flint, Michigan, applied for a license to operate a second station in Flint, proposing identical programming but different staffs and advertising rates. The jarring nature of Genessee's proposals made it clear they could not meet "the public interest" standard required by the Communications Act. Not only would the second station not genuinely compete against the first, it might prevent future entry by a competitor that would provide an alternative service. The FCC's antiduopoly policy, promoting diversity of control of broadcast communications, was born.[9]

As FM and television became available, the FCC codified its antiduopoly rules to prohibit any licensee from owning more than one station of each type (AM, FM, or TV) in a community. Furthermore, the Commission, in a series of rules, limited the number of stations of the same broadcast service that any licensee could own, no matter where located. The so-called 7-7-7 rules, finalized in 1953 and sustained in *United States v. Storer Broadcasting,* created finite limits on the potential of broadcast concentration by restricting the number of stations a licensee could own to seven of each type (AM, FM, and TV).[10]

Few applaud concentration of control of mass communications, and the Commission was no exception. "Centralization of control over the media of mass communications is, like monopolization of economic power, per se undesirable." When stations are owned by different entities, it is more likely that they will compete for the same audiences, and there is less chance that any given entity will have "inordinate" influence on public opinion. These views moved the Commission to conclude that "there is no optimum degree of diversification, and we do not feel competent to say or hold that any particular number of outlets of expression is enough." Bluntly, "60 different licensees are more desirable than 50, and even 51 are more desirable than 50." To effectuate this conclusion, the Commission adopted a series of prospective rules in the 1970s that prohibited both joint ownership of any local broadcast facilities (the one-to-a-market rules) and local broadcaster-newspaper combinations (the cross-ownership rules).[11]

In rhetoric outstripping reality, the Commission stated, "If our democratic society is to function, nothing can be more important than insuring that there is a free flow of information from as many divergent sources as possible." In fact the Commission did not even approach its rhetorical stance. Almost no divestiture was required under the cross-ownership rules (some sixteen "egregious" monopolies in metropolises like Mason City, Iowa, and Owosso, Michigan, were required to divest), and none was required under the one-to-a-market rules. Achieving the diversity to match the rhetoric could only come as local group owners sold their properties. Yet at best the rules would prospectively assist local diversity while quite possibly leaving national concentration unaffected, as witnessed by the local station swap of the *Washington Post* and the *Detroit Evening News* in what turned out to be an unneeded defensive anticipation of what the rules would require. The cross-ownership rules need not have any effect on national concentration, because they did nothing to limit the then-existing 7-7-7 (now 12-12-12) rules on the national level.[12]

The cross-ownership rules created a major First Amendment confrontation as newspapers, through the American Newspaper Publishers' Association (ANPA), challenged the ability of the Commission to preclude them from acquiring broadcast properties in communities in which they published. The National Citizens Committee for Broadcasting (NCCB), a media watchdog group, also challenged the rules, arguing that the Communications Act, as reinforced by First Amendment policies concerning diversity in the marketplace of ideas, required the Commission to order divestiture of all local cross-ownerships. The DC Circuit Court of Appeals agreed fully with the NCCB. Unimpressed by a divestiture requirement limited to the likes of Bluefield, West Virginia, the court noted that "limiting divestiture to small markets of 'absolute monopoly' squanders the opportunity where divestiture might do the most good . . . in the larger markets." Granting that divestiture would be beneficial in the sixteen affected markets, the Court nevertheless thought that the amount of diversity in larger markets "may in fact be no greater."[13]

At the Supreme Court, each side continued to rely on the First Amendment: the NCCB offensively, the ANPA defensively. This time, however, both sides lost. The Court had the least trouble rejecting the DC Circuit's embrace of the NCCB argument. Diversity of control was neither the exclusive nor the dominant policy in the Communications Act; and if the Commission wished to accommodate it to other policies, neither the act nor the Constitution mandated a contrary result. Somewhat more difficult in analysis, although ultimately also unanimous in result, was the rejection of the ANPA argument that even a prospective ban on cross-ownership unconstitutionally conditioned a newspaper's right to publish.[14]

The ANPA put forth two related arguments, both supplemented by an admonition to the Court not to let the novel form of regulation cause it to lose constitutional direction. The first was that there is an absolute constitutional right to publish, and forcing a newspaper to stop publishing in order to acquire a local broadcast station unconstitutionally conditioned that right. The second was that the regulations singled out newspapers for special, unfavorable treatment; and any regulations so doing necessarily ran afoul of the First Amendment. This latter argument failed immediately, because its necessary factual predicate—singling out newspapers for special, unfavorable treatment—was false. Commission rules equally precluded a television station from acquiring a broadcast property—or a newspaper—in its home community. All that the cross-ownership rules had done was bring the treatment of newspapers in line with the treatment of other major communications enterprises.

The Court was a bit disingenuous with the first argument—that it was unconstitutional to condition the receipt of a broadcast license on the licensee's not publishing a newspaper in the same community. The Court's answer was that "a newspaper owner need not forfeit anything in order to acquire a license for a station located in another community." This was nonresponsive to the issue of broadcasting in the same community; and it ignored a longstanding line of First Amendment cases that hold that "one is not to have the exercise of his liberty of expression in appropriate places abridged on the plea that it may be exercised in some other place." Under this well-established rule, the fact that the *Dallas Times Herald* can acquire a broadcast license in Houston is not an answer to why it may not obtain one in Dallas (where the *Morning News* does own a station). The answer must come from something beyond the availability of Houston.[15]

The Court had that additional answer and came to it by the end of that very paragraph: "The regulations are not content related; moreover, their purpose and effect is to promote free speech, not to restrict it." The regulations had no other purpose than to add additional voices to the market; such a purpose comports wonderfully with the First Amendment. That the effect of the regulations would be to promote free speech was less clear. Additional voices in the marketplace would most likely mean that different ideas would be available; but the different ideas might not necessarily be more ideas, because the second co-owned outlet need not be putting out the same ideas as the first. Indeed, the differences in coverage between print and broadcast might result in different issues being addressed in each of the two media.[16]

The Court's view that the purpose of the regulations was to enhance rather than restrict speech turned back to the beginning of the sentence, where the Court stated that the regulations are not content related. By this the Court meant that the regulations apply to all newspapers regardless of what they are saying. Content neutrality indicates a breadth of regulation that allows the reviewing court to conclude with some assurance that the regulating body is not motivated by a hidden agenda of silencing specific individuals or ideas. Yet it is inconceivable that the rules would have been promulgated if they were not viewed as influencing content. By preventing a media outlet in the community from acquiring another outlet in the same community, the rules do not dictate what will be said, but they certainly strive to ensure that what will be said will be different. The newspaper can say anything it wishes, and the FCC hopes that the broadcast outlet, in doing the same, will say something different. In essence, the Court saw the rules as having more to do with economics than with speech. The cross-ownership rules structured the delivery systems, not what was delivered. And, while the rules precluded dual ownership within the market, they did not prohibit any entity from acquiring one outlet and saying what it pleased.

*NCCB* is legally distinguishable from the factual situations described by Liebling and Bagdikian. As the Court recognized, it has consistently treated broadcasting as something special in the air. Indeed, the opinion contained the obligatory statements of its era in support of the technologically and economically silly notion that broadcasting is a scarce resource and print is not. Given the numbers of cities with four or five over-the-air television stations, fifteen to twenty-five radio stations, a three-dozen-channel cable system, and a single daily newspaper, this conclusion blinks reality. (And one could note, as I do at the end of this chapter, that this phenomenal expansion of radio and television is not unconnected with the decline of the daily newspapers.) Because I have treated this point fully in *American Broadcasting and the First Amendment,* I shall not pursue it further here, except to note that with scarcity better understood now, even by some members of the Court, as an untenable rationale, the substance of the broadcast/print distinction vanishes. When written, however, *NCCB* was open to the conceivable reading that broadcast frequencies, because they are "scarce," may be subjected to diversity regulation in ways more stringent than nonbroadcast media. Yet even as written, the strong affinity between *NCCB* and the 1945 antitrust decision in *Associated Press v. United States* suggests that the distinction, while present, was not controlling.[17]

At the beginning of World War II, there were three competing news services; Associated Press (AP), United Press, and International News Service; AP was dominant. AP had both an international and a domestic department collecting news and making it available to its members. The other two wire services could duplicate that, and, indeed, so could an individual newspaper, albeit on a smaller scale. Where AP was unique, and achieved its dominance, was its by-law requirement that all its members transmit all the local news they collect to AP and not to anyone else. In effect, every reporter of a member provided news to all other members via AP bureaus. Because of the size of AP membership (and a like agreement covering Canada), its ability to provide local news from all over North America was unparalleled. A paper excluded from AP could not hope to do as well.

By the time the government filed its antitrust suit, an earlier by-law that allowed any member to veto admission to AP had been repealed, and membership was theoretically available by simple majority vote. If the would-be new member was a competitor of an existing member, then the new member would have to pay an initiation fee of 10 percent of all annual assessments, dating back to 1900, which the AP had received from existing members in the new member's area. The initiation fee did not go into the AP treasury; instead it was immediately remitted to the new member's rivals in the same city (unless the rival chose to waive payment).

Willingness to pay the initiation fee—about $400,000 for a Chicago morning paper—was a moot point, however, because competitors of existing members could not achieve majority votes for membership. In the newspaper industry's version of senatorial courtesy, if a member competitor balked, then the would-be member's hopes were doomed. The *Washington Post* and *Washington Star* thought that membership for the *Washington Times Herald* would be a bad idea, and fellow AP members agreed by more than two to one. Similarly, Franklin D. Roosevelt's most strident newspaper critic, Colonel Robert R. McCormick and his *Chicago Tribune*, blocked the AP admission of FDR supporter Marshall Field's new *Chicago Sun*, which became the only morning newspaper in the United States with a circulation in excess of 25,000 that was not an AP member. Like the *Times Herald,* the *Sun* was rejected by more than two to one.[18]

The vote focused attention on AP, many of whose members knew that the by-laws were simply a means of restraining competition and were willing, if someone else took the initiative, to change them. But institutional conservatism and loyalty to associates prevailed even in the face of a potential antitrust suit by a Department of Justice that had every incentive to aid a prominent FDR supporter in the press. After a year of preparation, the Department of Justice determined to do good by doing well and filed the first antitrust suit ever against the press. The various by-laws limiting membership and restricting the flow of news from AP sources were, the government alleged, unlawful restraints of trade that had the intent and necessary effect of limiting competition (by making entry problematical) in the newspaper industry.[19]

There were two major theories available to the government. The first was a traditional Sherman Act approach, condemning the various practices found to restrain trade and limit entry. The second, both novel and broad, was being publicly advocated by Harvard's Zechariah Chafee, easily the most influential First Amendment scholar of the period. Chafee proposed a public-service principle— at a minimum, service without discrimination—and urged AP adopt it on its own, because expanding the flow of information was "the very essence of liberty of the press." Against these two theories was AP's argument that *any* regulation of the media, even to expand both AP's and the public's flow of information, was an infringement of the First Amendment. The case would be argued twice; once before a trial court consisting of three of the most eminent jurists in the nation, Learned Hand, his cousin Augustus N. Hand, and Thomas W. Swan; and once before the United States Supreme Court.[20]

At trial, the public-service theory prevailed by a Hands to Swan vote. Learned Hand—to whom Chafee had dedicated his seminal *Free Speech in the United States*—wrote the majority opinion along the lines of Chafee's public-service principle. The Court had to distinguish newspapers from other industries, and then to focus on consumer welfare rather than simply the interests of competitors. While the latter point seems obvious now, it was not then;

progressive jurists of the era did not think in terms of aiding competition in order to aid consumers.[21]

Hand had no trouble with the first point. "Even if this were a case of the ordinary kind: the production of fungible goods," it would be "a nice question" whether AP should prevail. But, the opinion went on, merging the two points, this was not an ordinary case; the interests of the industry were "neither exclusively, nor even primarily, conclusive" because this industry served "one of the most vital of all general interests: the dissemination of news from as many different sources as is possible." Then, in language that has become one of the most quoted statements on the First Amendment, Hand concluded that the interest was "closely akin to, if indeed it is not the same as the interest protected by the First Amendment; it presupposes that right conclusions are more likely to be gathered out of a multitude of tongues, than through any kind of authoritative selection. To many this is, and always will be, folly; but we have staked upon it our all."[22]

The implications of Hand's opinion, which a friend of Chafee's said "slavishly" followed Chafee, and which Chafee himself later more modestly stated "gave considerable support to the public service theory," were unclear. Public service sounded much like public interest, and the Supreme Court, through Justice Frankfurter, had just rejected a First Amendment challenge by the networks to FCC regulations that limited their ability to dominate their affiliates. Although the networks' First Amendment argument had been attenuated, there was ample reason for newspapers to fear the entering wedge of content regulation after Hand's decision. Chafee's advocacy of the public service concept had stated there was "no warrant" for fears of "putting a New Deal official at every editorial desk." But that caveat came on the heels of a very ambitious statement of Chafee's position: "The new conception of public service brings new responsibilities. Within reasonable limits *the public can shape* the nature of the services it receives. Prices, quality, wages paid, conditions of employment, etc., are subjected to regulations." It is no wonder the press was aghast; within four years Chafee himself would back down. Where government would use some content-neutral laws, there was the chance that content-specific regulation would follow. "Once they get going, they will move in many directions." Newspapers did not need to wait the four years with Chafee; they instinctively had those concerns.[23]

The Supreme Court, by a six-to-two vote, brought the case back into the more traditional restraint-of-trade rationale by affirming the decree without even mentioning the Hand-Chafee public-service theory. Concurring opinions by Frankfurter (favoring) and Douglas (seemingly rejecting) squared off on the public-service theory, but the other four justices in Black's majority wholly eschewed comment. After demonstrating that the intent and effect of AP's by-laws were "seriously to limit the opportunity of any new paper to enter" a city with an AP member, the Court turned in a single paragraph to AP's contention that the First Amendment granted it an immunity from the Sherman Act. The Court began by noting what appeared to be the "strange" assertion of AP that "the grave concern for freedom of the press which promoted adoption of the First Amendment should be read as a command that the government was without power to protect that freedom." Like Hand below, the Court found that the First Amendment "provides powerful reasons" for application of the antitrust laws to the press. "Surely a command that the government itself shall not impede the free flow of ideas does not afford non-governmental combinations a refuge if they impose restraints upon that constitutionally guaranteed freedom. Freedom to publish means freedom for all and not for some. Freedom to publish is guaranteed by the Constitution, but freedom to combine to keep others from publishing is not. Freedom of the press from governmental interference under the First Amendment does not sanction repression of that freedom by private interests."[24]

Although AP suffered a total loss at the Supreme Court, it could have been worse had a majority picked up the Hand-Chafee public-service concept. Under those circumstances the future might well have been uncharted. But as written, *Associated Press* was a standard antitrust case. And the aftermath was predictable. The *Chicago Sun* and other competing newspapers became AP members when the by-laws were invalidated.[25]

On the constitutional point, *Associated Press* broke no new ground. Eight years earlier, in a case involving application of the National Labor Relations Act to AP—forbidding AP from auto-

matically discharging unionized reporters—the Court had already
crossed the threshold with its conclusion that laws of general appli-
cability, which by definition would be content-neutral, could be
applied to the press. Furthermore, holding that the Sherman Act
could not be applied to the press would have been unthinkable.
Who, after all, could believe that the First Amendment would grant
a media corporation the right to monopolize (if it could) all the
communications in the United States? The Court was somewhat
too modest. Even Fred Siebert, the First Amendment expert retained to assist McCormick and AP in the case, concluded that
there was no case. AP's argument was not only "strange"; it was
unthinkable (save by the well-paid lawyers arguing on behalf of the
AP monopoly).[26]

# III

With the principle established that newspapers and the mass media
generally are subject to the antitrust laws, the natural reaction is to
associate media concentration with the need for more vigorous
enforcement of the Sherman Act. Hard on the heels of the *Associated Press* decision, the ACLU's Morris Ernst called for breaking up
the existing media monopolies. Some twenty years later, Philip
Hart, chairman of the Senate Antitrust Subcommittee, issued a
similar call to get down to the "arduous" work of "strict, aggressive, fearless application of the antitrust laws." Bagdikian did not
name his book *The Media Monopoly* by coincidence. He, too,
believed that our laws against monopolies had to be both improved
and brought into play against the ever-increasing concentration in
the field, and his 1987 edition went so far as to suggest a maximum
circulation for chains that grow by acquisition rather than creation.
These consistent calls for more and better antitrust enforcement are
not without force. Probably no industry has managed to engage in
such flagrant anticompetitive practices as the news industry while
attorneys in the Department of Justice (even when the Antitrust
Division was active) have looked elsewhere.[27]

At the local level, starting a newspaper or even keeping a second
one going is, as the statistics cited at the beginning of the chapter
demonstrate, difficult at best, impossible at worst. Over the past
fifty years fewer than five competing start-ups have continued to

exist independently, and the only one that appears to turn a profit—the *Slidell (Louisiana) Daily Sentry-News*—knocked its competitor out. Major areas have seen a number of failed attempts: New York (twice), Long Island, Philadelphia, Atlanta, Phoenix, Oklahoma City, to name just the largest cities. Up to fifteen years ago the start-up costs for a new paper—essentially acquiring the staff and the printing plant—were dauntingly high. Technology, however, has lowered these costs, although it remains to be seen how far. Any newspaper coming into being will need to achieve 40 percent of the area's circulation for a chance to survive; and that probably is unachievable, because newspapers enjoy tremendous economies of scale. It takes just about as much money to publish the next issue of an already existing newspaper as it does to publish the first issue of a new newspaper. Thus, although the costs of production are the same, the larger paper can spread its costs over a broader circulation base. Furthermore, advertisers have become exceptionally devoted to paying the lowest cost per thousand readers. A larger newspaper, then, even though it charges a higher price per line of advertising, can justify that charge by its distribution over a greater circulation. A smaller paper, even with a lower charge per line, still faces the problem of its lesser circulation. It simply costs less to reach each reader of the larger paper. Until these economic facts change, competing newspapers are not going to spring up, whatever the theoretical possibility that they might do so.[28]

Indeed, to some analysts newspapers appear to be natural monopolies. Thus economist Bruce Owen concludes that "head-on competition among newspapers in the same town is a disequilibrium situation, one that will eventually be succeeded by merger, failure of one newspaper, or a joint operating agreement, tantamount to merger. Antitrust action aimed at preserving competition in this sense is simply doomed to failure." While the very largest markets have seemed to be an exception, the demise of the *Los Angeles Herald-Examiner* in late 1989, leaving the *Los Angeles Times* with a monopoly, indicates that Owen's assessment may be perfectly accurate.[29]

Yet if nature creates these monopolies, human intervention seems unusually present as well. Various newspaper industry practices have as their primary logic the thwarting of competition. While a start-up newspaper can match an existing competitor in reporting local news with its own reporters, even after *Associated Press* it may have some difficulties nationally and internationally, depending on the amount of up-front payment the wire service requires. In AP's case, even after losing the antitrust case, the payment was high enough that a newspaper had to be established before it could obtain AP services, even though without them it might not be possible to get established. But even assuming that adequate wire services are readily available, a would-be competitor cannot match the existing paper in two important fillers: syndicated columnists and comics. Recall the happy announcement of the *Detroit News* that it had taken the best from the *Detroit Times*—eighteen comic strips. Prior to its untimely demise, the *Times* would have had the exclusive right to publish them. These exclusive contracts guarantee that new newspapers will have difficulty acquiring those comic strips that are most popular. In the case of syndicated columnists, many papers acquire exclusive rights to far more than they can or would use; that acquisition makes sense because it guarantees that those under contract, even if unused, cannot appear elsewhere in the area of territorial exclusivity. Functionally, such contracts reinforce the trend of newspapers deaths and single-paper monopolies.[30]

Economics inevitably leading to a single-paper monopoly is bad enough, but in some cities it could be worse for a would-be competitor, because the two existing papers operate as partners. Such partnerships, called joint operating agreements (JOAs), are in place in such cities as Seattle, San Francisco, Tucson, Salt Lake City, Columbus, Chattanooga, Nashville, Birmingham, and Pittsburgh. Typically, a JOA provides for pooling production facilities, combination rates for advertising, and profit sharing, leaving only editorial functions separate. Essentially, a JOA gives the two partners a shared monopoly, and no new newspaper has ever been created in a city with a JOA. While JOAs shut out competitors, they may (if the agreement lasts long enough) prevent one of the two papers from hitting a circulation spiral, in which its circulation and hence its advertising jumps sufficiently to cause its rival's circulation and advertising to spiral fatally downward. Thus, although a JOA will almost always (there are no exceptions yet) prevent the creation of a third paper, the pressures of economics probably would do that anyway; and a JOA does preserve an existing two where operation of those same pressures of economics might leave only one.[31]

Little can be done about natural monopolies, but whether daily newspapers are truly natural monopolies has been debated. Keith Roberts observed, "whatever the ultimate ability of competition to survive in the newspaper industry may be, the prevalence of anti-competitive practices in the circulation effort has prevented any fair test of it so far. Certainly, until these practices end, no ordinary man would lightly enter the newspaper industry as a competitor of existing papers." Yet even as Roberts wrote in 1968, the Antitrust Division did virtually nothing to remove artificial barriers to entry. Testifying before the House Antitrust Subcommittee in 1963, the general counsel of the American Newspaper Publishers' Association stated that there had been only eight important antitrust cases against the industry. Although the Antitrust Division was about to be more active, by 1969 fewer than a dozen cases had been initiated after the victory in *Associated Press.* Even after that case, no government agency can forget that a media litigant not only may rely on the First Amendment defensively, but may also use it offensively to attempt to portray the government adversely in the court of public opinion. The combination largely eliminated antitrust as a threat to newspaper practices and therefore, to at least some extent, guaranteed an absence of competition in the local markets.[32]

When the Antitrust Division finally went to court, it won. The Times Mirror Company, parent of the *Los Angeles Times,* had decided to enter the suburban market to the east, not by striving for increased circulation or by beginning a new paper (as it had with the *Orange Coast Daily Pilot* to the south) but by purchase of the *San Bernardino Sun,* the largest independent daily newspaper in Southern California. By adding in the *Sun*'s 54,000 daily circulation, the Times Mirror Company increased its morning market share in San Bernardino County from 24 to 99 percent, its evening share from 11 to 55 percent, and its Sunday share from 20 to 64 percent. A judicial victory for the Antitrust Division forced Times Mirror to divest itself of the *Sun.* Unfortunately, the new purchaser was Gannett (which has bequeathed the *Sun* five publishers and six editors in its twenty-year stewardship).[33]

Almost simultaneously, the Antitrust Division filed suit against the two Tucson papers, which since 1940 had been operating under a JOA that provided for splitting profits pursuant to an agreed formula as well as engaging in the price-fixing of ad rates. When the JOA was signed in 1940, one paper was losing money, while the other was making a modest profit. By 1964, the two had a pretax profit of over $1.7 million. In any other industry a profit-sharing monopoly and price-fixing would be per se violations of the Sherman Act—that is, illegal regardless of any preferred justifications. The Supreme Court, through Justice Douglas, held that they were illegal for newspapers as well.[34]

The papers relied on a judicially created exception to the Sherman Act, the failing-company doctrine, which authorizes an otherwise illegal merger when one of the two companies is certain to fail and there is no other available purchaser for it. The Court doubted that the *Tucson Citizen* was anywhere near failing in 1940, despite its operating losses; it further noted that no attempts had been made to secure any other purchaser than its sole competitor, the *Tucson Star.* As in *Associated Press,* the Court treated newspapers like any other industry, and in so doing easily found that the combination violated the Sherman Act.

Congressional reaction to the Tucson case was swift and sure. Bowing to massive newspaper lobbying which emphasized the need to preserve competing voices in the communities that were still fortunate enough to have them—it being better to have separate news and editorial voices without economic competition than a single voice as a result of the outcome of competition—an overwhelming majority in Congress voted for the Newspaper Preservation Act (NPA) of 1970. As initially drafted, the NPA would simply have reversed the Court; grandfathered permanently (that is, left standing and valid) the existing twenty-two JOAs; and expressly permitted price-fixing, profit pooling, and market control. But in the legislative process the act was expanded to authorize the creation of new JOAs, with the prior written consent of the attorney general, if one of two newspapers is "in probable danger of financial failure." The attorney general must find, however, that the JOA "would effectuate the policy and purpose" of the NPA.[35]

The premise of the NPA is that a two-newspaper city will continue that way even if the weaker of the two has a strong chance of failing. Unfortunately, economic realities cut exactly the other way. Why should the stronger of the two papers agree to share the monopoly it is about to enjoy, rather than let the weaker die and keep the monopoly profits to itself? The only economically sensible reason would be that the weaker is going to take a while to die and in its prolonged death throes will depress the stronger's revenues sufficiently to offset the future monopoly profits. But it makes just as much sense to let the weaker paper die, even if it takes a while, rather than forego the opportunity of a monopoly. The *Washington Post,* of course, did just that. Rather than enter a JOA, it let the *Washington Star* die (but it did not obtain its monopoly because the Unification Church then founded the *Washington Times,* which apparently never needs to turn a profit). Dwight Teeter aptly noted both that a truly failing newspaper is unlikely to be saved by the NPA and that papers saved by the NPA are unlikely to be truly failing. The stronger paper has an incentive to enter a JOA, not when it believes the future holds monopoly, but rather when it foresees continuing competition.[36]

When papers die in major cities because competitors will not join JOAs to save them, half of Teeter's observation is validated. Whether JOA papers are truly failing is harder to substantiate, if only because there have been only a handful of new JOAs since 1970. But many of these have tell-tale qualities suggesting that the weaker paper was not about to go under. The first case seeking the attorney general's approval arose in Anchorage, where the *Times* was in good shape, but the *Daily News* had such obsolete equipment that it was in serious trouble. The Department of Justice did not even think a hearing was necessary prior to approval. The JOA subsequently expired, and McClatchy came in with millions to upgrade the *Daily News*'s equipment, turning it into the larger of the two papers, although it still remains unprofitable (and maybe the *Times* now is, too). The willingness of outsiders to infuse money was squarely put in issue in the Seattle JOA between the afternoon *Seattle Times* and the weaker morning *Post-Intelligencer,* one of Hearst's mismanaged papers. There had been serious inquiries from potential buyers for the *P-I* in three separate years preceding the agreement to form the JOA, and the administrative law judge (ALJ) hearing the case in the Department of Justice found that the *P-I* in all probability could be sold at fair market value to a buyer who would keep it independent. The ALJ then ruled as a matter of law that alternative buyers were irrelevant. Although both the attorney general and the Ninth Circuit Court of Appeals agreed, it will take more than a court decision to convince either economists or reasonable people that a paper thought to have a substantial fair market value is truly heading for death. The very fact of potential buyers at fair market value indicates that there are people in the industry who believe the paper can make a go of it.[37]

Then came the Detroit JOA, which involved papers owned by two of the largest chains in the United States: Gannett and Knight-Ridder. Chains have shown an affinity for JOAs and their shared monopoly. About a quarter of the cities with JOAs have subsequently seen chains (especially Gannett) come in, but Detroit marked the first time that two giants asked to form a JOA. Both Detroit papers were losing millions each year, and given their prices—the all-day *News* at 20¢ per issue (no other Gannett paper goes for less than 25¢) and the morning *Free Press* at 15¢—one can see why. Their parent chains certainly were making money, and each could sustain its paper (although, sadly, the NPA makes the deep pocket of the parent irrelevant). Furthermore, in contrast to the situation in the other cities in which JOAs have been approved, in Detroit neither paper hit a circulation spiral indicating that it would die at some future date. The joint press release of the two said they had "fought to a virtual draw," although to comply with the language of the NPA, the two selected the *Free Press* to be the loser of the even battle. Logically, the fact that neither paper was dying should have precluded approval of the JOA, but the DC Circuit Court of Appeals sustained it, and the Supreme Court split four to four, thereby upholding a merger that some analysts believe will generate $100 million a year in profits within five years. Although that estimate seems unbelievably high, no one disputes that there is a lot of money to be made under the Detroit JOA.[38]

Despite strange occurrences like those in Anchorage and Seattle, the NPA is neither as bad as its critics claim, nor as charmed as its supporters (invariably newspapers) hold. First, it does not and cannot save newspapers that are on the wrong side of the circulation spiral; there is simply no incentive for the stronger to intervene and save the weaker—unless the stronger fears that a third paper will move in and purchase the weaker with an intent to compete. Second, it may not even save two voices in cities with a JOA. Miami, St. Louis, Bristol, Tennessee, and Franklin–Oil City, Pennsylvania, have each seen a newspaper in a JOA fold. In Miami, the Cox and Knight-Ridder chains reached an agreement to extend their NPA-grandfathered JOA through 2021, with Cox killing its weaker *Miami News* immediately, thereby freeing the *Miami Herald* from a drain on the JOA. The murder contract left Cox with 10 percent of the *Herald*'s profits for the next thirty years (and spared the *Herald* some $70 million in covering the anticipated losses of the *News* through 1996, when the first JOA was to expire). Miami and Detroit give strong support to the view that the NPA was raw special-interest legislation designed to line further the pockets of the already wealthy.[39]

Yet the fears of opponents of the NPA—that JOAs would prevent competition—appear overblown as well. To be sure, no new paper has entered into competition against a JOA, but no third paper has successfully entered into a two-paper market either. The economic forces that result in single-paper monopolies are simply too great for a start-up third paper to overcome. A much more valid fear was that JOAs would harm competing suburban papers by their ability to fix advertising prices. This fear was quite realistic, given the desires of most urban papers to find some legal way to crush their suburban competition. Yet it has not happened. Walter Niebauer studied six matched pairs of JOA and competitive newspaper markets for their impact on suburban papers; he found no differences in the numbers of suburban papers between the markets but substantial differences in the circulations of the sets of papers—to wit, that suburban papers in JOA markets had twice the circulation of the suburban papers in competitive markets.[40]

The NPA thus does not appear to have done much to harm or to help newspaper competition. Given the relevant economic forces, the act has little impact beyond enriching a lucky few. Therein lies one further problem. However gratifying it may be for Hearst, Knight-Ridder, Gannett, or even the *New York Times* (controlled by the Ochs Trust, which also controls the *Chattanooga Times*) to obtain a legal shared monopoly, there is something unseemly about a newspaper asking the attorney general of the United States for permission to do business in a specially privileged way. For a brief period, at least, the paper is compromised; and so, too, are our traditions of an independent press. This is not to say that an antitrust exemption violates the First Amendment, for it assuredly does not. Rather, it is to say that the exemption, like most favors, is not cost-free: not to the press; not, on a different basis, to the reading public. The NPA ensures that Liebling's dream of competing urban dailies will remain nothing more than a dream, divorced from reality; because, rather than compete, newspapers desire to merge. Even if the economics of the circulation spiral have placed the competitive urban market on the endangered species list, the NPA says that the antitrust laws cannot be brought to bear to do anything about it, even if we could think of something to be done.[41]

The ideal of the competing newspaper community has captured much of the discussion of antitrust and its possibilities, because everyone knows that a single newspaper is a monopoly. When we move from a local monopoly to the national level, to encounter issues such as increasing chain ownership or the formation of ever larger media holdings within conglomerates, "monopoly" no longer is the technically correct term. Yet the problem may even be greater, because at the national level our concern is that American readers have fewer and fewer options. While the problem of national concentration has seemed clear to media critics, what is less recognized is that the antitrust laws simply do not deal with the large structural problems of the media.

Let me begin with the chain ownership problem, whether it is Thomson with its one hundred small newspapers, Gannett with its ninety-plus scattered in middle-sized communities around the nation, or Newhouse and Knight-Ridder with their fewer papers but larger cities. Leaving aside the NPA, the antitrust laws work well at the local newspaper level because the laws are geared to reasonably interchangeable products within the same geographic market. When one local paper raises its subscription price or advertising rates, we would expect the competing paper to witness increased demand for its product. But when Gannett raises the price of its paper in Rochester, we would not expect any effect on the Gannett (or Knight-Ridder) paper in Detroit. The two are not in the same market, and in no sense compete with each other for readers or advertisers. Bluntly, chain ownership does not deal with the level of competition faced by a paper, and, like it or not, the antitrust laws do. As a former head of general litigation in the Antitrust Division noted, newspaper acquisitions that "may substantially lessen competition" in any line of commerce in "any section of the country" are illegal. But if the Antitrust Division "cannot find a provable economic effect in an identifiable market, there is no action we can take." The loss of independent voices when newspapers are acquired by a chain remains unfortunate, but the antitrust laws, as both written and interpreted, deal with economic competition, and chain ownership per se does not present the problem the laws deal with.[42]

The antitrust laws treat the media no differently from any other industry, and this requires a focus on particular markets. National effects of the usual newspaper merger are probably insignificant. Ironically, the local effects may justify action. Thus while Gannett can swallow newspaper after newspaper with no appreciable national effect, in 1968 when the Thomson and Brush-Moore chains completed a merger of thirty-five newspapers, the Antitrust Division stepped in to force divestiture of two newspapers: in Canton and Alliance, Ohio! Just like the FCC saving Norfolk, Nebraska, and Effingham, Illinois, from their cross-owned monopolies.[43]

The same helplessness occurs when the concern is conglomerate ownership. While there is much to be said for the idea that a democracy should not countenance conglomerates, the simple fact is that we do; and ever since the early 1980s, the merger mania of the United States has created larger and larger economic units. Too many of those units involve media corporations, but as long as the antitrust laws are not implicated by largeness per se, there is nothing to be done by law.[44]

# IV

The toothlessness of the antitrust laws need not be a permanent state. We can always change the antitrust laws to break up types of "concentration" that are deemed harmful. Whether wise or not, such a course of action raises no constitutional questions. But that general course of conduct is currently unlikely in the extreme. Concentration per se is rarely discussed as an evil thing, but media concentration is. Therefore the realistic course is to investigate what would happen if we adopted a media-specific antitrust policy, forcing divestitures of media holdings in circumstances where like holdings of any other type of company would be permitted.

While that has a wonderful sound to it, there may be unfortunate side-effects. Consider the Louisiana of sixty years ago, where Huey Long controlled the state by his stranglehold on rural voters and the avid support of the rural press. Long's wishes being commands in his fiefdom, he wished for a different stranglehold on the urban press. While running Louisiana as a US Senator, he hit on an ingenious idea to bring the opposition urban press to heel: the "two cents per lie tax." As he and his slavishly loyal replacement as governor, Oscar K. ("O.K.") Allen, explained the proposal, the big Louisiana newspapers "tell a lie every time they make a dollar." Long's "lie tax" was a 2 percent gross receipts tax that applied only to newspapers with a circulation of over 20,000 copies per week. There were thirteen of them, with twelve in the opposition camp. Of the 150 remaining papers in the state, there were several nearing the 20,000 cutoff, but they were Long supporters. The Kingfish felt bad about lumping the *Lake Charles American-Press* with his enemies but could not find a way to exempt it from the tax: "We did not think we could do it, but we would have done it if we could."[45]

In *Grosjean v. American Press* the Supreme Court unanimously struck down the tax. Before we look at the Court's reasoning, it is useful to reflect on what would have happened if there were no Fourteenth Amendment. *Grosjean* was decided in 1936, before even radio established itself as a news provider. Had the First Amendment been inapplicable to the states—as has recently been proposed in conservative legal circles—Louisiana (and potentially other states) could have been reduced to the information status of a third-world dictatorship. Fortunately, the Fourteenth Amendment guarantees the application of the First to the states, and the Court confidently analogized the circulation tax to the eighteenth-century English "taxes on knowledge," which attempted to drive up the cost of the more cheaply priced opposition papers. A tax on knowledge curtailed the ability of the citizens to discuss public affairs and was unconstitutional for three reasons: its historical abuse, its intent to limit circulation, and its pin-point hit at only a few newspapers.[46]

Taxes, per se, are hardly unconstitutional. Thus "the tax here involved is bad not because it takes money" from a newspaper. A year later the Supreme Court found frivolous a claim that newspapers enjoyed a constitutional immunity from a general non-discriminatory tax. General nondiscriminatory laws, such as the

Sherman Act, the National Labor Relations Act, the Fair Labor Standards Act, and most tax laws, can be applied to the press. But the line is drawn at special laws. The question remained, however, whether that line was drawn only around Huey Long's home.[47]

It wasn't—as Hubert Humphrey's and Walter Mondale's Farm-Labor Minnesota learned when its 1971 legislature ended the tax exemption for newspapers. Instead of applying the sales tax to the press, Minnesota adopted a use tax based on the cost of the paper and ink products consumed in producing newspapers. Two years later, the legislature gave newspapers a bit of a break when it modified the use tax to exempt the first $100,000 worth of ink and paper consumed each year (functionally a $4000 credit, given the 4 percent use tax). The intriguing aspect of the law was that had the legislature instead extended the 4 percent sales tax to newspapers, they would have paid vastly more than they did with the new use tax; indeed, had the sales tax been extended, the Minneapolis Star and Tribune Company would have paid about $1.8 million yearly, some three times the amount assessed under the use tax. Benefit or not, in *Minneapolis Star & Tribune v. Minnesota Commissioner of Revenue,* the use tax was held unconstitutional.[48]

Although Minnesota's tax was not tainted by the purpose of suppressing an opposition press as was Louisiana's, an illegal purpose is not necessary for a First Amendment violation. Justice O'Connor's opinion for the Court found several independent reasons why the use tax was unconstitutional. The clearest was that it was a tax on large newspapers. The $100,000 exemption resulted in the vast majority of Minnesota papers (some 358 of 374 with any paid circulation) paying no tax at all. Of the limited few that did incur liabilities, over two-thirds of the total was paid by the *Star Tribune.* Tailoring a tax to hit but a few members of the press, whether for evil reasons, as in *Grosjean,* or for benign reasons, is unconstitutional.[49]

But having declared the tax unconstitutional (with the votes of everyone but Rehnquist) because of its impact only on big papers, the Court went on to find the tax unconstitutional for two additional reasons. Both were based on the fact that the tax was special to the press. All nine justices agreed that had Minnesota simply extended the 4 percent sales tax to newspapers, there would have been no constitutional problems. But singling the press out for a special tax possibly loosened political constraints, depriving the press of the insulation normally provided by general legislation. The Court found no good reason for selecting a use tax as a substitute for the sales tax. Rehnquist's dissent had offered the reason that newspaper vending machines might thereafter have to demand 26¢ instead of 25¢ (and noted that the legislature could have considered the alternatives of the papers eating the tax or raising their prices to 30¢ as unattractive), and Rehnquist found that to be sufficient reason to look for alternatives to the sales tax. The majority's answer—that other low-priced goods are not exempted from the general sales tax—is not entirely responsive to Rehnquist's vending machine rationale, but underscores again the majority's conclusion that special taxes on the press are unconstitutional.[50]

Finally, and unnecessarily, the majority discussed whether it mattered that Minnesota's choices benefited the press because applying the sales tax would result in significantly higher liabilities. Despite wonderment whether this was true—coming in the form of a rare (and unfounded) display of judicial modesty that explained how difficult it was for judges to comprehend tax incidence—the Court felt that even if the press were better off with the current "*differential* treatment" it was nevertheless faced "with the possibility of subsequent differentially *more burdensome* treatment." Thus the Court speculated that the legislature might be able to keep the press tame by the implicit threat that the special low tax could be changed to a special high tax. Nowhere did the majority bother to explain why a press that was smart enough to fear the legislature's ratcheting the tax higher might not also be smart enough to know, as Rehnquist did, that the judiciary would not sit by and let stand a tax that uniquely burdened the press. The idea of potentially more burdensome taxes is not, on the Minnesota facts, a particularly compelling rationale. It does, however, again reinforce the essential rationale of the opinion that special press taxes are unconstitutional, while the application of general laws to the press need not be.[51]

The hostility to special laws against the press stole Senator Edward Kennedy's best 1987 Christmas present, which came from his friend Senator Ernest Hollings of South Carolina. Hollings had Communications Subcommittee staffers slip into the 471-page

Continuing Resolution (the funding for the federal government for fiscal year 1988) a nifty little provision that told the FCC it could not have any money if it allowed Rupert Murdoch to operate Boston's Channel 25 while he also owned the *Boston Herald*. Murdoch's *Herald* was a consistent thorn in Kennedy's hide, and Hollings, the chair of the Commerce Committee (parent of the Communications Subcommittee), bluntly stated that he inserted the divestiture requirement to help the senior senator of the Bay State. After all, what are friends for—and what's the Constitution among friends?

The words "Rupert Murdoch," "*Boston Herald*," and "Channel 25" do not appear in Hollings's innocuously worded amendment:

Provided, further, that none of the funds appropriated by this Act or any other Act may be used to repeal, or to retroactively apply changes in, or begin or continue a re-examination of the rules of the Federal Communications Commission with respect to the common ownership of a daily newspaper and a television station where the grade A contour of the television station encompasses the entire community in which the newspaper is published or to extend the time period of current grants of temporary waivers to achieve compliance with such rules. . . .

Not exactly deathless prose, but effective. Murdoch, an American citizen because the Communications Act prohibits aliens from being licensees, just happened to be the only person in the United States who had a current temporary waiver of the cross-ownership rules; because of his acquisition of Fox, he had waivers in both New York City and Boston. (The New York problem was mooted by Murdoch's sale of the *New York Post*.) As a result of the amendment, Murdoch would be forced immediately to sell, to buyers who would know he was in a legal bind, either the *Herald* or Channel 25. If he did not or could not, then the FCC would simply, by the automatic termination of its temporary waiver, "divest" Murdoch of Channel 25. If you don't like Rupert Murdoch's journalism— and many people from Edward Kennedy to Senator Timothy Wirth of Colorado (a former chair of the House Communications Subcommittee) to the author of this book don't—then Hollings's present necessarily makes journalism better. At the cost of the First Amendment.[52]

It would be nice if there were some cost-free way, consistent with the Constitution, to rid the media of the Rupert Murdochs and their debasing of the information stream of the American public. But there isn't, and resort to laser-beam precision legislation to obtain even a good end is, in the apt words of the DC Circuit Court of Appeals, "bound to raise a suspicion that the law's true target is the message" which, of course, would make the law unconstitutional. The DC Circuit then resorted to Supreme Court jargon and demanded that the government "show that its regulation is necessary to serve a compelling state interest and is narrowly drawn to achieve that end." Not surprisingly, a law that demands Rupert Murdoch sell Channel 25 to anyone—including the *Boston Globe*—but does not apply to *any* other waivers of the cross-ownership rules has a good ends-means fit only if its purpose is the unconstitutional one to harm Rupert Murdoch because of the content of his message.[53]

The courts are striving to protect the press from legislation animated by hostility to its printed content. *Grosjean* and *News America Publishing* make the point expressly; *Minneapolis Star & Tribune Co.* is more oblique but recognizes that taxing is a special power that always carries the potential to bring its targets to heel. A broad reading of the cases might suggest that special laws aimed at the media and challenged by their targets are always unconstitutional. But *NCCB v. FCC*, discussed earlier, cautions against such a broad reading of the cases. While their exact import may be debatable, they appear to indicate that the Court is ready to protect the press from content-neutral legislation that masks a content-specific purpose, and that a prophylactic rule is necessary in the tax area because of the ease with which taxes could mask that illegal purpose.

## V

The dominant economic characteristics of newspaper ownership today are local monopolies, JOAs, chain ownership, cross-ownership of a newspaper and television station in the same city, and media conglomerates. It is not an attractive picture. Yet between the NPA and the current limits of antitrust law, there is virtually nothing practical we can do without adopting some difficult changes. Following World War II the Hutchins Commission, appropriately taking a long-range view, concluded that if the "great concentrations" of private media power are "irresponsible, not even the First Amendment will protect their freedom from governmental control." Yet saying that a long-run solution may be available later provides small consolation for those who see a more immediate problem now and would rather do something about it sooner than later—when possibly the too concentrated media will be able to create a false consensus that immunizes it from change.[54]

In *Government and Mass Communications,* Chafee stated that the decision whether it was wise actively to employ the antitrust laws against concentration in the communications industry is "the most important problem discussed in my book, and also the most difficult." For the ACLU's Morris Ernst, writing just a year earlier in *The First Freedom,* it was a laydown: the antitrust laws were an important content-neutral mechanism to prevent concentrations that might distort the marketplace of ideas. What separated Chafee's perception of difficulty from Ernst's more typical response was a query about how effective the antitrust laws really were and a concern about excessive governmental involvement with the media.[55]

Chafee, unlike Ernst and other advocates of greater antitrust enforcement, thought that Sherman Act enforcement worked "none too well for commodity businesses." Time has validated the conclusion that antitrust actions are no panacea for guaranteeing competition among small units. It is therefore unlikely to prove effective in combating media concentration. Some solace from that conclusion may be found in the possibility that the problem of media concentration is not as great as has been suggested. Both Liebling and Bagdikian were print journalists from age cohorts that could not conceive of broadcasting as a potential claimant to the print tradition. (Indeed, in the summer of 1989 Bagdikian complained in Senate testimony of newspaper support for full First Amendment rights for broadcasters.) Possibly because they come out of this older print tradition, with its inability to see broadcasters as peers, their writings presume that once there was a better time.[56]

To be sure, it would be nice to have a choice of several local newspapers. Instead, for local information we must typically rely on a single local newspaper, three local television stations, and maybe a handful of radio stations. For national and international news, Americans once had all the information available in their competing local newspapers, supplemented by some weekly news magazines. Now the competing local daily is gone. But in its stead most Americans can find the *New York Times, USA Today,* or the *Wall Street Journal.* None, of course, has an afternoon edition. Their operations recognize the realities of the information market. Newspapers are for mornings; radio controls drive-time; and in the evening, television (now meaning PBS and Cable News Network in addition to the three networks), the most trusted news source, dominates. Today may not be as good as the good old days, but it is not a reinstitution of the Dark Ages either.

There are more giant companies out there, and giants pose dangers. But there are a fair number of competing outlets, too, and Americans, if they wish, can acquire a considerable diversity of information. Having said that, I do not wish to claim that things could not be better; my point is that they may not be as bad as some of the statements quoted in this chapter suggest. Acknowledging that they could be better offers an alternative to yearning for a return to a better past; it demands, as Bagdikian does, that we strive for a better future. If antitrust has not worked as well as hoped, that does not mean that it could not be improved.

It is possible to argue that *Grosjean* and *Minneapolis Star & Tribune Co.* stand as barriers against a media-specific antitrust policy; but both seem more naturally concerned with the potential of using special tax laws to force the media to conform. As noted earlier, they are prophylactic decisions, necessary to protect the First Amendment demands of content neutrality. In *NCCB* the Court unanimously sustained a major effort to diversify media holdings. It held that we may seek diversity of ownership because we believe it will provide diversity of views; and that does not make the structural regulation content-based, because *any* content then appearing is acceptable. While one could argue that the same principle would have made Senator Hollings's attack on Murdoch valid, there is a world of difference between a law applying to a single individual and one applying to numerous firms throughout an industry.

Forty years ago Justice Douglas wrote that "in matters relating to business, finance, industrial and labor conditions, health and the public welfare, great leeway is now granted the legislature, for there is no guarantee in the Constitution that the status quo will be preserved against regulation by government." First Amendment rights are different, he went on, because they "are placed separate and apart; they are above and beyond the police power; they are not subject to regulation in the manner of factories, slums, apartment houses, production of oil, and the like." Although Douglas's rhetoric may have run away with him—as this chapter notes, many general laws may be indeed applied to the press—he is obviously correct that the First Amendment is above and apart because of its essential relationship to democratic governance. Without information, there is no way the citizens can tell their government how to perform.[57]

The idea of media-specific antitrust law is attractive precisely because, as Learned Hand recognized in *Associated Press,* the media are essential to the preservation of a democratic society, and concentration of the media makes them less likely to produce the diversity of voices we would hope to have available. It may be that it will prove impossible to obtain new antitrust laws, although, as Bagdikian noted, the increase in concentration in the four years between his two editions forced him to offer politically unachievable proposals because they offer the only realistic solution. It may be that the economic forces acting in the communications industry will defeat any future changes made in the antitrust laws. But the Constitution does not stand as a bar to prevent the polity from taking steps to reduce concentration in the one industry most important to our well-being as a democracy. We should recall, though, Chafee's reminder that if we rely on the antitrust laws, we must nevertheless be wary of too great an association between government and the industry.[58]

This is, as Chafee further recognized, an exceptionally difficult problem, because on paper the solution seems so attractive, and yet reality cautions that easy solutions do not always yield the anticipated consequences. Nevertheless, a democratic polity cannot cede its ability to regulate the structure of the communications industry. The First Amendment, while prohibiting government from regulating content, does not leave the government without power to prevent and abate concentrations of power. That was Justice Black's message in *Associated Press,* and it is as valid now as the day it was written.[59]

■    ■    ■

# Part Three

# Models

# Overview

We have looked at the traditions of freedom of the press and at the major legal issues that confront the press. There have been hints that some theory of freedom of the press can explain many of the Supreme Court decisions, and the chapters which follow discuss popular models of freedom of the press that promise some descriptive and considerable prescriptive accuracy; that is, models having some judicial support and offering the ability to suggest outcomes across a range of cases.

No phrase has captivated those speaking for the media more than "the public's right to know." This post–World War II phrase has such an attractive ring that it often becomes synonymous with freedom of the press. Of its many attractive qualities, none exceeds its absence of any connotations of special privilege, which often accompany the concept of freedom of the press. Yet the public's right to know is neither self-defining nor self-executing. Its ambiguities lead to two entirely different models of freedom of the press. One would grant the press preferred status among all communicators, complete with the special legal privileges that entails. This right-to-know model elevates the press as the public's surrogate in vindicating the public's rights. The other, pointing in the opposite direction, uses the government as a surrogate for the public and regulates the press in those ways essential to seeing that the public's right to know receives vindication in fact as well as rhetoric. These two models and their interrelation are discussed in Chapter 8.

Chapter 9 takes its title "The Fourth Estate" from the memorable phrase of Edmund Burke. Like the right to know, the "Fourth

233

Estate" phrase has been used with more frequency in the last twenty years—especially after it received extrajudicial support from an important speech by Justice Stewart. The press, as the Fourth Estate, retains its independence from the other three—Lords Spiritual, Lords Temporal, and Commons, which have in modern times been subsumed into one: the government. The press is autonomous, functioning as a watchdog on the government, publicizing abuses, and, one hopes, arousing the citizenry. The cornerstone of the discussion in Chapter 9 is *Miami Herald v. Tornillo*, a case in which the Supreme Court validated the necessary autonomy of the press.

*Chapter Eight*

# The Right to Know

The Hand decision in *Associated Press* was but one of a series of events giving the press a bad name. Franklin D. Roosevelt's driving, acerbic, and very able FCC chairman, James Lawrence Fly, had told a press conference at the annual meeting of the National Association of Broadcasters that the leadership of the industry reminded him of "a dead mackerel in the moonlight—it both shines and stinks." Such universal condemnation was appropriate for print, too, because no matter how well FDR performed, the vast majority of daily newspapers were certain that whoever was selected by the Republican National Convention could do a better job. William Allen White, when president of the American Society of Newspaper Editors, told his colleagues to stop looking elsewhere for someone to blame and instead put their own house in order. Against this background, Henry Luce of Time-Life decided that what the press could use was a substantial restatement of its importance to American democracy, and he provided $200,000 for a Commission on Freedom of the Press to do the restating.[1]

With the donation of the money and selection of the chairman, University of Chicago President Robert Maynard Hutchins, the boy-wonder of American higher education, Luce's role was over. Thereafter Hutchins, Dean of the Yale Law School at the age of 28, president of the University of Chicago just two years later, a supernova if there ever was one, took over. He put together what may be the most star-studded private commission ever created: the poet and Librarian of Congress Archibald MacLeish; the theologian Reinhold Niebuhr; the Harvard historian Arthur M. Schlesinger,

Sr.; Charles E. Merriam, chair of the political science department at Chicago; and Harold Lasswell, the director of war communications research at the Library of Congress and one of the leading political scientists of his generation. Ten of its thirteen members were of such importance that they are discussed at least briefly in one of the important studies of American thought from 1920 to 1945, Edward A. Purcell's *The Crisis of Democratic Theory*. Two of the three who were not, Zechariah Chafee and the Harvard philosopher (emeritus) William Ernest Hocking, had national reputations within their fields and were well versed in theories of freedom of the press.[2]

This was no modern commission of notables, where staff members prepare high-sounding documents to be ratified by the famous. Instead the commission met extensively over a three-year period before producing its controversial report, *A Free and Responsible Press*, not to mention six individually authored books (including Chafee's *Government and Mass Communications*). On one hand the report talked about rights, but on the other hand it tied them to responsibilities: "Since the claim of the right is based on the duty of a man to the common good and to his thought, the ground of the claim disappears when this duty is ignored or rejected."[3]

The commission believed that the press was not meeting its obligation to fully and fairly inform the public and that economic forces were driving the press in directions where its responsibilities would be further eroded. These beliefs, when coupled with the report's use of common-carrier analogies and its labeling of the press "a business affected with the public interest," could be, and were, taken as calls for government regulation despite explicit statements to the contrary.[4]

Hutchins, undoubtedly anticipating a hostile press reaction, accurately noted that there was nothing "startling" about the commission's recommendations. A. J. Liebling agreed, finding the report not strong enough to suit him. The tone of the report and its general failure to sing the press's praises resulted in its being mostly ignored—an unconscionable slight, given the commission's membership—and invariably condemned by the few who noticed it. Its central question, however, could not be so easily dismissed. If the press has special guaranteed rights and those rights carry with them responsibilities, then what remedies, if any, are appropriate to ensure that the responsibilities are met? It is useful to look at various justifications for protecting freedom of expression, before focusing specifically on the claim that freedom of the press is protected to fulfill the public's right to know.[5]

# I

The ringing reaffirmation Luce desired would have found its roots in John Milton and John Stuart Mill, with more modern antecedents in Justices Holmes and Brandeis. Holmes captured the tradition in a phrase when he introduced the dominant First Amendment metaphor, the marketplace of ideas: "But when men have realized that time has upset many fighting faiths, they may come to believe even more than they believe the very foundations of their own conduct that the ultimate good desired is better reached by free trade in ideas—that the best test of truth is the power of the thought to get itself accepted in the competition of the market."[6]

Brandeis, in a wonderful six-word sentence, observed: "Men feared witches and burnt women." How else, except through discussion, can irrational fears be exposed for what they are? As Milton had observed centuries ago, "who ever knew Truth put to the worse, in a free and open encounter?" Even *New York Times v. Sullivan,* which is identified with a different justification than the marketplace, found it impossible to avoid the metaphor's power. The First Amendment "was fashioned to assure unfettered interchange of ideas." Erroneous statements are bound to be made, but the breathing space necessary for uninhibited debate protects them. Furthermore, even falsity serves a function in the marketplace, as Mill observed, by bringing about "the clear perception and livelier impression of truth, produced by its collision with error."[7]

Although other theories of freedom of expression exist, none has as long a lineage or as distinguished a group identified with it. In fact, it is difficult to avoid Holmes's marketplace metaphor because it manages to capture so much. It recognizes change; it resonates with an adversarial and competitive system that lawyers and economists find congenial; and it offers a more neutral arbiter of truth than the appraisal of a single individual or government. It is not without limitations, however, and over the years alternative explanations have proven more popular with those writing in the area.

Although *New York Times* has language supporting the marketplace metaphor, it is, as Chapter 3 shows, most closely identified with Alexander Meiklejohn's competing conception: that freedom of speech is protected because it is an essential aspect of self-governance. Meiklejohn expects self-governing citizens to vote on behalf of wise policies, and that is impossible without all relevant information. How else can the people know what policies and politicians to favor? Only if citizens are free to discuss everything that relates to public policy can a democracy thrive. Meiklejohn's approach has the added attraction of tying in perfectly with American views that sovereignty exists in the citizenry. Those who temporarily govern are merely agents, and naturally, agents have no authority to limit the information their superiors need.[8]

Just as Meiklejohn's conception shades into marketplace ideas at one end—citizens must decide—it shades into another justification of freedom of speech at the other. Historically governments, too, often even our own, have viewed freedom of speech as carrying delegitimizing potential. Only a very secure government tolerates such open questioning of its justifications. John Roche captured this beautifully when he modified Lord Acton's famous dictum on power corrupting to read: "Power corrupts but the prospect of losing power corrupts absolutely." Those holding government office too often wish to use state power to control the dangerous ideas of the opposition, as illustrated by the Sedition Act, the prosecution of World War I dissenters, and the efforts to deny employment to those perceived as too red or pink in the 1950s. Santayana was right that those who forget their history wind up repeating it; and one of the important lessons learned is that a strong protection of freedom of speech is essential to check the propensity of government to win a debate, and thereby engage in a particular course of action, by fiat rather than by votes or reason. The checking theory, unlike both the marketplace and self-government theories, is bottomed in neither truth nor rationality, but rather in distrust. It assumes a darker side of human nature and holds that those who wield governmental power will be prone to overreaching, and thus that it is essential to provide information for a resisting citizenry.[9]

The three foregoing justifications are all avowedly instrumental; they turn on consequences. Each protects freedom of speech, not for its own sake, but because freedom of speech is a means to an end worth achieving: ascertaining truth, promoting self-government, checking government abuses. Because each is justified as leading to certain results, each can be subjected to empirical verification (assuming that appropriate measuring tools exist). And anything that can be subjected to empirical verification, may, in the process, be shown false. Because no one really wants the justifications for freedom of speech to be refuted, some scholars have justified speech on noninstrumental grounds, thereby guaranteeing that no set of facts could upset their theory.

The principal treatment of speech as an end in itself intertwines speech with an individual's self-actualization and dignity. In his justly famous *Whitney* concurrence, Brandeis wrote that "those who won our independence believed that the final end of the State was to make men free to develop their faculties. . . . They valued liberty both as an end and a means. They believed liberty to be the secret of happiness and courage to be the secret of liberty." Resting partially on Brandeis for their judicial authority and partially on the weaknesses of the instrumental justifications, some modern theorists, especially C. Edwin Baker, have focused exclusively on the liberty aspect of speech, treating speech as an integral part of human self-realization. To be truly a human being, one must have a free mind. To cabin thoughts and discussions is an exercise of illegitimate despotic control by the state over the individual.[10]

None of the justifications of freedom of speech is without its difficulties. The marketplace model rests on a belief in objective truth and in the predominance of rational thought, and an almost religious faith that truth will prevail, all of which beliefs have suffered greatly in this century. It also raises issues, such as those discussed in Chapter 7, about entry barriers and oligopoly power. Meiklejohn's rationale carries the potential to exclude from protection anything that does not provide information about issues on which citizens may be called on to vote. Furthermore, it seems to describe more of an Athenian polity (actually his model was a New England town meeting) rather than a huge nation where voter participation rarely reaches 50 percent. Nor does it explain well why those very same self-governing citizens might not determine that some information was so harmful to the polity—the H-bomb problem is illustrative—that it must be suppressed regardless of the views of the few who would like to discuss it.

The checking value assumes that abuse by government is more harmful than abuses by concentrations of private power, because the government can act uniformly across jurisdictions. Furthermore, the checking value gains textual force from the language of the First Amendment itself, which is, after all, directed toward governmental, not private, abuses. Like Meiklejohn and the marketplace, it, too, has an elite, antidemocratic strain that decides for the governing majority that its long-run needs and values should trump their more strongly held short-run desires. It also rigidly dichotomizes speech from all other human activity, in which government participation is seen, at least by those who are not doctrinaire libertarians, as beneficial rather than harmful. The same rigid dichotomy is present in the self-realization theory, which is often perceived by critics as limitless in its thrust. Speech is but one example of an activity that is self-realizing—sex, smoking crack, or riding a motorcycle at 90 miles an hour without a helmet are others—and the theory often seems better suited to libertarianism than freedom of speech.[11]

Thomas Emerson, who with Kalven dominated the post-Chafee generation, realized, as too many others have not, that looking for a single explanation for the importance of freedom of speech is a futile search. Each of the theories has explanatory power. Each has serious weaknesses. Each one, taken on its own, fails to provide an adequate basis for heightened protection of freedom of expression. Emerson's great insight, implicit in Brandeis's *Whitney* concurrence, was that the whole is stronger than the sum of its parts. There is a synergy among the various explanations for freedom of expression that is lost when the discussion deals with the strengths and weaknesses of a single theory. Hence, when only one theory of freedom of expression is put forward, the claim for heightened protection will be weaker than if the full panoply of justifications were brought to bear on the problem, as section III of this chapter shows.[12]

I have gone through this abbreviated analysis of freedom of speech because it is important to realize that many writers justify freedom of the press by only a single theory—necessarily an instrumental one. Although, as the history recounted in Chapter 1 illustrates, the framers thought of freedom of the press before freedom of speech, modern analysis places freedom of the press as a subset of freedom of speech in the various theories of freedom of expression. Freedom of the press, like free speech, can advance truth, provide useful information for self-governing citizens, and operate to check governmental abuses. Because it can fit within each theory (and its fit within the checking theory is more precise than that of free speech), it is subject to whatever limitations each has.

It is rarely perceived that freedom of the press can also fit within a liberty theory—although unlike freedom of speech it is unclear whose self-realization is at issue: that of the reporters, the editors, the publishers, or the owning corporation (a logical impossibility— but the human components, at least, are capable of seeing what is published in a newspaper as being important to their self-realization). Although I, too, place little emphasis on the self-realization value, it is important to realize that in some circumstances it will arise in a discussion of freedom of the press. Nevertheless, editors, publishers, and most academic theorists explain freedom of the press in purely instrumental terms. We do not protect the press for itself, but rather because it serves to guarantee other fundamental values. Thus the Hutchins Commission report, as well as Hocking's separate volume, based freedom of the press on the national need to have a morally responsible body politic with the necessary information to make intelligent decisions. Hocking quoted the commission's staff director, Robert Leigh, who noted that freedom of the press "has changed its point of focus from the editor to the citizen."[13]

## II

Despite similar instrumental justifications for freedom of expression and freedom of the press, public discussions of the two are typically quite different. Occasionally speakers are required to justify their exercise of freedom of speech, but the questions will not place at issue all freedom of speech. The right is too universal. Freedom of the press is different for just that reason. As the quotation from Liebling at the beginning of Chapter 7 trenchantly notes, only those who can afford to own a press can exercise the rights of freedom of the press, whatever they are. It is a privileged position, and privileges are not well respected in American debate, as the press knows too well. As a result, discussions of freedom of the press become doubly instrumental. First, for the reasons just discussed, a self-realization justification for press freedom is difficult and often factually impossible. Therefore, instrumental justifications—whether marketplace, self-government, or checking—predominate. But the issue of privilege introduces a second, and more directly instrumental, justification into the debate, for typically the press justifies itself somewhat along the lines of "we do it all for you" or, as Dan Rather facetiously offered, "[our] cause is America."[14]

Walter Cronkite wondered why the beneficiaries of freedom of the press had so much difficulty comprehending its value. "Why can't the American people see that freedom of the press is not some privilege extended to a favored segment of the population but is purely and simply their own right to be told what their government and its servants are doing in their name?" Cronkite's statement, made during Watergate, offers a checking value view of the press; yet, in 1973, many Americans were not as interested as the press in checking Richard Nixon's government. An alternative and more prevalent formulation at the time was articulated by Justice Douglas: "The press has a preferred position in our constitutional scheme, not to enable it to make money, not to set newsmen apart as a favored class, but to bring fulfillment of the public's right to know." Douglas, always well attuned to the outside world impacting on the First Amendment, was presenting for the press its own best case in its own terms. "We do it all for you" means "our" profession vindicates your "right to know."[15]

Kent Cooper, a high corporate official with Associated Press, claims to have popularized the phrase "right to know" in a speech he gave at the end of World War II and then promoted in a similarly titled book written in the mid-1950s. Although often tied specifically into demands for freedom of information statutes and open meeting laws, the right to know gained a momentum of its own and was, by the end of the 1960s, treated by the media as a synonym for freedom of the press. The linguistic switch had immediate benefits for the press. The democratic connotations of "right to know" jettisoned the problem of privilege, while the elasticity of the phrase provided a cover for any issue facing an embattled and litigious national press.[16]

The logical implications of the right to know, as well as the momentum from the peak years of the Warren Court (discussed in Chapter 3), led the press to litigate in the 1970s for special—but allegedly necessary—press rights. The right to know implied a preferred position within the Constitution; and there had been an antecedent.

Shortly after the New Deal established hegemony over the judiciary in the late 1930s, the Supreme Court had announced that First Amendment freedoms enjoyed a "preferred position" among constitutional rights. This rhetoric lasted well over a decade, until it was overwhelmed by the Court's acquiescence in the national purge of reds and pinks in the 1950s. When the Court emerged from the trauma, the preferred position was already an anachronism—for with the bulk of the Bill of Rights being applied to the checking of state governments, it was apparent that the Court liked the whole Bill of Rights, except for the Second Amendment's right to bear arms and the Seventh's right to jury trial in civil cases. Flushed with judicial victories, major scoops, and an important extrajudicial speech by Potter Stewart, and filled with the hubris that the right to know invites, the press modified the old preferred-position debate. Not only was the First Amendment special, but within the First the press enjoyed a preferred position, because only the press served all Americans. The *New York Times* lawyer Floyd Abrams, a skilled and scholarly advocate, and the insightful Melville Nimmer demonstrated that the preferred-position argument had constitutional force, if not authority, behind it.[17]

The press's preferred-position argument debuted in *Branzburg;* the outcome was a defeat. But how much? Three justices had taken the press position on its own terms, and Douglas accepted the logic of the right to know so fully that he would have given the press more than it dared to ask. Then there was Powell's Solomon-like vote, indicating that he had some sympathy with the preferred-position argument in some circumstances. Maybe it wasn't such a defeat at all.

It was all downhill from there. Whether in the context of access to prisons, or of a newsroom search for evidence of third-party criminality, or of "editorial privilege" in *Herbert v. Lando,* or of access to the preliminary hearing in *DePasquale,* defeat followed defeat for the preferred-position, much as night follows day. It was an idea whose time came and went in a flash. The white flag of surrender was raised by Laurence Tribe, arguing for the newspapers in *Richmond Newspapers.* Asked by Justice Stewart whether his clients were not the press, he responded that he was "not making a point of their status" beyond observing that he would be distressed if they were treated *worse* than others. Chief Justice Burger, whose personal dislike for the press geometrically increased when he heard preferred-position arguments, then interjected: "Is there any difference in whether a person wants to attend to write something or just make a speech about it?" "None," Tribe responded, "nor if he just wanted to inform himself as a citizen."[18]

With surrender came victory. *Richmond Newspapers* closed the preferred-position argument while opening courtrooms, with the likely beneficiaries being those newspapers that assign reporters to cover trials—and therefore the reading public, who, while not able to take the time and effort to attend, can nevertheless be informed about the functioning of the system of justice. Then the special tax cases, litigated without preferred-position arguments, in fact granted the press a special position when to do so was necessary to protect its autonomy.

The specifics of the cases rejecting a preferred position were detailed in Part Three. Some cases could have gone the other way, but the totality of the preferred-position argument was a loser. The press was claiming privileges that would have been accorded no one else. At a time when major institutions of private power, whether corporations or universities, were coming under increased scrutiny by the government and public, it was somewhat unworldly to believe that one major institution could not only remain immune, but indeed garner special legal privileges as well. The very rationale that caused the press to grab hold of the right to know as a synonym for freedom of the press—the problem of privilege—almost mandated the outcome of the litigation seeking a preferred position. The law, and especially the Constitution, grants privileged status with reluctance and only for the most compelling reasons. However much the press argued that it really needed the right in question, its own vigorous behavior belied the assertion. An arrogant, cantankerous, adversarial press could remain "uninhibited, robust, and wide-open" with very little assistance from the legal system beyond the guarantee of the right to publish.

### III

The press's efforts to gain a preferred constitutional status under the press clause were paralleled by a development that pointed in the opposite direction, to a position where the press would be subordinate to other communicators. Ironically, this development, too, had its roots in Warren Court decisions.

After the *New York Times* decision was handed down, Meiklejohn told Kalven that it was an occasion for dancing in the streets. While they were dancing, Jerome Barron was preparing his article, "Access to the Press—A New First Amendment Right," which contested both the older Holmesian marketplace and the newer Meiklejohnian synthesis. Barron had not been a part of the earlier First Amendment debates where the discussions addressed how better to protect more speech. His specialty was broadcasting, and his scholarship vigorously supported its regulation. Furthermore, as a citizen he was concerned with the one-sided pro-war position of the media. These coalesced to create the insights of "Access."[19]

Barron argued that *New York Times* was not a landmark for freedom of expression but rather was a missed opportunity. The Court had simply perpetuated the romantic myth of a smoothly functioning, self-correcting marketplace of ideas. If that market ever had existed, it no longer did. Instead, concentration of ownership, canned editorials, and syndicated columnists had diminished the "robust" debate for which Brennan called and had effectively excluded most of the public from participation in the debate.

Barron's thesis was thus a radical attack on both the Supreme Court's jurisprudence and the best of the academic writing on freedom of expression. Part of his critique had been anticipated, although not from the usual sources of debate on First Amendment jurisprudence. Conservative economists had tweaked the hegemonic academic belief that although marketplaces of goods and services needed government regulation in order to function in the public interest, the marketplace of ideas was guided by an "invisible hand." What these lonely economists wanted from the academy was praise for markets and condemnation of government regulation. What Barron gave them instead was agreement that there was an anomalous difference in the way we treated the markets, coupled with a ringing cry that the treatment must be brought into harmony. The government, Barron argued, must accept its duty to remedy the defects of a concentrated marketplace of ideas.[20]

For Barron the issue was the quality of debate in the marketplace. Citizens could not hope to own printing presses and were generally excluded from the pages of papers. Yet the Court in *New York Times* took a powerful institution and gave it yet another right. As Mark Tushnet would later (and perhaps excessively) put it, "The First Amendment, usually thought of as a vehicle by which otherwise powerless people can gain power, became another one of the assets held by the powerful." Rather than protection from libel, Barron believed that the opportunity in *New York Times* had been to advance debate by fashioning a right to reply to a libel, as a hoped-for prelude to readers' rights of response generally to articles appearing in the paper.[21]

Unlike Meiklejohn, who wrote in 1948 and received the Court's imprimatur in 1964, Barron did not have long to wait for judicial validation. Just two years after "Access" appeared, the Supreme Court decided *Red Lion Broadcasting v. FCC* and sustained the constitutionality of the FCC's Fairness Doctrine, requiring that broadcasters (1) present controversial issues of public importance to their audiences and (2) ensure that both sides of the issues are available.[22]

With *New York Times* but five years old and clearly in its expansive phase, it is hardly surprising that broadcasters analogized their plight under the Fairness Doctrine to that of newspapers under the chill of libel law. Yet despite Kalven's proclamation that *New York Times* was *the* First Amendment decision, it was to have no influence on *Red Lion*'s outcome. It was cited but a single time, in conjunction with a reference to Holmes's *Abrams* dissent and in the context of an assertion that the purpose of the First Amendment was to "preserve an uninhibited marketplace of ideas in which truth will ultimately prevail."[23]

The difference in tone between that quotation and Brennan's "uninhibited, robust, and wide-open" signaled that the Court was going elsewhere. It was still going with Meiklejohn, albeit a very different aspect of Meiklejohn than that celebrated by Kalven and

*New York Times.* The key to Meiklejohn's analysis was his belief in the rational citizen-governor who would consider the options fully and then "vote wise decisions." Adopting the mode of a New England town meeting, Meiklejohn looked to structured debate with Robert's Rules of Order prevailing. He focused not on "the words of the speakers, but the minds of the hearers." Thus, "what is essential is not that everyone shall speak, but that everything worth saying shall be said." With the focus on the listeners rather than the speakers, the state may play a moderating role to ensure that ideas essential to decision making are brought forward and redundancies limited. It was this part of Meiklejohn's argument that *Red Lion* embraced.[24]

The Court took the noncontroversial starting point that "the people as a whole retain their interest in free speech by radio and their collective right to have the medium function consistently with the ends and purposes of the First Amendment." First Amendment scholars would expect at this point a reference to Brandeis's *Whitney* opinion covering the various purposes of the First Amendment. Instead, the Court followed with a statement which, to someone unfamiliar with Meiklejohn, would be startling: "It is the right of the viewers and listeners, not the right of the broadcasters, which is paramount."[25]

The Court squarely adopted a listeners'-right-to-know model, which explains the previous sentence about the ends and purposes of the First Amendment. Instead of the usual concern with governmental interference with the marketplace, *Red Lion* took the metaphor in a different direction, toward improving the marketplace; it thereby provided a tremendous reinforcement for Barron's thesis. The switch in focus from speakers to listeners demanded an inquiry into what occurs when the marketplace malfunctions by creating unjustifiable barriers to the entry of new ideas into the competitive mix. The answer, following Barron, was that government might, indeed must, selectively intervene to remove entry barriers, thereby promoting efficiency. That, after all, is the basic theory behind much of antitrust law, whether the market in question be widgets or ideas. But *Red Lion* was not stopping at antitrust; the positive role government could play was not limited to structural regulation. A listener-oriented right-to-know model requires some implementing scheme. One, following Barron directly, would have listeners come forward and state what they wish to hear (by whatever mechanism that could be accomplished). A second would have a government mediator decide what listeners want or need to hear. The ink was barely dry when the two models were put in collision in *CBS v. Democratic National Committee [DNC]*.[26]

*CBS v. DNC* was a case, like *Branzburg*, that had already become famous under another name; at the FCC and the DC Circuit Court of Appeals it was known as *BEM* (for *Business Executives' Move for Vietnam Peace*). The DC Circuit had ruled that if a broadcaster accepted any advertising, then it could not refuse those wishing to purchase editorial advertising. There was, the court ruled, an "abridgeable" First Amendment right to purchase advertising on broadcast stations. Neither before nor since, and with good reason, has a court ever created a new First Amendment right by using the adjective "abridgeable."[27]

The Supreme Court would have none of the DC Circuit's reasoning. Random advertorials (as they were called) could undermine the structured debate promised by the Fairness Doctrine. Those wishing to speak could hardly be relied on to judge the value of their own ideas or the public's need to hear them. That was the function of broadcasters, as supervised by the FCC. "Determining what best serves the public's right to be informed is a task of great delicacy and difficulty." In the first instance the broadcaster makes the decisions, subject of course to overruling by the government mediator whose task it is to follow the "admonition of Professor Meiklejohn that '[w]hat is essential is not that everyone shall speak, but that everything worth saying shall be said.'" Although the listeners'-rights model remained intact, access was rejected as a solution, because it could not, as supposedly the FCC could, ensure the true fruition of listeners' rights to information.[28]

The defeat of access in *CBS v. DNC* was nothing compared to its unanimous trouncing a year later in *Miami Herald v. Tornillo*, a case squarely testing Barron's thesis and, appropriately enough, argued by Barron himself. *Tornillo*, which is the centerpiece of Chapter 9, embraced a Fourth Estate checking model and rejected the right-to-know model for the print media. It thus stands as a bar to imposing broadcast-like obligations on the press. Nevertheless, almost immediately a newer generation of academics found a need to reconsider *Tornillo*'s rationale and its implications.[29]

*Tornillo* did not kill the right-to-know model; it limited it. The model itself received a substantial boost in *Virginia State Board of Pharmacy v. Virginia Citizens Consumer Council,* where the Supreme Court held that the First Amendment precluded a state from banning advertising for legal commercial products. The decision implied, and subsequent cases so held, that protections afforded commercial speech would be more limited than normal, as the state had a greater interest in protecting listeners from advertisements that might mislead them (the paternalistic facet of the listeners'-right-to-know model). That the case was purely a listeners'-rights decision was dramatically illustrated by the lack of a willing speaker. The plaintiffs who brought the suit wanted to *hear* comparison-price advertising. The Virginia Board of Pharmacy was sued because it was the regulatory body precluding such ads. But for the first, and only, time in a domestic speech case, there was not even a nominal would-be speaker.[30]

*Virginia Pharmacy* could not undo the crimp *Tornillo* put on full fruition of a listeners'-rights model, especially after the Court decided *Buckley v. Valeo* and *First National Bank of Boston v. Bellotti,* a pair of highly controversial campaign finance cases. These two cases explicitly rejected arguments, coming from *Red Lion,* that because a fair election debate is essential, governments could limit the amount that private citizens and corporations spend to support candidates and ballot propositions. "The concept that government may restrict the speech of some elements of our society in order to enhance the relative voice of others," the Court held, "is wholly foreign to the First Amendment."[31]

By holding that spending could not be limited, *Buckley* and *Bellotti* allowed the better-funded campaigns to buy more access to the public arena of debate than their poorly funded competitors. This allowed the possibility—and to some the near certainty—that the marketplace of ideas would become the preserve of the privileged. "Unchecked political expenditures, no less than crass regulation of ideas, may drown opposing beliefs, vitiate the principles of political equality, and place some citizens under the damaging and arbitrary control of others." Wealth, not talent or the merit of ideas, is the ticket to the public's ear. The political market simply becomes another reflection of the unequal distribution of income rather than of the distribution of ideas held by citizens of the polity.

With political action committees raising money in an unceasing harvest, and with corporations, such as those in the tobacco and nuclear power industries, spending massively to defeat referenda aimed at their products, the underlying First Amendment theory of *Buckley* and *Bellotti* did not appear as neutral in fact as it was in theory.[32]

My colleague Sanford Levinson has aptly noted: "If both political views and the propensity to spend money on politics were distributed randomly among the entire populace, it is hard to see why anyone would be very excited about the issue of campaign finance." Levinson's trenchant point is that there is no such randomization; with F. Scott Fitzgerald we believe that the rich are different, that they think differently from the rest of us, and, more ominously, that they are willing to spend their money as necessary to convince us that we ought to accept their views.[33]

*Buckley* and *Bellotti* shattered the decades-old First Amendment consensus of the academy, that more speech is better. Once, statements about speech rebutting speech had carried the day; now they sounded very abstract and unconvincing. Money translates too easily into power, and power into domination and distortion of the marketplace of ideas. In the 1980s a number of academics, notably Owen Fiss and Judith Lichtenberg, concluded that some regulation of concentrations of private power, including the print media, was constitutionally allowable and politically necessary.

Admittedly influenced by Charles Lindblom's *Politics and Markets,* Fiss wished to counter the distorting power of wealth, especially the wealth of corporations (including media corporations), on the political process. As Fiss saw the marketplace of ideas, it is a fit candidate for government countervailing power, which historically has been a necessary antidote to the distortions created by "grossly unequal distributions of power." Where but with the state can we find power to equal that of CBS? Who else but the state can "supplement" the marketplace of ideas? Fiss offered a First Amendment solution that is wholly instrumental, designed to achieve that "rich public debate" necessary for self-government and assisting a people with a "limited capacity . . . to learn all that they must to function effectively as citizens." If the appropriate debate does not exist, or if the government believes there are ideas that are not being heard, or not being heard enough, then it has both the "power" and duty to act. "The state must put on the agenda issues that are systematically ignored and slighted and allow us to hear voices and viewpoints that would otherwise be silenced or muffled." The state may act as it finds necessary, even if that means "frustration of would-be speakers" when their speech would "drown out the voices of others or systematically distort the public agenda."[34]

Lichtenberg, who, unlike Fiss, focused explicitly on the press, saw many of the same problems highlighted by Fiss. Editors, rather than providing information, can restrict it. They stand as important censors in the system of information distribution, censors with real power to influence and distort the marketplace of ideas. With Fiss, Lichtenberg was concerned with the excessive power of the privileged few who can own a newspaper.[35]

Lichtenberg wrote that "nothing guarantees that all valuable information, ideas, theories, explanations, proposals, and points of view will find expression in the public forum. . . . [To the contrary,] the range of views considered respectable enough to appear regularly in the American mass media is extraordinarily narrow. As a result, we are more ignorant and more provincial than we could be, and we may be worse off in other ways as well." The Hutchins Commission would not have had to change a word. The Hutchins Commission, however, was content to offer tame or hortatory solutions. Lichtenberg, by contrast, was willing to concede that freedom of the press is "a nearly unchallengeable dogma," even as she simultaneously readied to do battle to bring the necessary information to the public.[36]

Because both Fiss and Lichtenberg find obvious defects in the marketplace, especially in the potential of the wealthy to drown out competing voices, there are necessarily marketplace overtones in their analysis. Yet the marketplace is but a backdrop to a listeners'-rights model. Instead, both see the necessity of a government mediator to assist the citizenry in receiving that information which intelligent citizens should, but do not, have. Without a government mediator, implementation of the public's right to know is impossible. Both Fiss and Lichtenberg are monistic theorists, and as Mark Yudof, Frederick Schauer, and Steven Shiffrin have demonstrated, monistic First Amendment theory is inherently weak and undervalues the whole range of interests that the First Amendment protects. As monistic theorists, Fiss and Lichtenberg isolate a single strand of First Amendment justification and attack it separately, as if there were nothing else on the field. By ignoring the synergy among rationales, they mistakenly treat a division as if it were a platoon.[37]

There are major assumptions implicit in the desire to correct information defects by a governmental mechanism that would supervise the print media. To explore these assumptions it is helpful to envision a new agency, the Mass Media Regulatory Commission, at the outset, and watch it work. Because its job is to guarantee that all the necessary information reaches the American people, it will be staffed with individuals having the requisite knowledge. That is, they will know which ideas and information are not known or are insufficiently known and then act to correct the defect.

Pointing out the shortcomings of our mass media, Lichtenberg's Reagan-era example is "the narrowness [which] is evident . . . in the debate about providing military aid to the Nicaraguan Contras—no one argues that we ought to support the Sandinistas." That's true; the debate was framed between the Reagan administration's efforts to fund the Contras for military action and the congressional Democrats' varying positions, either that aid should be halted entirely or that it should be limited to "humanitarian" provisions (in the myopic view that buying someone bandages will not free up other money for bullets). Now let's switch to the deliberations of the Mass Media Regulatory Commission.[38]

*Commissioner*
    *One:*      Hey, have you all been following the Central American debate?

*Commissioner*
    *Two:*      Of course we have; our job is to monitor the news available to the American people, and remedy the defects as necessary.

    *One:*      But have you noticed how one-sided and narrow the debate is?

    *Two:*      No kidding. That's why I think President Reagan has such troubles with the Congress. The media always seem to favor cutting off aid to the Freedom Fighters rather than giving them a chance to free their homeland from its oppressive rule.

We should pause for a moment to consider two possible scenarios. In the first, Commissioner One picks up Lichtenberg:

> *One:* Wait a minute. You're not doing your job as surrogate for the American people. Don't you realize that the press is not carrying stories that favor giving aid to the Sandinistas so that they can defeat the Contras and develop the type of society they wish to create? Don't you realize that if the press carried stories about the good that aid to the Sandinistas could do, we might have a fuller debate in the US and a better society in Central America?
>
> *Two:* Hey, I hadn't thought of that.

The commissioners recognize the need—a failure to explore the pro-Sandinista view—and are ready to correct it.

Now to the second scenario. In it, Commissioner Two successfully presses his point that President Reagan's excellent policies do not prevail because the prevailing liberal bias in the media wrongly tilts the debate against the Contras. Does not the second of these scenarios seem vastly more likely to occur between two commissioners both appointed by President Reagan? If so, then the Mass Media Regulatory Commission's intervention will have made us worse off by a government-mandated tilt in the debate toward its own policies; whereas not implementing the first scenario, not broadening our views, simply fails to make us better off.

How could Lichtenberg, who is correct in saying that the press is more narrow than it need be—it did not discuss invading Nicaragua either—think the pro-Sandinista, rather than the pro-Reagan, scenario would be chosen by the proposed commission? To use the phrase of Robert Nagel, she is "captured by the lure of the possible." Like Clarence Dill, Senate sponsor of the Radio Act of 1927, she believes that the commission would be staffed by "men [and women] of big abilities and big vision."[39]

Lichtenberg's confident assumption is that appointees will be quality, nonpartisan people just like herself. This flounders quickly at the intersection of reality (regulatory commissions lack both prestige and pay) and the Constitution (the power of appointment is vested in the president). Thus Richard Nixon and Ronald Reagan, no less than John Kennedy and Franklin Roosevelt, get to appoint when vacancies occur during their presidencies. We are as likely to see Reagan appointing Edward and not Anthony Kennedy to the Supreme Court as Reagan appointees finding fault with the mass media for not discussing aid to the Sandinistas. Nothing in broadcast regulation, which is the nearest analogy, suggests the contrary.

Fiss, who knows how the staffing would work, nevertheless answers that we must have faith. He asserts that there is no reason to presume that the state will be more likely than any other institution to use its power "to distort public debate," and that state suppression of a would-be speaker should not be presumed to be unconstitutional. Mark Yudof had persuasively argued to the contrary; that with all its resources and prestige, government has a powerful incentive to influence public debate in ways that favor those currently holding power. But this is not for Fiss, who holds instead that in First Amendment analysis there can be no presumptions against the state.[40]

Presumptions provide guidance in areas of factual ambiguity and uncertainty. Their use is either to support common sense or to move an outcome toward the predetermined result. Fiss's presumptions are that government regulation of the marketplace of ideas would work; and that even if it did not work, nothing else works the way it should, either, and so government regulation would leave the country no worse off.

Stanley Ingber writes that there are scholars who "view government regulation of mass media as a threat to First Amendment freedoms of speech and the press." The perfect accuracy of Ingber's statement is not what makes it remarkable; it is rather that he thought it worth saying. If everyone agreed, presumably there would be no need for notice. After all, one geographer does not feel compelled to note that other geographers think the world is round. For Fiss, Ingber, and Lichtenberg, the tradition of no government regulation lacks the givenness it once had. Somehow, its rationale seems lost. Yet there is still every reason to fear that government would attempt to tilt the debate its way; and under these circumstances Justice Holmes had a better solution: "This is not a matter for polite presumptions; we must look facts in the face."[41]

Thomas P. Scanlan summed up a considerable scholarly literature in writing that "where political issues are involved governments are notoriously partisan and unreliable." The federal government, especially the executive branch, has the ability to speak in the area of freedom of expression with one voice, creating a risk of uniformity and the smothering of dissent. Fiss mistakenly finds that risk no greater than we run with private media power. But in our pluralistic society, private power over ideas and information is not monolithic. The power of the federal government can be; that is why it may stifle if it wishes. And that explains why, had there been no Watergate, the specter of a second term of Richard Nixon's attitudes and initiatives with respect to the media is so haunting. Scanlan underscores the powerful insights Thomas Emerson brought together as "the Dynamics of Limitation." The rather elemental point is that American history ought not to be erased by presumption (although some day a government functionary, duly charged, may try).[42]

# IV

Perceptive scholars, such as Lillian BeVier and William Van Alstyne, and insightful media representatives, such as Anthony Lewis, recognized quickly that the two differing right-to-know theories were logically inseparable. The initial charm of the right to know was its ability to remove the press from its seeming position of privilege. Had the right to know stopped there, Kent Cooper could have taken pride in his creation, and few others would have cared. But the media often took the right to know quite seriously and stood by its implications, which appeared to necessitate a new privileged position for the press. Thus Cooper's slogan, attempting to substitute a democratic ideal for a perceived special privilege, turned out to imply an even greater special privilege for the press—and worse, to invite the press to focus upon it, as a too often arrogant press did during the 1970s.[43]

The Hutchins Commission was not alone in its ability to tie rights to responsibilities. The law with regularity has taken privilege and added to it responsibility. It should have taken very little time for any serious look at the right to know to come to the conclusions that special responsibilities might be implicit therein. To the question, In what respects is the press special? Van Alstyne (who believed it wasn't) suggested, "One answer is that they are to be 'specially' accountable, i.e., more answerable than laymen." Van Alstyne early demonstrated that while at the hands of friends the language of special privileges can be soothing, "the rhetoric that special privileges carries with [them] special responsibility will not be long in coming, and it is a rhetoric which enemies of press freedom can use with telling effect." It is therefore a rhetoric that friends of press freedom should be wary of encouraging.[44]

Hocking had taken an early swing at the rhetoric of the right to know: "We say recklessly that they [the public] have a 'right to know'; yet it is a right which they are helpless to claim, for they do not know that they have the right to what as yet they do not know." Hocking's citizens were helpless because the right to know is not self-executing. Some body must act before the citizens can enjoy their rights. The press would quickly answer, It's us. But it need not be, as both Fiss and Lichtenberg demonstrated. In their views, the government would be the implementing body in deciding what the public needed to know and how they could be helped in knowing it.[45]

Typically, the right to know is aimed at government, and it demands more knowledge of what is happening, what is to happen, and why. If taken seriously, and to some extent it should be, this means that the primary responsibility for added information should lie with the government. To the extent this means that governmental officials have responsibility to facilitate added access to places and information, well and good. But primary responsibilities can be exercised in a number of ways, and one of these might be competing information outlets: a real government press (as opposed to the layered independence of Public Broadcasting). Responsibility could also be exercised in the form of added supervisory functions, which Fiss and Lichtenberg perceive as essential.

Why should there be a reporter's privilege? To guarantee added information that will allow the public to better understand. Why should reporters have access to prisons and other off-limits places? To bring to the public information which they could not otherwise acquire. Why should newsroom searches (with, of course, a search warrant) be banned? To guarantee that the press cannot be intimidated by government. Why should the laws of libel be tilted more toward freedom to publish and away from reputational interests? To remove the chilling effect on public discussions.

All the answers make perfectly good sense. Each ties in to an informing function of the press. Each is instrumental, and therefore we can ask how well promise matches performance. How well is the press exercising its informing function? Is the press meeting its responsibilities, indeed its sole purpose, in vindicating the public's right to know? Why is there so much _____ (fill in the blank with whatever excess comes to mind: sensationalism, puffery, negativism) in the media? Can the public have the information it needs when the press wastes so much of its space on whatever filled in the blank? If the public does have a right to know, then the press ought not be complaining if the public (through some mechanism) demands an accounting.

Chief Justice Burger opened some of this questioning in his *Pentagon Papers* dissent: "It is not disputed that the *Times* has had unauthorized possession of the documents for three to four months, during which it has had its expert analysts studying them, presumably digesting them and preparing the material for publication. During all of this time, the *Times,* presumably in its capacity as trustee of the public's 'right to know,' has held up publication for purposes it considered proper and thus public knowledge was delayed." Where was the public's right to know during March, April, May, and early June, 1971? Where is the public's right to know when a story is killed (as initially happened when several different news organizations suppressed the story of the CIA– Howard Hughes contract to have the *Glomar Explorer* raise a sunken Russian submarine, only to have the story later spring to the front pages)? All editing restricts the right to know, because editing requires decisions about what to withhold.[46]

The right to know is not a right; it's a slogan. Furthermore, it is a dangerous slogan, because it instantly invites inquiry into the actual performance of a newspaper. Instead of giving the press more rights, it runs the risk of denying the press its most sacred possession, its autonomy.

The string of defeats from *Branzburg* to *Gertz* to *Zurcher v. Stanford Daily* (the newsroom search) to *Herbert v. Lando* to *DePasquale* left the press reeling and its argument for special privileges in shambles. But no case took away press autonomy and its right to publish as it chooses. No case treated the press worse than any other citizen. Paul Branzburg had to comply with a subpoena, but so, too, did Richard Nixon. CBS underwent discovery, but the *Washington Post* did the same to William Tavoulareas. The *Stanford Daily* was searched, but with a warrant any business may be searched, even, as in *Zurcher,* for evidence of third-party criminality; and in many cases the warrant requirement has been dispensed with altogether. The preliminary hearing in *DePasquale* was closed, and that was an outrage, but an outrage perpetrated on anyone wishing to witness Seneca County justice in operation.

Nor did the cases prevent legislation from giving the press special privileges. In *Branzburg* the majority noted that some states had adopted shield laws; following *Branzburg,* other states were added to the list. *Richmond Newspapers* guaranteed that trials would be open, not on a preferred press theory, but because the public has the right to attend. Yet once they are open, special seating for the press is allowable and, as Chief Justice Burger noted, even encouraged. The public is not invited to a presidential press conference, but some members of the press are. The same is true for the crossing of police or fire barricades.[47]

Nor did the cases themselves preclude heightened constitutional protections for the press under some circumstances. While the access-to-places cases did reject the press argument, *Branzburg* stated that it was not suggesting "that news gathering does not qualify for First Amendment protection; without some protection for seeking out the news, freedom of the press could be eviscerated." What was rejected was a claim of confidentiality in the circumstances of a grand jury investigation. Following *Branzburg,* numerous lower courts have authorized specific claims of confidentiality when the competing interests called for it. More specifically, the press tax cases did recognize a special privilege for the press. No other industry could have prevailed in those cases, but taxation has such a powerful potential to bring the press to heel that the Court created special rules to ensure press independence.[48]

The press takes its win-loss record before the Supreme Court too literally. Instead of asking which cases it has to win and which cases it can afford to lose (without precipitating the fall of civilization as we know it), the press sees all cases as of equal significance—after all, each involved *the* First Amendment. In *Branzburg* the claim of reporter's privilege was less than fifteen years old, whereas the demand for open courts in *Richmond Newspapers* had preconstitutional lineage; yet they were seen as the same. Had the press focused on the cases it had to win, it would have noted that it won them. Then-professor Robert Bork once noted that "journalists might say that even paranoids have enemies, but I think the appropriate reply, based on the judicial record, is that even paranoids have friends." Unfortunately, tunnel vision causes the major media sources to focus on their own cases to the virtual exclusion of others. Furthermore, possibly because "press" is explicitly mentioned in the First Amendment, the press takes a hometown approach that causes it to systematically undervalue the civil liberties protected elsewhere, even elsewhere in the First. Sure *Branzburg* stung, but *Greenburgh Civic Association,* where the Court held that the Post Office could prevent citizens' groups from inserting fliers into home mailboxes because their fliers lacked stamps, passed without mention. Yet the Court did Anatole France one better. Some of the more affluent would be subsidized with bulk mailing rates, while the less affluent were stuck with a first class stamp per flier. The editorial blasts that obligingly follow press losses were silent, probably because *Greenburgh Civic Association* matters only to those for whom stamps are a real expense, and newspapers can pay the postage. It appears never to have occurred to the press that it was being treated no worse than anyone else, and in some cases better.[49]

When it really counted, the Supreme Court guaranteed that the press could perform its various roles in our democracy. But, apart from Justice Douglas, and with the exception of some overblown dicta from other justices, the Court never saw the right-to-know model as a viable First Amendment doctrine. Whether out of distrust of the press, distrust of its own abilities, or faithfulness to a simpler constitutional ideal, the Court never embraced either side of the right to know. In rejecting that theory, however, it never endangered the essential autonomy of a free press.

# Chapter Nine

# The Fourth Estate

The same year that Justice Brennan assured his fame with *New York Times v. Sullivan,* Justice Potter Stewart wrote a one-paragraph concurring opinion in an Ohio case where the state supreme court had found the movie *Les Amants* obscene—even though the rapid-sequence love scene that supposedly justified the criminal prosecution was "so fragmentary and fleeting that only a censor's alert would make an audience conscious that something 'questionable' [was] being portrayed." Unwilling to join Justices Black and Douglas in finding that the Constitution precluded all obscenity regulation, Stewart nevertheless wished to call a halt to the nonsense that Victorian-minded state courts kept imposing on books, magazines, and, especially, movies. He argued that governmental power only reached "hard-core pornography." Then, in a sentence that would haunt him for the rest of his career, he admitted he could not define what he meant, but added, "I know it when I see it."[1]

Stewart always enjoyed a trip north to his New Haven alma mater. On one such trip, the dean of the law school introduced him by saying: "This is Justice Potter Stewart. He comes to the Yale Law School with frequency. We know him when we see him." On another of those trips to Yale—to address the Sesquicentennial Convocation at the law school—his extrajudicial remarks cut more important new ground than his opinions. Telling his audience that the framers intended the press clause to guarantee "the institutional autonomy of the press," Stewart emphasized that the clause is a "*structural* provision" operating to create "a fourth institution outside the government to check the potential excesses of the other three branches." He explicitly acknowledged Edmund Burke who, according to Thomas Carlyle, "said there were Three Estates in Parliament; but, in the Reporters' Gallery yonder, there sat a Fourth Estate more important far than they all." Stewart's address defined and legitimated the Fourth Estate model of the press. Avowedly instrumental, it protects the press as an autonomous, independent check on government.[2]

Just a few months earlier, the Court decided a case where the *Miami Herald* had turned its editorial pages against Pat Tornillo, a feisty teacher's union leader who was running for the state legislature. Major newspapers rarely get so exercised over a candidate for a large, statewide representative body, but the *Herald* thought Tornillo was something special. So, too, was a long-forgotten Progressive Era statute guaranteeing a candidate attacked by a newspaper the right to reply. When the Supreme Court, in *Miami Herald v. Tornillo,* struck down the Florida law, it validated the Fourth Estate model, in operation if not in name, and guaranteed the press the necessary autonomy to perform the checking function that model envisions.[3]

## I

Turn-of-the-century Southern newspapers, both the rural weeklies and the city dailies, existed for politics, and editors had the least charity for state legislators. The Southern pattern held true in Florida, where irresponsible reporting was not limited to any particular segment of the state. The urban press was conservative, and it slanted stories accordingly. The more numerous rural papers, for their part, found Southern demagogues especially seductive.[4]

With the demise of the Republican party in the 1890s went the need for unhesitating support for any Democrat. Newspapers could thus "appraise the chief executives on a factional basis." The dominant figure of the period, Florida's best-known governor, Napoleon Bonaparte Broward, knew only too well that he had "no greater foes" than the conservative urban press, although he had more than ample support in its rural counterpart. Urban newspaper attacks led Broward to devote 10 percent of his 1907 message to the legislature to the need for criminalizing newspaper lies, proposing to "make public mendacity a misdemeanor and punish any newspaper writer or editor or publisher who deliberately and intentionally writes or publishes an article that is untrue, and mak[e] the public printing of an untruth prima facie evidence of the misdemeanor." His message singled out the Jacksonville *Florida Times-Union* for special criticism. The *Times-Union* then helped prove Broward's point by printing what it claimed to be the entire text of his message while deleting all the pejorative references to itself.[5]

The legislature took no action on Broward's newspaper proposal; but six years later, under Governor Park Trammell, Florida attempted to clean up its primaries. Trammell's election reforms added sections to the Corrupt Practices Act to bring newspapers under its coverage. Rather than embracing Broward's suggestion to criminalize the publication of falsehood, Trammell tried to ensure that voters had the opportunity of seeing a bigger picture than just one-sided accusations. The act gave those candidates whose character or conduct were assailed in newspaper columns a right to reply, in space equally conspicuous, to the charges. It also placed a limit on campaign spending, prohibited bribing newspapers to support a candidate, and forbade attacks on candidates in the last eighteen days of a campaign unless the candidate was first personally served with the charges.

Like the Minnesota Gag Law a decade later, the Trammell Corrupt Practices Act enjoyed newspaper support. The act was sponsored and managed in the Florida House by an editor of the Plant City *Courier*. In the House, all five newsmen-members voted yes; their votes were sufficient to have carried the bill, since only four noes were registered. (The vote was 58 to 4.) The three newsmen-senators split two to one in favor; the Senate passed the law by a 21 to 6 vote. The right-of-reply statute, often misperceived as a post-Watergate phenomenon, thus entered the Florida statute books.[6]

## II

In 1967 Pat Tornillo helped lead the first statewide teachers' strike in US history. A transplanted New Jersey teacher, Tornillo had abandoned Dade County classrooms for the executive offices of the Dade County Classroom Teachers' Association (CTA). By the time of the strike Tornillo was well known in Florida. Everything he said or advocated seemed to generate controversy. While his mission in life, amply reflected in the press, appeared to be ever higher teachers' salaries, he also pushed for unpopular causes—aid for Cuban refugees' children, the Head Start program for blacks, and faster desegregation of the schools. He showed a real knack for gaining publicity, such as sending telegrams in July 1967 to both the Republican and the Democratic national committees urging them to stay away from Miami in 1968 for their conventions because of the pathetic state of education in Dade County.[7]

The 1967 strike was strange and senseless, precipitated by Governor Claude Kirk's grandiose presidential ambitions and a teachers' union that created so much momentum for a strike that it walked out to force Kirk not to veto a funding bill that the union publicly labeled unacceptable! Because of the convoluted motivations of the union, the press had genuine difficulties explaining why over half of the state's teachers submitted resignations (teachers' strikes were illegal) and stayed away from their classrooms for three weeks and then suddenly reappeared the Monday after Kirk publicly abandoned a losing position by declaring he had "broken" the strike and would let the funding package become law without his signature.[8]

The intense opposition to the strike by the press, including the *Herald,* was understandable. Few newspapers like labor unions. Fewer still like public employee unions, and there are almost none that support illegal strikes by public employees—especially when the strike appears wholly unnecessary. Don Shoemaker, who ran the *Herald* during these events, later conceded in an interview that the paper, though not antiworker, was unquestionably antiunion.

If the strike made no newspaper friends, it certainly did no damage to Tornillo's career as a union leader. In the two-year period following the strike, Tornillo was in the pages of the *Herald* at least monthly, and twice the *Herald* ran editorial attacks on him. One of these, in March 1969, coined the name "Boss Tornillo," subsequently "Czar Tornillo." Interestingly, the *Herald's* attorney, Dan Paul, believes that the *Herald's* contempt for Tornillo, which was apparent from the way the paper treated him, turned him from just another union leader into an important public figure. The *Herald* made him.

In both 1970 and 1972 Tornillo ran for the state legislature.

Without the Supreme Court's 1964 reapportionment decision, *Reynolds v. Sims,* that would have been inconceivable. While the population had been growing explosively in the south of Florida, the pre-*Reynolds* legislature reflected the fact that for most of its existence, Florida's citizens lived mainly in the northern sections of the state. Prior to reapportionment by a federal district court, Dade County had a single senator and three representatives. Following the plan adopted by the court, Dade jumped to nine senators and twenty-two representatives. Reapportionment opened new offices and allowed individuals like Tornillo a chance. Subsequent reapportionment after the 1970 census added four additional representatives.[9]

In his 1970 campaign, Tornillo was one of three challengers to a four-term incumbent. The incumbent got 34,562 votes in the primary and Tornillo ran second with 20,359. The other two received enough votes to force a runoff, in which Tornillo was slaughtered, 70,009 to 44,364. The *Herald* did not editorialize; indeed it scarcely covered the race. Although Shoemaker, who made the decisions to editorialize against Tornillo in 1972, states he cannot remember the 1970 race, both he and Tornillo speculate that no one thought Tornillo had a chance and so the *Herald* ignored him. Tornillo wishes that had been the case two years later.[10]

Tornillo stayed active in both the union and politics. Indeed, he thought it important that the two converge. When the 1972 Democratic National Convention arrived, he was selected as a Humphrey delegate, but on the eve of the convention he shifted to McGovern. Then in late July he announced his candidacy for Florida House District 103.[11]

There were two other candidates, Alan Becker and Hugh Duval. Coverage of the campaign was sparse, but with thirty-five races for the legislature plus numerous judicial and law enforcement races in Miami, coverage would necessarily be minimal. According to Tornillo, he was the least liberal of the three. This could not be inferred from the *Herald*'s preelection edition on Sunday, September 10, which reflected an anti-Tornillo bias. All three were discussed, but Tornillo was last and received the least space. Neither alphabetical order—Duval preceded Becker—nor age—Becker was the youngest, a mere 27—can explain this. When I brought this to Shoemaker's attention, he agreed it was "unfair" to Tornillo.

Maybe to the *Herald*'s surprise, Tornillo ran a strong second. Becker received 13,113 votes, Tornillo 11,967, and Duval 8,206. In three weeks Tornillo and Becker would meet in the runoff, with the winner assured of a seat in the statehouse.[12]

There were few substantive differences between the two. Each had his own constituency, Tornillo with the teachers and Becker, an aggressive tenants' rights attorney, with renters. In fact the only "genuine issue" between the two was whether Becker lived in the 103d district. Becker and his wife had an apartment elsewhere, but for the race they moved into the district with his wife's grandparents, and he assured voters that he would soon find his own residence there. But where Becker lived and would live was unimportant. When the *Herald* went at Tornillo in a pair of editorials, it confirmed that he was the issue.

The first of the two was triggered by Tornillo's attempt to find an issue. He had attacked Becker for failure to make a timely filing of campaign contributors as required by Florida law. The *Herald* did not, however, report this in a news story. Instead, on September 20 the *Herald* editorialized under the title "The State's Laws and Pat Tornillo." The editorial was fairly short and offered what was, for the *Herald*, a simple truism: that a man who had led an "illegal" strike "against the public interest" was hardly in a position to refer, as Tornillo had, to an opponent as lacking "the knowledge to be a legislator." The editorial ended by stating: "We cannot say it would be illegal but certainly it would be inexcusable of the voters if they sent Pat Tornillo to Tallahassee."[13]

Tornillo was outraged. On reading the editorial he called Elizabeth duFresne, the partner of his then-vacationing lawyer, Tobias (Toby) Simon, at home. She recalls Tornillo being so mad that she had to hold the phone at arm's length to protect her ear. As soon as duFresne reached her office, Tornillo was on the phone again blasting the *Herald*. She then began to research. Turning to Florida's libel statutes, she found a cross-reference to "right of reply." In less than an hour she turned up the long-neglected provision of the 1913 Corrupt Practices Act.

Tornillo did nothing about the *Herald* editorial for a week. Why did he wait? He has no recollection. Dan Paul, the *Herald*'s lawyer, thought that Tornillo and Simon did not expect the *Herald* to publish the reply and that the delay was to get the best timing for publicity from the lawsuit they would file—publicity that would assist Tornillo's campaign (which Paul felt was going nowhere). Paul, however, was unaware that Simon had been out of town. It is possible that the delay stemmed from the decision to wait for Simon to return and offer his evaluation of the right-of-reply law.

On Thursday, September 28, Tornillo called Fred Sherman, the *Herald*'s editorial writer, to say that he and Simon would be coming over just before noon, and asked that Shoemaker be present at the meeting. Shoemaker, however, had other appointments, and it was Sherman who met with Tornillo and Simon. Simon informed Sherman of the right-of-reply law; Tornillo gave him a typed response in the same number of words as the editorial, and they demanded that the *Herald* run it. They pointed out that the right-of-reply law carried criminal penalties.

After Tornillo and Simon left, Paul was consulted. There were also internal discussions between Sherman and Shoemaker. All came out the same way. Paul told Shoemaker the law was unconstitutional, and Shoemaker likened the situation to having a gun pointed at his head. With these conclusions, the *Herald* would not run the reply. The discussions also foreclosed the possibility of running the reply as a letter to the editor.

At the time of the meeting between Tornillo and Sherman, the *Herald*'s second editorial on Tornillo was already written. It ran the next day. Entitled "See Pat Run," it begins with a large picture of an empty classroom with chairs neatly stacked on top of desks. Beneath this picture, the editorial begins: "From the people who brought you this—the teacher strike of '68—come now instructions on how to vote for responsible government." It goes on to blast Tornillo and the CTA on issue after issue. No one could miss the point.[14]

With the election just four days away, the right-of-reply statute on the books, and the *Herald* refusing to comply, Tornillo's only hope was a quick judicial order. He wrote and delivered a response to the second editorial, knowing that only a judge could get it in the *Herald*. Simon and duFresne, meanwhile, prepared papers for an immediate hearing on Monday morning to consider a request for injunctive relief.

They got the hearing but not the injunction. Because the constitutionality of a state statute would be at issue in the hearing, the trial judge, Francis Christie, notified the Florida attorney general, Robert Shevin. Seven months earlier, in the first reported case involving the right-of-reply statute, a Daytona trial judge had held the statute unconstitutional, and Shevin, believing the decision correct, elected not to appeal. He adhered to that position, and Judge Christie adopted it also. Paul won without even having to answer Tornillo's complaint.[15]

A day later Tornillo lost in the more significant forum, 21,135 votes to 13,444. He believed the *Herald* had "done him in." Yet several things point to the contrary. The first is that despite an increase in voter turnout, Tornillo was barely able to add to his primary total. Almost all of Duval's votes went to Becker. Second, Tornillo's assessment of the *Herald*'s influence seems dubious. A percentage split of 57 to 43 hardly seems the type where the final outcome can be influenced by a pair of editorials, no matter how good. This is especially the case where a person, like Tornillo, has been so much a part of the local news for years that his positions, even if distorted, must be known to those willing to take the trouble to vote. Furthermore, the evening *Miami News,* albeit with a circulation a fifth of the *Herald*'s, endorsed Tornillo.[16]

Nevertheless, whatever the real facts, Tornillo believed the *Herald* was to blame; and at a minimum he was correct in his conclusion that the paper had treated him very unfairly. The paper wrote a self-satisfied editorial about the election results, quoting Tornillo's postmortem comment, "I think people believe what they read in the newspaper," and responding, "We appreciate the endorsement, Mr. Tornillo, and are pleased that now we have found an opportunity to compliment your judgment." Tornillo again wrote a reply. This time, the election and the right-of-reply law behind, the *Herald* printed it in full.[17]

## III

The election may have been over, but the hard feelings were not. An important principle—power in the democratic process—was at stake; at least Tornillo so believed. The *Herald,* too, thought an important principle—the freedom of the press from governmental coercion—was involved. Neither party liked the other, and there was still the lawsuit. Because only principle was at stake, the suit could not be settled out of court. It would go on until a winner emerged.

Three weeks after the election, Judge Christie held a hearing and reaffirmed his earlier conclusions. Tornillo had now lost the emergency hearing, the election, and the final judgment. But he decided to appeal. The hurried posture of the case meant that the appeal would involve the simple legal issue of whether a legislature could authorize a right of reply for a candidate for public office who had been attacked by a newspaper.[18]

If the attorney general would not defend the statute, Simon was able to find even better support in Jerome Barron, who had left the George Washington Law Center for what turned out to be a brief sojourn as dean of the Syracuse Law School. Barron presented to the United States Supreme Court the major test of the First Amendment theory that he had been elaborating for the prior half-dozen years. (duFresne dropped out of the case with an insight that will bring joy to the hearts of most who do not teach constitutional law and many who do: "I was happy to leave it. It wasn't law at all. Just politics.") Barron's seminal "Access" article in the *Harvard Law Review,* discussed in section III of the previous chapter, had argued that citizens needed an increased opportunity to expand the existing debate in the mass media via the mechanism of a right to reply. Barron had argued for judicial creation of such a right, but Florida offered a superior solution; its statute eliminated any issues of judicial usurpation of the legislative function. Tornillo's case was as good as the current state of American law would provide. Florida's right-of-reply law might be seen as more limited than the already constitutional Fairness Doctrine, since the right of reply looked analogous to the FCC's more limited personal-attack rules sustained in *Red Lion Broadcasting v. FCC.* Thus if Tornillo could prevail, Barron would have achieved a necessary first step in moving his compulsory-access idea from the pages of law reviews and the lacunae of broadcast regulation into the fabric of freedom of the press.[19]

The Florida Supreme Court would certainly not have been the *Herald's* first choice of venue. There was bad blood between the two institutions, and a major scandal was about to break. Three of the justices would be confronted with possible impeachment; a fourth was being asked to justify the court's unusual intervention in a parole board matter on behalf of a robber with good connections to the criminal underworld; and a fifth was having a bout with the bottle. The *Herald,* as messengers are wont to learn, was seen as part of the problem. As the problems increased, a written and initialed notation on a court document was discovered that "indicated a strong personal bias" against the *Herald.* The *Herald* could be forgiven for not believing the pro forma denial that followed.[20]

But the *Herald* got no choice of forum; it was off to the Florida Supreme Court, where Tornillo prevailed. The decision tracked the arguments of Barron and other contributors to the access literature and added a touch of the press's own arguments, put forward just a year earlier in *Branzburg*'s losing effort to secure a constitutionally protected reporter's privilege. Although the opinion did not cite the secondary literature, it fairly reflected it.[21]

The opinion coalesced around two basic ideas. First, writing within the right-to-know framework, the court emphasized the importance of information in a democracy. The court used the Madison quote which opened Chapter 6: "A popular Government without popular information or the means of acquiring it is but a Prologue to a Farce or a Tragedy; or, perhaps both." The public's need for information is greatest during an election, and a newspaper's attack on a candidate not only hurts the candidate, it hurts the electorate by denying it both sides of the controversy. After all, the First Amendment's guarantee of a free press is "not for the benefit of the press so much as for the benefit of us all."[22]

Second, drawing heavily on, but not citing, the access literature, the court painted the picture of media concentration:

The right of the public to know all sides of a controversy and from such information to be able to make an enlightened choice is being jeopardized by the growing concentration of the ownership of the mass media into fewer and fewer hands, resulting ultimately in a form of private censorship. Through consolidation, syndication, acquisition of radio and television stations and the demise of vast numbers of newspapers, competition is rapidly vanishing and news corporations are acquiring monopolistic influence over huge areas of the country.

"Freedom of expressions was retained by the people through the First Amendment *for all the people* and *not merely for a select few.*" When newspapers may attack candidates with impunity, "the pub-

lic interest in free expression suffers." The court made clear that
Red Lion was persuasive on the speech-enhancing function of the
right of reply and concluded that the statute was "consistent with
the First Amendment."[23]

The Herald petitioned for a rehearing. Simon, confident of maintaining the victory, did not even respond. He was rewarded again
when the court denied the petition, in an unusual way, by writing
an opinion affirming the prior decision. The concluding sentence in
the opinion denying the petition hit hard: "In conclusion, it must be
remembered that the First Amendment Freedom of the Press is for
the benefit of all the people and not just those who have invested
money in the publishing business."[24]

Now it was the Herald's turn. The next encounter would be in a
forum less unfavorable to the paper. Now joined by virtually the
entire media establishment, the battle was waged on two fronts, in
the Supreme Court and in the media. If the nine-to-zero trouncing
Tornillo, Barron, and Simon were to get at the Supreme Court
seems one-sided, the media trouncing they received while the case
was pending was in the same league.

The Florida Supreme Court decision shocked the press. Never
reticent about using their own pages to assert their own interests,
newspaper after newspaper editorialized about the threat to press
freedom in the Florida decision. The Herald then printed these as
guest editorials on its own pages. Simon, attempting to present the
other side, wrote a letter to the editor explaining the decision, but it
was not printed. Friends at the Herald told him that a decision had
been made "upstairs" to print nothing he wrote. (Once, however,
during the pendency of the case at the Supreme Court, the Herald
ran an op-ed piece by Tornillo—at the same time as it ran a piece by
a deputy attorney general of Florida on the unconstitutionality of
the right of reply.)

Simon then had Barron write a letter which was sent to one
hundred major newspapers. About six weeks later Simon sent a
follow-up letter asking whether Barron's piece had been run. Naturally not every newspaper replied, but of those that did, only one
said it had run the Barron letter. With that paper could be included
the South Dade News-Leader of Homestead, which stood alone in
editorializing in favor of the Florida Supreme Court.[25]

When Gilbert Cranberg, then the editorial writer of the Des

*Moines Register,* wrote Simon asking about the case, Simon responded with passion about his inability to present his side to the public. After noting that he had been a cooperating lawyer with the American Civil Liberties Union since its Florida chapter opened, he hit on the refusal of newspapers to recognize two sides of the issue:

There seems to be something terribly wrong with all of this if "freedom of the press" means that our side will never even be published because it is critical of a position near and dear to the hearts of newspaper publishers. . . . In other words, if I had some mental reservations about the necessity for a right to reply, the treatment I have been accorded during the past twelve months has completely erased all doubts from my mind.

At least the Supreme Court would hear Simon's side. Winning in the media may be satisfying, but winning in court is much more so.[26]

At oral argument Barron was buffeted by hostile questions from both the right and the left. Justice Rehnquist wanted to know whether Barron "was suggesting that the First Amendment intended that one man could commandeer another man's printing press for his own use." Justice Marshall, at the end of a couple of questions to Barron, announced: "So, anyone could silence the press by simply becoming a candidate!" Although Barron retained a small hope of garnering five votes, it was no more than a hope. The opinion, handed down three months later, was unanimously against him.[27]

In the longest section of the opinion, Chief Justice Burger presented the argument for access in such a manner that, were it not for the Court's use of phrases like "access advocates," a person reading it and stopping there would assume that Barron, Simon, and Tornillo had won. The case Burger presented reflected almost perfectly the arguments developed in the legal literature commencing with Barron's initial article. At the time of ratification of the Bill of Rights there was a broadly representative, albeit highly partisan, press. "A true marketplace of ideas existed in which there was relatively easy access to the channels of communication." But in the past half-century vast changes had occurred. Newspapers became big business. Newspaper chains swallowed formerly independent papers, and economics caused the competing daily almost to vanish and prevented the creation of new papers.[28]

If these changes resulted in concentration in fewer hands, other changes were cutting further into diversity. The rise of syndicated commentary added another homogenizing note. The combination of these processes has resulted in the public's losing its "ability to respond or to contribute in a meaningful way to the debate on issues." As the Hutchins Commission had noted: "The right of free public expression has . . . lost its earlier reality." Media concentration has created a situation fundamentally inconsistent with our "profound national commitment to the principle that debate on public issues should be uninhibited, robust, and wide-open."[29]

Having presented the access arguments persuasively, the Court stated two separate reasons why a right of access was inconsistent with the First Amendment. First, it accepted the argument offered by the *Herald* that instead of promoting controversy, the effect of an access statute would be to chill debate. The Court immediately moved to its second reason in the next paragraph (the opinion's last): "Even if a newspaper would face no additional costs . . . and would not be forced to forgo publication of news or opinion . . . the Florida statute fails to clear the barriers of the First Amendment because of its intrusion into the function of editors." The choice of what is and is not printed is exclusively within the control of the editors, and government may not intrude. Period. It was not explained; it was not wordy; and it was not ambiguous.[30]

## IV

The Court devoted but two paragraphs to the chilling effect. The first stated that the right of reply "exacts a penalty" in the form of costs imposed: "printing and composing time and materials." The second stated that these penalties "might well" cause editors to "conclude the safe course is to avoid controversy." "Might well" immediately became "would." "Therefore under operation of the Florida statute, political and editorial coverage would be blunted or reduced."[31]

It is not surprising that the chilling effect would feature prominently in the decision; as previous chapters have demonstrated, it is an important argument in press litigation. One way around it might have been for the Court to return to *Red Lion*, where it had myopically decided that the Fairness Doctrine did not chill broadcast discussions. But Barron understood that *Red Lion's* conclusion of no chill was unlikely to be transported to newspapers, and therefore he argued that broadcasting and the Fairness Doctrine were irrelevant.

For chilling-effect purposes, broadcasting is anything but irrelevant, unless there is some reason to believe that the cause of the chilling effect in broadcasting might not operate with regard to newspapers. Is there? Initially, many newspapers might well avoid a chill because newspapers have a history of being willing to stand up to government—the result, presumably, of their internalized belief in the Fourth Estate model and the importance of checking government transgressions. But if access claims were made and sustained (by whatever mechanism), it would be otherworldly to assert or expect that newspapers would not at least think about the possible consequences of having to print a reply to any particular story they were thinking of running.[32]

Thinking is the first step toward getting cooler. There can be no chilling effect without an actor's understanding how a given law might affect his or her speech activities. What happens after that thought will be the test of whether there is a chilling effect. If the stories are always run the way they would have been, then the pause to think does not represent a chill. If stories are watered down or killed, as we saw with "Ivy Bells" in Chapter 5, then there is a chill.

Suppose for a moment that a federal right of reply had been on the books in 1972. What would the *Washington Post's* Watergate coverage have looked like between July and November? Even assuming the *Post* could not be deterred, there would have been some difference in the paper. On those days that the *Post* did not choose to run the White House disclaimer as a separate story, instead of Ron Ziegler's routine denial being placed in the fifth paragraph of the principal story, the denial itself would run as a (front page) story. Even if that would not deter the *Post*, it might well convince other newspapers that the effort was not worth it.

Still, the *Post*, like the *Herald*, is a major, profitable newspaper with a sizable institutional ego. Although its resources (including pages) are not infinite, they are substantial. It may be possible for a large, powerful metropolitan paper to ignore the effect of a right of reply and continue business as usual by simply acknowledging that op-ed stories would from time to time appear on page one.

Smaller newspapers have less space, profits, and ego. And it has always been the case that the weaker are likely to cool down more quickly than the strong. Smaller papers may not be significant in the larger scheme of things, but whatever freedom of the press means, it applies just as much to the *Citrus County Chronicle* as to the *Washington Post*. Furthermore, larger papers are likely to be in areas where there are abundant media outlets and greater opportunity for alternative views to be presented (their actually being heard is more speculative). Smaller papers generally serve areas with fewer alternative media outlets, although word of mouth may function as an information medium in such areas.

After the Florida Supreme Court's initial decision, a number of smaller newspapers filed friend-of-the-court affidavit-briefs relating how the law might affect them. Although Simon privately poked fun at them, their concerns reflected the problems that exist for smaller newspapers. The Brooksville *Sun-Journal* asked "who decides whether I leave out the Church column or Miss Perch's women's news." The Anna Maria *Islander* wondered about vagueness in the context of politicians' well-known thin skin: "any story or editorial that doesn't make him appear to be in favor of God and motherhood is [likely] reason enough to demand rebuttal space." Demand, yes; receive, no. A right of reply may well chill, but it should not force editors to reach for their parkas every time some politician is not portrayed as his mother would have him seen.[33]

The more tight, narrow, and almost self-executing a statute is, the less chill there should be; the more it covers, the more important the identity of the decision maker—as the discussion between the two hypothetical commissioners in Chapter 8 illustrates. We know it is not going to be Bill Moyers or George Will, but knowing who it is not does not tell you who it is. I doubt if someone is going to jump around a Georgetown cocktail party pointing with pride to a recent appointment as right-of-reply czar. In a world where an appointment to the FCC is a fairly low-level political payoff (useful largely for the private-sector career it will lead to later), how much lower would be a person who makes right-of-reply determinations, especially on the state or local level? Yet this person would be on the front line of what are likely to be frequent First Amendment determinations. The FCC experience demonstrates that the regulations favor incumbents and that even when the regulations themselves are neutral, the Commission will apply them to favor incumbents. It is inconceivable that a similar experience would not occur under a right of reply or an access scheme.

Maybe these problems of decision maker biases could be minimized, as in Tornillo's case, by applying to a judge for the order. But Lee Bollinger and Laurence Tribe have expressed concern that there will always be a danger of manipulation by the decision maker, even if he or she is a judge. Some judges will lack the necessary knowledge, others the independence. The only way to reduce this potential chill would be to minimize the scheme's coverage; there is no way to eliminate the chill completely.[34]

There is one further aspect to the chilling-effect argument: regardless of how the chill is measured, it might be outweighed by the good the right of reply accomplishes. It is important to remember that even if a chill exists, a law will be constitutional if the countervailing benefits are sufficient, as my discussion of the constitutional status of libel laws illustrates. If the chill is insufficient there, it could easily be argued that it is a fortiori insignificant with a right of reply, for there are no astronomical jury awards in the picture.

This extended discussion reveals that the chilling-effect argument has several problems which could not be disposed of in two paragraphs, as Chief Justice Burger tried to do. Indeed, attempting to do so in two paragraphs may have served to demonstrate to skeptics how weak the chilling-effect argument really is. Even a narrow right of reply would cause some chill to smaller papers, and a broader statute would spread the chill to the larger papers; but the degree of chill remains speculative. It is hard to win a speculative chilling-effect argument. "Cool" is met with the response "warm"—or "warm enough." A neutral person may be able to determine who has the better of the debate; but chilling-effect arguments, unless they are lay-downs, are much more likely to persuade the already committed than to bring others into the fold.

The better rationale was Chief Justice Burger's conclusion that the Constitution locates all authority of inclusion and exclusion with editors. This conclusion both recognized the necessity of choice in the composition of a newspaper and found that the First

Amendment placed that choice with a paper's editors. Newspapers are not put together by natural selection, but by decisions on what to include, with how much space, and where the story should be placed. Because such decisions are unavoidable, someone must have the authority to make them.

The principal argument for a right of reply is that under a certain defined set of circumstances, editorial discretion can be improved upon, because a reply will enhance public debate by placing more information in the public domain. Yet this assertion is incorrect and misleading. A reply does not make more information available to the newspaper's readers; rather, it makes different information available. Consequently, the argument for a right of reply must be downsized a bit. At its strongest, it would be that a right of reply provides a fairer, more complete picture of one significant issue; and that whatever is cut from the paper will be the most trivial items. This may turn out to be true, but it need not; nor in fact is it likely to be true.

If we are to speculate on what will be cut, it is most realistic to expect that a reply to an editorial will displace material that would otherwise appear on the editorial pages and therefore will not displace material in the newspaper's Lifestyle section. Under the Florida statute, and under most likely proposals, a reply must be as prominent as the original story. To allow otherwise would invite the newspaper to bury the reply in the most inconspicuous place possible. Furthermore, since readers of newspapers are drawn to the paper for a variety of reasons, the mix already created by the paper is the one it has concluded best serves its readers. It is unrealistic to conclude that political news will displace "soft" news.

Under these, the most likely, circumstances, a reply will add information about a subject already discussed, with the result that some other subject, otherwise fit for the editorial pages, will receive less attention or none at all. Thus a right of reply will have the effect of suppressing other items—probably other current affairs topics—that an editor would otherwise have included.

A legislature has concluded that we are better served by more information about a person already discussed in the news than by knowing whatever other information it displaces. We may be sure also that the author of the reply will share this conclusion. It is not clear, however, whether it is accurate, or whether any readers of the newspaper will believe they are better served by the substitution. If a newspaper carries a certain amount of church news and that news is cut to carry a reply, those who value church news will probably not believe they were well served. The same can be said with regard to any subject, including anything otherwise fit for the editorial pages. What makes the legislative choice appear attractive is that it deals with the paramountcy of political debate and is coupled with the unexplored (and probably inaccurate) assumption that soft news is the likely target for deletion.

Of course a newspaper could print the information the reply displaces and not print something else, or it could just add pages to the paper and print everything. But newspapers do not print "everything." Each day choices are made; vastly more is excluded than printed, and there is no *a priori* reason why the reply material is more important than information already deemed insufficiently important to be included.[35]

In some way, these choices about inclusion and exclusion must be made. If Chief Justice Burger was correct in his conclusion that the editing function is protected by the First Amendment, then a right of reply violates the First Amendment.

This conclusion is bolstered by the one further aspect of freedom of the press that everyone agrees is part of the First Amendment tradition both past and present: no (or almost no) prior restraints. As detailed in Chapter 5, government is forbidden to order nonpublication (except, now, in very compelling circumstances). The principle that holds that government cannot tell people what they may not say is broad enough to prevent government from telling people what they must say. Were it not, government would be able to indirectly prevent publication by excessive demands to publish information. The principle that covers these circumstances is editorial autonomy. Within its scope it is indivisible. Someone has the final say: either the editor, the would-be replier, or the government.

Because editorial autonomy is indivisible, it must be absolute. It is either there or it is not. Benno Schmidt found *Tornillo* "a stark and unexplained deviation" from the Court's avoidance of absolutism in First Amendment adjudication. Floyd Abrams responded that *Tornillo* "is hardly absolutist; rather it is representative of the vast freedom afforded the press at the apex of its first amendment protection." Abrams is right that *Tornillo* represents the First

Amendment at its apex, but there is no need to shy away from recognition of absolutism. When decisions must be made there must be a decision maker. Someone must say what is printed and what is not. The principle of editorial autonomy cannot be divided between editor and judge; in a disputed case, someone must prevail.[36]

When the choice is what must appear, editors prevail; when the choice is what may appear, there are modest chinks in editorial autonomy that come largely from criminalization of certain subject matter. Criminalization of subject matter, whether illustrated by *Morison* and the leaking of spy satellite photos or by *Pittsburgh Press* and gender-based want ads, reflects a judgment that either the material or the way it is presented is exceptionally harmful. In the context of a right of reply, such a judgment would be based on the view that if a newspaper savages someone, it owes to that person and its readers a duty to present the other side. The principle of editorial autonomy has its claims, but so too, the argument would go, may other competing principles such as fairness. An access proponent could concede that autonomy is absolute within its proper sphere, but hold that just as the criminal law represents a boundary, so does fairness.[37]

The problem here—assuming, as I do, that text, purpose, history, and tradition are valid sources of constitutional interpretation—is figuring out how fairness became either a First Amendment value or a limitation on the First Amendment. The First Amendment, after all, does not refer to press "responsibility" even in the limited sense of the "abuse" clause found in most state constitutions. Nor can we look to the Bill of Rights generally, or to the press of the late eighteenth century, or even to evolving traditions, to import fairness into the First Amendment. Some parts of the Bill of Rights, such as the "fair trial" provisions, promote fairness; others, such as the right against self-incrimination, do not. The First Amendment, to the extent that the framers would have thought about it in that way, is a provision that would not promote fairness. The framers knew a partisan and scurrilous press, not a fair one. Two hundred subsequent years may have toned the press down, but even since the advent of so-called objective journalism it is still debatable whether fairness has become a journalistic norm.[38]

Indeed, our traditions are clear. A fair press, as determined by a government mechanism, is not a free press. A free press may be fair; we hope it will not be irresponsible; but, as Blasi so powerfully demonstrates, for the press to serve as a check on the government it must be free to gather and report information about government and those who do or would govern. A government official deciding which stories necessitate replies is both historically and theoretically inconsistent with this. Therefore, fairness, seen either as a value or as a limitation on the First Amendment, would cut to the core of the press's Fourth Estate function. We can have a free press or a fair one, but, as Chief Justice Burger recognized, we cannot have both.

## V

Suppose, however, that the allure of a better world proved irresistible, that a right of reply was felt to be so ethically compelling that, despite chilling-effect and autonomy arguments, it was found consistent with the Constitution. Suppose that Pat Tornillo had prevailed. What might have happened?

Whether because the press had the political power to prevent any legislative ox-goring or because other states felt respect for the long tradition of press autonomy, in 1974 only Florida had a right-of-reply statute on its books. In some states the status quo might continue, because of either or both of the two suggested reasons, albeit with a little more emphasis on the first. But could anyone believe that the status quo would remain everywhere? Are legislators such a selfless breed that a judicial validation of their right to protect their interests in the public debate would not result in some states passing new laws? Certainly not the ones I look at.

In 1971 the House of Representatives passed a measure that would have granted candidates for federal office the right to purchase newspaper space at bargain-basement rates. This is about as minimally intrusive as a reply (or more accurately in this case, access) statute could get. The House bill thus brought newspapers and broadcasters under a new section 312(a)(7) of the Communications Act. The Senate version took the standard view that broadcasting was entitled to less First Amendment protections than print, and accordingly that candidate access could be constitutionally applied only to broadcasters. In conference the Senate prevailed. If

*Tornillo* had gone the other way, the House version would be a highly likely candidate for the United States Code.[39]

More intrusive measures would also be constitutional if *Tornillo* had prevailed; they therefore would have become possible. After argument at the Supreme Court, both President Nixon and Senator John McClellan warmly supported the idea of a federal reply law, with the former noting that it would both "enhance" debate and encourage "good and decent people" to run for office without fear of scurrilous attacks. Barron's retrospective address to the Association for Education, less than two months after *Tornillo,* has a perfect summation: "With such friends, the cause of right to reply had less to fear from its enemies." That Nixon's support was the kiss of death in 1974—and Barron believes it was the most important factor in his defeat—would not have foreclosed the possibility of a federal statute at a later date.[40]

Even if no federal statute was forthcoming, what about the states? Probably there would be a variety of measures, with most tracking whatever the Supreme Court said was okay. But here and there the little laboratories of experimentation would go farther, providing an interesting array. I would assume that the farthest reaches of legislation would be a "Politicians' Day-in-the-Paper Act," tracking the concerns of the editor of the *Islander* mentioned earlier: anything not pleasing to the subject of an editorial would merit a right of reply.

The legislative process would have broken a barrier. For good or ill, newspapers would be even more a part of the political process and would find it necessary to attempt to protect themselves against adverse legislation (rather than the current position of trying to push favorable legislation). And legislation that can affect the content of a newspaper would have a more routine quality about it. Tribe rightly warns that access regulation in the print media would be seen as a "profound break" with tradition, transforming "the boundaries of the legally thinkable and [creating] a corresponding increase in pressure to regulate still more deeply."[41]

Given its resources, the press might do all right in the legislative process; but since the legislation in question would be likely to pit politicians' interests against those of the press, the press probably would do less well than if the legislators were neutral arbitrators between competing interests. But press resources do guarantee that, as night the day, litigation would follow legislation.

Here we all know the outcome. After about a decade of decisions the Supreme Court would "finally" settle the area. Some wonderful four-part test would be announced to determine when a right of reply is appropriate. A not implausible choice might be that access would be granted (1) if the person attacked did not have access to an alternative equivalent media outlet; (2) if the other side of the story was not generally available to the reading public; (3) if the mechanism for determining when a reply shall be granted was plain, efficient, and speedy; and (4) if the statute as applied in the case enhanced rather than abridged the quality of debate.[42]

The fact that there is a rule matters more than its precise content. Not only would the legislatures of the nation have had practice passing legislation for newspapers, the judges, too, would have gained practice and, in the process, acquired confidence in the ascertainment of appropriate limits. The Supreme Court's "rule" would allow them to weigh the needs of the local marketplace of ideas and the merits of the newspaper's and would-be replier's claims. It would be a different world.

No area of law worth the costs of litigation is static. When an area produces litigation, it is moving. This is why it is so essential in civil liberties litigation to win the first case testing an area of settled rights. To lose that initial case is to open up a whole new area for exploration, as mandatory drug testing currently illustrates.

Fortunately, *Tornillo* reaffirmed our ninth-grade civics understanding of freedom of the press: that old South Carolina flag with its rattlesnake and motto "Don't Tread on Me." *Tornillo* left the old rights where it found them and preserved the status quo, thereby guaranteeing that press energies can be spent writing about governmental abuses rather than lobbying legislatures in attempts to stave off unfavorable legislation. Chief Justice Burger's opinion meshed perfectly with the defensive nature of the *Herald*'s claim. After fully stating the arguments in favor of a right of reply, he just said no.

Schmidt was so outraged by the lack of engagement that he concluded, "the Court's skimpy justification is certain to create doubts about the constitutional rule announced." Chief Justice Burger's failure to engage, so annoying to Schmidt and other commentators, is in fact a great strength of the opinion. Nice debates about our traditional rights are fine in the legal journals, but in the public forum there is no need to reason about old rights. We have them. If the discussion is open, then at least one possible outcome is bad. Why legitimate the inquiry by engaging in the debate? We can debate some other issue instead of the taking away of rights that Americans have long enjoyed and understood.[43]

I should not be misunderstood. I am not making the ironic point that the First Amendment, while facilitating debate, cannot itself be debated. My conclusion that Chief Justice Burger's failure to debate is praiseworthy is not an assertion that some principles, especially those of the First Amendment, cannot hold their own in an open debate. But I am concerned with the locale of debate and the effects of any such debate on our rights as citizens. I believe that we must debate our fundamental values when differences appear. But the arena of the debate may well affect the perception of the values. Quite frankly, I do not believe that a twenty-page Supreme Court opinion meeting all the standards of craft (that all considerations are ventilated fully and that the opinion be of publishable quality for a good legal journal) can as effectively protect the right of press autonomy as the blunt rejection in *Tornillo*.

Imagine this longer, better-reasoned opinion. It will be scrutinized; glimmerings of this or that will be picked up—and apart; and maybe a wedge, already thought virtually certain by some commentators despite zero judicial encouragement, could be found for more litigation and experimentation. Given the way judicial decisions are dissected, I would not find it inconceivable that the newer, better, *Tornillo* would lead to a situation where a rejection of a powerful claim is nevertheless translated at the enforcement level into the possibility of further action. I realize that in the very next case the Court could announce that it said "no" in *Tornillo* and "no" is what it meant. But litigation is not a precise art, much less an exact science, and claims do not always come out the way they go in. The Court might find a subsequent case inappropriate for review; or the Court might decide to let the area sort itself out for a while; or it might decide that whatever was happening in the trenches was not so bad and therefore that *Tornillo* overreached in its negativism.

Given the principle of press autonomy, what was essential in

*Tornillo* was an immediate halt to the notion that newspapers have enjoyed too many rights and should be placed under some legal duties to the reading public. If this movement were not halted in one shot, then the traditional barrier would be down, and the legislative experimentation might begin. Where the process would then stop would be anyone's guess. Whether we would still think of freedom of the press in terms of its fierce independence from government would also be open.

Over a half-century ago, Justice Brandeis wrote that *Boyd v. United States* was "a case that will be remembered as long as civil liberty lives in the United States." Now *Boyd* is both gone and forgotten. Since civil liberties still live in the United States, Brandeis got his prediction wrong. And even an opposite result in *Tornillo* would still have left civil liberties and freedom of the press in the United States. They would, however, be different; we cannot know if they would be better (or worse), for it is impossible to know futures we cannot live.[44]

The complexities of modern life apparently made *Boyd*'s protections, involving freedom from intrusive searches of private papers, too costly. Faced with near panic over the issues relating to drugs, the Supreme Court is currently finding more and more searches and seizures to be constitutionally acceptable. Retrenchment of the rights we traditionally have enjoyed is deemed necessary to keep the Constitution up with the times. Barron's scholarship presented similar claims: abandon the romantic myth of the First Amendment and face modern press realities.

The synergy of text, purpose, history, and ongoing tradition have combined to validate an absolute right of press autonomy from government in decisions about what and what not to publish. A break in that right, even for the best of reasons, would begin what I suspect would be an irresistible movement toward a government umpire.

It has long been assumed that civil liberties are not lost wholesale but rather retail, at quite good prices and therefore, initially at least, for the best of reasons. There is no way to put this to an empirical test, and no one would wish to accidentally begin on a path that, if uncorrected, would make a prediction like Brandeis's come true.

Pat Tornillo challenged a part of the traditional core of freedom of the press, albeit for very good reasons. Barron has consistently and persuasively expressed those reasons. Subsequently Vincent Blasi added another point when, after demonstrating in detail the consistency between the checking value and the traditional hands-off rule, he switched to argue that some access statutes should be sustained because of the checking value. He concluded that the Florida statute was overbroad because it gave a reply to officeholders, but a narrower statute giving "a right to reply only to nonincumbents like Mr. Tornillo should be upheld." Had the Florida Supreme Court given the right of reply a narrowing construction to exclude officeholders, a not inconceivable possibility, Blasi would have found in favor of Tornillo on the ground that a local news organization "may actually form a part of an abusive local oligarchy" and that incumbents, but presumably not challengers, "typically have ample opportunities to disseminate their views."[45]

Nevertheless, acceding to the arguments for a right of reply, even a bit, breaks the barrier and starts the legal momentum going. Not even proponents of access know what the ultimate outcome would be. Would it provide a useful check—maybe even a modest but appropriate chill—on papers like the *Manchester Union Leader* and thus provide better service for the citizens of New Hampshire and other places in need of diversity? Or would it result, as Blasi could not have known, in people like Pat Tornillo, exceptionally well known in their communities, being given a legal basis for additional publicity while leaving the vast bulk of the population in the same position as they are now? We are being asked to partially abandon the constitutional rights we have known for a speculative balance that may or may not work. About the only thing that would be certain is that it would be unlikely for our system to start on the road and then turn back. The force needed to break the existing barriers would probably be too great to permit a full return even if, to many, that seemed wise.

Thus *Tornillo* got it just right: a perfect tone for the correct result, preserving our preexisting rights. Barron's argument, despite its persuasive power, did not merit a full judicial response. A succinct rejection was the best way to demonstrate that the old constitutional rights were still valid. Further discussion would just have opened the door to further litigation, and the point of the Court's opinion was that no matter how compelling a right of reply might seem, further litigation was not needed because, as Justice Jackson noted in a different context, the First Amendment "was designed to avoid these ends by avoiding these beginnings."[46]

The content of freedom of the press has a traditional core in editorial autonomy from government: one part is no prior restraints; the other is the inability of government to dictate coverage. They combine to enable the press to perform its Fourth Estate role, a role more secure than the nebulous and inconsistent possibilities in the public's right to know. In his last opinion, Justice Black wrote that the function of freedom of the press was to allow the press to "censure the Government. Only a free and unrestrained press," he continued, "can effectively expose deception in government." All this was potentially at stake and therefore preserved in *Tornillo*. If Chief Justice Burger did not say it with the eloquence of a Black, a Brandeis, or a Jackson, well, no one else does either; what he did was say it just right. For that he deserves a lot more credit than he typically receives.[47]

## VI

Legality is not synonymous with right, nor unconstitutionality with wrong. Descriptively, Barron was on target. A concentrated, homogenized press will overreport some stories and underreport (or ignore) others to the detriment of us all. While there are no easy solutions, the press has not been its normal complacent self in dealing with these problems.

During Tornillo's unnoticed 1970 campaign, the *New York Times* editorially announced a new policy. Henceforth, the *Times* would open its op-ed page several times a week to contributions from outside the industry. The *Times* hoped "to afford greater opportunity for exploration of issues and presentation of new insights and new ideas by writers and thinkers who have no institutional connection with the *Times* and whose views will very frequently be completely divergent from our own." Other papers, including the *Miami Herald,* have followed suit with one or more of the following responses: opening the op-ed pages, allocating more space for letters to the editor, and, as with the *Washington Post,* creation of an ombudsman.[48]

These new approaches still leave the discretion of what to print with an editor of the paper. Tornillo still would not get his two replies published under the same circumstances as prevailed in 1972. This does not mean, however, that the changes are cosmetic only. Nevertheless, would-be contributors are only incidental beneficiaries of the new approaches; the changes are designed to serve the readers of the paper. Sometimes the editorial choices will seem capricious, other times perfect; that is the nature of editorial choice.

Although Barron lost his legal war, the concerns he articulated motivated others voluntarily to take steps in the direction he pointed. The new approaches deal with his prime concern: that different voices be heard and different issues addressed. The solutions are not perfect, but with such an intractable problem they could not be. Furthermore, as voluntary responses to a widely perceived problem, changes can be made as experience dictates. These attempts, even if imperfect, are better than errors of legislation—a possibility that lurked within *Tornillo*.[49]

Law professors typically lose interest in the litigants once a judicial opinion has been published. An epilogue on *Tornillo* indicates that there is value in asking what happened next.

In Florida, political events moved swiftly in the period following the US Supreme Court decision. The looming scandal at the Florida Supreme Court resulted in a rapid transfusion of personnel. Within two years of *Tornillo*, four of the seven judges had been replaced. In the Florida legislature, the statute books were cleaned of the unconstitutional right to reply. Still, some members could not resist tweaking the press. An amendment to the repealer was proposed that would let the public vote on the hiring and firing of managing editors of newspapers. It was defeated by only seven votes.[50]

Tornillo never tried elective politics again, but he remains firmly in control of his union. The old CTA has changed both its name and its affiliation: It became the United Teachers of Dade and dropped the NEA and joined the American Federation of Teachers. UTD's lawyer is Elizabeth duFresne, who kept Tornillo as a client after Toby Simon's death. She is now a senior partner in the Miami firm that currently represents the *Herald!*

Shoemaker has retired, but the *Herald* remains one of the outstanding newspapers in the United States; it was responsible for bringing down the 1988 presidential candidacy of the Democratic front-runner Gary Hart. It has a monopoly now, because, as discussed in Chapter 7, its joint operating agreement with the *Miami News* was extended as part of a deal to kill the *News*.

Time does heal: Tornillo's relations with the *Herald* are quite good, and he finds his way into the paper, including letters to the editor, with frequency. Both Tornillo and Shoemaker look back on the events and see their positions as ones of principle which left no alternatives. Tornillo, at least, believes that some time in the future his position on the right of reply will prevail. Shoemaker still believes the *Herald* had no choice but to refuse to print Tornillo's replies. John Knight, president of the chain owning the *Herald,* was unhappy about the suit but fully backed it. Nevertheless, Knight had a simple message for Shoemaker: "Don't do it again."

Fortunately, once was enough. Had *Tornillo* gone the other way, it is too possible to imagine what the reaction of a financier who borrowed heavily to gain control of a newspaper chain might be: Don't do anything that could make waves and run up litigation costs. Fortunately also, Knight and Shoemaker, as real newsmen, could think of themselves as heirs of John Peter Zenger and act accordingly. Their willingness to stand for what they believed right bequeathed us the unanimous opinion most fully supporting the Fourth Estate model of the press. While Justices Black and Douglas typically staked out positions far beyond where their brethren would go, on the issue of the press autonomy needed to perform a checking function, they brought everyone in.

# Conclusion

Freedom of the press is guaranteed "not for the benefit of reporters," Dan Rather asserted. And certainly not for the benefit of those lucky enough to own a newspaper. Oh no, as he continued, "it is for the benefit of listeners and viewers and readers. The cause is America." Rather, not surprisingly, has bought fully into the instrumental view of the press that disassociates its power from its privileges. He, and his colleagues, do it all for us.[1]

Rather may disassociate power from privilege, but it is much harder for those looking at the realities of media ownership to do the same. By the time of A. J. Liebling's death, the idea of competing daily newspapers had died in all but the major cities. Subsequently even Los Angeles and Miami have become single-daily-newspaper cities, and other cities, most recently Detroit and Seattle, have had their daily newspapers join forces in an anticompetitive arrangement that promises great profits and, perhaps, the continued existence of a second paper in partnership with its former competitor. Furthermore, the great profits from ending competition hold special allure for newspaper chains, thereby reinforcing the view that chains don't like competition in the first place. While the number of chains has diminished, the reason is chain mergers with chains, thereby creating even larger concentrations. All this has been topped off, as Ben Bagdikian so painstakingly demonstrated, by concentration of ownership of all types of communications organizations.

Concentrations of power, whether big oil or big labor (as it once appeared) or big media, leave Americans uneasy. At almost the same time that Rather was asserting that the press did it all for us, oil prices were skyrocketing and big oil made a similar assertion (national security and all that). When I hear claims that someone is doing it all in my interests, I always hold tighter to my wallet. Rather's complaint, like that of big oil, is that if government regulation (in this case requests for the names of sources) would just go away, he could do his job better and thereby improve our lives. Maybe so, but such arguments are not only self-serving, they are notoriously unsuccessful when coming from giants. Thus Martin Shapiro notes, "increases in concentration inevitably lead to increased interest in regulation." Why the state? asks Owen Fiss. The answer, corroborating Shapiro's point, is: to regulate.[2]

As long as concentration of the media keeps increasing, their power will appear to be increasing, and there will be discussions of potential regulation, whether based on equality-oriented theories such as Fiss's or on more purely majoritarian theories ("the people have already decided that issue [adversely to the press]"). The Hutchins Commission report in its nuanced style predicted as much, recognizing the correlation between right and responsibility. The right—freedom of the press—offers, in its modern manifestation, the potential of power. With power goes responsibility, and the important questions are whether an accounting will be called for and if so, who will do it and by what means.

As to the once universal love of freedom of expression, my colleague Jack Balkin writes, "it's not that way any more." The shift from universal support began, unintentionally and imperceptibly, two decades ago, when much of the best constitutional law scholarship focused on issues of equality. Indeed, Fiss was a major contributor to this literature. The discussions of equality did not mention either freedom of speech or freedom of the press. But whatever formal equality there may be between the majority of Americans and those who own newspapers, substantive equality is lacking; and the scholarship aimed to create conditions of substantive equality. A separate strand of this scholarship emphasized the need of heightened judicial protection for minorities—and the authors did not mean the newspaper-owning minority. Any writing driven by concerns about equality will question privileges, and freedom of the press is a privilege. Nor is this an area where equality can be achieved by raising the bottom; greater equality necessarily involves leveling down. Thus when a First Amendment scholar writes that some scholars "view government regulation of mass media as a threat to First Amendment Freedoms," the obvious and ominous corollary is that others do not.[3]

The battle for regulation will be fought first in the academic world, just as the battle against the Supreme Court's acquiescence in the McCarthy hysteria was. Like many a battle in the legal journals, it will be over theory rather than practice. Good, and preferably grand, theory has a captivating mystique that leaves it all but immune to questions about how it would work in fact. Unlike in the real world, decision makers in a theoretical model always know enough to produce the correct results, and they are never torn by conflicting pressures. Within the confines of the theoretical model, decision makers need not deal with the instabilities and inconsistencies that (Arrow's Theorem explains) necessarily face their real-world counterparts. Thus Judith Lichtenberg does not pause to ask how her proposal would work; the fact that it is a good idea is sufficient. Eschewing Holmes's maxim, theorists tend to be driven more by their own logic than by experience, which they often lack. They are readily attracted by some version of the right-to-know model, to supplant the Fourth Estate model.[4]

Whether and how the press is to be held accountable represents the important intellectual gulf between the right-to-know model and the Fourth Estate model of the press. The logic of the former calls for an accounting at some time, while in the latter, autonomy precludes an accounting for performance.

While precluding an accounting, autonomy nevertheless explains performance (and does not render a critique impermissible). Tom Patterson and John Peter Zenger could have justified their writings in marketplace terms; they could have explained them in discussions about speech and its necessary relationship to self-government; they could have explained how self-realizing it is to discuss such important matters (although in Zenger's, but not Patterson's, case that would have been difficult, since Zenger was a printer, not an editor); but in fact the two were exercising the press's checking function. They were calling public servants to task, demanding an accounting—one that the governing agents always owe, but are rarely called upon to give. It is here, rather than in Holmes's marketplace or Meiklejohn's self-government or Baker's

self-realization, that the press, by both its power and its independence, plays a unique role in our democracy.[5]

The Fourth Estate model explains the choices made in Part Two
and highlights the areas where governmental action should be of
special concern. Libel law is important when the plaintiff is a public
official or a public figure who is tied into public issues. In these
situations, a libel action may be a disguised way of preventing the
press from performing a checking function; and because of the
specter of astronomical damage awards, all of libel law carries the
potential to chill the necessary discussions of how the public business is transacted. Similarly with prior restraints. When the press
has information about governmental actions, that information is
already available to too many in the public domain. The very
futility of a prior restraint on politically sensitive information is
sufficient reason—there are others—to recognize that Blackstone's
two-hundred-year-old position continues to make sense.

If the demands to know confidential sources came from within
the Beltway, then there would be reason to postulate that the
government was attempting to break the reporter-source relationship to protect itself. But Woodward and Bernstein were not sub-
poenaed, whereas Myron Farber was; and as long as that pattern
holds, the Fourth Estate model operates, including its essential
reliance on confidential sources for reporting on what government
is doing. Similarly, as discussed in Chapter 7, those structural
regulations—such as individualized taxation—that could threaten
the independence and therefore the autonomy of the press, should
be unconstitutional. The highly profitable JOAs fit very uneasily
here, because when the press comes hat-in-hand to government for
multi-multimillion dollar bonuses, dollars may trump independence. Those chains most interested in JOAs were so thrilled with
the Nixon administration's backing of the Newspaper Preservation
Act that they threw their support behind Nixon's reelection efforts.
Had he been opposed by a real candidate, instead of George Mc-
Govern, we would have a better idea of the actual workings of
autonomy and the desire for special privileges.[5]

Freedom of the press, like other essential civil liberties, had its
origins in times when the government's claim to sovereignty was
not based on consent of the people. Freedom of the press, as Zenger

and other colonial dissenters knew, rested partially on the foundations of popular support against an unpopular government. With the transformation of sovereignty and the establishment of universal suffrage, freedom of the press necessarily is exercised against a popularly supported government. The change is highlighted by the switch in jury behavior from Zenger's trial to those of the World War I dissenters, to the Selective Service convictions during the early period of the Vietnam War, and to the past 15 years of libel decisions. Juries may, and often do, lash out at people and institutions they perceive to be threatening to a status quo with which they are satisfied.

A powerful and privileged press checking a popularly elected and powerful government creates tensions that cannot be removed without compromising press autonomy. When the press performs at its best, exemplified by the *Washington Post* during Watergate, it will face not only an angry government but substantial numbers of angry citizens as well. "Who elected you?" is a question that cannot be answered on its own terms; there is an unavoidable tension between the belief that privilege requires justification and the knowledge that autonomy cannot exist without independence. Learned Hand, in his *Associated Press* opinion, recognized that tension and resolved it by emphasizing the need for faith: "To many this [avoidance of authoritative selection] is, and always will be, folly; but we have staked upon it our all."[6]

Faith may not satisfy those who ask "Who elected you?" Their concerns are more secular and immediate, but also harder to implement quickly against a right as basic as freedom of the press. Faith is a central response, however, to those who, like Fiss and Lichtenberg, perceive a systemic slighting of issues they hold dear and a corresponding emphasis on issues designed to make the overall status quo (with a little lessening of the legal pressures on business) appear the natural order of things. These two authors posit the need for change as part of a long-run view. Example and counterexample are insufficient responses from their perspective, because they postulate a general failure of the system (and those who do not see that failure are considered to be living examples of how the system has improperly narrowed the available options). Both hold to an alternative view of faith, one that embraces the government.

Thus Fiss quite expressly embraces the New Deal regulatory model and explains his desire to regulate public debate in part as an effort to rekindle regulation generally.

While a look at broadcast regulation would seem essential to their positions—and would decisively refute the view of a beneficent neutral government arbiter—neither Fiss nor Lichtenberg indicates the slightest awareness of the realities of government regulation. Fiss cites to the soaring language of the Fairness Doctrine and hears the ideal of neutral, detached presentation of public issues without indoctrination, operating to produce an enlightened citizenry without manipulation of voters. As a theorist he appears wholly unconcerned about how the doctrine works (and with his ready presumptions he can overcome the facts if necessary). It is sufficient that the doctrine reads well—just as his public-debate principle reads well; that is often the charm of good theory. For the rest of us, who will be stuck with the consequences of good theory, facts matter. The broadcast experience with a regulated First Amendment offers the best evidence that a free press must be an autonomous press.[7]

Still, perhaps the mistakes of the past can be corrected; perhaps a learning curve exists, as the Supreme Court itself demonstrated in the decisive changes between the era of World War I and the period, described in Chapter 3, from *Times* to *Times*. Guesses like these must be made with reference to the past, but ultimately, as Hand knew, they are guesses made more by faith than science.

That Hand turned to faith ought not be surprising. A similar faith exists regarding other parts of our constitutional system that check the exercise of governmental authority. Thus there is an important parallel between the justification of the Fourth Estate model and that of the Supreme Court's ability to hold federal and state statutes unconstitutional (although, unlike freedom of the press, judicial review is not textually explicit but arises by necessary inference). Both checking functions are exercised against policies formally adopted by popularly elected officials. Both are exercised by unelected and unaccountable individuals. Yet both are perceived as essential components of our democracy (with emphasis on *our*, for it is possible to have a democracy without judicial review, though not without freedom of the press—however, other democracies do have considerably less freedom of the press than ours).

Like judicial review, freedom of the press has its good times and its bad times. We think of judicial review's spectacular blunders, such as upholding "separate but equal" and validating the march to segregation in *Plessy v. Ferguson* (which in fact had a solid major-itarian consensus behind it). More recently the Supreme Court's abortion decisions, whether right or wrong, have been contentious in the extreme. A growing literature, mostly from the right, would have considerably less judicial review. Yet judicial review is integral to our constitutional fabric; even if the Court blows a few, its constitutional review of legislation nevertheless serves an impor-tant function in our body politic.[8]

The same can be said, with considerably more confidence I think, about freedom of the press. True, press performance during the McCarthy period was as acquiescent as the Supreme Court's; the idea of checking McCarthy was largely after the fact. But just as the Court had Black and Douglas dissenting, there was a minority of the press that dissented from the hysteria and kept the standards of civil liberties alive and before some of the public. There is no reason to suppose that had Fiss's and Lichtenberg's regulatory apparatus been in place, coverage would have been any better. Instead, there is every reason to believe it would have operated contrary to their faith, hopes, and presumptions by lessening criticism of McCarthy. CBS was the only network that took on McCarthy, and to say it was unhappy and reluctant is an understatement. Even then, Ed-ward R. Murrow and Fred Friendly waited long enough so that Murrow was able to read, during his program, editorial denuncia-tions of the Wisconsin demagogue from the nation's leading news-papers. When the next crisis came, again only CBS risked any preelection analysis of the looming Watergate scandal, and even that was too little, too late (and, after a phone call from White House operative Chuck Colson, it was cut back on the orders of CBS owner William Paley). Yet if the regulated broadcasters were too timid, at least some newspapers were willing to risk potentially serious consequences to stand up to the government. That is what freedom of the press allows when it recognizes autonomy, and that is precisely what is threatened when autonomy is threatened.[9]

Furthermore, for all the talk about power, it has been a long time since the press sent American youths to die in faraway lands. Some news stories are highly controversial, but it is hard to point to any as being in the same league as *Dred Scott* and its Civil War facilitating conclusion that Congress had no power over slavery in the territories. The press is far better at its Fourth Estate function of checking than it is with the right-to-know duty of initiating. Its power, at its peak, is that of agenda setting; it does not, and cannot, force action. Thus for all Woodward and Bernstein's great reporting, had not Judge Sirica taken matters into his hands, the Watergate disclosures might have come to a premature halt early in Nixon's second term. And it was not the *Post* or the *Times* that gave the House impeachment inquiry its momentum; it was the instant gut reaction of the American people to Nixon's sacking of Archibald Cox, Elliot Richardson, and William Ruckelshaus in the Saturday Night Massacre. Finally, Westmoreland's efforts to the contrary notwithstanding, the Vietnam War was lost in Southeast Asia, not on American television—a point recognized today by the Army's official Center of Military History.[10]

Like judicial review, freedom of the press has proven to be a guarantor of civil liberties. The message may be initially unpalatable, but as the urge to kill the messenger passes, the message is evaluated. Sometimes it will remain unpopular and bring the press into collision with the passions of the time. Then the tensions become all too visible, the costs obvious, the benefits (from the view of those questioned) perceptibly less. Nevertheless, no one has yet suggested a better alternative, and the examples of less democratic countries with their controlled newspapers present a powerful reinforcement of the idea that America has been doing something right for a long time.

The Hutchins Commission warned that if the newspapers of the nation were "irresponsible, not even the First Amendment will protect their freedom from governmental control." When the Hutchins Commission wrote "irresponsible" the members presumably shared a common definition. But subsequently it is clear that responsibility is very much in the eyes of the beholder. Ask Richard Nixon and Barbara Jordan about Watergate. Ask Frank Church and William Colby about the publishing of the Pike Report on the misdeeds of the CIA. Ask Gary Hart and George Bush about the *Miami Herald*'s following Donna Rice to a Georgetown townhouse and then staking it out. America is a large, diverse, and, at times, contentious polity. Too often, "responsible" and "irresponsible" become labels placed on the carcass of the gored ox. Nowhere was this better illustrated than in the opposite attitudes toward Otto Otepka, who delivered three State Department Security files to the Senate Subcommittee on Internal Security, and Daniel Ellsberg, who, just eight years later, leaked the Pentagon Papers. Everyone who applauded Otepka condemned Ellsberg, and vice versa. The right saw Otepka as a lonely hero in the fight against communism, Ellsberg as a virtual traitor. Indeed, on May 20, 1971, the *Washington Post* reached back to Otepka's disclosure and editorialized against giving him a sinecure position on the toothless and functionless Subversive Activities Control Board—citing his "past conduct in the handling of security affairs." Thus, although the Hutchins Commission prediction remains apt, it is necessary to recognize that *irresponsible* necessarily means not performing adequately or properly in the minds of a significant segment of the society. It lacks the inherent meaning the Hutchins Commission postulated.[11]

Justice Jackson wrote that the "very purpose of a Bill of Rights was to place certain subjects beyond the reach of majorities. . . . One's right to life, liberty, and property, to free speech, a free press, freedom of worship and assembly, and other fundamental rights may not be submitted to vote; they depend on the outcome of no elections." The Bill of Rights did not, however, put them beyond question. The tensions inherent in the checking function and majoritarian decision making ensure that the press, even as it serves its various functions, will be challenged, sometimes from the right, sometimes from the left, and maybe even sometimes by everyone.[12]

Pollsters tell us press credibility varies. That is how it should be. If it did not vary, the press would not be doing its job. Its job—and its performance—cannot be rendered immune from criticism, whether from George Bush, Michael Dukakis, Gary Hart, William Westmoreland, Owen Fiss, Judith Lichtenberg, or Patrick Buchanan. Criticism comes with the territory. That territory requires the press to perform many functions, and although I have emphasized its checking function, that is but one. The press is an essential ingredient in the democratic dialogue in America. It is a participant, not a referee—history ultimately wears the zebra shirt—and therefore it needs feedback. Its myopia amuses. Its size worries. Its errors hurt. Its arrogance angers. Like other institutions, it professes ideals that exceed its very human capacities.

At its best, the Constitution supports an informed public, creating a representative democracy, reflecting a common good, and being ultimately respectful of the needs of all. While the Constitution authorizes more than sufficient authority to achieve its goals, it nevertheless creates important checks. Power, when loosened from restraint, destroys more readily than it creates. Therefore the Constitution contains, both in its body and in the Bill of Rights, important safeguards—staggered and lengthy senatorial terms, two-house concurrence, presidential appointment, an independent judiciary, federalism, religious freedom, and other individual freedoms—to guarantee that the experiment in freedom would not be lost in a season of panic or a mistaken episode of collective certainty about our past and therefore our future. Freedom of the press is an integral part of the checks that strive to preserve a delicate balance, which simultaneously energizes and restrains. Thornton Wilder wrote that "every good and excellent thing in the world stands moment by moment on the razor-edge of danger and must be fought for—whether it's a field, a home, or a country." Or those great and basic rights that make us free.[13]

# Notes

## Introduction

1. F. Little, *Thomas M. Patterson*, 11 Rocky Mountain Law Review 149 (1939) is the best piece available on Patterson. L. Hafen, COLORADO 264–65 (Denver: Peerless Publishing, 1933); L. Dorsett, THE QUEEN CITY 68, 75, 79, 130–42 (Boulder: Pruett Publishing, 1977); R. De-Lorme, *Turn-of-the-Century Denver: An Invitation to Reform*, 45 Colorado Magazine 1 (1968).

2. DeLorme, *Turn-of-the-Century Denver* at 9; R. Perkin, THE FIRST HUNDRED YEARS: AN INFORMAL HISTORY OF DENVER AND THE ROCKY MOUNTAIN NEWS 407–10 (Garden City, N.Y.: Doubleday, 1959).

3. The secondary sources just say that Adams apparently won. In Patterson's answer to the show-cause order, he stated that the margin was 9000 votes according to the "official returns." *People ex rel. Attorney General v. News-Times Publishing Co.*, 35 Colo. 253, 284–90 (1906). Although not so detailed, the secondary literature agrees. P. Fritz, COLORADO 377 (New York: Prentice-Hall, 1941); Hafen, COLORADO at 267–68. Adams was not the usual "two-time former" governor. He had served single terms in 1887 and 1897.

4. *Marbury v. Madison*, 5 U.S. (1 Cranch) 137 (1803).

5. *News-Times Publishing*, 35 Colo. at 303; Fritz, COLORADO at 377; Hafen, COLORADO at 267–68. I realize that the Pinckney example is not perfect because the 1800 election precipitated the Twelfth Amendment; thus neither Pinckney nor Aaron Burr was in the electoral college officially as a vice-presidential candidate.

6. *People v. Johnson*, 34 Colo. 143 (1905).

7. *Denver Times*, June 24, 1905, reprinted in *News-Times Publishing*, 35 Colo. at 256–57.

8. *Rocky Mountain News*, June 25, 1905, reprinted in 35 Colo. at 257–58.

9. *Denver Times,* June 26, 1905, reprinted in 35 Colo. at 259–63.

10. *Rocky Mountain News,* June 30, 1905, reprinted in 35 Colo. at 271–75.

11. Justice Steele's solo dissent reproduced in full Patterson's statement to the court why he should not be held in contempt (*News-Times Publishing,* 35 Colo. at 395–99). Steele's dissent ends with an apt comment on the majority's ruling truth irrelevant: "In the very nature of things, those who before believed the charges to be true are now confirmed in their belief, and those who did not believe them, now have their confidence in this court shaken solely because of the action of the court in refusing the respondent a hearing, and denying him the right to offer proof in support of the charges" (id. at 461).

12. Colorado Constitution art. II, § 10 (emphasis added).

13. *News-Times Publishing,* 35 Colo. at 361–62, 392–94, 356.

14. *Patterson v. Colorado,* 205 U.S. 454, 462 (1907). Justice Harlan dissented on the merits; Justice Brewer dissented without indicating a view on the First Amendment issue. (Whether the First Amendment applied to the states will be discussed in Chapter 2.) W. Blackstone, 4 Commentaries on the Laws of England 151 (Oxford: Clarendon Press, 1769).

15. J. Alexander, A Brief Narrative of the Case and Trial of John Peter Zenger 8 (S. Katz, ed.) (Cambridge, Mass.: Belknap Press, 1963). This is the indispensable source for the Zenger case: Alexander's "Brief Narrative," written shortly after the trial, is republished along with a superb introductory essay by Stanley N. Katz and three useful appendices. For the facts leading up to the trial I have relied exclusively on Katz's excellent introduction. For the trial itself I relied on Alexander's narrative, which I have interpreted as a lawyer taking apart another's case.

16. Katz, *Introduction* to Alexander, Brief Narrative at 2.

17. Id. at 3–4, 6–7.

18. Id. at 9.

19. Id. at 10–11, 13.

20. Id. at 17.

21. Id. at 17–19; Alexander, Brief Narrative at 49.

22. Alexander, Brief Narrative at 49.

23. Id. at 62.

24. Id. at 51–55.

25. Id. at 56; Katz, *Introduction* at 21–22; L. Wright, *Milestones and Concepts of the Lawyer-Citizen,* 41 American Bar Association Journal 797 (1955).

26. Alexander, Brief Narrative at 65, 66.

27. Id. at 62, 68, 69.

28. Id. at 69.

29. Id. at 74.

30. Id. at 75 (emphasis omitted).

31. Id. at 84, 81.

32. Id. at 96, 98, 99.

33. Id. at 101.

34. Katz, *Introduction* at 29–30.

35. Consider the Espionage Act trial of Jacob Abrams that ultimately led to Justice Holmes's eloquent dissent in *Abrams v. United States,* 250 U.S. 616 (1919). Abrams, a Russian immigrant and alien, was on the stand and being questioned by the trial judge, Henry DeLamar Clayton, Jr., whose younger brother had been killed by a German bomb in France just five months earlier. Abrams, who spoke with a soft voice and distinct Yiddish accent, was attempting to justify his anarchist beliefs: "This government was built on a revolution. . . . When our forefathers of the American revolution—" Clayton interrupted instantly, "Your what?" "My forefathers," responded Abrams. Clayton: "Do you mean to refer to the fathers of this nation as your forefathers?" R. Polenberg, FIGHTING FAITHS 95–102, 118–25 (New York: Viking Penguin, 1987). On the day of sentencing, Clayton delivered a two-hour tirade at the defendants and then sentenced Abrams to twenty years.

36. D. Teeter, A Legacy of Expression: Philadelphia Newspapers and Congress During the War for Independence 13 (Ph.D. dissertation, School of Journalism, University of Wisconsin, Madison, 1966); William Cushing to John Adams, February 18, 1789, quoted in L. Levy, THE EMERGENCE OF A FREE PRESS 199 (New York: Oxford University Press, 1985).

## Chapter 1

1. "Official Notice of Ratification" (March 1, 1792), reproduced in B. Schwartz, 2 THE BILL OF RIGHTS: A DOCUMENTARY HISTORY 1203 (New York: Chelsea House, 1971).

2. This is the position taken by Leonard Levy's influential books: LEGACY OF SUPPRESSION (New York: Oxford University Press, 1960), enlarged and republished as EMERGENCE OF A FREE PRESS (New York: Oxford University Press, 1985). My own research, as well as that of others relied upon in this chapter, was in large measure stimulated by Levy's seminal LEGACY. Although I, like others, dispute Levy's legal conclusions, his superb research is indispensable to an understanding of the colonial meaning of freedom of the press.

3. Kenneth Bowling entitled his dissertation A Tub to the Whale: The

Adoption of the Federal Bill of Rights (unpublished dissertation, University of Wisconsin, Madison, 1968), using Jonathan Swift's story to explain the Federalists' expedient conversion to the Bill of Rights. "Sea-men have a Custom when they meet a *Whale*, to fling him out an empty *Tub*, by way of Amusement, to divert him from laying violent Hands upon the Ship." A Tale of a Tub, in The Writings of Jonathan Swift 284 (R. Greenberg, ed.) (New York: Norton, 1973). R. Buel, Securing the Revolution 246 (Ithaca, N.Y.: Cornell University Press, 1972).

4. The First Amendment was, in fact, the third submitted to the states. The first two, as submitted, were dear to elected officials' hearts: one dealt with population for congressional districts, the other with congressional compensation. Furthermore, as David Anderson notes, "freedom of the press or speech was never first on anyone's list. It was the last right mentioned in the Address to the Inhabitants of Quebec. It was article twelve of the Pennsylvania Declaration of Rights, the sixteenth of twenty amendments proposed by the Virginia Ratifying Convention, and the second clause of the fourth proposition in Madison's proposed bill of rights." *The Origins of the Press Clause*, 30 UCLA Law Review 455, 482–83 (1983) (footnotes omitted).

5. G. Wood, The Creation of the American Republic 132 (Chapel Hill: University of North Carolina Press, 1969).

6. Id. at 281–92; F. McDonald, Novus Ordo Seclorum 58–59 (Lawrence: University of Kansas Press, 1985).

7. Wood, Creation of the American Republic at 285; Anderson, *Origins of the Press Clause* at 464; D. Rabban, *The Ahistorical Historian: Leonard Levy on Freedom of Expression in Early American History,* 37 Stanford Law Review 795, 828 (1985). A shorter version of Rabban's article, stating his conclusions without the focus on Levy, appears as *The Original Meaning of the Free Speech Clause of the First Amendment,* in R. Simmons, ed., 6 The United States Constitution at 36 (Manchester: Manchester University Press, 1989). Only Connecticut and Rhode Island did not join the constitution drafting; they continued under their colonial charters.

8. F. Hall, *The Common Law: An Account of its Reception in the United States,* 4 Vanderbilt Law Review 791, 798–800 (1951); M. Horowitz, The Transformation of American Law 4 (Cambridge, Mass.: Harvard University Press, 1977); Levy, Emergence of a Free Press at 183.

9. Quoted in Hall, *Common Law* at 798, 799nn.

10. J. Trenchard and T. Gordon, 1 Cato's Letters; or, Essays on Liberty, Civil and Religious, and Other Important Subjects 100 (New York: Da Capo Press, 1971); Schwartz, 1 Bill of Rights at 235, 342.

11. Id. at 266, 277. Both of the unique Pennsylvania provisions were also adopted by Vermont when it formed its constitution a year later. Pennsylvania's radical constitution was replaced in 1790. R. Brunhouse, THE COUNTER-REVOLUTION IN PENNSYLVANIA (Harrisburg: Pennsylvania Historical Society, 1942).

12. "Narrow conservatism" is Levy's characterization of Blackstone in EMERGENCE OF A FREE PRESS at xv. From the point of view of the Radical Whigs this is, if anything, an understatement.

13. Rabban, *Ahistorical Historian* at 828; Rabban, *Free Speech Clause* at 40.

14. Rabban, *Free Speech Clause* at 39–43.

15. D. Teeter, A Legacy of Expression: Philadelphia Newspapers and Congress During the War for Independence 13 (Ph.D. dissertation, School of Journalism, University of Wisconsin, Madison, 1966); M. Yodelis, WHO PAID THE PIPER? PUBLISHING ECONOMICS IN BOSTON, 1763–75, Journalism Monographs no. 38, at 42 (Lexington: University of Kentucky Press, 1975).

16. D. Teeter, *Press Freedom and Public Printing: Pennsylvania, 1775–83*, 45 Journalism Quarterly 445, 446 (1968); N. Rosenberg, PROTECTING THE BEST MEN 45 (Chapel Hill: University of North Carolina Press, 1986).

17. Teeter, *Press Freedom and Public Printing* at 446, 447. When the British were approaching Philadelphia in 1777, Congress took steps to protect printers and their equipment. "It was feared that all the printers would flee, interrupting the state's—and Congress'—main method of financing the war: printing paper money." Teeter, Legacy of Expression at 95.

18. M. Jensen, Book Review, 75 Harvard Law Review 456, 457 (1961) (reviewing Levy, LEGACY OF SUPPRESSION); Levy, EMERGENCE OF A FREE PRESS at x; R. Buel, *Freedom of the Press in Revolutionary America*, in B. Bailyn and J. Hench, eds., THE PRESS AND THE AMERICAN REVOLUTION 59, 81 (Boston: Northeastern University Press, 1981).

19. Teeter, *Press Freedom and Public Printing;* Legacy of Expression.

20. Teeter, Legacy of Expression at 21; D. Teeter, *The Printer and the Chief Justice: Seditious Libel in 1782–83*, 45 Journalism Quarterly 235, 236 (1968); J. Wheeler, THE MARYLAND PRESS 19–36 (Baltimore: Maryland Historical Society, 1938).

21. *New York Times v. United States*, 403 U.S. 713 (1971); *Independent Gazetteer*, June 22, 1782, quoted in Teeter, Legacy of Expression at 207.

22. Teeter, Legacy of Expression at 120; *Press Freedom and Public Printing* at 449.

23. Teeter, Legacy of Expression at 241, 244.

24. *Independent Gazetteer,* June 23, 1783, quoted in Teeter, Legacy of Expression at 250.

25. Teeter, Legacy of Expression at 127; *Independent Gazetteer,* April 21, 1781, quoted in D. Teeter, *Decent Animadversions: Notes Toward a History of Free Press Theory,* in D. Bond and W. McLead, eds., NEWSLETTERS TO NEWSPAPERS: EIGHTEENTH-CENTURY JOURNALISM 237, 240 (Morgantown: School of Journalism, West Virginia University, 1977); *Freeman's Journal,* May 23, 1781, quoted in Teeter, *Decent Animadversions* at 240.

26. *Pennsylvania Packet,* July 3, 1779, quoted in Teeter, *Press Freedom and Public Printing* at 450.

27. Teeter, *Press Freedom and Public Printing* at 450.

28. Teeter, Legacy of Expression at 97, 107–09.

29. *Pennsylvania Evening Post,* June 25, 1778, quoted in Teeter, Legacy of Expression at 111.

30. Teeter, Legacy of Expression at 144–45; D. Teeter, *From Revisionism to Orthodoxy,* 13 Reviews in American History 518, 521–22 (1985).

31. Teeter, Legacy of Expression at 149.

32. A. Schlesinger, PRELUDE TO INDEPENDENCE 189 (New York: Alfred A. Knopf, 1958): "Liberty of speech belonged solely to those who spoke the speech of liberty." J. Kettner, THE DEVELOPMENT OF AMERICAN CITIZENSHIP, 1608–1870 (Chapel Hill: University of North Carolina Press, 1978) at 183, notes that execution of Tories for treason was rare during the war. "The death penalty seems to have been carried out only when there was clear evidence of active disloyalty; even then the purpose was as much to warn other potential traitors as to satisfy a patriotic bloodlust."

33. Teeter, Legacy of Expression at 121.

34. *Independent Gazetteer,* September 28, 1782, quoted in Teeter, *The Printer and the Chief Justice* at 237.

35. *Independent Gazetteer,* December 17, 1782; Oswald to Lamb, November 26, 1782, both quoted in Teeter, *The Printer and the Chief Justice* at 238, 239.

36. *Independent Gazetteer,* December 31, 1782, and January 4, 1783, quoted in Teeter, *The Printer and the Chief Justice* at 240, 241.

37. Quoted in Rosenberg, PROTECTING THE BEST MEN at 53; Levy, EMERGENCE OF A FREE PRESS at xvi.

38. H. Nelson, *Seditious Libel in Colonial America,* 3 American Journal of Legal History 160 (1959).

39. Id. at 161, 164, 169–70; Buel, *Freedom of the Press in Revolutionary America* at 70.

40. Nelson, *Seditious Libel in Colonial America* at 163–64; J. Smith,

PRINTERS AND PRESS FREEDOM 9 (New York: Oxford University Press, 1987).

41. Levy, EMERGENCE OF A FREE PRESS at 182.

42. C. Rossiter, SEEDTIME OF THE REPUBLIC 141 (New York: Harcourt, Brace, 1953); Trenchard and Gordon, 1 CATO'S LETTERS 249; 3 CATO'S LETTERS at 299, 302–03.

43. Trenchard and Gordon, 1 CATO'S LETTERS at 246–47, 253.

44. Rabban, *Free Speech Clause* at 40; Buel, *Freedom of the Press in Revolutionary America* at 74–75; Rabban, *Ahistorical Historian* at 827; Levy, EMERGENCE OF A FREE PRESS at 113; Smith, PRINTERS AND PRESS FREEDOM part 1. Rabban expressly acknowledges his debt to the historians of civic republicanism, especially Bernard Bailyn, Gordon Wood, and Buel.

45. J. Smith, *A Reappraisal of Legislative Privilege and American Colonian Journalism,* 61 Journalism Quarterly 97 (1984).

46. Smith, PRINTERS AND PRESS FREEDOM at 5–7; Rabban, *Ahistorical Historian* at 832–34; Rabban, *Free Speech Clause* at 41.

47. Levy, EMERGENCE OF A FREE PRESS at 182. In *Garrison v. Louisiana,* 379 U.S. 64 (1964), the Supreme Court took the "reckless disregard" standard of *New York Times v. Sullivan* (to be discussed in Chapters 3 and 4) and applied it to criminal libel on facts where the alleged criminal libel against certain judges was functionally the same as seditious libel. When Levy wrote, he thought that a country with a law of seditious libel could not have a libertarian tradition. Yet this was prior to *Garrison;* and even now, after *Garrison,* it is conceivable (although I think it unlikely) that a person could be convicted of seditious libel if his or her libelous statements were intentionally false.

48. *Independent Gazetteer,* November 9, 1782, quoted in Teeter, *The Printer and the Chief Justice* at 239–40.

49. *Independent Gazetteer,* October 19, 1782 and November 9, 1782, both quoted in Teeter, *The Printer and the Chief Justice* at 239–40.

50. *Independent Gazetteer,* November 9, 1782 and December 7, 1782, quoted in Teeter, *The Printer and the Chief Justice* at 239–40.

51. Rosenberg, PROTECTING THE BEST MEN at 62.

52. Id. at 62–63.

53. Id. at 63.

54. Cushing to Adams, February 18, 1789, quoted in Levy, EMERGENCE OF A FREE PRESS at 199.

55. Id.

56. Id. at 199, 200.

57. Adams to Cushing, March 7, 1789, quoted in Levy, EMERGENCE OF A FREE PRESS at 200; Cushing to Adams, quoted at id.

58. Schwartz, 1 BILL OF RIGHTS at 437–39. A fuller account of the "legislative history" of the press clause than this section attempts is available in Anderson, *Origins of the Press Clause* at 462–86.

59. P. Ford, ed., ESSAYS ON THE CONSTITUTION OF THE UNITED STATES 289 (Brooklyn, N.Y.: Historical Printing Club, 1892); J. Wilson, *An Address to a Meeting of the Citizens of Philadelphia* (1787) in Schwartz, 1 BILL OF RIGHTS at 529.

60. Quoted in Levy, EMERGENCE OF A FREE PRESS at 270.

61. Anderson, *Origins of the Press Clause* at 471–73; Schwartz, 2 BILL OF RIGHTS at 842; D. Laycock, *Nonpreferential Aid to Religion: A False Claim About Original Intent,* 27 William and Mary Law Review 875, 907 (1989); 1 THE DEBATES AND PROCEEDINGS IN THE CONGRESS OF THE UNITED STATES [ANNALS], 1st Cong. 456, 457 (J. Gales ed. 1834). This superb speech by Madison receives the attention it warrants in D. Laycock, *Notes on the Role of Judicial Review, the Expansion of Federal Power, and the Structure of Constitutional Rights,* 97 Yale Law Journal 1711 (1990).

62. ANNALS, 1st Cong. at 452, 690, 784.

63. Id. at 759, 808.

64. JOURNAL OF THE FIRST SESSION OF THE SENATE 70 (J. Gales and W. Seaton, printers, 1820). Douglas Laycock makes a similar point with respect to the debate over nonpreferential aid to religions. Had the framers wished to authorize nonpreferential aid, they knew how to word it; one draft of the establishment clause did so. But, like the Blackstonian draft of the press clause, it was rejected. *Nonpreferential Aid to Religion* at 879–83.

65. JOURNAL at 70–71, 77; ANNALS, 1st Cong. at 939.

66. Anderson, *Origins of the Press Clause* at 486.

67. A number of writers have emphasized the federalism aspects of the First Amendment, but no scholar has done a better job than William Van Alstyne in explaining that knowing what the states were permitted to do tells nothing about what the federal government supposedly lacks power to do. *Constitutional Power and Free Speech: Levy's Legacy Revisited,* 99 Harvard Law Review 1089 (1986). His argument is nevertheless overstated. What occurred at the state level respecting freedom of the press—and especially religious establishment—is relevant to what the founding generation thought about the meaning of those terms. Laycock, *Nonpreferential Aid to Religion* at 894–902.

68. Levy, LEGACY OF SUPPRESSION as interpreted by Levy in *Liberty and the First Amendment: 1790–1800,* 68 American Historical Review 22 (1962); D. Anderson, *Levy v. Levy,* 84 Michigan Law Review 777, 782–83 (1986).

69. Anderson, *Origins of the Press Clause* at 533; Levy, EMERGENCE OF A FREE PRESS at 236.

70. McDonald, NOVUS ORDO SECLORUM at 57–96; G. Wood, *Ideology and the Origins of Liberal America*, 44 William and Mary Quarterly 628, 634 (1987); Buel, *Freedom of the Press in Revolutionary America* at 70.

71. Rosenberg, PROTECTING THE BEST MEN at 70.

72. Z. Chafee, FREE SPEECH IN THE UNITED STATES (Cambridge, Mass.: Harvard University Press, 1941).

73. Teeter, *From Revisionism to Orthodoxy* at 523; Rabban, *Ahistorical Historian* at 799–801; Anderson, *Levy v. Levy* at 783–85.

74. Anderson, *Origins of the Press Clause* at 534; Levy, EMERGENCE OF A FREE PRESS at 272 (emphasis in original). As David Anderson notes, the quoted language is expressly contrary to Levy's thesis in LEGACY OF SUPPRESSION and inconsistent with points in EMERGENCE OF A FREE PRESS: "To conclude that they intended to preserve seditious libel and Blackstone, and that they also intended to reject Blackstone and preserve the seditious press with which they were familiar, is not revision but confusion." Anderson, *Levy v. Levy* at 786.

## Chapter 2

1. Z. Chafee, FREE SPEECH IN THE UNITED STATES 79 (Cambridge, Mass.: Harvard University Press, 1941).

2. R. Wiebe, THE OPENING OF AMERICAN SOCIETY 3–125 (New York: Random House, 1984); J. Miller, THE FEDERALIST ERA 84–125 (New York: Harper and Row, 1960).

3. Wiebe, OPENING OF AMERICAN SOCIETY at 67–89; R. Buel, SECURING THE REVOLUTION 93–135 (Ithaca, N.Y.: Cornell University Press, 1972).

4. Buel, SECURING THE REVOLUTION at 37; Wiebe, OPENING OF AMERICAN SOCIETY at 72, 87; R. Buel, *Freedom of the Press in Revolutionary America*, in B. Bailyn and J. Hench, eds., THE PRESS AND THE AMERICAN REVOLUTION at 82–83 (Boston: Northeastern University Press, 1981).

5. Wiebe, OPENING OF AMERICAN SOCIETY at 73; P. Foner, ed., THE DEMOCRATIC-REPUBLICAN SOCIETIES, 1790–1800: A DOCUMENTARY SOURCEBOOK 64 (Westport, Conn.: Greenwood Press, 1976); D. Rabban, *Ahistorical Historian*, 37 Stanford Law Review 795, 844 (1985).

6. Foner, DEMOCRATIC-REPUBLICAN SOCIETIES at 64; E. Link, DEMOCRATIC-REPUBLICAN SOCIETIES, 1790–1800, at 162 (New York:

Columbia University Press, 1942); Buel, SECURING THE REVOLUTION at 103–04; Rabban, *Ahistorical Historian* at 845.

7. Wiebe, OPENING OF AMERICAN SOCIETY at 72–73; Rabban, *Ahistorical Historian* at 845; N. Rosenberg, PROTECTING THE BEST MEN 73 (Chapel Hill: University of North Carolina Press, 1986).

8. Rosenberg, PROTECTING THE BEST MEN at 71–73; Buel, SECURING THE REVOLUTION at 99–101.

9. J. Appleby, CAPITALISM AND A NEW SOCIAL ORDER 77 (New York: New York University Press, 1984).

10. Rosenberg, PROTECTING THE BEST MEN at 74–78; Appleby, CAPITALISM AND A NEW SOCIAL ORDER at 75–76; J. Smith, FREEDOM'S FETTERS 14, 21 (Ithaca, N.Y.: Cornell University Press, 1956).

11. Smith, FREEDOM'S FETTERS at 5–6.

12. Id. at 7.

13. Id. at 14.

14. Id. at 102–03, 193–95; J. Miller, CRISIS IN FREEDOM 63–64 (Boston: Atlantic–Little, Brown, 1951).

15. Miller, CRISIS IN FREEDOM at 69; Miller, FEDERALIST ERA at 231; L. Levy, EMERGENCE OF A FREE PRESS 297 (New York: Oxford University Press, 1985). The Sedition Act, 1 US Statutes at Large 596–97 (1798), is reprinted in Smith, FREEDOM'S FETTERS at 441–42.

16. D. Anderson, *The Origins of the Press Clause,* 30 UCLA Law Review 455, 516–19 (1983).

17. Otis stated that the objections to the Act "might be reduced to two inquiries. In the first place, had the Constitution given Congress cognizance over the offences described in this bill prior to the adoption of the amendments of the Constitution? and, if Congress had that cognizance before that time, have those amendments taken it away?" THE DEBATES AND PROCEEDINGS IN THE CONGRESS OF THE UNITED STATES [ANNALS], 5th Cong. 2145–46 (1798).

18. J. Cooke, ed., THE FEDERALIST no. 84 (A. Hamilton) at 579 (Middletown, Conn.: Wesleyan University Press, 1961).

19. ANNALS, 5th Cong. at 2146.

20. Id. at 2165, 2167.

21. *United States v. Worrell,* 2 U.S. (2 Dall.) 384 (1798); *United States v. Hudson,* 11 U.S. (7 Cranch) 32 (1812); C. Warren, 1 THE SUPREME COURT IN UNITED STATES HISTORY 434–35 (Boston: Little, Brown, 1922).

22. Alexander Addison quoted in Buel, SECURING THE REVOLUTION at 256 (emphasis in original); Levy, EMERGENCE OF A FREE PRESS at 305–08.

23. Rabban, *Ahistorical Historian* at 850–51; Smith, FREEDOM'S FETTERS at 324–25, 153–55; Cooke, FEDERALIST no. 71 at 483–84.

24. Miller, CRISIS IN FREEDOM at 137; Smith, FREEDOM'S FETTERS at 101; Harper: ANNALS, 5th Cong. at 1179, 2102–03; Allen: id. at 2093–2100.

25. Smith, FREEDOM'S FETTERS at 130; Miller, FEDERALIST ERA at 234.

26. Smith, FREEDOM'S FETTERS at 21, 26; ANNALS, 5th Cong. at 2110; Buel, SECURING THE REVOLUTION at 235; Miller, FEDERALIST ERA at 235; Anderson, *Origins of the Press Clause* at 515–16; ANNALS, 6th Cong. at 93, 922, 952 (1801).

27. Miller, CRISIS IN FREEDOM at 85; ANNALS, 5th Cong. at 2162.

28. Wiebe, OPENING OF AMERICAN SOCIETY at 94–95. The Virginia Resolutions, the Kentucky Resolutions, and Madison's *Report on the Virginia Resolutions* are reproduced in Volume 4 of the enlarged edition of J. Elliot's DEBATES ON THE FEDERAL CONSTITUTION at 528 (Philadelphia: J. B. Lippincott, 1907).

29. Elliot, 4 DEBATES at 569.

30. Id. at 569–70.

31. Id. at 569; ANNALS, 5th Cong., 2nd sess. at 2160–61, ANNALS, 5th Cong., 3rd sess. at 3003–14; Levy, EMERGENCE OF A FREE PRESS at xii, 284–349; Rabban, *Ahistorical Historian* at 851–54; Anderson, *Origins of the Press Clause* at 529–33.

32. S. Levinson, CONSTITUTIONAL FAITH 9–11 (Princeton, N.J.: Princeton University Press, 1988); Rosenberg, PROTECTING THE BEST MEN at 80; H. Powell, *The Original Understanding of Original Intent,* 98 Harvard Law Review 885 (1985).

33. ANNALS, 1st Cong., 1st sess. at 456. The more common phrase "parchment barriers" appears in *Federalist* no. 48, but it refers to provisions regarding separation of powers and not, as too commonly assumed, to a bill of rights.

34. Elliot, 4 DEBATES at 578 (Madison's *Report*), 545 (Kentucky Resolution of 1799).

35. Madison to Edward Everett, August 30, 1830, published in the October 30, 1830, *North American Review,* reprinted in M. Meyers, ed., THE MIND OF THE FOUNDER at 532–44 (Indianapolis: Bobbs-Merrill, 1973).

36. Elliot, 4 DEBATES at 568.

37. *Gitlow v. New York,* 268 U.S. 652, 672 (1925) (dissenting); *Abrams v. United States,* 250 U.S. 616, 624 (1919) (dissenting); *Schenck v. United States,* 249 U.S. 47 (1919); *Patterson v. Colorado,* 205 U.S. 454, 462 (1907); Holmes to Zechariah Chafee, June 12, 1922, quoted in

D. Rabban, *The Emergence of Modern First Amendment Doctrine,* 50 University of Chicago Law Review at 1265 (1983).

38. Quoted in H. Peterson and G. Fite, OPPONENTS OF THE WAR, 1917–18, at 14 (Madison: University of Wisconsin Press, 1957).

39. T. Gregory, *Suggestions of Attorney-General Gregory to the Executive Committee in Relation to the Department of Justice,* 4 American Bar Association Journal 305, 306 (1918); Z. Chafee, FREE SPEECH IN THE UNITED STATES 37 (Cambridge, Mass.: Harvard University Press, 1948); J. O'Brian, *Civil Liberty in War Time,* 42 Report of the New York State Bar Association 275, 277 (1919).

40. S. 2, 65th Cong. 1st sess. § 4 (1917); Title 1, § 3 of the Espionage Act, 40 US Statutes at Large 217 (1917); Title 12, id.; H.R. Report no. 69, 65th Cong., 1st sess. 19 (1917); H. Edgar and B. Schmidt, *The Espionage Statutes and Publication of Defense Information,* 73 Columbia Law Review 929, 946–66 (1973).

41. Gregory, *Suggestions* at 306; Wilson to Representative Edwin Webb, Chairman of the Judiciary Committee, May 22, 1917, read by Webb on the House floor, 55 Congressional Record 3144 (1917); T. Carroll, *Freedom of Speech and of the Press in War Time,* 17 Michigan Law Review 621, 624 (1919).

42. Rabban, *Emergence of Modern First Amendment Doctrine* at 1218–19; Edgar and Schmidt, *Espionage Statutes* at 941.

43. 55 Congressional Record 1594, 1595 (1917).

44. *Debs v. United States,* 249 U.S. 211 (1919).

45. H. Nelson, D. Teeter, and D. Le Duc, LAW OF MASS COMMUNICATIONS 331–33 (Westbury, N.Y.: Foundation Press, 6th ed. 1989); Rabban, *Emergence of Modern First Amendment Doctrine* at 1219–23; Peterson and Fite, OPPONENTS OF THE WAR at 95.

46. Rabban, *Emergence of Modern First Amendment Doctrine* at 1223; 55 Congressional Record 1822 (1917).

47. P. Murphy, THE MEANING OF FREEDOM OF SPEECH 18 (Westport, Conn.: Greenwood Publishing, 1972); R. Wiebe, THE SEARCH FOR ORDER: 1877–1920 at 287–88 (New York: Hill and Wang, 1967); B. Bailyn, D. Davis, D. Donald, J. Thomas, R. Wiebe, and G. Wood, THE GREAT REPUBLIC 1024 (Boston: Little, Brown, 1977); M. Graber, TRANSFORMING FREE SPEECH (Berkeley and Los Angeles: University of California Press, 1991).

48. *Schenck; Debs,* 249 U.S. at 214; D. Rabban, *The First Amendment in Its Forgotten Years,* 90 Yale Law Journal 514 (1981).

49. *Frohwerk v. United States,* 249 U.S. 204 (1919); Brief for Plaintiff in Error at 1–4, *Frohwerk.*

50. *Schenck,* 249 U.S. at 51, 52.

51. *Frohwerk,* 249 U.S. at 209.

52. Id. at 208; *Schenck,* 249 U.S. at 52; Rabban, *Emergence of Modern First Amendment Doctrine* at 1261.

53. Rabban, *Emergence of Modern First Amendment Doctrine* at 1232; Alfred Bettman to Zechariah Chafee, October 27, 1919, quoted in id. at 1296.

54. J. Daniels, THE WILSON ERA 116 (Chapel Hill: University of North Carolina Press, 1944); Josephus Daniels, Diary, August 7 and 16, 1917, in A. Link, ed., 43 THE PAPERS OF WOODROW WILSON (Princeton, N.J.: Princeton University Press, 1983).

55. Max Eastman, Amos Pinchot, and John Reed to Woodrow Wilson, July 12, 1917, in Link, 43 PAPERS OF WOODROW WILSON (listing twelve excluded publications); S. Miller, VICTOR BERGER AND THE PROMISE OF CONSERVATIVE SOCIALISM 194 (Westport, Conn.: Greenwood Press, 1973) ("fifteen major socialist publications").

56. Wilson to Burleson, September 4 and 24, October 11, 18, and 30, in Link, 44 PAPERS OF WOODROW WILSON; Burleson's notation is at the bottom of Wilson's letter of September 24; R. Baker, ed., 7 WOODROW WILSON: LIFE AND LETTERS 165 n. 1 (Garden City, N.Y.: Doubleday, 1939).

57. Burleson to Wilson, July 16, 1977, in Link, 43 PAPERS OF WOODROW WILSON.

58. Burleson to Wilson, October 16, 1917, in Link, 44 PAPERS OF WOODROW WILSON; Wilson to Arthur Brisbane, September 24, 1917, in id.; Wilson to Herbert Croly, October 22, 1917, in id.

59. 20 US Statutes at Large 355 (1879); *Lewis Publishing v. Morgan,* 229 U.S. 288, 304 (1913).

60. The circulation figure comes from Justice Brandeis's dissent in *United States ex rel. Milwaukee Socialist Democratic Publishing Co. v. Burleson,* 255 U.S. 407, 418 (1921). Surprisingly, Miller in VICTOR BERGER does not provide circulation figures for the paper.

61. Miller, VICTOR BERGER at 198.

62. Id. at 199, 201, 202, 205; Peterson and Fite, OPPONENTS OF THE WAR at 164–65.

63. *Milwaukee Socialist Democratic Publishing,* 255 U.S. at 413, 414, 436. Chafee, FREE SPEECH IN THE UNITED STATES at 303, brought my attention to the Food Control Act decision, *United States v. L. Cohen Grocery Co.,* 255 U.S. 81 (1921).

64. L. Powe, *Justice Douglas After Fifty Years: The First Amendment, McCarthyism and Rights,* 6 Constitutional Commentary 269 (1989); V. Blasi, *The Pathological Perspective and the First Amendment,* 85 Columbia Law Review 449 (1985).

65. *Gilbert v. Minnesota*, 254 U.S. 325, 327, 333 (1920).

66. Chafee, FREE SPEECH IN THE UNITED STATES at 56–57; Rabban, *Emergence of Modern First Amendment Doctrine* at 1232. The latter notes that even jury instructions "unusually sensitive to free speech" generally resulted in jury verdicts to convict.

67. *Milwaukee Socialist Democratic Publishing*, 255 U.S. at 414.

## Chapter 3

1. H. Kalven, THE NEGRO AND THE FIRST AMENDMENT 3 (Chicago: University of Chicago Press, 1965).

2. *New York Times*, March 19, 1960; T. Branch, PARTING THE WATERS: AMERICA IN THE KING YEARS, 1954–63 at 288–89 (New York: Simon and Shuster, 1988).

3. *NAACP v. Alabama ex rel. Patterson*, 357 U.S. 449 (1958), 360 U.S. 240 (1959), 368 U.S. 16 (1961), culminating with 377 U.S. 288 (1964).

4. Branch, PARTING THE WATERS at 287–89.

5. Id. at 293–97.

6. Id. at 309–11.

7. *New York Times*, March 29, 1960. A large blow-up of the ad is appended to both the petition for certiorari and the petitioner's brief on the merits, *New York Times v. Sullivan*, 376 U.S. 254 (No. 606, October Term 1962, and no. 39, October Term 1963).

8. I have inserted a dash before "and millions of others"; in the original ad, only the dash following this phrase was printed.

9. Branch, PARTING THE WATERS at 289.

10. Brief of Petitioner, *New York Times v. Sullivan* at 18–19 (No. 39, October Term 1963).

11. ACLU Amicus Brief, *New York Times v. Sullivan* (No. 39, October Term 1963)—the appendix lists every reported Alabama libel case in the twentieth century.

12. Id. at 5–6.

13. Brief of Petitioner at 19–21; ACLU Amicus Brief at 5–6; H. Salisbury, WITHOUT FEAR OR FAVOR 383–84 (New York: Times Books, 1980).

14. Brief of Petitioner at 25–28; Salisbury, WITHOUT FEAR OR FAVOR at 384. The Bessemer indictments hung over Salisbury "for several years since no DA was willing to take the political risk of dismissing them. Finally one quiet day three or four years later (I forget the exact date)" they were dismissed (Salisbury to author, May 11, 1989).

15. H. Kalven, *The New York Times Case: A Note on the "Central Meaning of the First Amendment,"* 1964 Supreme Court Review 191,

194–97; H. Kalven, A WORTHY TRADITION 62 (New York: Harper and Row, 1988).

16. Branch, PARTING THE WATERS at 371.

17. Id. at 370–71; Brief of Respondent at 14–15.

18. Kalven, *New York Times Case* at 196.

19. Id. at 195–96; Kalven, WORTHY TRADITION at 62; D. Anderson, *The Case for Libel Reform* (forthcoming); Branch, PARTING THE WATERS at 391; *Parks v. New York Times Co.* 308 F.2d 474 (5th Cir. 1962), reversing 195 F. Supp. 919 (M.D. Ala. 1961) (Judge Frank Johnson refusing to remand to state court). Because of the Supreme Court decision in Sullivan's case, these remaining cases never went to trial.

20. J. Goodale, "Is the Public 'Getting Even' with the Press in Libel Cases?" *New York Law Journal,* August 11, 1982, at 1–2. In this regard, it bears noting that the *New York Herald Tribune,* beset with similar problems, died in 1966; given the way strikes were wracking both papers, it was not inevitable that the *Times,* rather than the *Herald Tribune,* would be the survivor. This is not to suggest, however, that the similar problems of the two papers were identical—the *Herald Tribune* was losing money each year, whereas the *Times* operated under "perilously thin profit margins." R. Kluger, THE PAPER: THE LIFE AND DEATH OF THE NEW YORK TRIBUNE at 717 (New York: Alfred A. Knopf, 1986).

21. *New York Times v. Sullivan,* 273 Ala. 656, 144 So. 2d 25, 29, 51 (1962).

22. On the NAACP, see the cases in note 3 above, plus *NAACP v. Button,* 371 U.S. 415 (1963), and *Gibson v. Florida Legislative Investigating Committee,* 372 U.S. 539 (1963). On the constitutionality of state libel laws, see *Chaplinsky v. New Hampshire,* 315 U.S. 568, 571–72 (1942); *Pennekamp v. Florida,* 328 U.S. 331, 348–49 (1946); *Beauharnais v. Illinois,* 343 U.S. 250 (1952); *Roth v. United States,* 354 U.S. 476, 483 (1957); *Konigsberg v. State Bar of California,* 366 U.S. 36, 49–50 (1961). It should be noted, however, that in the same term that the Supreme Court stated in *Chaplinsky* that libel was a category of unprotected speech, the Court split four-four (Jackson not participating) on that very question in *Schenectady Union Publishing Co. v. Sweeney,* 316 U.S. 642 (1942). The only legal literature on the issue consisted of a paper by Harry Kalven written a decade earlier, cited in Kalven, *New York Times Case* at 192 n. 4, and Justice Black's views that the First Amendment protected all speech "absolutely." See E. Cahn, *Justice Black and First Amendment "Absolutes": A Public Interview,* 37 New York University Law Review 549 (1962). Natchman is quoted in 16 Media Law Reporter, April 11, 1989.

23. Brief of Petitioner at 49–50, *New York Times v. Sullivan* (No. 39,

October Term 1963). Wechsler summarized his strategy twenty-five years later: "If you feel that the environment is on your side, that legal trends are on your side, the problem of counsel is to present the court with adequate materials to support that case." 16 Media Law Reporter, April 11, 1989.

24. *New York Times v. Sullivan,* 376 U.S. 254, 276 (1964).

25. A. Meiklejohn, FREE SPEECH AND ITS RELATION TO SELF-GOVERN-MENT (New York: Oxford University Press, 1948).

26. *New York Times v. Sullivan,* 376 U.S. at 271, 279; *Speiser v. Randall,* 357 U.S. 513 (1958).

27. *New York Times v. Connor,* 365 F.2d 567 (5th Cir. 1966); Salisbury, WITHOUT FEAR OR FAVOR at 389–90.

28. Kalven, *New York Times Case.* In his closing footnote Kalven also gave Meiklejohn's imprimatur: "It is an occasion for dancing in the streets" (id. at 221 n. 125).

29. L. Tribe, CONSTITUTIONAL CHOICES 190–92 (Cambridge, Mass.: Harvard University Press, 1985); L. Powe, *Making the Hard Choices Easy,* 1986 American Bar Foundation Research Journal 57, 68.

30. L. Powe, *Justice Douglas After Fifty Years: The First Amendment, McCarthyism and Rights,* 6 Constitutional Commentary 269 (1989).

31. *Dennis v. United States,* 341 U.S. 494, 509 (1951); *New York Times v. Sullivan,* 376 U.S. at 270.

32. *Rosenblatt v. Baer,* 383 U.S. 75 (1966); *Monitor Patriot v. Roy,* 401 U.S. 265 (1971); *Ocala Star-Banner v. Damron,* 401 U.S. 295 (1971).

33. Branch, PARTING THE WATERS at 657; *Associated Press v. Walker,* 388 U.S. 130, 140–42 (1967) (decided as *Curtis Publishing v. Butts*).

34. Quoted in *Butts,* 388 U.S. at 142.

35. *Butts,* 388 U.S. at 163–64 (separate opinion).

36. Kalven, *New York Times Case* at 221; *Rosenbloom v. Metromedia,* 403 U.S. 29, 32–34, 40, 43 (1971). The quotations are from Justice Brennan's plurality opinion, which was joined by Chief Justice Burger and Justice Blackmun. Although Justice Douglas did not participate in *Rosenbloom,* his position was that *all* libel suits are unconstitutional. When this and Justice Black's identical position are counted in, there were at least five justices who would agree with the Brennan position as the constitutional minimum. See *Rosenbloom,* 403 U.S. at 58–59 (opinion of Justice White).

37. *Garrison v. Louisiana,* 379 U.S. 64 (1964); *St. Amant v. Thompson,* 390 U.S. 727, 731 (1968); *Greenbelt Publishing Association v. Bresler,* 398 U.S. 6 (1970); *Time, Inc. v. Hill,* 385 U.S. 374 (1967). See generally H. Kalven, *The Reasonable Man and the First Amendment,* 1967 Supreme Court Review 267. Richard Nixon made his only Supreme

Court appearance as counsel in *Time, Inc. v. Hill;* Leonard Garment has published an interesting reminiscence on Nixon and Hill, "Annals of Law (Nixon and Privacy)," *New Yorker,* April 17, 1989, at 90.

38. *LaMont v. Postmaster General,* 381 U.S. 301 (1965).

39. *DeGregory v. New Hampshire,* 383 U.S. 825 (1966); *Elfbrandt v. Russell,* 384 U.S. 11 (1966); *Keyishian v. Board of Regents,* 385 U.S. 589 (1967); *United States v. Robel,* 389 U.S. 258 (1967).

40. *Jacobellis v. Ohio,* 378 U.S. 184, 197 (1964); *Ginzburg v. United States,* 383 U.S. 463 (1966); *Mishkin v. New York,* 383 U.S. 502 (1966); *Memoirs v. Massachusetts,* 383 U.S. 413 (1966); *Redrup v. New York,* 386 U.S. 767 (1967). Thirty-one cases were Redrupped. *Miller v. California,* 413 U.S. 15, 22 n. 3 (1973).

41. *Stanley v. Georgia,* 394 U.S. 557 (1969); *United States v. Reidel,* 402 U.S. 351 (1971); *United States v. 37 Photographs,* 402 U.S. 363 (1971); *Interstate Circuit v. Dallas,* 390 U.S. 676, 704 (1968).

42. *Bond v. Floyd,* 385 U.S. 116 (1966).

43. *Brandenburg v. Ohio,* 395 U.S. 444, 447 (1969). F. Strong, *Fifty Years of "Clear and Present Danger,"* 1969 Supreme Court Review 41; H. Linde, *"Clear and Present Danger" Reexamined,* 22 Stanford Law Review 1163 (1970); G. Gunther, *Learned Hand and the Origins of Modern First Amendment Doctrine,* 27 Stanford Law Review 719 (1975).

44. *Cohen v. California,* 403 U.S. 15, 24–25 (1971).

45. *O'Brien v. United States,* 391 U.S. 367 (1968).

46. S. Ungar, THE PAPERS AND THE PAPERS 19 (New York: E. P. Dutton, 1972); Salisbury, WITHOUT FEAR OR FAVOR at 82; F. Abrams, "The Pentagon Papers Case a Decade Later," *New York Times Magazine,* June 7, 1981, at 22.

47. Salisbury, WITHOUT FEAR OR FAVOR at 57–63, 228; S. Hersh, THE PRICE OF POWER 328–29 (New York: Summit Books, 1983).

48. Salisbury, WITHOUT FEAR OR FAVOR at 121, 126–27.

49. *New York Times,* June 13, 1971, at 1. The remaining important story was of the United States counseling India and Pakistan to exercise caution in the crisis that was about to change East Pakistan into the independent Bangladesh. The four diplomatic volumes which Ellsberg protected were routinely available to reporters during his trial in 1973, but subsequently were placed under court seal. Hersh, PRICE OF POWER at 321 n.

50. Salisbury, WITHOUT FEAR OR FAVOR at 233–36, 213–15; Hersh, PRICE OF POWER at 386.

51. Salisbury, WITHOUT FEAR OR FAVOR at 223–28, 235–36; Hersh, PRICE OF POWER at 383–89; Abrams, "Pentagon Papers Case."

52. Salisbury, WITHOUT FEAR OR FAVOR at 243–47. Lord, Day, and

Lord's refusal to defend was not without consequences; the *Times* abandoned the firm.

53. Abrams, "Pentagon Papers Case"; Salisbury, WITHOUT FEAR OR FAVOR at 259–62. Although his performance that day (only) might lead to a different conclusion, Gurfein, a distinguished lawyer with strong ties to Thomas Dewey, was not a Nixon loyalist.

54. Ungar, THE PAPERS AND THE PAPERS at 130–46; Salisbury, WITHOUT FEAR OR FAVOR at 292–94.

55. Salisbury, WITHOUT FEAR OR FAVOR at 294; Ungar, THE PAPERS AND THE PAPERS at 151–58.

56. Salisbury, WITHOUT FEAR OR FAVOR at 322–23; Ungar, THE PAPERS AND THE PAPERS at 204. Amazingly, the Gayler supplement to his affidavit, which produced a discussion that sounds very much like a trial hearing, occurred before the DC Circuit Court of Appeals.

57. *United States v. New York Times,* 444 F.2d 544 (2d Cir. 1971); *United States v. Washington Post,* 446 F.2d 1327 (D.C. Cir. 1971).

58. *United States v. Washington Post,* 446 F.2d at 1330.

59. I was Justice Douglas's law clerk at the time. My recollection is that with the term winding down (wound down for me), there was not the earlier time pressure, and over leisurely lunches in the law clerks' private dining room, the clerks closely followed the progress of the cases.

60. Griswold, "Secrets Not Worth Keeping," *Washington Post,* February 15, 1989, at A25; Salisbury, WITHOUT FEAR OR FAVOR at 327–29; Ungar, THE PAPERS AND THE PAPERS at 221–23.

61. R. Woodward and S. Armstrong, THE BRETHREN 139–50 (New York: Simon and Shuster, 1979) contains, as usual, a remarkably accurate account of the Court's internal deliberations about this case. The most interesting aspect of this account is the report that James Reston, a senior columnist and vice-president of the *Times,* called Burger to ask for a meeting about the case. Harrison Salisbury doubts that it happened—"the supposed episode would seem to be a product of the hysteria of the period"—because Reston (a) has no recollection of calling Burger, (b) would never think of lobbying the chief justice, and (c) "wrote his last column for *The Times* before departing on June 26 and it was published Sunday June 27. He left the next day for China." WITHOUT FEAR OR FAVOR at 348 n. There seem to be several possibilities: (1) Harlan, to whom Burger told the story, was wrong; (2) Burger made it up; (3) Reston tried before he left for China. I am 100 percent sure that Burger told the story to Harlan, because Harlan reported it contemporaneously to his clerks and would not have told them if it were not so, and his clerks would have had no reason to make up such a story and tell others, myself included. "Hysteria" it may be, but either Burger was lying to Harlan or

Reston's recollection, intentionally or not, caused him to mislead Salisbury. Salisbury has written to me that Reston has a notoriously bad memory, and so his failure to remember ought not to count. But his datebooks should; and they make it unlikely that he called Burger. On that basis I agree with Salisbury that, for reasons of his own, Burger created the incident. Salisbury to author, May 28, 1989.

62. *New York Times v. United States,* 403 U.S. 713 at 749, 750, 752 (Burger), 753 (Harlan), 763 (Blackmun).

63. Ungar, THE PAPERS AND THE PAPERS at 250–51; Salisbury, WITHOUT FEAR OR FAVOR at 336, 347–48. Abrams, "Pentagon Papers Case," is an interesting retrospective by one of the *Times*'s legal team.

64. R. Nixon, RN: THE MEMOIRS OF RICHARD NIXON 510–14 (New York: Grosset and Dunlap, 1978); Salisbury, WITHOUT FEAR OR FAVOR at 337–39, 445–46.

65. *New York Times v. United States,* 403 U.S. at 728.

66. Id. at 717.

67. *De Jonge v. Oregon,* 299 U.S. 353, 365 (1937).

## Chapter 4

1. A. Lewis, *New York Times v. Sullivan Reconsidered,* 83 Columbia Law Review 603 (1983).

2. F. Schauer, *Public Figures,* 25 William and Mary Law Review 905, 911–12 (1984); *St. Amant v. Thompson,* 390 U.S. 727, 731 (1968); *Gertz v. Robert Welch, Inc.,* 418 U.S. 323 (1974); D. Robertson, *Defamation and the First Amendment,* 54 Texas Law Review 199 (1976) (*Gertz* necessary to check press power); D. Anderson, *A Response to Professor Robertson: The Issue Is Control of Press Power,* 54 Texas Law Review 271 (1976).

3. Lewis, *New York Times v. Sullivan Reconsidered;* H. Johnston and H. Kaufman, "Annenberg, *Sullivan* at Twenty-Five and the Question of Libel Reform," 7 *Communications Lawyer* 3 (Winter 1989).

4. *Bose Corporation v. Consumers Union,* 466 U.S. 485 (1984); *Philadelphia Newspapers v. Hepps,* 475 U.S. 767 (1986); *Hustler Magazine v. Falwell,* 485 U.S. 46 (1988).

5. *Edwards v. National Audubon Society,* 556 F.2d 113, 120 (2d Cir. 1977); *Ollman v. Evans,* 750 F.2d 970, 1002 (D.C. Cir. 1984) (concurring); *Milkovich v. Lorain Journal Co.,* 110 S. Ct. 2695, 2706 (1990).

6. L. Tribe, AMERICAN CONSTITUTIONAL LAW 865 (Mineola, N.Y.: Foundation Press, 2d ed. 1988); R. Epstein, *Was New York Times v. Sullivan Wrong?* 53 University of Chicago Law Review 782 (1986); Lewis, *New York Times v. Sullivan Reconsidered.*

7. B. Brewin and S. Shaw, VIETNAM ON TRIAL (New York: Atheneum, 1987); R. Adler, RECKLESS DISREGARD (New York: Alfred A. Knopf, 1986); R. Smolla, SUING THE PRESS 182–237 (New York: Oxford University Press, 1986); *Tavoulareas v. Piro*, 817 F.2d 762 (D.C. Cir. 1987) (en banc), cert. denied, 484 U.S. 870 (1987); J. Soloski, *The Study and the Libel Plaintiff*, 71 Iowa Law Review 217, 219 (1985).

8. M. Newcity, *Libel Law Then and Now*, 1989 Wisconsin Law Review 359, 362, 379–82.

9. R. Bezanson, G. Cranberg, and J. Soloski, LIBEL LAW AND THE PRESS (New York: Free Press, 1987); M. Franklin, *Winners and Losers and Why*, 1980 American Bar Foundation Research Journal 455; M. Franklin, *Suing the Media for Libel*, 1981 American Bar Foundation Research Journal 797.

10. Bezanson, Cranberg, and Soloski, LIBEL LAW at 7–11.

11. Soloski, *The Study* at 219; Bezanson, Cranberg, and Soloski, LIBEL LAW at 13–15. Franklin, in his sample, found that public officials were more often accused of crime than incompetence (*Suing the Media for Libel* at 812–13).

12. Bezanson, Cranberg, and Soloski, LIBEL LAW at 15–17.

13. Id. at 21–28.

14. Id. at 30–53; Smolla, SUING THE PRESS at 187; G. Cranberg, *Fanning the Fire*, 71 Iowa Law Review 221, 223, 224 (1985).

15. Bezanson, Cranberg, and Soloski, LIBEL LAW at 55–77.

16. Id. at 77, 58–59; Franklin, *Suing the Media for Libel* at 801–02.

17. Bezanson, Cranberg, and Soloski, LIBEL LAW at 133–34, 144–46.

18. Id. at 179; Franklin, *Suing the Media for Libel* at 829. Tavoulareas is quoted in Smolla, SUING THE PRESS at 256.

19. Bezanson, Cranberg, and Soloski, LIBEL LAW at 129–30.

20. Smolla, SUING THE PRESS at 184–85; *Herbert v. Lando*, 441 U.S. 153, 176 (1979).

21. Bezanson, Cranberg, and Soloski, LIBEL LAW at 142–44. Robert Post's brilliant and sophisticated article, *The Social Foundations of Defamation Law: Reputation and the Constitution*, 74 California Law Review 691 (1986), illustrates that the dignity component of reputation is quite capable of explaining much of the jury behavior.

22. Bezanson, Cranberg, and Soloski, LIBEL LAW at 178, 153, 289 n. 131; Franklin, *Winners and Losers and Why* at 473; Franklin, *Suing the Media for Libel* at 805.

23. Bezanson, Cranberg, and Soloski, LIBEL LAW at 3, 199 (quoting Robert Sack).

24. D. Anderson, *The Case for Libel Reform* (forthcoming).

25. *Gertz*, 418 U.S. at 329; 680 F.2d 527 (7th Cir. 1982).

26. *Dun & Bradstreet v. Greenmoss Builders*, 472 U.S. 749 (1985).

27. *Pring v. Penthouse*, 695 F.2d 438 (10th Cir. 1982); Smolla, SUING THE PRESS 162–64.

28. *Tavoulareas;* Smolla, SUING THE PRESS at 182–97.

29. *Time, Inc. v. Firestone*, 424 U.S. 448 (1976).

30. *Green v. Alton Telegraph Printing Co.*, 107 Ill. App. 3d 755, 438 N.E.2d 201 (1982); Smolla, SUING THE PRESS at 74.

31. *Othello*, act 3, sc. 3, lines 155–61; Post, *Social Foundations of Defamation Law;* Smolla, SUING THE PRESS at 8–9, 13, 24–25; W. Van Alstyne, *First Amendment Limitations on Recovery from the Press*, 25 William and Mary Law Review 793, 794–95 (1984); M. Franklin, *A Critique of Libel Law*, 18 University of San Francisco Law Review 1, 9 (1983).

32. Anderson, *Case for Libel Reform;* D. Laycock, MODERN AMERICAN REMEDIES 591–613 (Boston: Little, Brown, 1985).

33. Anderson, *Case for Libel Reform*.

34. *Herbert v. Lando*, 568 F.2d 974 (2d Cir. 1977).

35. *Herbert v. Lando*, 441 U.S. 153 (1979); G. Cranberg, "Libel Judges Are Setting the Standards for the Press," *Washington Journalism Review*, September 1989 at 42; M. Franklin, *Reflections on Herbert v. Lando*, 31 Stanford Law Review 1065 (1979); W. Brennan, *Address*, 32 Rutgers Law Review 173, 179–81 (1979).

36. J. Lubell quoted in a Mobil Corp. advertisement, *New York Times*, September 25, 1983, at 25; R. Cunningham, *The Eight Most Common Complaints*, EDITOR AND PUBLISHER, March 19, 1983, at 40; Anderson, *Case for Libel Reform*.

37. Schauer, *Public Figures* at 927.

38. Id. at 927 n. 100. For a contrast, even if overstated, with Schauer's optimism about press behavior, see M. Hertsgaard, ON BENDED KNEE: THE PRESS AND THE REAGAN PRESIDENCY (New York: Farrar, Straus, Giroux, 1988).

39. A. France, THE RED LILY 75 (W. Stephens, trans.) (London: John Lane, 1924).

40. S. Brill, *American Lawyer* July/August 1985 at 33; Johnston and Kaufman, "Libel Reform" at 8.

41. B. Fein, NEW YORK TIMES V. SULLIVAN: AN OBSTACLE TO ENLIGHTENED PUBLIC DISCOURSE AND GOVERNMENT RESPONSIVENESS TO THE PEOPLE (WASHINGTON D.C.: AMERICAN LEGAL FOUNDATION, 1984); M. FRANKLIN, *What Does "Negligence" Mean in Defamation Cases?* 6 Comm/Ent Law Journal 259 (1984); M. Franklin, *Public Officials and Libel*, 5 Cardozo Arts and Entertainment Law Journal 51, 66–69 (1986).

42. *Rosenbloom v. Metromedia,* 403 U.S. 29, 62 (Harlan, dissenting), 78 (Marshall, dissenting) (1971).

43. D. Anderson, *Reputation, Compensation and Proof,* 25 William and Mary Law Review 747 (1984); *Aware, Inc. v. Faulk,* 14 N.Y.2d 899, 252 N.Y.S.2d 95, 200 N.E.2d 778 (1964), cert. denied, 380 U.S. 916 (1965); J. Faulk, FEAR ON TRIAL (Austin: University of Texas Press, 1983).

44. Anderson, *Case for Libel Reform;* L. Forer, A CHILLING EFFECT (New York: Norton, 1987); *Faulk.*

45. Smolla, SUING THE PRESS at 242; Van Alstyne, *Limitations on Recovery from the Press* at 803–09; F. Abrams, "Why We Should Change the Libel Law," *New York Times Magazine,* September 29, 1985, at 34, 93; *Browning-Ferris Industries v. Kelco Disposal, Inc.,* 109 S. Ct. 2909 (1989).

46. Most of the Winter 1989 issue of *Communications Lawyer* is given over to discussions of the proposal.

47. Cranberg, "Libel Judges Are Setting Standards for the Press," *Washington Journalism Review,* September 1989 at 42, 44.

48. Johnston and Kaufman, "Libel Reform" at 4; E. Roberts, "When Freedom of Expression Becomes a Financial Burden," remarks on receiving the John Peter Zenger award, November 13, 1987, quoted in H. Nelson, D. Teeter, and D. Le Duc, LAW OF MASS COMMUNICATIONS at 143 (Westbury, N.Y.: Foundation Press, 6th ed. 1989); Bezanson, Cranberg, and Soloski, LIBEL LAW at 49: "Attend a meeting of editors and chances are you will hear complaints, accompanied by nods of approval from colleagues who had similar experiences, about how the editors were misquoted in their own papers. Studies of press credibility by journalism groups invariably concluded that inaccuracy and unfairness are major parts of the credibility problem."

49. M. Franklin, *A Declaratory Judgment Alternative to Current Libel Law,* 74 California Law Review 809 (1986). Franklin proposes some delicate fee-shifting arrangements whereby the prevailing party would receive reasonable attorneys' fees, subject to several exceptions that appear intended to swallow the rule. The key exception would preclude the awarding of attorneys' fees to a successful defendant where plaintiff brought the action with a reasonable chance of success and attempted (prior to the suit) to present evidence to the defendant that the statement it published was false.

50. Anderson, *Case for Libel Reform.*

51. *Gertz,* 418 U.S. at 340–41; *Greenmoss Builders,* 472 U.S. at 757–61.

52. Brewin and Shaw, Vietnam on Trial 90–91; *Chicago Tribune,* February 19, 1989.

53. Franklin, *Declaratory Judgment Alternative* at 828.

54. *New York Times,* December 18, 1983; Brewin and Shaw, Vietnam on Trial at 314, 352–53.

## Chapter 5

1. J. Elliot, ed., 4 Debates on the Federal Constitution 569 (Philadelphia: J. B. Lippincott, 1907).

2. S. Barnett, *The Puzzle of Prior Restraint,* 26 Stanford Law Review 539 (1977); F. Schauer, *Fear, Risk, and the First Amendment,* 58 Boston University Law Review 685, 725–30 (1978); J. Jeffries, *Rethinking Prior Restraint,* 92 Yale Law Journal 409 (1982); M. Redish, *The Proper Role of the Prior Restraint Doctrine in First Amendment Theory,* 70 Virginia Law Review 53 (1984); M. Scordato, *Distinction Without a Difference,* 68 North Carolina Law Review 1 (1989); O. Fiss, The Civil Rights Injunction 69–74 (Bloomington: Indiana University Press, 1978). The classics supporting the traditional hostility toward prior restraints are T. Emerson, *The Doctrine of Prior Restraint,* 20 Law and Contemporary Problems 648 (1955) and V. Blasi, *Toward a Theory of Prior Restraint,* 66 Minnesota Law Review 11 (1981).

3. *Near v. Minnesota,* 283 U.S. 697 (1931).

4. J. Milton, *Areopagitica,* in J. Patrick, ed., The Prose of John Milton 326 (New York: New York University Press, 1968); F. Friendly, Minnesota Rag 13 (New York: Random House, 1981). The final quotation in the text is slightly modified; Friendly actually wrote "published by some Duluth religious nut."

5. Friendly, Minnesota Rag at 18–22.

6. *Near,* 283 U.S. at 704; Friendly, Minnesota Rag at 49–50.

7. *Near,* 283 U.S. at 706; Friendly, Minnesota Rag at 26, 51–54; *State ex rel. Olson v. Guilford,* 174 Minn. 457, 219 N.W. 770 (1928); 179 Minn. 40, 228 N.W. 326 (1929). Guilford operated the *Saturday Press* with Near, but Guilford, "bored with the glacial pace of the litigation," eventually "sold his interest in the paper to Near (some say no cash changed hands)." Guilford was then severed from the case. Minnesota Rag at 60, 82.

8. *Near,* 283 U.S. at 719–20.

9. Id. at 712, 713.

10. Id. at 713.

11. Id. at 716, citing Z. Chafee, Freedom of Speech 10 (New York: Harcourt, Brace and Howe, 1920); S. Godofsky, *Protection of the Press*

*from Prior Restraint and Harassment Under Libel Laws,* 29 University of Miami Law Review 462, 471–72 (1975) (one of the *Post*'s lawyers explaining their litigation strategy); E. Griswold, *Teaching Alone Is Not Enough,* 25 Journal of Legal Education 251, 258 (1973).

12. *Nebraska Press Association v. Stuart,* 427 U.S. 539, 567 (1976).

13. Barnett, *Puzzle of Prior Restraint,* was a discussion of *Nebraska Press Association.*

14. The agreement is reproduced in *United States v. Marchetti,* 466 F.2d 1309, 1312 n. 1 (4th Cir. 1972).

15. *Snepp v. United States,* 444 U.S. 507 (1980); *Alfred A. Knopf, Inc. v. Colby,* 509 F.2d 1362 (4th Cir. 1975), cert. denied, 421 U.S. 992 (1975).

16. *Washington Post,* April 6, 1980; *Freedman v. Maryland,* 380 U.S. 51 (1965); V. Marchetti and J. Marks, THE CIA AND THE CULT OF INTELLIGENCE xxv, 14 (New York: Alfred A. Knopf, 1974). The initial CIA refusal to clear the quoted sentence came prior to Allende's assassination.

17. *Alfred A. Knopf,* 509 F.2d at 1369–70.

18. *Near,* 283 U.S. at 716.

19. L. Tribe, AMERICAN CONSTITUTIONAL LAW 1047 (Mineola, N.Y.: Foundation Press, 2d ed. 1988); *Pittsburgh Press Co. v. Pittsburgh Commission on Human Relations,* 413 U.S. 376, 390 (1973).

20. H. Kalven, *Forward: Even When a Nation Is at War—,* 85 Harvard Law Review 3, 32 (1971); D. Laycock, MODERN AMERICAN REMEDIES 363 (Boston: Little, Brown, 1985).

21. *Bloom v. Illinois,* 391 U.S. 194 (1968); *Gompers v. Bucks Stove & Range Co.,* 221 U.S. 418 (1911); D. Dobbs, HANDBOOK ON THE LAW OF REMEDIES 96–98 (Minneapolis: West Publishing, 1973); H. Monaghan, *First Amendment "Due Process,"* 83 Harvard Law Review 518, 526–32 (1970); W. Mayton, *Toward a Theory of First Amendment Process,* 67 Cornell Law Review 245, 277 (1982).

22. *Walker v. City of Birmingham,* 388 U.S. 307, 321 (1967); *Shuttlesworth v. City of Birmingham,* 394 U.S. 147 (1969).

23. *Carroll v. President and Commissioners of Princess Anne,* 393 U.S. 175 (1968); *Walker,* 388 U.S. at 315, 318; Fiss, CIVIL RIGHTS INJUNCTION at 68–74; Barnett, *Puzzle of Prior Restraint* at 553–58; Jeffries, *Rethinking Prior Restraint* at 431–34; Redish, *Proper Role of the Prior Restraint Doctrine* at 93–99. Blasi is less sure that jettisoning the collateral bar rule would bring prior restraints and subsequent punishment sufficiently close together; he is treated in section IV of the chapter. Blasi, *Toward a Theory of Prior Restraint* at 35–38, 85–92.

24. *Nebraska Press Association,* 427 U.S. at 559; Emerson, *Doctrine*

*of Prior Restraint* at 659; Blasi, *Toward a Theory of Prior Restraint* at 52–53; Mayton, *Toward a Theory of First Amendment Process* at 250–51; A. Bickel, THE MORALITY OF CONSENT 61 (New Haven, Conn.: Yale University Press, 1975).

25. Bickel, MORALITY OF CONSENT at 61.

26. H. Salisbury, WITHOUT FEAR OR FAVOR 290 (New York: Times Books, 1980); *United States v. Progressive, Inc.,* 467 F. Supp. 990 (W.D. Wis.), dismissed mem., 610 F.2d 819 (7th Cir. 1979). The *Progressive* case is more fully discussed in L. Powe, *The H-Bomb Injunction,* 61 University of Colorado Law Review 55 (1990).

27. E. Knoll, *National Security: The Ultimate Threat to the First Amendment,* 66 Minnesota Law Review 161 (1981); L. Hand, *The Deficiency of Trials to Reach the Heart of the Matter,* in 3 LECTURES ON LEGAL TOPICS 87, 105 (New York: Association of the Bar of the City of New York, 1926); J. Faulk, FEAR ON TRIAL (Austin: University of Texas Press, 1983).

28. Knoll, *National Security* at 161; H. Morland, THE SECRET THAT EXPLODED 176, 179, 204–06 (New York: Random House, 1981). Morland, the author of the *Progressive* story on the H-bomb, also notes the disappointment that the Camp David peace accords dwarfed the *Progressive* the evening the injunction was made final. Id. at 193.

29. *United States v. Morison,* 844 F.2d 1057 (4th Cir. 1988) cert. denied, 109 S. Ct. 259 (1988); L. Powe, *Espionage, Leaks and the First Amendment,* 42 Bulletin of the Atomic Scientists 8 (June/July 1986); Morison's exact sentence was four two-year terms to run concurrently; 10 *News Media and the Law* 3–6 (Summer 1986).

30. Barnett, *Puzzle of Prior Restraint* at 551; Blasi, *Toward a Theory of Prior Restraint;* Jeffries, *Rethinking Prior Restraint;* Schauer, *Fear, Risk, and the First Amendment.*

31. S. Ungar, THE PAPERS AND THE PAPERS 175–92 (New York: E. P. Dutton, 1972); Salisbury, WITHOUT FEAR OR FAVOR at 319; Judge Roger Robb in oral argument, quoted id. at 322.

32. Morland, SECRET THAT EXPLODED 197, 203. "Spring Berg" was undoubtedly Friedwardt Winterberg of Reno, who had published in British and German scientific journals, and who brought accurate diagrams published in *New Solidarity* to the *Progressive*'s attention.

33. Morland, SECRET THAT EXPLODED at 183, 192, 194–96, 202–03, 223, 226–27; E. Teller, *Hydrogen Bomb,* 14 ENCYCLOPEDIA AMERICANA 654–56 (New York: Americana, 1979).

34. P. Wright, SPY CATCHER (New York: Viking, 1987); on the efforts of the Thatcher government to block publication, see M. Turnbull, THE SPY CATCHER TRIAL (London: Heinemann, 1988) ("I am very grateful to

everyone who made the case possible and, in particular, to Peter Wright and Margaret Thatcher, without whose not dissimilar determination a thoroughly unmeritorious piece of litigation would never have seen the light of day"), and Note, *The Spycatcher Cases,* 50 Ohio State Law Journal 405, 409 (1989). Both the books are inconsistent, from covers to inside pages, as to whether they think *spy catcher* should be one or two words; I chose two words because that is how the title is pronounced, and that is the way the Tarlton Law Library at The University of Texas has catalogued the books. Morland, SECRET THAT EXPLODED at 202. H. Linde, *Courts and Censorship,* 66 Minnesota Law Review 171, 197 (1981).

35. Knoll, *National Security* at 168–69. The hint of stronger measures, however, is mine.

36. I heard Knoll make the remark at a conference at the University of Minnesota celebrating the fiftieth anniversary of *Near,* June 1981.

37. Hearings on H.R. 5623 before a Subcommittee of the Senate Committee on the Judiciary, 70th Cong., 1st sess. 75–76 (1928); see also E. Borchard, DECLARATORY JUDGMENTS 341–49 (Cleveland, Ohio: Banks-Baldwin Law Publishing, 1934) and 764–801 (2d ed. 1941).

38. *Dombrowski v. Pfister,* 380 U.S. 479 (1965); *Younger v. Harris,* 401 U.S. 37 (1971); *Steffel v. Thompson,* 415 U.S. 452 (1974); *Doran v. Salem Inn,* 422 U.S. 922 (1975) (preliminary relief available to protect the status quo); O. Fiss, *Dombrowski,* 86 Yale Law Journal 1103 (1977); D. Laycock, *Federal Interference with State Prosecutions,* 46 University of Chicago Law Review 636 (1979); H. MacGill and A. Soifer, *The Younger Doctrine,* 55 Texas Law Review 1141 (1977). Laycock's article makes clear that *Dombrowski* was misperceived as revolutionary and that it was in fact an essential, if accidental, step toward *Younger.*

39. *Cohen v. California,* 403 U.S. 15 (1971).

40. Blasi, *Toward a Theory of Prior Restraint* at 49–63.

41. Jeffries, *Rethinking Prior Restraint* at 427 n. 57; Redish, *Proper Role of the Prior Restraint Doctrine* at 67; *Dennis v. United States,* 341 U.S. 494 (1951).

42. Respondent's Brief at 2–3, *Seattle Times v. Rhinehart,* 467 U.S. 20 (1984) (No. 82–1721). A different analysis of the case may be found in R. Post, *The Management of Speech: Discretion and Rights,* 1984 Supreme Court Review 169.

43. Abrams, "The Pentagon Papers Case a Decade Later," *New York Times Magazine,* June 7, 1981, at 78; Morland, SECRET THAT EXPLODED at 144, 154, 178.

44. E.g., 2 *News Media and the Law* 38 (October 1978) (federal district judge orders NBC to inspect a copy of a television documentary scheduled to air that evening; overturned by appellate court five hours

later), and 40 (Minnesota trial judge orders weekly newspaper not to publish an account of an open court hearing; state supreme court reverses a week later).

45. Morland, SECRET THAT EXPLODED at 165.

46. Powe, *H-Bomb Injunction* at 75.

47. *Progressive, Inc.*, 467 F. Supp. at 996; Morland, SECRET THAT EXPLODED at 154.

48. Morland, SECRET THAT EXPLODED at 41, 50, 153.

49. *Speiser v. Randall*, 357 U.S. 513 (1958).

50. *Near*, 283 U.S. at 720; Friendly, MINNESOTA RAG.

51. Morland, SECRET THAT EXPLODED at 154; *Progressive, Inc.*, 467 F. Supp. at 966.

52. Morland, SECRET THAT EXPLODED at 50, 153, 171–73.

53. Id. at 166, 197.

54. Id. at 140, 142, 146, 176; Blasi, *Toward a Theory of Prior Restraint* at 51.

## Chapter 6

1. Madison to W. T. Barry, August 4, 1822, in 9 THE WRITINGS OF JAMES MADISON at 103 (G. Hunt, ed.) (New York: Putnam's Sons, 1910).

2. *Buckley v. Valeo*, 424 U.S. 1, 14 (1976).

3. A. Meiklejohn, FREE SPEECH AND ITS RELATION TO SELF GOVERNMENT at 75 (New York: Oxford University Press, 1948).

4. R. Woodward and C. Bernstein, ALL THE PRESIDENT'S MEN (New York: Simon and Shuster, 1974); *New York Times*, December 22, 1974, at A1; *Chicago Sun-Times*, April 26, 1981; *Washington Post*, January 8, 1982, at A1; *Chicago Sun-Times*, July 27, 1983; *Washington Post*, October 2, 1986, at A1.

5. T. Emerson, *Colonial Intentions and Current Realities of the First Amendment*, 125 University of Pennsylvania Law Review 737 (1977); *Legal Foundations of the Right to Know*, 1976 Washington University Law Quarterly 1; *Houchins v. KQED*, 438 U.S. 1, 32 (1978) (Stevens dissenting); *Saxbe v. Washington Post*, 417 U.S. 843, 862–68 (1974) (Powell dissenting).

6. 42 United States Code §§ 2014(y)(1), 2274, 2277 (restricted data defined as design, manufacture, or utilization of atomic weapons); 50 United States Code § 421 (prohibits any person with authorized access to classified information from disclosing any information identifying a covert agent as part of a "pattern of activities intended to identify or expose covert action"); National Security Secrets and the Administration of Justice: Report of the Senate Select Committee on Intelligence, 95th Cong., 2d sess. 18 (1978); 108 Congressional Record 23140–41 (1962); Es-

pionage Laws and Leaks: Hearings Before the Subcommittee on Legislation of the House Permanent Select Committee on Intelligence, 96th
Cong., 1st sess. 146 (1979).

7. 18 United States Code § 641 (conversion); § 793 (unauthorized
disclosure); § 794 (disclosure to foreign government).

8. *Haig v. Agee*, 453 U.S. 280 (1981).

9. L. Tribe, AMERICAN CONSTITUTIONAL LAW 965 (Mineola, N.Y.:
Foundation Press, 2d ed. 1988).

10. Both "it would be the easy thing to do" and "it would be wrong"
joined the political vocabulary thanks to Richard Nixon. His May 14,
1969, "Address to the Nation on Vietnam" stated in its third sentence: "I
know that some believe that I should have ended the war immediately
after inauguration by simply ordering our forces home from Vietnam."
He followed with: "This would have been the easy thing to do. It might
have been the popular thing to do. But . . ." PUBLIC PAPERS OF THE
PRESIDENT OF THE UNITED STATES: RICHARD NIXON 365 (Washington,
D.C.: Government Printing Office, 1971). "It would be wrong" is a
Watergate statement found on the tapes. It was so prevalent that William
Safire quipped that his "job in the Nixon administration was to turn out
the lights after a meeting was over and call back into the darkened room,
while unknown recorders still whirred, 'But it would be wrong!' " He
twice used the story: *New York Times,* May 29, 1989, at 23 and *New
York Times,* June 19, 1983, § 6 at 8.

11. *Landmark Communications v. Virginia,* 435 U.S. 829, 845 (1978);
*Florida Star v. B.J.F.,* 109 S. Ct. 2603, 2609–12 (1989); *Seattle Times v.
Rhinehart,* 467 U.S. 20 (1984).

12. "Government may not prohibit or punish publication of that information once it falls into the hands of the press, unless the need for secrecy
is manifestly overwhelming." *Landmark Communications,* 435 U.S. at
849; 50 United States Code § 421.

13. M. Langley and L. Levine, *Branzburg Revisited,* 57 George Washington Law Review 13, 25–32 (1988); M. Linsky, IMPACT 169, 198 (New
York: W. W. Norton, 1986).

14. Linsky, IMPACT at 197, 238–39.

15. *Garland v. Torre,* 259 F.2d 545 (2d Cir. 1958), cert. denied, 358
U.S. 910 (1958).

16. Caldwell Affidavit at 17a; *Branzburg v. Hayes,* 408 U.S. 665
(1972) (No. 70–57).

17. Appendix at 3a–4a, *Branzburg,* 408 U.S. 665 (No. 70–85).

18. *New York Times,* December 14, 1969.

19. Caldwell Affidavit at 19a, *Branzburg,* 408 U.S. 665 (No. 70–57).

20. Department of Justice Memorandum No. 692 (September 2, 1970)
quoted in *Branzburg,* 408 U.S. at 733 (dissent).

21. *Branzburg,* 408 U.S. at 702.

22. Id. at 690–91.

23. Id. at 703–08.

24. Id. at 709–10.

25. Langley and Levine, *Branzburg Revisited.*

26. T. White, "Why the Jailing of Myron Farber 'Terrifies Me,'" *New York Times Magazine,* November 28, 1978, at 27; Linsky, IMPACT at 185–87; Morris, *Eight Days in April,* 17 Columbia Journalism Review 25 (Nov./Dec. 1978); *New York Times,* February 13, 1985, at A1.

27. E.g., *Miller v. Transamerican Press, Inc.,* 621 F.2d 721 (5th Cir. 1980).

28. D. Laycock, MODERN AMERICAN REMEDIES 652–56 (Boston: Little, Brown, 1985).

29. M. Farber, "SOMEONE IS LYING" (Garden City, N.Y.: Doubleday, 1982). There is a typo in the book that sets the *Times*'s fine at $286,000. Id. at 350.

30. *Matter of Farber,* 78 N.J. 259, 394 A.2d 330 (1978), cert. denied, 439 U.S. 997 (1978).

31. *New York Times,* August 6, 1978.

32. Farber, "SOMEONE IS LYING" at 270–71, 283; *Roviaro v. United States,* 353 U.S. 53 (1957); *Jencks v. United States,* 353 U.S. 657 (1957); *Alderman v. United States,* 394 U.S. 165 (1969).

33. M. Langley and L. Levine, *Broken Promises,* 27 Columbia Journalism Review 21 (July/Aug. 1988).

34. *Cohen v. Cowles Media Co.,* No. 799806 (Minn. Dist. Ct. Hennepin County, June 19, 1988) reported in 14 Media Law Reporter at 1460 and *National Law Journal,* August 1, 1988, at 8, aff'd in part, 445 N.W.2d 248 (Minn. Ct. App. 1989).

35. *Cowles Media Co. v. Cohen,* 457 N.W.2d 199 (Minn. 1990).

36. A. Lewis, *A Preferred Position for Journalism?* 7 Hofstra Law Review 595, 618 (1979).

37. *Pell v. Procunier,* 417 U.S. 817 (1974); *Saxbe,* 417 U.S. 843; *Houchins,* 438 U.S. 1.

38. *Gannett v. DePasquale,* 443 U.S. 368, 375, 391–93 (1979).

39. Brief of Petitioner at 29, *Gannett* (No. 77–1301); Appendix at 32a–51a, id.

40. Even after the guilty plea was entered, what transpired at the preliminary hearing has never come out; none of the opinions in the New York courts and none of the briefs filed with the cases states what the judge ruled or to what lesser included offenses the defendants pleaded guilty.

41. *Gannett,* 443 U.S. at 404–05.

42. D. O'Brien, THE PUBLIC'S RIGHT TO KNOW 135 (New York: Praeger, 1981).

43. *Stevenson v. Commonwealth,* 218 Va. 462, 237 S.E.2d 779 (1977); Appendix at 34a, *Richmond Newspapers v. Virginia,* 448 U.S. 555 (No. 79–243), reproducing *Richmond News Leader,* May 31, 1978, at 59.

44. *Richmond Newspapers,* 448 U.S. at 559–61.

45. Brief of Appellant at 42 n. 37, *Richmond Newspapers* (No. 79–243). (The footnote also explains the difficulties, beyond simple audio problems, of getting the hearing transcript even after the tape recording of the trial was supposedly made available.)

46. *Washington Post,* September 17, 1979, at C1; *New York Times,* August 11, 1979, at 43; *Richmond Newspapers.*

47. *Richmond Newspapers,* 448 U.S. at 564–77.

48. W. Brennan, *Address,* 32 Rutgers Law Review 173 (1979); *Richmond Newspapers,* 448 U.S. at 587–88.

49. *Richmond Newspapers,* 448 U.S. at 582.

50. J. Goodale, "Gannett Is Burned by Richmond's First Amendment 'Sunshine Act,'" *National Law Journal,* September 29, 1980, at 24; White, "Jailing of Myron Farber." An excellent skeptical piece on the whole problem is L. BeVier, *An Informed Public, an Informing Press,* 68 California Law Review 482 (1980).

51. R. Woodward and S. Armstrong, THE BRETHREN (New York: Simon and Shuster, 1979).

52. *Globe Enterprise v. Superior Court,* 457 U.S. 596 (1982); *Press Enterprises [I] v. Superior Court,* 464 U.S. 501 (1984); *Press Enterprises [II] v. Superior Court,* 478 U.S. 1 (1986); *Douglas Oil Co. v. Petrol Stops Northwest,* 441 U.S. 211, 218, quoted in *Press Enterprises II,* 478 U.S. at 9.

53. *Powell v. Alabama,* 287 U.S. 45 (1932); *Gideon v. Wainwright,* 372 U.S. 335 (1963); W. Lockhart, Y. Kamisar, J. Choper, and S. Shiffrin, CONSTITUTIONAL LAW 845 (Minneapolis: West Publishing, 6th ed. 1986).

54. *Richmond Newspapers,* 448 U.S. at 577–78; A. Adler, LITIGATION UNDER THE FEDERAL FREEDOM OF INFORMATION ACT (Washington, D.C.: American Civil Liberties Union Foundation, 14th ed. 1989).

55. *Betts v. Brady,* 316 U.S. 455 (1942).

## Chapter 7

1. *Hazelwood School District v. Kuhlmeier,* 484 U.S. 260 (1988); M. Yudof, *Personal Speech and Government Expression,* 38 Case Western Reserve Law Review 671 (1988).

2. A. Liebling, THE PRESS 32 (New York: Pantheon Books, 2d revised ed. 1981) (from his *New Yorker* column "The Wayward Press" of May 14, 1960). Eighty-two of the ninety-six "Wayward Press" columns from

May 19, 1945, through April 13, 1963, were written by Liebling. When he died the *New York Times,* December 30, 1963, editorialized: "He was, by his own description, 'a chronic, incurable, recidivist reporter,' and his admiration for skill in reporting was boundless. His death stills a pen that could inspire as well as wound. The press will be duller for the loss of his barbs."

3. M. Emery and E. Emery, THE PRESS AND AMERICA 622–23 (Englewood Cliffs, N.J.: Prentice Hall, 6th ed. 1988) has 1676 as the total for 1986, down from a postwar high of 1785 in 1954; media analyst John Morton, in the *Washington Journalism Review* at 56 (April 1988), lists the current number of dailies at 1649.

4. Liebling, THE PRESS at 63, 66–67; B. Bagdikian, THE MEDIA MONOPOLY 72 (Boston: Beacon Press, 1983) and 69–70 (2d ed. 1987); A. Smith, GOODBYE GUTENBERG 45 (New York: Oxford University Press, 1980); B. Rucker, THE FIRST FREEDOM 22 (Carbondale: University of Southern Illinois Press, 1968); B. Compaine, C. Sterling, T. Guback, and J. Noble, WHO OWNS THE MEDIA 37 (White Plains, N.Y.: Knowledge Industry, 2d ed. 1982); Emery and Emery, THE PRESS AND AMERICA at 623.

5. Liebling, THE PRESS at 47–48.

6. Emery and Emery, THE PRESS AND AMERICA 627; Smith, GOODBYE GUTENBERG at 46.

7. Jerome Barron, *Access to the Press—A New First Amendment Right,* 80 Harvard Law Review 1641 (1967). Barron's ideas and influence will be discussed more fully in Chapters 8 and 9.

8. Bagdikian, MEDIA MONOPOLY at 8–21 (1st ed.) and 18–25 (2d ed.). The "Private Ministry of Information and Culture" is the title of Part 1 of the book.

9. *Genessee Radio,* 5 FCC 183 (1938).

10. 5 Federal Register 2382, 2384 (1940); 6 Federal Register 2282, 2284 (1941); *United States v. Storer Broadcasting,* 351 U.S. 192 (1956).

11. *Multiple Ownership of Standard, FM and TV Broadcast Stations,* 22 F.C.C.2d 306, 310–11 (1970); *Amendment of Multiple Ownership Rules,* Pike and Fisher, 2 RADIO REGULATION 2d, at 1588, 1592 (1964); *Second Report and Order,* 50 F.C.C.2d 1046 (1975), on reconsideration, 53 F.C.C.2d 589 (1975). Of course, the FCC's looks at newspaper-broadcast ownership have not always been benign, as I discussed in Chapter 5 of AMERICAN BROADCASTING AND THE FIRST AMENDMENT (Berkeley and Los Angeles: University of California Press, 1987).

12. *Second Report and Order,* 50 F.C.C.2d at 1079; D. Polsby, *F.C.C. v. National Citizens Committee for Broadcasting and the Judicious Use of Administrative Discretion,* 1978 Supreme Court Review 1, 8; *Multiple*

*Ownership,* 100 F.C.C.2d 17, on reconsideration, 100 F.C.C.2d 74 (1984). No group owner may reach an audience in any one service exceeding 25 percent of the US population. At the time the commission adopted the cap, Metromedia had the largest reach at 23.89 percent.

13. *National Citizens Committee for Broadcasting v. FCC,* 555 F.2d 938, 966 (D.C. Cir. 1977).

14. *FCC v. National Citizens Committee for Broadcasting [NCCB],* 436 U.S. 775 (1978).

15. The quotation comes from the beginning case in the line, *Schneider v. Town of Irvington,* 308 U.S. 147, 163 (1939).

16. *NCCB,* 436 U.S. at 801.

17. *Associated Press v. United States,* 326 U.S. 1 (1945).

18. Z. Chafee, GOVERNMENT AND MASS COMMUNICATIONS 542–48 (Chicago: University of Chicago Press, 1947); M. Murphy, *The United States v. the Associated Press,* 1974 Montana Journalism Review 40–46. The *Chicago Sun* was defeated 684 to 247; the *Washington Times-Herald,* 514 to 242. Id. at 41.

19. Chafee, GOVERNMENT AND MASS COMMUNICATIONS at 549; D. Smith, ZECHARIAH CHAFEE, JR. 97 (Cambridge, Mass.: Harvard University Press, 1986); Powe, AMERICAN BROADCASTING AND THE FIRST AMENDMENT at 68–74.

20. Smith, CHAFEE at 97. Chafee's written debate with Fred S. Siebert was published "in several major newspapers," but it was rejected by the likes of the *New York Times,* the *New York Herald Tribune,* and the *Washington Post* (id. at 96; Murphy, *United States v. the Associated Press* at 42). For historical reasons, antitrust litigation initiated by the Department of Justice was tried before three-judge district courts. The practice ceased in 1976.

21. Z. Chafee, FREE SPEECH IN THE UNITED STATES (Cambridge, Mass.: Harvard University Press, 1921).

22. *United States v. Associated Press,* 52 F. Supp. 362, 372 (S.D.N.Y. 1943).

23. Smith, CHAFEE at 98 (emphasis added) and 107 (quoting an exchange, whether oral or written is unclear, with ACLU attorney Morris Ernst); Chafee, GOVERNMENT AND MASS COMMUNICATIONS at 554; *National Broadcasting Company v. United States,* 319 U.S. 190 (1943), discussed in Powe, AMERICAN BROADCASTING AND THE FIRST AMENDMENT at 33–37.

24. *Associated Press,* 326 U.S. at 13, 20.

25. Chafee, GOVERNMENT AND MASS COMMUNICATIONS at 563.

26. *National Labor Relations Board v. Associated Press [NLRB v. AP],* 301 U.S. 103 (1937). The case was decided the same day as *NLRB v.*

*Jones and Laughlin Steel,* 301 U.S. 1 (1937), and by the same five-to-four vote that established the constitutionality of the National Labor Relations Act under the commerce clause in that case. Furthermore, the four dissenters—Sutherland, Van Devanter, Butler, and McReynolds (the Four Horsemen of Reaction)—had also been the dissenters in *Near;* so taking their First Amendment dissent in *NLRB v. AP* seriously is all but impossible. Nevertheless, if one imagines the dissent to be written by a Douglas instead of by Sutherland, there is in fact a real power to the opinion that is too easy to overlook. Forty years later the Court took a parallel argument very seriously in the context of NLRB jurisdiction over lay teachers at parochial schools. *NLRB v. Catholic Bishop of Chicago,* 440 U.S. 490 (1979) (without a clear expression of congressional intent, NLRB held to lack jurisdiction). F. Siebert, *My Experiences with the First Amendment,* 56 Journalism Quarterly 446, 449 (1979).

27. M. Ernst, THE FIRST FREEDOM 250–52 (New York: Macmillan, 1946); P. Hart, *The Congressional Perspective of Competition in the Communications Industries,* 13 Antitrust Bulletin 973, 977 (1968); Bagdikian, MEDIA MONOPOLY ch. 13, "To Undo Excess."

28. J. Morton, "The Business of Journalism: Second Papers Don't Flourish," *Washington Journalism Review,* September 1989, at 6. Freedom of Expression: Hearings before the Committee on Commerce, Science and Transportation, U.S. Senate, 97th Cong., 2d sess., serial 97-139, at 141 (1982).

29. B. Owen, ECONOMICS AND FREEDOM OF EXPRESSION 52–53 (Cambridge, Mass.: Ballinger, 1975).

30. The best of the articles in the field is K. Roberts, *Antitrust Problems in the Newspaper Industry,* 82 Harvard Law Review 319 (1968), which also cites many of the extensive congressional hearings in the area.

31. S. Lacy, *Content of Joint Operation Newspapers,* in R. Picard, J. Winter, M. McCombs, and S. Lacy, eds., PRESS CONCENTRATION AND MONOPOLY 147–50 (Norwood, N.J.: Ablex, 1988); D. Coulson, *Antitrust Law and Newspapers* in id. at 179–80.

32. Roberts, *Antitrust Problems in the Newspaper Industry* at 341; Arthur Hanson in Hearings on the Concentration of Ownership in the News Media before the Subcommittee on Antitrust of the House Committee on the Judiciary, 88th Cong., 1st sess. 260 (1963).

33. *United States v. Times Mirror Co.,* 274 F. Supp. 606 (C.D. Cal. 1967), affirmed, 390 U.S. 712 (1968). For those for whom the distinction matters, the holding was based on § 7 of the Clayton Act rather than on the Sherman Act. J. Morton, "Media Control: What If . . . ," *Washington Journalism Review,* April 1988, at 56.

34. *Citizen Publishing Co. v. United States,* 394 U.S. 131 (1969).

35. Newspaper Preservation Act, 15 United States Code §§ 1801–04 (1970). A number of discussions of the NPA are included in the excellent bibliography in Picard et al., PRESS CONCENTRATION AND MONOPOLY.

36. D. Holder, "Joint Operating Agreements: If You Can't Beat 'Em, Join 'Em," *Washington Journalism Review,* November 1982, at 20, 22 (quoting Teeter); S. Barnett, "Court Review to Affect Newspaper Industry Structure," *Legal Times of Washington,* November 15, 1982, at 15; Coulson, *Antitrust Law and Newspapers* at 188–89.

37. Morton, "Business of Journalism"; *Committee for an Independent P-I v. Hearst Corp.,* 704 F.2d 467 (9th Cir. 1983) cert. denied, 464 U.S. 892 (1983); A. Carlson, *The Newspaper Preservation Act: The Seattle Application,* 1982 University of Illinois Law Review 669.

38. S. Barnett, *Monopoly Games—Where Failures Win Big,* 19 Columbia Journalism Review 40 (1980); S. Barnett, *Detroit's High-Stakes "Failure" Game,* 27 Columbia Journalism Review 40 (1988); *Michigan Citizens v. Thornburgh,* affirmed by an equally divided Court, 110 S. Ct. 398 (1989); *New York Times,* November 14, 1989, at 29.

39. Lacy, *Content of Joint Operation Agreements* at 148–49; J. Morton, "The *Miami News'* Profitable Death," *Washington Journalism Review,* December 1988, at 46.

40. W. Niebauer, *Effects of the Newspaper Preservation Act on the Suburban Press,* 5 Newspaper Research Journal 41–49 (1984); Lacy, *Content of Joint Operation Agreements* at 151–52; Coulson, *Antitrust Law and Newspapers* at 187–90.

41. S. Barnett, "Regulating Newspapers: Novel Problems for Justice," *Legal Times of Washington,* September 1, 1980, at 11, 15.

42. Emery and Emery, THE PRESS AND AMERICA at 627–30; C. Mahaffie, *Mergers and Diversification in the Newspaper, Broadcasting and Information Industries,* 13 Antitrust Bulletin 927, 931 (1968).

43. Mahaffie, *Mergers,* at 932.

44. Coulson, *Antitrust Law and Newspapers* at 195 (although he believes that "imaginative application" of the antitrust laws could be successful).

45. Record at 43, *Grosjean v. American Press,* 297 U.S. 233 (1936).

46. *Grosjean,* 297 U.S. at 246–51. If there were no Fourteenth Amendment, the Court might have determined that the "republican form of government" clause of Article IV of the Constitution was judicially enforceable; but the point remains that if the federal courts could not act, Louisiana or any other state might be reduced to state-controlled information.

47. *Giragi v. Moore,* 301 U.S. 670 (1937).

48. *Minneapolis Star & Tribune Co. v. Minnesota Commissioner of Revenue,* 460 U.S. 575 (1983).

49. Id. at 591–92.

50. Id. at 587 and 602 (dissent).

51. Id. at 588.

52. The exact language is printed only in the 1194-page Making Further Continuing Appropriations for the Fiscal Year ending September 30, 1988, H.R. Report no. 498, 100th Cong., 1st sess. 34 (1987).

53. *News America Publishing, Inc. v. FCC,* 844 F.2d 800, 814, 810 (D.C. Cir. 1988) (quoting *Arkansas Writers' Project v. Ragland,* 481 U.S. 221 (1987), a case invalidating a tax scheme that exempted newspapers and "religious, professional, trade and sports journals," but not other types of publications).

54. Coulson, *Antitrust Law and Newspapers* at 180; R. Leigh, ed., A FREE AND RESPONSIBLE PRESS 80 (Chicago: University of Chicago Press, 1947).

55. Chafee, GOVERNMENT AND MASS COMMUNICATIONS at 537; Ernst, THE FIRST FREEDOM at 249–53.

56. Chafee, GOVERNMENT AND MASS COMMUNICATIONS at 594; Smith, CHAFEE at 107; Media Ownership: Diversity and Concentrations: Hearings before the Subcommittee on Communications of the Senate Committee on Commerce, Science and Transportation, 101st Cong., 1st sess., no. 101-357, at 86–89 (1989).

57. *Beauharnais v. Illinois,* 343 U.S. 250, 286 (1952) (dissenting opinion).

58. Bagdikian, MEDIA MONOPOLY at 225–26.

59. C. Baker, HUMAN LIBERTY AND FREEDOM OF SPEECH 266–70 (New York: Oxford University Press, 1989).

## Chapter 8

1. "Fly Blasts Nets," *Broadcasting Magazine,* May 19, 1941; M. Blanchard, THE HUTCHINS COMMISSION, THE PRESS AND THE RESPONSIBILITY CONCEPT, Journalism Monographs no. 49, at 9, 11 (Lexington: University of Kentucky Press, 1977). This is an appropriate place to correct a typo in my AMERICAN BROADCASTING AND THE FIRST AMENDMENT at 69. In stating the opposition of the press to FDR, I had intended to use his figure of 75 percent; I never caught the "95 percent" until after the paperback edition appeared.

2. E. Purcell, THE CRISIS OF DEMOCRATIC THEORY (Lexington: University of Kentucky Press, 1973). The third member who did not make Purcell was Robert Redfield, an anthropologist who was dean of social sciences at Chicago. By 1947, when the commission report was issued,

Lasswell was on the Yale Law School faculty. Luce was true to his commitment to keep his hands off and even refrained from public comment on a final product he found disappointing. H. Ashmore, Unseasonable Truths 294 (Boston: Little, Brown, 1989).

3. R. Leigh, ed., A Free and Responsible Press 9 (Chicago: University of Chicago Press, 1947); Ashmore, Unseasonable Truths at 294.

4. Leigh, Free and Responsible Press at 18, 128, 90–96.

5. Id. at viii; A. Liebling, Book Review, *The Nation*, April 12, 1947, at 427. The report underwhelmed Liebling, as his characteristically humorous review demonstrates. The reaction to the report is discussed in Blanchard, Hutchins Commission at 29–50.

6. *Abrams v. United States*, 250 U.S. 616, 630 (1919) (dissent).

7. J. Milton, *Areopagitica*, in J. Patrick, ed., The Prose of John Milton 327 (New York: New York University Press, 1968); *Whitney v. California*, 274 U.S. 357, 376 (1927) (concurring); *New York Times v. Sullivan*, 376 U.S. 254, 269, 279 n. 19 (1964); J. Mill, On Liberty 15 (Oxford: Blackwell, 1947).

8. A. Meiklejohn, Free Speech and Its Relation to Self-government (New York: Oxford University Press, 1948). As I note in Chapter 6, this theory is somewhat overdrawn.

9. Vincent Blasi's seminal *The Checking Value in First Amendment Theory*, 1977 American Bar Foundation Research Journal 521, is the modern genesis of "checking."

10. *Whitney*, 274 U.S. at 376; C. Baker, Human Liberty and Freedom of Speech (New York: Oxford University Press, 1989).

11. F. Schauer, Free Speech: A Philosophical Inquiry (Cambridge: Cambridge University Press, 1982) provides the best critique of the various theories although, quite naturally, supporters of any one of the theories are quite able to critique the others.

12. T. Emerson, The System of Freedom of Expression (New York: Random House, 1970); L. Powe, *Scholarship and Markets*, 56 George Washington Law Review 172, 179 (1987); S. Shiffrin, *The First Amendment and Economic Regulation: Away from a General Theory of the First Amendment*, 78 Northwestern University Law Review 1212 (1983); M. Yudof, When Government Speaks (Berkeley and Los Angeles: University of California Press, 1983).

13. Baker, Human Liberty and Freedom of Speech at 253–55, is that rare exception who see aspects of freedom of the press in liberty terms (albeit because he sees all First Amendment issues in liberty terms); W. Hocking, Freedom of the Press 169 (Chicago: University of Chicago Press, 1947).

14. T. Bethell and C. Peters, "The Imperial Press," *Washington Monthly,* November, 1976, at 29.

15. C. Whalen, YOUR RIGHT TO KNOW at x (New York: Random House, 1973); *Branzburg v. Hayes,* 408 U.S. 665, 721 (1972) (dissenting).

16. K. Cooper, THE RIGHT TO KNOW at iv (New York: Farrar, Straus and Cudahy, 1956); J. Merrill, IS THERE A RIGHT TO KNOW? Freedom of Information Center Publication no. 002 (Columbia, Mo.: Freedom of Information Center, 1967); J. Merrill, *The "People's Right to Know" Myth,* 45 New York State Bar Journal 461 (1973).

17. *Jones v. Opelika,* 316 U.S. 584, 608 (1942) (Chief Justice Stone dissenting), adopted as the opinion of the court on rehearing, 319 U.S. 103 (1943) (per curiam). A quick but hostile history of the preferred position is provided in Justice Frankfurter's concurring opinion in *Kovacs v. Cooper,* 336 U.S. 77, 89 (1949); P. Stewart, *"Or of the Press,"* 25 Hastings Law Journal 631 (1975); F. Abrams, *The Press Is Different,* 7 Hofstra Law Review 563 (1979); M. Nimmer, *Introduction—Is Freedom of the Press a Redundancy?,* 25 Hastings Law Journal 639 (1975).

18. The questions from the bench and Tribe's answers are from Anthony Lewis's notes of oral argument. A. Lewis, *A Public Right to Know about Public Institutions,* 1980 Supreme Court Review 1, 19; *First National Bank of Boston v. Bellotti,* 435 U.S. 765, 795–802 (1978) (concurring). Burger's concluding sentence reads: "In short, the First Amendment does not 'belong' to any definable category of persons or entities: It belongs to all who exercise its freedoms."

19. H. Kalven, *The New York Times Case,* 1964 Supreme Court Review 191, 221 n. 125; J. Barron, *Access to the Media—A New First Amendment Right,* 81 Harvard Law Review 1641 (1967); J. Barron, *In Defense of Fairness: A First Amendment Rationale for Broadcasting's "Fairness" Doctrine,* 37 University of Colorado Law Review 31 (1964); J. Barron, *The Federal Communications Commission's Fairness Doctrine,* 30 George Washington Law Review 1 (1961).

20. A. Director, *The Parity of the Economic Marketplace,* 7 Journal of Law and Economics 1 (1964).

21. M. Tushnet, *Corporations and Free Speech,* in D. Kairys, ed., THE POLITICS OF LAW at 253, 257 (New York: Pantheon Books, 1982).

22. *Red Lion Broadcasting v. FCC,* 395 U.S. 367 (1969).

23. Id. at 390.

24. *New York Times v. Sullivan,* 376 U.S. at 270; Meiklejohn, FREE SPEECH at 24–28.

25. *Red Lion Broadcasting,* 395 U.S. at 390.

26. *CBS v. Democratic National Committee,* 412 U.S. 94 (1973).

27. *Business Executives' Move for Vietnam Peace v. FCC*, 450 F.2d 642, 655 (D.C. Cir. 1971).

28. *CBS v. DNC*, 412 U.S. at 102, 122.

29. *Miami Herald v. Tornillo*, 418 U.S. 241 (1974); Powe, *Scholarship and Markets* at 178–80.

30. *Virginia State Board of Pharmacy v. Virginia Citizens Consumer Council*, 425 U.S. 748 (1976).

31. *Buckley v. Valeo*, 424 U.S. 1, 19 (1976); *First National Bank of Boston v. Bellotti*, 435 U.S. 765 (1978).

32. J. Wright, *Money and the Pollution of Politics*, 82 Columbia Law Review 609, 637 (1982). The statement in text that wealth, not talent is the ticket to the public's ear is not accurate. It is not wealth per se, but some level of affluence combined with the conclusion that economic self-interest requires spending, that brings money into the political marketplace. L. Powe, *Mass Speech and the Newer First Amendment*, 1982 Supreme Court Review 243, 265. For simplification (and therefore with distortion) I have accepted the terms of debate as the rich versus us.

33. S. Levinson, *Regulating Campaign Activity*, 83 Michigan Law Review 939, 945 (1985).

34. C. Lindblom, POLITICS AND MARKETS (New York: Basic Books, 1977); O. Fiss, *Why the State?* 100 Harvard Law Review 781, 785–88 (1987); O. Fiss, *Free Speech and Social Structure*, 71 Iowa Law Review 1405 (1986).

35. J. Lichtenberg, *Foundations and Limits of Freedom of the Press*, 16 Philosophy and Public Affairs 329 (1987).

36. Id. at 329–30.

37. Yudof, WHEN GOVERNMENT SPEAKS; Schauer, FREE SPEECH; Shiffrin, *First Amendment and Economic Regulation;* Powe, *Scholarship and Markets.*

38. Lichtenberg, *Foundations and Limits* at 330 n. 3.

39. R. Nagel, CONSTITUTIONAL CULTURES 4 (Berkeley and Los Angeles: University of California Press, 1989); 67 Congressional Record 12352 (1926).

40. Fiss, *Why the State?* at 786–87.

41. S. Ingber, *The First Amendment in Modern Garb: Retaining System Legitimacy—A Review Essay of Lucas Powe's American Broadcasting and the First Amendment*, 56 George Washington Law Review 187, 204 (1987); *Frank v. Mangum*, 237 U.S. 309, 349 (dissenting).

42. T. Scanlan, *Freedom of Expression and Categories of Expression*, 40 University of Pittsburgh Law Review 519, 534 (1979); Powe, AMERICAN BROADCASTING AND THE FIRST AMENDMENT at 121–41; T. Emerson,

TOWARD A GENERAL THEORY OF THE FIRST AMENDMENT 16–25 (New York: Vintage Books, 1966).

43. W. Van Alstyne, *The Hazards to the Press of Claiming a "Preferred Position,"* 28 Hastings Law Journal 761 (1977); W. Van Alstyne, *The First Amendment and the Free Press,* 9 Hofstra Law Review 1 (1980); L. BeVier, *An Informed Public, an Informing Press,* 68 California Law Review 482 (1980); A. Lewis, *A Preferred Position for Journalism?* 7 Hofstra Law Review 595 (1979); Lewis, *Public Right to Know.*

44. Van Alstyne, *The First Amendment and the Free Press* at 19; R. Bork, "The First Amendment Does Not Give Greater Freedom to the Press than to Speech," *Center Magazine,* March/April 1979, at 28, 34.

45. Hocking, FREEDOM OF THE PRESS at 170–71.

46. *New York Times v. United States,* 403 U.S. 713, 750 (1971) (dissenting); H. Salisbury, WITHOUT FEAR OR FAVOR 540–45 (New York: Times Books, 1980).

47. *Richmond Newspapers v. Virginia,* 448 U.S. 555, 573 (1980).

48. *Branzburg,* 408 U.S. at 707.

49. Bork, "First Amendment" at 34; *United States Postal Service v. Greenburgh Civic Association,* 453 U.S. 114 (1981).

## Chapter 9

1. *Jacobellis v. Ohio,* 378 U.S. 184, 197–98 (1964).

2. P. Stewart, *"Or of the Press,"* 26 Hastings Law Journal 631, 633–34 (1975).

3. *Miami Herald v. Tornillo,* 418 U.S. 241 (1974). Tornillo is pronounced tor-nil-lo (not tor-nee-yo). The remainder of this chapter is condensed from my article *Tornillo,* 1987 Supreme Court Review 345, which has both additional information and more extensive footnoting.

4. T. Clark, THE SOUTHERN COUNTRY EDITOR 283 (Indianapolis: Bobbs Merrill, 1948).

5. Clark, SOUTHERN COUNTRY EDITOR at 295–96; J. Dovell, 2 FLORIDA 711–12 (New York: Lewis Historical Publishing, 1952), quoting 1907 Message to the Legislature from the House Journal at 70; T. Hoffer and G. Butterfield, *The Right to Reply,* 53 Journalism Quarterly 111, 112 (1976).

6. Hoffer and Butterfield, *Right to Reply* at 113–14.

7. *Miami Herald,* October 22, 1965; November 22, 1965; March 2, 1966; June 28, 1966; July 14–17, 1967.

8. Powe, *Tornillo* at 352–56.

9. *Reynolds v. Sims,* 377 U.S. 533 (1964); C. Tebeau, A HISTORY OF FLORIDA 449 (Coral Gables: University of Miami Press, 1971).

10. *Miami Herald,* September 9, 1970; September 30, 1970.

11. *Miami Herald,* July 12, 1972.

12. *Miami Herald,* September 13, 1972.

13. The full text of the editorial (*Miami Herald,* September 20, 1972) reads:

### The State's Laws and Pat Tornillo

LOOK who's upholding the law!

Pat Tornillo, boss of the Classroom Teachers Association and candidate for the State Legislature in the Oct. 3 runoff election, has denounced his opponent as lacking "the knowledge to be a legislator, as evidenced by his failure to file a list of contributions to and expenditures of his campaign as required by law."

Czar Tornillo calls "violation of this law inexcusable."

This is the same Pat Tornillo who led the CTA strike from February 19 to March 11, 1968, against the school children and taxpayers of Dade County. Call it whatever you will, it was an illegal act against the public interest and clearly prohibited by the statutes.

We cannot say it would be illegal but certainly it would be inexcusable of the voters if they sent Pat Tornillo to Tallahassee to occupy the seat for District 103 in the House of Representatives.

14. The full text of the second editorial (*Miami Herald,* September 29, 1972) reads:

### See Pat Run

FROM the people who brought you this—the teacher strike of '68—come now instructions on how to vote for responsible government, i.e., against Crutcher Harrison and Ethel Beckham, for Pat Tornillo. The tracts and blurbs and bumper stickers pile up daily in teachers' school mailboxes amidst continuing pouts that the School Board should be delivering all this at your expense. The screeds say the strike is not an issue. We say maybe it wouldn't be were it not a part of a continuation of disregard of any and all laws the CTA might find aggravating. Whether in defiance of zoning laws at CTA Towers, contracts and laws during the strike, or more recently state prohibitions against soliciting campaign funds amongst teachers, CTA says fie and try and sue us—what's good for CTA is good for CTA and that is natural law. Tornillo's law, maybe. For years now he has been kicking the public shin to call attention to his shakedown statesmanship. He and whichever acerbic prexy is in alleged office have always felt their private ventures so chock-full of public weal that we should leap at the chance to nab the tab, be it half the Glorious Leader's salary or the dues checkoff or anything else except perhaps mileage on the staff hydrofoil. Give him public office, says Pat, and he will no doubt live by the Golden Rule. Our translation reads that as more gold and more rule.

15. *State v. News-Journal Corp.,* 36 Fla. Supp. 164 (Cir. Ct. Volusia County 1972).

16. *Miami Herald,* October 4, 1972; *Miami News,* September 11, 1972, at 30A; October 2, 1972, at 30A. The *Herald's* circulation was

354,408, while that of the *News* was only 78,119. EDITOR AND PUB-
LISHER YEARBOOK 61, 62 (New York: Editor and Publisher, 1973).

17. *Miami Herald,* October 5, 1972; October 7, 1972. Tornillo signed
the letter: "Pat 'Boss' Tornillo."

18. *Tornillo v. Miami Herald,* 38 Fla. Supp. 80 (Cir. Ct. Dade County
1972).

19. J. Barron, FREEDOM OF THE PRESS FOR WHOM? (Bloomington: Indiana University Press, 1973); *Access to the Press—A New First Amendment Right,* 80 Harvard Law Review 1641 (1967); *An Emerging First
Amendment Right of Access to the Media?* 37 George Washington Law
Review 487 (1969); *Access—The Only Choice for the Media?* 48 Texas
Law Review 766 (1970); *Red Lion Broadcasting v. FCC,* 395 U.S. 367
(1969).

20. R. Fisher, *And Who Will Take Care of the Damrons?* in THE TRIAL
OF THE FIRST AMENDMENT at 16 (Columbia, Mo.: Freedom of Informa-
tion Center, 1975). This little pamphlet was commissioned by Knight-
Ridder, owner of the *Herald,* for a pretty tidy sum.

21. *Tornillo v. Miami Herald,* 287 So. 2d 78 (Fla. 1973).

22. Id. at 81–83.

23. Id. at 82, 83, 84 (emphasis in original).

24. Id. at 91.

25. *South Dade News-Leader,* July 25, 1973; Simon to Paul Brook-
shire (editor of *South Dade News-Leader*), August 9, 1973.

26. Simon to Cranberg, January 8, 1974, at 3.

27. Fisher, *Who Will Take Care?* at 13.

28. *Tornillo,* 418 U.S. at 248, 253.

29. Id. at 250, quoting the Hutchins Commission report at 4.

30. Id. at 256–58.

31. Id. at 257.

32. V. Blasi, *The Checking Value in First Amendment Theory,* 1977
American Bar Foundation Research Journal 521.

33. Simon told Tornillo of the newspapers' filings, listed them by
name, and then wrote: "Do you realize the amount of attorney's fees you
are generating? This is unquestionably contributing to the enormous
inflation overtaking the United States." Simon to Tornillo, August 14,
1973. Brief of *The Citrus County Chronicle* as Amicus Curiae at 2; Brief
of *The Islander* as Amicus Curiae at 2.

34. L. Bollinger, *Freedom of the Press and Public Access,* 75 Michigan
Law Review 1, 31 (1976); L. Tribe, AMERICAN CONSTITUTIONAL LAW
1002 (Mineola, N.Y.: Foundation Press, 2d ed. 1988).

35. E. Hynds, AMERICAN NEWSPAPERS IN THE 1970S, at 17 (New
York: Hasting House, 1975), states that advertising constitutes 40 to 75

percent of a paper. I have never heard anyone previously place the figure below 60 percent. According to the standard media text, E. Emery and M. Emery, THE PRESS AND AMERICA 233 (Englewood Cliffs, N.J.: Prentice-Hall, 4th ed. 1978), advertising space reached 50 percent by World War I. Regardless of the exact amount of advertising space, a newspaper cannot just print everything. The amount of advertising sets a limit on the amount of news that will be printed.

36. B. Schmidt, FREEDOM OF THE PRESS VS PUBLIC ACCESS 233 (New York: Praeger, 1976); F. Abrams, *In Defense of Tornillo,* 86 Yale Law Journal 361 (1976).

37. *United States v. Morison,* 844 F.2d 1057 (4th Cir. 1988) cert. denied, 109 S. Ct. 259 (1988); *Pittsburgh Press Co. v. Pittsburgh Commission on Human Relations,* 413 U.S. 376 (1973).

38. A typical "abuse" clause reads as follows: "No law shall be passed to curtail, or restrain the liberty of speech, or of the press, and any person may speak, write and publish his sentiments, on all subjects, being responsible for the abuse of that liberty." GEORGIA CONSTITUTION art. I, § 1, para. 5. Forty-two states have similar provisions.

39. 17 Congressional Record 43163–64 (1971); Senate Conference Report 92-580. The statute was sustained in *CBS v. FCC (Carter-Mondale),* 453 U.S. 367 (1981).

40. *New York Times,* March 12, 1974, at 17; *Washington Post,* March 13, 1974, at 26 (editorial); *Reflections on the Tornillo Case,* in J. Barron, PUBLIC RIGHTS AND THE PRIVATE PRESS 1, 2 (Toronto: Butterworths, 1981).

41. Tribe, AMERICAN CONSTITUTIONAL LAW at 700; see also Bollinger, *Freedom of the Press and Public Access* at 31. Blasi sees this as an important symbolic value because even if press regulation has "limited material impact," it nevertheless tarnishes the image of a totally free press (*Checking Value* at 624; but see id. at 628, quoted in text at note 45 below).

42. When I presented this at a faculty colloquium, my colleagues understood that my four-part test was facetious, but several told me they thought it was nevertheless sound. Therefore, let me briefly explain its flaws. (1) It is probably impossible to find an equivalent to a daily newspaper, given their scarcity and probable market dominance. Thus the first part of the test is likely either to be always satisfied or to provide an interesting discussion of how many radio stations equal a newspaper. (2) What does "reading public" mean? How is it different from the public? Does "generally available" have any different content from "alternative equivalent media outlet"? (3) This sounds nice, but still it is a mechanism

that could be abused. (4) The requirement is conclusory and assumes, as discussed, that reading the reply is of more benefit to the public than whatever story is omitted to make room for the reply.

43. Schmidt, FREEDOM OF THE PRESS at 231. Alexander Bickel decried a story of faculty members debating with students over whether to burn an ROTC building. "The matter was ultimately voted upon, and the affirmative lost—narrowly. But the negative taken by the faculty was only one side of a debate which the faculty rendered legitimate by engaging in it. Where nothing is unspeakable, nothing is undoable." A. Bickel, THE MORALITY OF CONSENT 73 (New Haven, Conn.: Yale University Press, 1975).

44. *Boyd v. United States,* 116 U.S. 616 (1886); *Olmstead v. United States,* 277 U.S. 438, 474 (1927) (dissenting).

45. Blasi, *Checking Value* at 628.

46. *West Virginia v. Barnette,* 319 U.S. 624, 641 (1943).

47. *New York Times v. United States,* 403 U.S. 713, 717 (1971).

48. *New York Times,* September 21, 1970, at 42; Jim Hampton (editor of the *Herald*) to author, June 15, 1987: "I've opened our Op-Ed Page far more than in Shoemaker's day. Nothing to do with Tornillo; just my own recognition that, as the only real game in town, we have an obligation to provide an accessible soapbox for those of opposing views. We give priority in our Reader's Forum to letters opposing us, for the same reason." The *Herald* does not have an ombudsman. E. Hynds, AMERICAN NEWSPAPERS IN THE 1980S, at 294–95 (New York: Hasting House, 1980); D. Shaw, JOURNALISM TODAY chap. 6 (New York: Harper's College Press, 1977); C. Tate, *What Do Ombudsmen Do?* 23 Columbia Journalism Review 37 (1984).

49. One ambitious project, announced with much fanfare in the *Columbia Journalism Review,* was a National News Council. It was proposed by the Twentieth Century Fund as "an independent forum for public and press discussion of important issues affecting the flow of information." 11 Columbia Journalism Review at 44 (1973). With foundation funding, its goal was "to receive, to examine, and to report on complaints concerning the accuracy and fairness of news reporting," thereby increasing public trust in journalism by assessing complaints about the work of major news organizations. Id. at 43. The *Columbia Journalism Review* reported the council's decisions, but many newspapers refused to cooperate, others cooperated tepidly, and the *New York Times* was vigorously opposed to the council. *New York Times,* March 21, 1984, at 19. The Council eventually wound up so moribund that its death went unnoticed in the *Columbia Journalism Review.* P. Brogan, SPIKED:

THE SHORT LIFE AND DEATH OF THE NATIONAL NEWS COUNCIL (New York: Priority Press, 1985).

50. *Editor and Publisher,* May 3, 1975, at 40.

## Conclusion

1. T. Bethell and C. Peters, "The Imperial Press," *Washington Monthly,* November 1976, at 28, 29.

2. M. Shapiro, *Libel Regulatory Analysis,* 74 California Law Review 883 (1986); O. Fiss, *Why the State?* 100 Harvard Law Review 781 (1987).

3. J. Balkin, *Some Realism About Pluralism: Legal Realist Approaches to the First Amendment,* 1990 Duke Law Journal 375, 376; O. Fiss, *The Fate of an Idea Whose Time Has Come,* 41 University of Chicago Law Review 742 (1974); O. Fiss, *Groups and the Equal Protection Clause,* 5 Philosophy and Public Affairs 107 (1976); O. Fiss, *The Forms of Justice,* 93 Harvard Law Review 1 (1979); S. Ingber, *The First Amendment in Modern Garb: Retaining System Legitimacy—A Review Essay of Lucas Powe's American Broadcasting and the First Amendment,* 56 George Washington Law Review 187, 204 (1987).

4. K. Arrow, SOCIAL CHOICE AND INDIVIDUAL VALUES (New York: Wiley and Sons, 2d ed. 1963); D. Mueller, PUBLIC CHOICE (Cambridge: Cambridge University Press, 1979). In colloquial form, Arrow's Theorem demonstrates that inconsistency and instability are inherent in group decision making, an idea informally captured in the folk saying that a camel is a horse designed by a committee. In simplified, but more technical, form, Arrow's Theorem demonstrates that no conceivable voting system can enable one to move from (a) the individual ordinal preference rankings of three or more options by three or more voters to (b) a social ranking of the options in question, without violating one or more of the plausible criteria of rationality that the theorem delineates.

5. B. Bagdikian, THE MEDIA MONOPOLY 101–02 (Boston: Beacon Press, 1983).

6. *United States v. Associated Press,* 52 F. Supp. 362, 372 (S.D.N.Y. 1943).

7. L. Powe, AMERICAN BROADCASTING AND THE FIRST AMENDMENT (Berkeley and Los Angeles: University of California Press, 1987); L. Powe, *Scholarship and Markets,* 56 George Washington Law Review 171, 184–86 (1987).

8. *Plessy v. Fergusson,* 163 U.S. 537 (1896); R. Bork, THE TEMPTING OF AMERICA (New York: Free Press, 1989); R. Nagel, CONSTITUTIONAL CULTURES (Berkeley and Los Angeles: University of California Press, 1989).

9. J. Persico, EDWARD R. MURROW 377–80 (New York: McGraw-Hill Publishing Co., 1988); AMERICAN BROADCASTING AND THE FIRST AMENDMENT 138–41.

10. *Scott v. Sandford*, 60 U.S. (19 How.) 393 (1857). *Boston Globe*, August 31, 1989, at 1, discussing William Hammond, THE MILITARY AND THE MEDIA, 1962–68: THE US ARMY IN VIETNAM (Washington, D.C.: Center for Military History, 1988).

11. R. Leigh, ed., A FREE AND RESPONSIBLE PRESS 80 (Chicago: University of Chicago Press, 1947); *New York Times*, November 6, 1963, at 1; *Washington Post*, May 20, 1971, at A18.

12. *West Virginia v. Barnette*, 319 U.S. 624, 638 (1943).

13. T. Wilder, THE SKIN OF OUR TEETH: PLAY IN THREE ACTS 139 (New York: Harper and Bros., 1942).

# Index

Compositor: Keystone Typesetting, Inc.
Text: 11/13 Sabon
Display: Sabon
Printer: Edwards Brothers, Inc.
Binder: Edwards Brothers, Inc.